Darren Coffield is a British artist. He has exhibited at venues ranging from the Courtauld Institute, Somerset House, to the Voloshin Museum, Crimea. In the early nineties Coffield worked with Joshua Compston on the formation of Factual Nonsense, the centre of the emerging Young British Artists scene. A book by Coffield about this period in British art, *Factual Nonsense: The Art and Death of Joshua Compston*, was accompanied by an exhibition curated by Coffield at Paul Stolper Gallery. He lives and works in London.

OXFORD STREET

SOHO

SQUARE

Great Chapel Street

WARDOUR STREET

Dean Street

Frith Street

Greek Street

CHARING CROSS

Meard St

Bateman Street

Old Compton Street

Romilly Street

Rupert St

WARDOUR STREET

Archer St

Cambridge Circus

SHAFTESBURY AVENUE

Gerrard Street

Lisle Street

Leicester St

Key:

1. Caves de France
2. Birch & Conran
3. Colony Room Club
4. The Gargoyle
5. Groucho Club
6. Blacks
7. Janus (Sex Shop)
8. French House
9. Golden Lion

10. Dumpling Inn
11. The Sphinx
12. The Music Box
13. Gerry's (first club)
14. Wheeler's
15. Kettner's/Soho House
16. Coach & Horses
17. David Archer's Bookshop
18. Palace Theatre
19. Gerry's Wine & Spirits

20. Ronnie Scott's
21. Carlisle House
22. Au Jardin des Gourmets
23. Thea Porter's Shop
24. St. Martin's School of Art
25. Charlie Chester's
26. Havajah Club
27. Dog & Duck
28. Swiss Tavern
29. St. Anne's Church

Tales from the Colony Room

SOHO'S LOST BOHEMIA

Darren Coffield

unbound

Also available by the author

Factual Nonsense: The Art and Death of Joshua Compston

First published in 2020
This paperback edition first published in 2021

Unbound
Level 1, Devonshire House, One Mayfair Place, London W1J 8AJ
www.unbound.com

Text design by Ellipsis, Glasgow

A CIP record for this book is available from the British Library

ISBN 978-1-80018-028-4 (paperback)
ISBN 978-1-78352-816-5 (hardback)
ISBN 978-1-78352-817-2 (ebook)

Printed in Great Britain by Clays Ltd, Elcograf S.p.A

3 5 7 9 8 6 4 2

For Muriel, Ian and Michael

A NOTE ON LIBEL

It is obvious that many of the people in this book existed in a dimly lit small green room in one form or another. But any similarity between these people and other people is purely coincidental.

Contents

Foreword

by Barry Humphries

The Colony Room was, for me at the time, a wonderful discovery. It provided an atmosphere of delectable depravity for the select company of alcoholics and would-be artists who managed to win the reluctant approval of Muriel Belcher, the gorgon-like proprietrix. A long flight of stairs led to this louche establishment, and Muriel sat at the entrance, perched on a stool, resembling nothing so much as a Nazi anti-Semitic caricature. Her barman and sidekick was Ian 'Bawd', an evil-looking catamite with a name as Dickensian and descriptive as Muriel's. They were a double act, and only a very select few of London's upper-class riff-raff earned their approval.

Here, in this small, smoke-filled room could be found, on almost any night of the week, Francis Bacon in black leather doling out champagne, and Malcolm Williamson, Master of the Queen's Musick, noodling at the keyboard in a dark corner. Elizabeth Smart, that intelligent and glamorous Canadian beauty, poet and mistress of the poet George Barker, was always there, and the critic John Davenport, 'half seas over', as they used to say.

Who else can I see through the fumes of Gitanes and Senior Service? Who stands at that nasty little bar and looks at me over the parapet of nearly sixty years? 'The Two Roberts' of course, Robert MacBryde and Robert Colquhoun, two artist 'partners' who painted identical pictures in the 'Post-War' style. My countryman, Colin MacInnes, great-grandson of Edward Burne-Jones and chronicler of Notting Hill and Soho, would certainly be there with a couple of his black protégés, turning more vicious with every drink. A glimpse, perhaps, of Tom Driberg, saturnine journalist, MP and putative spy, cruising the room in search of rough trade. He once took me to the nearby Mandrake Club and quizzed me about a writer friend of mine in Prague. And there was always a distinguished personage addressed by Muriel as 'The Commander'. No doubt he was. A tall, John Cleese-like gent in command of submarines, I later heard, and mostly in command of himself; but after fifteen gins, his old seaworthy eyes flickered in the direction of one of the dolly birds who occasionally fluttered into this *cage aux folles*.

There were certainly some lovely girls there, drawn to the dissolute atmosphere of the club and its habitués, most of whom resembled characters in one of Simon Raven's more scabrous novels. Amongst the lovely girls would be Georgina Barker, with whom I long ago enjoyed the most intimate of all human connections, and that charming artist Sally Ducksbury, and Sandy Fawkes, reckless redhead journalist and fashion editor, who was later to cohabit with an American serial killer. Of course, that celebrity drinker and celebrator of self-destruction, Jeffrey Bernard, would frequently loiter in the Colony when he wasn't down the road at Gerry's club on Shaftesbury Avenue. But Muriel didn't like him much. And in the company of Frank Norman, the jailbird playwright with an ominous razor scar on his soft pink face, Jeffrey became truculent. 'His parents sent him to the wrong school and he never got over it,' said Elizabeth Smart enigmatically. A permanent member was Daniel Farson, flâneur, journalist and biographer of Francis Bacon, whose face changed over the years from angelic blond boy to, well, a Francis Bacon portrait.

So what was Muriel's secret? What did that ogress and her malevolent elf Ian use to entice us to that infernal club? As she grew even uglier and he transformed from lah-de-dah rent boy to a booze-bitten queen with a strawberry nose, we still climbed those fateful stairs. Their secret was: 'The Slate'. No one paid. It was the alcoholics' paradise. You merely ran up a slate. Later, much later, came the reckoning, but you never knew how they arrived at the astronomical total, and alkies like to pay more anyway. It's our reward and our punishment. When they called the men 'fuck-face' and the women 'cunty', we still came back for more. We thought we were all on 'life's threshold', when we were actually at the terminus.

Introduction

HEALTH WARNING:
This book contains strong language, sex, violence and extreme wit.

Viewed as a tiny green oasis by some and a blurred drinking hellhole by others, the Colony Room Club functioned both as a bar and a cultural barometer. 'Muriel's', as it was affectionately known, was heroically bohemian; London's answer to Bricktop's in Paris, Dean's in Tangier and Harry's Bar in Venice. The club was dominated, indeed created, by two personalities – that of its owner and founder, Muriel Belcher, who opened the Colony Room in 1948, and the artist Francis Bacon, who was one of her first customers. In this book we witness these future legends gravitating together and coming of age with their circle of friends, such as John Deakin, Lucian Freud, Daniel Farson, Frank Norman and Jeffrey Bernard. It's a story of being adrift in a world of fractious friendships, casual sex, passion, loss and desire, deep in the heart of Soho.

Everyone who frequented the Colony can clearly remember the first time they went there. Like the recipient of a major shock stumbling upon a murder scene, the club left its mark on anyone who entered. Everyone has their own peculiar story of how they came across the club. I arrived there in the 1980s with my former sparring partner, the artist Joshua Compston. I had read about the club in a book of Francis Bacon interviews, *Brutality of Fact*, but this was scant preparation for the experience of first walking through the door. I had no preconceptions of what it would be like, but it far exceeded my expectations. The club was tiny, the size of a small living room, decorated in a melancholic green, with a bar at one end and a single unisex toilet at the other. Like so many before me, I felt completely at home, washed up on the shore of a luscious green bohemian paradise.

It seemed an unusual place to frequent as I was an art student at the time and there was hardly anyone there under the age of thirty. Most of my tutors were astonished and horrified that I had become a member as they had all been abused and thrown out by the then proprietor and former barman, Ian Board, who ruled the club with a rod of iron – like a cross between Oscar Wilde and Hitler. Fortunately for me, it was Ian himself who took me under his wing and made me a member. He would often ask at the end of the evening, 'How's your handbag, dear?', meaning, are you going to be okay getting home or do you need money for a taxi? He knew the perils and pitfalls of being a young, unknown artist, and could recall how difficult money was to come by for Francis Bacon, Lucian Freud and countless other artists he had known over the years.

The Colony was not just a bar, but also an artistic support centre, psychiatrist's couch, local post office (members left notes and letters to one another behind the bar), unemployment bureau and marriage guidance centre ('It will all end in tears, dear!'). The members came and behaved as a wayward family. They were empathetic to one another and would help each other out. As Ian Board informed me, 'The most important thing in life is empathy, you can't quantify kindness, you can pat a dog on the head and be kind, so what? Empathy is everything. Empathy is the most important thing to have between people.'

With most private clubs you are joining a clique or crowd, and have to behave accordingly. With the Colony there was no clique, crowd, way to dress, or act, and no required station in life in order to become a member. The club was a place of release and relief: it was a very fluid place. Walking in the dark, anonymous doorway off the street, passers-by would look at you as if you were visiting a call girl. Climbing the rickety staircase and pushing open the club's heavy green door felt like a clandestine act in itself. The drinking laws were draconian before 1988. All pubs were closed between three p.m. and six p.m., so unless you were a member of a private club, there was nowhere to drink.

These ghastly English laws, you can't have a drink, can't do anything. Do you think they'll ever change them? . . . I can take you up that awful Colony Room if you like.

– Francis Bacon

The club was also a great litmus test. There was never one person I met and liked who dismissed the place. Many of the club's members were extraordinary eccentrics, never destined to become famous due to the nature of their professions, but nevertheless integral to the atmosphere. I can recount bizarre afternoons spent chatting to Myra Hindley's psychiatrist, or karate play-fighting with the actor Burt Kwouk (Cato in the Pink Panther films). However, the club's most famous member was Francis Bacon, who drank there for four decades and for whom it was a second home. No matter where Bacon travelled and worked – Tangier, Paris, Monte Carlo – the one constant in his life, to which he could always return, was the Colony. It was his lodestar.

Unlike Bacon, many other talented people squandered their artistic wealth in Soho. Long before the advent of mobile phones the club formed part of Soho's Bermuda Triangle: the French (House), the Coach & Horses and the Colony Room Club – a diabolical trinity where loved ones could enter, dissipate and not be heard of again for what seemed an eternity. Soho, as a beacon of counterculture, attracted the talented, like moths to a flame. Many members were shooting stars, shining brightly and fading out far too young. The artist John Minton committed suicide in 1957, aged forty, and from my artistic generation alone Joshua Compston died drinking ether, aged twenty-five, and Angus Fairhurst hanged himself, aged forty-one.

Why were so many extraordinary artists attracted to a drinking club? Well, alcohol is one of the few intoxicating substances you can take and continue to produce work of a reasonable standard whilst still having some control over it. In other words their critical faculties would be impaired by drugs but not necessarily obliterated by drink. Bacon experimented with painting whilst drunk or with very bad hangovers. He would say, 'I find the worse the hangover the more the mind seems to crackle with energy.'

Bacon was the draw for the younger generation, such as Michael Clark, Damien Hirst and Marc Quinn, who in the seventies, eighties and nineties beat a path to the Colony. As an artist you have to feed on those that have gone before you, so you might as well feast on the best, and the artists of the Colony were the greatest post-war figurative painters of the twentieth century. When people look for schools of art they look for similarities in the work. The artists who went to the Colony were all very diverse. Primarily they were so diverse that there was no 'School of Colony'. Many other well-known artists drank in the club alongside Bacon: Craigie Aitchison, Michael Andrews, Frank Auerbach, Clive Barker, Peter Blake, Edward Burra, Henri Cartier-Bresson, Patrick Caulfield, John Craxton, Barry Flanagan, Lucian Freud, Alberto Giacometti, Nina Hamnett, Augustus John, R.B. Kitaj, John Latham, Eduardo Paolozzi, Isabel Rawsthorne, Keith Vaughan. The list goes on and on.

However, it must be said that the club was not just a place for artists – indeed poets, painters, writers, tailors, sailors, editors, African chiefs, lords, landowners, barrow boys, musicians, singers, strippers, stagehands and petty crooks all drank there and the club's membership ran the gamut of types, trades and professions who lived or worked in the West End. They drank, caroused, gossiped and entertained one another with their anecdotes, which in turn sometimes gave rise to mythical events that never happened, such as the poet Dylan Thomas throwing up over the Colony Room carpet. Nevertheless, part of the charm and potential pitfall of a book about drinkers is their tendency to embellish, enlarge and conflict in their anecdotes.

I remember Dylan Thomas, of course, dear. A little man who couldn't get a word in edgeways. His wife was someone with whom I had a few differences of opinion.

– Muriel Belcher

Running a successful private drinking club in Soho was a balancing act to be marvelled at. You had to be tough enough to get the gangsters to respect you and leave you alone to prosper; urbane and witty enough to collect aristocratic clients around you; worldly enough to hold court over hardened businessmen; tolerant enough to empathise with all the strange flotsam and jetsam of mixed morals that are inevitable in Soho; and above all, have the knowledge of a ringmaster and the skill of a diplomat. On top of all this you also needed a good barman who would not allow himself or the customers to rob you blind. It wasn't easy money and could only be achieved by the type of person who could run a successful military coup.

In its sixty-year history the Colony had just three proprietors. The first, Muriel Belcher, began the mad party in 1948 and somehow it managed to carry on in one form or another into the twenty-first century. Famous for her wit, infamous for her devastating put-downs, Muriel greeted her favourite members with the cheery greeting, 'Hello Cunty', upon their arrival. She referred to Francis Bacon as 'Daughter' and he called her 'Mother', so close was their relationship.

Muriel's Colony was steeped in the tradition of the salon – a gathering of people with an inspiring hostess, held to amuse, refine the taste and increase the knowledge of the participants through conversation. Women were traditionally a powerful, and historically overlooked, influence on the salon. They were the centre of the salon's life and carried a very important role as regulators, selecting their guests and deciding the subjects of their meetings whilst mediating and directing the discussion.

In a regimented, class-ridden and sexually repressed post-war London, Muriel's attracted professional drinkers to a man, woman or something in-between, since sexual nonconformity always played its part in the mix. The club echoed the salon's absence of social hierarchy and encouraged socialising between different social ranks, races, sexes and sexualities, breaking down the social barriers and taboos that other establishments operated under.

Francis Bacon was aware of Gertrude Stein's salon in pre-war Paris and brought talented people into Muriel's orbit, as Picasso had done before for Stein. There are some other notable similarities – both were lesbians, and like Muriel's, entrée into the Stein salon was a sought-after validation. Both women also became a combination of mentor, critic and guru to those who gathered around them. Stein's salon brought together the confluences of talent that would help define pre-war modernism in literature and art in Paris – becoming synonymous with Picasso and Matisse – whilst Muriel's became a fixture of post-war London, and will be forever associated with the artistic milieu of Francis Bacon and Lucian Freud.

After Muriel's death in 1979, the club was taken over by her loyal barman, Ian Board. Verbally agile, a vigorous persecutor of bores and a tremendous raconteur, he was amazingly charismatic and repulsive at the same time. Ian was notoriously fearsome. He was short, square-jawed with enormous tinted spectacles framing a huge red nose, which pulsated like a rancid tomato – a testimony to his years of alcohol abuse. During Ian's reign of terror, the club would veer from a salon to a theatre of cruelty with alarming regularity. Although famous for his swearing and violent outbursts, he was also a self-effacing and kind man when he thought he should drop his guard and take someone into his confidence. He kept the club going in tribute to Muriel, whom he had idolised all his life, until finally joining her in that great celestial bar in 1994.

The third and final proprietor, Michael Wojas, was Ian's loyal barman from 1981 onwards, and took over running the club upon his death. Just as some, who affectionately knew the club as Muriel's, could never quite accept the reign of the 'upstart barman', Ian Board, taking over when Muriel died, history repeated itself with Michael's reign. A man of many attributes and faults, if it weren't for him, the club would have probably ground to a halt within a few years. Michael managed to re-energise the club, making it the 'in' place for a whole new generation.

Like many strange tales, this book came about through an unexpected twist of fate. Before his early demise, Michael Wojas gave me some tapes, which contained interviews with old club members. I didn't really know what to do with them at the time, so I put them away in a drawer and forgot about them. A few years later, whilst working on Joshua Compston's biography, *Factual Nonsense*, it occurred to me that a similar oral biography and interview format would work with a book on the Colony Room Club. I had spent most of 2005 helping Michael Wojas try and complete the documentary he had begun filming in 1998 for the fiftieth anniversary of the club – viewing over two hundred hours of footage meant I was very well versed in the club's history. I also had my own peculiar chequered past, working behind the bar for a day after Ian Board died, and having the dubious honour of being the only member to throw an all-night stag party in the club. This, combined with the fact that I had been a member for twenty years, and knew, from my early days of drinking in Soho, many of the faces from the area's post-war golden age, put me in good stead to take on the book.

Many infamous Colony characters are gathered together within these pages; nevertheless, there are some that somehow slipped by the wayside, such as the photographer Harry Diamond, whose portrait by Lucian Freud can be seen at the Tate Gallery, Stephanie 'Steve' Storey, a pinstriped besuited lesbian getaway driver, and Ian Dunlop, aka 'The Greying Mantis'. Over time, previously well-known figures have unfairly faded into obscurity: for example, Michael Nelson, a writer famous for his Captain Blossom autobiographical novels and Anthony Carson, whose appetite for alcohol and falling in love was related with much humour as a newspaper columnist long before Jeffrey Bernard. However, a list of all those who frequented the establishment would be a tome about as much fun to read as a telephone directory. On the contrary, this book is predominantly an oral biography of the club and its members. This literary form gives the reader a real flavour of what it was like to frequent the Colony and its environs. With a glass in hand, the reader moves through the decades listening to personal reminiscences, opinions and vitriol from the authentic voices of those who were actually there.

After twenty-seven years of working at the Colony, Michael Wojas decided to call last orders for the final time and closed the club after its sixtieth anniversary in December 2008. Now that the club is no more and Soho is being sanitised, people ask 'Where is Bohemia?' Sadly, Soho's Bohemia is no more – but fortunately for Wojas, as with so many before, whether it be Bacon, Bernard, Farson or Freud, the story never ends. They become Soho legends, the object of bar-room talk, whispers and spurious truth. Such is the legacy of the Colony Room Club. Would you like to join? Sorry, the membership list is now closed. But if you really want to know what it was like to be there, pour yourself a large drink, imagine you are perched on a stool at the end of the bar eavesdropping in, and read on.

Soho Intro

MICHAEL HEATH: Francis Bacon, Muriel Belcher, Ian Board – their lifestyles are the stuff of legend; they were terrifying people. These people don't really exist any more. The health system in this country is designed to stop people from doing what they want to do, whether it's smoking, drinking, gambling . . . even getting angry – there's probably a pill they could give you. People back then were self-medicating with alcohol, the doctors too. Brandy and scotch were both deemed medicinal, but now the corporate world, the great bores, have taken over Soho. I look back now and think how lucky I was to be alive then.

NORMAN BALON: People say Soho has changed, I don't think it has, maybe outwardly. One end of Old Compton Street now has got the name of the 'gay capital of Europe'. Soho at one time was ruled by the Maltese and was the 'vice capital of Europe'. One of the Kings of England used to have a room over the road above Kettner's restaurant, where he would entertain his mistress Lillie Langtry. Soho has always been naughty. The characters we knew have gone – we've lost Daniel Farson, Jeffrey Bernard, Francis Bacon, but all those years ago when they first came to Soho, no one had heard of them.

⎯•⎯

FRANCIS BACON: I knew Soho when I was only twenty in 1930, and I liked it very much. Across Oxford Street there was a pub called the Black Horse where John Minton and a whole crowd of people used to meet and then, of course, drift down to Soho. There were so many little clubs, but now they're gone and the area is diminished. What excited me was that there were no barriers against age, race, class or sex. It was nothing to do with 'gayness'. Gay is a ridiculous word.

⎯•⎯

GRAHAM MASON: Gay culture? I've no idea what gay culture is about in Soho these days. I despise them because for the most part they are sashaying up and down the pavement, giving off such an air of 'I am-ness', whereas in my 'gay' world in the 1960s there was no need for 'gay style'. It seems horribly unimportant, it shouldn't matter. I don't give a damn if someone is gay, lesbian or loves horses, whatsoever!

MARSH DUNBAR: What about heterosexuals?

GRAHAM MASON: Oh no, I can't stand them! People say, Soho's not what it used to be. But Ian Board used to say, 'It never bloody was, was it?' I suppose so, but who wants to have a gay coffee on Old Compton Street, inhaling taxi fumes with your gay haircut? It's too silly, sitting out on the pavement baffles me, I think they are all crazy. Lovely young things I'm sure, but it's not my Soho.

MAID MARION: At least it's open and acceptable nowadays. It wasn't easy being gay in the fifties and sixties. You had to watch yourself. The area was full of prostitutes, pornographers and villains. Soho back then is nothing like it is today. Old Compton Street is now full of gay bars. It was more sinister years ago.

***

SANDY FAWKES: Soho has always changed with the times. It has been glamorous (witness the elegant layout of the streets and remaining houses in Soho Square), seedy, violent and industrious. The seediness came from the fact that the rents were cheap . . . There was a time when a flat or an office in Soho spoke of impecunity; elderly persons climbing stairs to a room with a sink, a gas ring and probably a chamber pot under the bed; or it could be an aspiring literary publisher in a linoleum-floored office, heated by a one-bar electric fire, paying poets out of a tin cash box.

***

SUGGS: Soho was full of bohemians because it was the arse end of the West End. Once it became expensive, the bohemians were driven out and it became full of bores, bankers and city bods who think it's a bit risqué. Many of the afternoon drinking clubs closed down in 1988 when they changed the licensing laws to allow pubs to open all day.

***

DOUGLAS SUTHERLAND: The years immediately after the war saw the heyday of London as the vice capital of Europe – a title it was eventually to yield only to Hamburg with its notorious Reeperbahn area. In the West End, when the lights went up again, the prostitutes lined the streets, the youngest and prettiest spaced every few yards along brilliantly illuminated thoroughfares like Piccadilly and Bond Street while their mothers lay in wait in the darker, more deeply recessed doorways. And in the back streets of what was dubbed 'the square mile of vice', illegal clubs mushroomed, their lights flashing a baleful welcome to the lonely and bored.

FRANCIS BACON: When I first knew Soho, the prostitutes were all over the area, and it would be true to say the streets were more fun and amusing because there were these images of people around that gave a living sense of the area.

FRANK NORMAN: Soho, like anywhere else, is a place you either love or hate, though I do not think it is possible to hate it entirely. It has great charm and loads of character, and one of its amenities is bound to appeal to you. It will be a crying shame when it has all gone, for go it must. However, so long as the restaurants continue to serve good food, the people will come. And until a law is passed banning sex, the clients will patronise the girls.

DANIEL FARSON: Sex has always been part of Soho's attraction. Soho without sex would be a *sham* . . . If I described a Soho type of person, it would be someone who enjoyed drink and food and conversation and laughter, who would never cash a cheque at a bank but always with a friend or pub or shop, who'd probably cry quite a lot and enjoy it, and would miss the train back home if a party was going on.

JEFFREY BERNARD: Why did I fall in love with Soho? It's the only place where people will accept you for what you are . . . I am interested in what is called loss. Property developers, like Paul Raymond, have ruined Soho. The attractive thing about it was, I hate to say 'village', but it was a village in a way. Everyone who worked here, lived here. It was a community, which one could never say about Chelsea or Hampstead. Soho has always meant freedom for me. People behaved exactly as they wanted to in Soho without anyone being judgemental about it.

DARREN COFFIELD: Soho appealed to those who sought non-conformity, creativity and sex. The lifestyle was a death sentence for some. Francis Bacon appeared immune to the satanic zeal of Soho; he was a Dorian Gray figure, who never seemed to age. He thrived on the bohemian lifestyle, often going back to work after epic drinking sessions. There has always been an inexhaustible supply of eager young souls to fuel the fires of Soho. Few people are actually born there, although many are destined to die there.

GEORGE MELLY: Back then we were not concerned with legends or concepts, we simply did what entertained us. We never thought, Would that be good for my image? Because we didn't know what an image was, which made it much more realistic. There was none of that posturing or posing that there is now.

FRANK NORMAN: My London is Soho, that square mile which has by turns destroyed and enriched my soul and pocket. I have walked its streets without food for three days, or proper sleep for a week. I have trod the same pavements with several hundred pounds in my pocket and the future as bright as a newly minted sixpence. I have been chased by the police around Soho Square and cried for the loss of a lover in Italian restaurants . . . I perpetually complain about how much the place has changed in recent years, but hardly a week passes without my visiting Muriel Belcher at the Colony Room in Dean Street . . .

1

Muriel's

FRANK NORMAN: In Soho alone there are reputed to be five hundred clubs. The boldest, campest, most written and talked about is Miss Muriel Belcher's Colony Room Club in Dean Street . . . When the 'In London Last Night' used to appear in the *Evening Standard*, there was hardly a week went by without some mention of the Colony Room Club or one of its seven hundred members who are as mixed a bunch as you are ever likely to meet: some are very rich and many are very poor . . . on a good night they all get along with each other like a big happy family. On a bad night they snap and snarl at each other like a pack of mongrel bitches in a slum alley.

GEORGE MELLY: The Colony is a small room, which holds the magic of my youth. I think the problem looking back is we embellish things with hindsight. If you'd gone up to Muriel Belcher and asked her if she'd started a club to help make the world a freer, more liberal place, she'd have said, 'Fuck off.'

MAID MARION: The drinking laws were different then, you could not consume alcohol in a public bar between three and six p.m., only in a private members' club. The original attraction of the Colony was that when the pubs had to shut at three in the afternoon, that's when Muriel opened. Once the early evening came and the pubs reopened, they didn't rush off, they stayed.

FRANK NORMAN: Clubland is a place all of its own, and the people who live in it are not of this world. Its citizens have only one interest in life and that is booze, though some do have a few other minor interests such as sex and death . . . In point of fact, some of the people who use these clubs are to be admired, for they have completely given up their struggle for survival. Their only interest is in drinking, and laying people, sex optional. Many of them have been successes of one kind or another at some time in their lives, and then after their meteoric rise to fame have crashed to the ground, some because they did not like success and others because they ran out of whatever talent they had . . . They are creatures of the night, their habitat is dark rooms with worn carpets and faded wallpaper in basements and back alleys, their faces are pale and blotchy and their clothes are tawdry. The conversation is liable to be extravagant and camp, but in spite of all this there is something enchanting about these people.

MAID MARION: The Colony could be found at 41a Dean Street. Its dingy, ill-lit passage was filled with boxes of empty wine bottles from the Italian restaurant, which occupied the basement and ground floor of the building. The entrance was dustbin-lined and dirty. The waft of the garlic and the waiters screaming at each other in their foreign tongue gave you the feeling of being in another land. The club occupied the first floor of the building. It was a small front room in a tiny Georgian house, and not particularly comfortable. The fascination was with the assortment of people who went there. Muriel never allowed the club to become typecast and that was her genius as a club owner.

IAN BOARD: When the club first opened, it was full of homosexuals and lesbians. The word 'gay' wasn't used then. Homosexuals in public, back then, had to be seen with a woman, and I suppose Muriel was what would be known nowadays as a fag hag. It wasn't known of in those days. The bar was originally a wonderful mahogany and there was bamboo all along the front. Before the cream-coloured walls became festooned with pictures, there were tropical plants riddled about the place. The bar stools and banquettes were all leopardskin. It looked like a sophisticated jungle, all paid for by the rich homosexuals who drank here. Of course the club has changed over the years. Everything changes, doesn't it? We change our knickers every day, don't we? Eventually the nails started falling out of the bamboo, the plants had to be watered and it all got too much. So we redecorated and the club's been 'Buckingham Green' ever since.

MAID MARION: Muriel's kingdom is a small, darkish-mirrored room. The carpet and banquettes are green and faded, worn out by her army of followers – the bar faces us, with mirrored shelves behind, holding bottles of spirits and various shaped drinking glasses. In the middle of the shelving is an old till, stripped of its covering, its mechanism exposed. In front of the bar are seven bar stools, one is high-backed and situated to the left of the bar, next to the door. To the right are two windows with a large mirror in-between. There are bunk seats below with a television set in the corner. To the left is a large mirror and a picture of Ginger Rogers and Fred Astaire hanging on the mud-green walls. A small piano sits in the recess, the front covered with photographs of various club members all showing their allegiance to Muriel.

MOLLY PARKIN: I was teaching at an art school in the Elephant & Castle and some of my colleagues took me along to the Studio Club in the West End, which had been started by John Minton. There I met a very nice, effeminate man called Tony Tooth of the Tooth Gallery, Mayfair. We just clicked and he said, 'If you think this club is good, I know another even better place.' The name, the Colony Room, conjured images of chandeliers, an exclusive clientele, chaise longues on which anything could happen. He took me through Soho to a dingy doorway and we began to climb the stairs. It was filthy, I thought I'd come to the wrong place. But I'd seen too many Hollywood films set during the Depression to know that you can't judge a club by the sleaziness of its exterior. Behind the shabby door I knew I'd find champagne and glamour. Tony rapped on the first-floor door and it swung open. I was totally unprepared for Muriel – as who indeed would not be in instant, bowel-voiding terror of that beak-nosed presence – perched there on her hallowed stool? The people in the club were extraordinary, I'd never seen such well-trodden faces. I didn't realise what alcohol could do to a face and I'd never been anywhere where there were so many upper-class accents. Muriel commanded me to stand next to her whilst banishing Tony to the other end of the bar. 'Now,' she said cosily, 'you common little cunt, who are you when you are at home, eh?' When I stammered that I was a painter, her eyes glinted with approval. 'Thought you was a fucking secretary from them awful clothes.' Someone said to me, 'You look like a champagne girl,' and quipped, 'Can we have some champagne for the girl?'

GRAHAM MASON: Isn't it funny how we can all remember when we first went to the Colony, just like when President Kennedy was shot; such an awful event, I suppose, changes your life. I'm not going to say it was a privilege. It bloody wasn't, one had to work at the cunts. But it was marvellous that they bothered to know me and what a wonderful enlivening thing to have known them all. The first time I went, I was intimidated by Muriel, which was her job. If someone brand new walked in, they had to be examined – 'Who are you? Members only!' That frightening shriek. Muriel was keen on money – you've got to be quite plain about this – she liked the moneybags. But if you were too goddamn boring, it didn't matter how much money you spent, that was it – 'OUT!' She wouldn't let you back in – 'Yes, what do you want?' – 'But I'm a member!' – 'Well, it was a mistake I made. Out, I'm sorry but I don't want you here, you're boring people.' The only unforgivable sin in the club was to be boring. It was sparkling times.

MARSH DUNBAR: I first went when I was seventeen with a student of John Minton's called Bobby Hunt. There used to be a huge mirror outside the entrance where you could check yourself before entering the club. Muriel frightened the arse out of me. If you didn't walk in with confidence she would have you. Verbally slaughter you, fucking kill you, baby. 'Shut that door! The wind is blowing right up my cunt.' Absolutely terrifying. I loved her, best bird in the world. She was such enormous fun to be with. She used to tell me how cheaply I could feed my children – 'Chicken wings! Go to Sainsbury's and buy chicken wings, terribly cheap for feeding those boys of yours.' There was however no question of the vodka, gin or whisky being any cheaper. I had a beautiful MG sports car, which I had to eventually sell to pay my bar bill. Mind you I shouldn't have been driving as I was pissed most of the time; I could have killed myself.

GERALD McCANN: Muriel's clientele was of a certain grandeur, the Maharajah of Cooch-Behar was a member. New members would go through the ritual of being ignored and finally being accepted. At the beginning one doesn't like new people on purpose, why should one? Until they prove themselves by buying one a drink or telling an extremely witty or dirty story. Only then do they have the possibility of being accepted.

IAN BOARD: This is a members' club and the rules must be observed. Should a friend be with you, you'd be asked to sign them in – an important ritual, although ninety-nine per cent of signatures are illegible. Non-members may not drink until that is done, nor may they buy drinks. Muriel was very strict on this. If a friend wanted to be a member, it was by no means automatic, and the applicant, even if vouched for and seconded by a member, would be sized up by Muriel over several visits.

GEORGE MELLY: There were many different clubs in Soho – some were crooks' clubs, police clubs, jazz clubs, some were even taxi drivers' clubs! One didn't measure out whether one liked the Colony because it was important in the social sense, or if one would get to know people who could be influential on one's life later; it wasn't like that. It was to do with fun, maliciousness also – everyone was tough on each other. It had a womb-like feeling. Once one left the noise of Soho and went up those disgusting stairs, one was in this little room with Muriel presiding on a stool by the door.

IAN BOARD: Sitting on a stool by the door as one does all day in the club is extremely uncomfortable. A lot of people say, 'How lucky.' Well yes, you are sitting there from three to eleven p.m. drinking, talking, listening to famous people, etc. But it isn't that, it's very hard work, but Muriel coped with it marvellously, it was her whole being.

MAID MARION: Her members' signing-in book was always at the ready. She sat upright on her perch and ruled the Colony as befitted her title 'Queen of Soho'. I asked Muriel, 'Where did you get the name of the Colony from?' She replied, 'I had a club called the Music Box with another woman. We fell out and I decided to open my own club but didn't know what to call it. The people who knew me well said, "You know what you will have? You will have your own following, your own Colony."'

COLIN MacINNES: To open a members' club, you gather together twenty-five ratepayers and you apply to the chief inspector of police of your area for permission to open up. The inspector – or, in fact, one of his minions – looks into you and the twenty-five, and, if all is well, in three months' time, a permit costing five shillings is granted by the magistrates' court. Meanwhile you have rented premises, which the sanitary inspector and the police once more must examine and approve. Then you stock up on booze, hang out a neon sign, and a new club has joined the five hundred-odd that are said to exist in the district round W1.

GRAHAM MASON: It was unheard of for a woman to be a proprietor of a bar in those days. She owned the place. She invented it. She put her money in it and created it from nothing. She was ahead of her time – well before the pink pound, she realised a lot of homosexuals had spare cash and nowhere to go. The Colony was a bolthole for queers at a time when they needed somewhere to hide, along with peers, politicians and a lot of luminaries who didn't dare appear in the queer pub down the road. Muriel loved them being around because they were funnier, brighter and spent more, which above all is what Muriel liked. But you certainly didn't have to be homosexual to be a member, by no means. People felt utterly safe and secure.

LADY ROSE McLAREN: As a woman alone, the Colony was the only place I felt comfortable in. One saw the world go by and people from all over the place and in all sorts of conditions . . . Muriel knew how just to handle all who came to the club.

MURIEL: 'Members only' . . . I can't stand respectability just for the sake of respectability. Nor people who bore the shit out of me, unless I feel in the mood for a bit of camping . . . The world outside may have altered, but our talk has always been very loose. We have a wonderful thing: if someone we don't know puts his face around the door, we can change the conversation at once. We might be chatting blue murder and it'll be 'how's your mother' in a flash.

GEORGE MELLY: Muriel's barman, Ian Board, in those days was very good-looking and quiet. Far from the noisy old splay-nosed harridan he became later.

IAN BOARD: When I come to think of it, it was the luckiest thing that ever happened in my life. I met Muriel when I was seventeen years old working as a commis waiter. From the first moment we met, there was a rapport. Muriel fulfilled the role of a 'queen's moll' at Le Jardin. Just before she was about to open the Colony Club, she said to me 'Here, girl,' – she was an outspoken woman – 'I am opening a club around the corner. If you'd like a job, I'd like you to come work for me.' She opened here on December 15th 1948. Muriel was a natural. Nothing I can say against that woman, never ever! If I ever hear anyone say anything against her, I would kill them. She was mother, brother, sister, father to me. I worked behind the bar for over twenty-five years before I took over. I had to be very prim and proper with a white coat, flat tight-fitting trousers, white shirt and bow tie. I had to call men 'Sir' and ladies 'Madam'. I was given £5 a week and lived off tips when I started work behind the bar. Mind you I used to do a lot of whoring on the side.

MAID MARION: Muriel was the attraction. She was a good conversationalist and read the papers back to front every day before she started work. She was slightly built and about 5 feet 4 inches tall. It was her face and hands you noticed most. She had a very unusual face, very sharp features, her long, bony nose arched and protruding over her shallow cheeks, proudly revealing her Jewish ancestry. Her deep-set eyes and eyebrows were pencilled black and her black shoulder-length hair, thin from years of dyeing, was brushed severely back over her ears. Her face defied anyone to challenge her authority or her request, 'Which one of you lot are going to buy me a drink?' When not holding a glass, she held a cigarette regally in her hand. She drew lightly on it and never inhaled. She would clasp her long, bony hands, twisted by Paget's disease, in her lap – raising them in mock horror, relief or joy of good news, a joke – or sometimes coming down on some unsuspecting member (who'd not bought her a drink) like a clap of thunder.

DARREN COFFIELD: Muriel was a true, though not direct, descendant of Teresa Cornelys, the quintessential Soho hostess: talented and inventive, her string of lovers included Casanova. In 1760 she rented Carlisle House, on the corner of Soho Square, and established it as London's most fashionable venue, a forerunner of the private drinking club, where she threw lavish parties. One audacious guest demonstrated an exciting new invention called 'roller skates' on the dance floor and crashed into a huge mirror. It shocked and enthralled London society. Like Teresa, Muriel was full of style, wit and generosity.

SANDY FAWKES: Muriel had an arrogant nose that could sniff the contents of a wallet across a crowded room . . . She was very generous with the money too; it was drinks all round, and that included poverty-stricken poet Paul Potts and every down-on-his-luck actor, writer or painter present, who could not dream of returning the compliment . . . She entertained lavishly at all the best restaurants on the manor, regaling the company with scandalous gossip . . .

PAUL POTTS: What makes her difficult to describe is her originality, a kind of non-ecclesiastical cardinal or perhaps a delinquent saint . . . She could have run a great hospital if she had wanted to, but drink and conversation were her materials, and she caused a large amount of happiness to come people's way.

MOLLY PARKIN: Like all Colony Room habitués, I gained infinitely more from Muriel than mere acceptance. I came to regard her as one of the touchstones of my life, she was what I wanted to be. It seemed to me that she had all the essential qualities – unbounded generosity; shrewd judgement of character; passionate concern for the underprivileged, particularly children; an avid interest in scurrilous gossip; a formidable capacity for alcohol; an admirable vocabulary of expletives; an affinity with eccentrics; a talent for extracting – and gleefully betraying – confidences; and a magical knack of getting everyone pissed. No one ever left Muriel's Colony sober or with their dreams diminished. Muriel was unfailingly sympathetic to the sensitive and insecure. She was a life-enhancer, an inspiration by example.

IAN BOARD: Muriel was born in 1908 to a strict Jewish family. Her father was a moneylender who died penniless and they hated each other. The family were always running away from creditors, but her parents were wealthy at one point and ran Birmingham's New Alexandra Theatre. A nervous child, she stammered so badly that she never went to school but had a nanny and a governess at home, and claimed that it was only when she learned to swear that she stopped stuttering. She first ran away to London at sixteen, after being slapped by her father for wearing lipstick. She was very close to her mother, who died just before she started the club.

MURIEL: I had one nice brother who died. My nanny was a real bastard and the governess would have had more hair on her chin than Che Guevara except that she shaved it every day . . . My mother, brother and I came to live in London after my father died, which was freedom enough for us all.

MAID MARION: She was reticent about her past. Muriel had a cousin who was gay and would come in from time to time. She

11

would go, 'Oh fuck him', she never had much time for him. He knew too much about her background, that was the real reason she didn't want him around. When she first came to London, she worked briefly in Harrods sports department and ran a dress shop in Streatham with her friend, Dolly, with whom she later started her first two clubs. They had flats next to each other in Mornington Crescent.

DARREN COFFIELD: Muriel had been part of clubland for over ten years before she created the Colony. In 1937, she opened her first club with Dolly Myers – the Sphinx in Gerrard Street. Then they ran the Music Box at 4 Leicester Street. Members included Brian Howard, a key figure in London's 'Bright Young Things', the fashionable set of partygoers satirised in Evelyn Waugh's *Vile Bodies*.

DANIEL FARSON: The members were theatrical, though not necessarily of the stage. One was Elvira Barney, who had been involved in a sensational murder case when she shot her lover after a party . . . [eventually] she was acquitted, though crowds booed her afterwards, and I have been told club-owners dreaded her arrival because she made dreadful scenes with the cry, 'I've murdered one bugger and got away with it. Don't think I'd hesitate again!' Muriel remembers her as 'enchanting'.

MURIEL: She fell in love with a poof called 'Spider' and later killed him. But she had what I'd call friends in high places.

DARREN COFFIELD: Then Muriel fell out with Dolly over her disastrous marriage to Alf Burger. So Dolly bought the lease on Le Boeuf sur le Toit at 11 Orange Street, renaming it the Romilly Club. The resident pianist was Leonard Blackett, a war hero and in later life Colony 'hostess'. Although the Romilly was once the most luxurious and fashionable gay club in London, it was Muriel who was to achieve lasting fame with the Colony Room Club in the 1950s.

MURIEL: I don't disapprove of much except spongers and bad manners . . . but anyone who makes an anti-Semitic remark, I knock them.

ELIZABETH SMART: Her Jewishness was important. She was proud and partisan – 'You've got to admit that a nice Jewish boy is superior.'

IAN BOARD: Muriel taught me some Yiddish, so we had a secret language and would have a chat about some of the people in the club. Muriel, of course, was a frightful snob. Everyone is a snob about something, wine snobs, music snobs, art snobs; everyone has some sort of snob quality to them. To me she was a woman riddled with style. Her humour was a form of high camp left over from the 1930s. Words ended in 'kins', as in 'give us a kissikins, dear', or in 'ette' as in 'would you like a drinkette?'

DICK WHITTINGTON: Muriel's wit came from so much more than her words. The delivery, the body language, the coarse juxtapositions and the wonderful communication of a sense of shared absurdity, all played their part in what was a well-rehearsed act interspersed with lines of Ortonesque originality.

MURIEL: Language is effective in getting them to let their hair down. I've created something . . . I'm a chatterer. I'd work at the club if I'd won the pools – I just couldn't sit on my arse. It's the social life. I love it here. I am always here.

HENRIETTA MORAES: She could be incredibly kind and generous. If anyone got into trouble, she would rustle up money for them. I went through a phase of being a cat burglar and was sent to prison for a fortnight. When I came out there was £1,000 waiting for me at the Colony, which was amazing. She was very much like that if she liked you.

MAID MARION: I'd heard of Muriel as a tough, rude, outspoken, old battleaxe, so when my friend George brought me to the club, I was tense and excited. Before I had time to look around, I heard a shrill voice saying, 'Hello George, how are you love? Is this cunt with you? Sign him in then.' Half looking at me, she said, 'Hello Cunty, what's your name?' I had already been told that if she called you a cunt twice in quick succession, she liked you. 'Get us a drink George, don't be a meanie. Ian and I are only drinking singles.' She said it so easily you almost apologised to her for paying for the drink, since she made you feel she had bought it. Muriel looked me up and down, 'How are you, Cunty?' – 'Hello, I'm fine.' – 'What are you drinking, Cunty?' – 'Whisky and water please.' After a while she turned to me and said, 'David, I do hope you'll come back here. What do you like about this place?' – 'Well, as soon as I walked in and first met you, I felt this is home.' – 'That's lovely, thank you,' she said.

INDIAN AMY: Unlike the rest of society, there was never any racial, religious or sexual division in the club. It was never an issue in the Colony. Up until 1967 it was a crime to be homosexual. It was Queen Victoria's fault. She couldn't believe two women would do anything sexual together and wouldn't pass a law banning lesbian sex. Men, however, in her opinion were more than capable and so she passed the law making homosexuality an offence. If Muriel had been a gay man running the club in 1948 with her risqué language, she wouldn't have got away with it.

DARREN COFFIELD: For Francis Bacon's generation, the club provided a support network in a hostile world. With its absence of social hierarchy, mixing of different social ranks, races and sexes, Muriel's Colony was a continuation of the tradition of the salon. But not the salon of civility, polite conversation and reasoned debate but rather a salon of absolute freedom of expression – to the point of nihilism.

GERALD McCANN: She had a dog called Nosher, which was slang for someone who performed cunnilingus. He sat on her lap, listening to all the gossip – it was said that he was the best-informed dog in town and should have had his own gossip column. It was such bubbly fun.

MAID MARION: The film star Eric Portman visited the club a lot until Nosher bit him in the leg and he never returned. Eventually Nosher got so bad-tempered that Muriel had to leave him at home. I looked after Nosher when they all went abroad for Francis' exhibition. I didn't like taking him out for walks in Soho. In those days the prostitutes were in every door-way, taking the piss out of me, making kissing noises whilst I walked this effeminate dog around. One night a friend asked me out. I had Nosher with me, so we went and took him back round to Muriel. We had a few drinks and I kissed Muriel goodbye. My friend went to do the same when Nosher barked at him and lunged. I heard this awful scream. I thought, Oh no, you must be joking. Nosher had bitten him on the kisser; it looked like he had a hare lip. Muriel was ever so worried about it all and thought he was going to sue her. Eventually she had to have Nosher's balls cut off to try and calm him down.

GEORGE MELLY: Muriel was a kind of magician, a witch, not necessarily a very kindly one. She could turn on people, she was rather mercenary, she weighed up whether someone was valuable. It was said that she had a remarkable eye for painting and a nose for literature – that was wrong! She had hardly ever read a book and I don't think she knew one picture from another. But she did have a remarkable eye for painters, and a nose for writers. She could tell if someone had potential immediately and she would cultivate them. In retrospect it was extraordinary to think it was there. She kept this cauldron on the boil and would occasionally throw in another ingredient that took her fancy. There were as many celebrated authors who climbed up and staggered down those odiferous stairs as there were painters and sculptors. That the list of painters who drank at the Colony Room should coincide so closely to a list of the best British post-war artists is more than a coincidence. Muriel was herself a work of art and much loved. Painting is a lonely business. The other side of that heavy door sat the charming antidote to the empty studio.

MAID MARION: Muriel had no interest in art so the artists could come and know that the one subject that would not be discussed was art.

GEORGE MELLY: The important thing was that the artists were attracted to her. They found her a witty, foul-mouthed mother figure and a generous one too. Under her occasionally beady eye, they were entirely at ease. The Colony was the nearest thing to a Paris café this bleak city could offer since the great days of the Café Royal.

GERALDINE NORMAN: I'd read about how the Impressionists gathered in Café Guerbois, and I always thought how attractive it must be to have some actual geographic place where you could go and know your friends are going to be there day or night. That was what struck me as exceptional about the Colony.

FRANCIS BACON: It's like a tank to which I climb and enter. It's different to anywhere else. Here we laugh more, we enjoy ourselves more. It's because of Muriel. Her tremendous ability to create an atmosphere of ease. After all, that's what we all want, isn't it, a place to go to where one feels free . . .

DARREN COFFIELD: Francis Bacon was always centre stage at the Colony – Muriel knew there was something extraordinary about him – long before he became famous. In 1948 he returned to London from Monte Carlo and exhibited at the Redfern Gallery that summer. Then, a few weeks before Christmas, he came across Muriel and the Colony.

MURIEL: When [Francis] first came here, she didn't have a pot to piss in . . . my Jewish JC said to me, 'Go over and talk to her. She'll mean something to you.'

IAN BOARD: Of course when many of the members first began to drink here, they were all unknown, and now they are all extremely famous because Muriel gave them a helping hand. Francis worked here for a period of time, Muriel called him a 'hostess'. They got on beautifully together, marvellously. He respected her. Francis was paid a commission on the drinks consumed by the members at the end of each week. But he always spent his money as soon as he got it. Of course he was getting far less for his pictures in those days.

DANIEL FARSON: You came to the Colony the day before it opened, didn't you?

FRANCIS BACON: Yes, I went there with Brian Howard. I met the old bastard across the road and he said, 'There's a new club opened, come across with me.' For some reason I liked it so much I went back the next day, and Muriel came over and spoke to me. She thought I knew a lot of rich people, which was untrue. She knew I didn't have much money, so she said, 'I'll give you £10 a week and you can drink absolutely freely here, don't think of it as a salary. Just bring in people when you feel like it.' I loved Muriel enormously. After Muriel's, at eleven o'clock we would go across the road to the Gargoyle Club, which was open until four or five in the morning. So if you weren't working or anything like that, it was a continuous party.

GEORGE MELLY: The Gargoyle was really high society. It was full of mirrors and original artworks by Matisse. The members were mainly aristocracy, who loved painting, as well as novelists and artists.

DANIEL FARSON: It had a strange entrance. There was a tiny lift that took you to the top and then you went all the way down into a room designed by Matisse. It was all very bizarre. All the customers were falling about. John Minton was always there with a table of sailors, the latest favourite was always at the top.

FRANCIS BACON: It also made for rows, if you remember, because my first meeting with you, if you do remember, you came across and said, 'Are you Francis Bacon?' I said, 'Yes,' and you threw a pint of beer in my face and that was my first meeting with you!

DANIEL FARSON: God, how memory fogs the brain. Francis, I remember it well, I met you in the afternoon . . .

FRANCIS BACON: My memory has not fogged my brain at all!

DANIEL FARSON: John Deakin introduced you to me in the Colony and we went over to the Gargoyle and I had a friend who went over and bought a drink. He might have thrown it over you . . .

FRANCIS BACON: It was you! It was you who did it . . .

DANIEL FARSON: On the contrary. I have never thrown a pint of beer over anyone in my life!

FRANCIS BACON: It's part of your charm when you're drunk!

DANIEL FARSON: I don't even drink beer!

FRANCIS BACON: Well, you got hold of it . . . Some glass of *filth*.

DANIEL FARSON: I went over to Francis to apologise and you said, 'It's bad enough I should pay for your friend's drinks without having your boredom as well.' We met the next day and became friends after that.

DARREN COFFIELD: Francis stopped being a Colony 'hostess' in 1950 and went to South Africa to visit his family. On his way back, the following year, his childhood nanny Jessie Lightfoot died at his London home. She had been his closest companion and confidante, helping him cook (she slept on the kitchen table), shoplift and organise illegal gambling parties. Francis was inconsolable – she was the most important woman in his life and his devotion to her was like that of a son. Upon her demise, Francis grew closer to Muriel.

GRAHAM MASON: Muriel adored Francis, he would call her 'Mother' and she in return called Francis 'Daughter'. Francis was a founder member and unstintingly loyal to Muriel, bringing lots of wealthy people into her orbit. Oh, she liked the readies and the handbags being opened – 'How's your handbag today, dear? *Get that handbag out, girl!'* – An awful woman but so charming and above all so wonderfully funny. But when she was going to be horrid, my God, she was a horrid girl!

DARREN COFFIELD: Whenever a guest outstayed their welcome, Muriel had a foolproof way of getting rid of them. 'Now let's all have a drink with this lovely Miss So-and-So,' she'd announce loudly to Ian Board, who would have already started pouring the drinks. 'Open your handbag, dear,' she'd instruct her victim, who'd have to grimace to a chorus of 'Cheers!' from a room full of hostile strangers. The cost of such a round was ruinous since her drinks were said to be the most expensive in London. 'They can't be so clever if they pay my prices,' quipped Muriel. However she allowed her 'daughter' unlimited credit – Francis ran up a £2,000 champagne bill at one point, an immense sum in the fifties.

DANIEL FARSON: 'Muriel Belcher. Muriel Belcher!' exclaimed my angry bank manager, threatening to return my cheques. 'Who is this woman you're keeping?'

GRAHAM MASON: Once I went absolutely potty and did a three-day violent binge, and of course I ran out of money right at the outset and would cash cheques every twenty minutes or so. Oh God! The courage it took to creep back in there and say to Muriel, 'Sorry, these cheques are going to come back.' – 'What! The whole shooting match?' You've got to remember in those days cashing a biggish cheque across the counter was about £3.

MARSH DUNBAR: She had the most enormous handbag, in which she had all one's bounced cheques with 'REFER TO DRAWER' stamped on them.

GRAHAM MASON: She made me then sign something like ten post-dated cheques, month by month paying it off. They didn't want to lose your custom. They wanted to make money out of you. Muriel would say, 'Don't be such a cunt dear and buy us all a drink.'

COLIN MacINNES: Credit, according to the regulations, 'is illegal', but is often given, since the illusion of getting drinks for free encourages further spending. The belief is strong, among club habitués, that the 'bill', when finally presented, is always inflated beyond the sum actually drunk.

ALIX COLEMAN: Muriel Belcher has her areas of shyness and sensibility. She gets angry with members who don't settle up, and writes them excommunicatory letters late at night . . . I've had letters, says one member, 'covered with drink, saying pay your bar bill. They're sweet, deteriorating at the bottom.' – 'Like me dear,' says Muriel.

MRS SIXPENCE: She referred to the club's mechanical cash register as her 'Jewish Piano'. She liked the sound of the old-fashioned rings and bells, so she could hear how much was going in. When they had wealthy people there, Ian would nick their champagne and pour a glass for the cash-poor person at the end of the bar. Or if you were rich and not drinking your champagne fast enough in Ian's opinion, he would pour half of it down the sink and say, 'You're running out. Do you want another bottle?' It was real skulduggery. If he had four bottles of champagne open on the counter, he wanted to get rid of them so he could take more money and open more bottles. We always paid for our drinks in cash. Others went in with no money and ran up a tab and paid it at the end of the month, but I wouldn't have trusted any of them at all. Bottles were never allowed on top of the counter, so if you bought a bottle of champagne, they would pour your glass behind the counter, not directly in front of you. Ian would then go up and down the counter depending on your liquidity with money. It was a bit like Robin Hood; if he thought you couldn't afford it and you had a charming or witty personality, he would pour you a glass of champagne from someone else's bottle.

MICHAEL HEATH: I was first taken to the Colony in 1958 by Jeffrey Bernard. Muriel was there – 'Who's this *cunt*?' she said. There was an old-fashioned one-arm bandit machine in the corner, which I played idly. I had beginner's luck and won the jackpot, £40, which showered out in loose change. I collected my winnings and left. Ian Board followed me out and started shouting abuse at me. It transpired that anybody who won the jackpot had to buy a round of drinks in the club, otherwise you'd be barred. So I went back, bought a round of drinks and lost my £40.

COLIN MacINNES: Club owners are various in temperament, but it's in the nature of the job that they must be patient, obliging, firm, shrewd and tactful – all attractive qualities. As for the profit they make, if you work it out, even roughly, what their wages bill must be, add rent in an expensive quarter, and other likely charges, it's clear it can't be terrific. But the charm of their calling is the life: the constant exercise of social flair. In the words of one of them (now retired): 'It's a perpetual party where your friends pay for the liquor.' And it's a tribute to their popularity that the club is always known not by its real name, but by theirs . . .

DARREN COFFIELD: 'Muriel's', as it was affectionately known, worked so well because the members were friends of Muriel, attending her slightly mad party. Many relished listening to Muriel's malicious gossip concerning mutual friends – until they departed and her knife became firmly planted in their own backs.

MERILYN THOROLD: My husband always said our marriage wasn't broken up by another man, it was the club. He was right, absolutely right.

MURIEL: I can listen to three conversations at once, dear. The whole lot. It doesn't matter about my temper. No one would dare answer me back. I can be as bad-tempered as I like. Anyhow, we're not used to insults. We're only used to the highest compliments. I give people one minute to get down the stairs, then my tongue begins to wag.

ELIZABETH SMART: I remember once, wavering and weaving and a bit above myself, beside the high stool where she always sat, and seeing her reflected in the dark mirrors opposite, and thinking, It's Francis Bacon's Pope! And I still think so, impertinently, in spite of Velazquez.

FRANK NORMAN: I have yet to meet someone who is a match for Muriel when it comes to a verbal punch-up. I have seen her render even the toughest of her members helpless under a barrage of abuse, the intensity of which leaves them inarticulate, chattering imbeciles.

DARREN COFFIELD: Muriel and her members could observe one another indirectly in the pieces of mirror dotted around the club's walls. The long shards acted like one of Francis Bacon's paintings, pulling people to bits and putting them back together in unlikely ways. They evoked the dislocation of things in the room. The subdued lighting gave it an air of foreboding.

DANIEL FARSON: Muriel is the only person I know with eyes in the back of her head, or else there is a most skilful use of mirrors. She carries on a conversation with a volley of asides to people apparently behind her: 'Can you keep a secret, Charlie?' she asks Charles Campbell, who replies, 'Of course not, Muriel.' – 'Hello darling, where's your beautiful wife?' to someone who has just entered, and then to an advertising man well-known for wangling trips abroad, who is crouched on the floor behind the piano, playing with a husky dog: 'Hold on to your sleigh, girl, or he'll bum a free ride to Alaska.' Both the dog and the man look up astonished. She adds, 'Glad to see you got the message,' and continues the conversation conspiratorially, 'Well Charlie, I'll tell you anyway.' She tells Charles Campbell a story about a rather rich friend of theirs who answered a 'husband and wife want to meet an interesting companion' ad. He had to travel a long way on a suburban train to a suburban house where he met a suburban couple, and while he tussled on the carpet with the lady wife, the husband was happily engaged on the bed. Afterwards he complained bitterly to Muriel that the poor-quality carpet had badly frayed his elbows. 'I think he was more used to the Aubusson or the Wilton, dear,' said Muriel. Then – 'Oh, Ian, look who it is,' as someone else came in, 'it's old . . . old . . .' having plainly forgotten his name.

ELIZABETH SMART: . . . the Colony also was a kind of continuing multiple serial story. You got the latest developments in people's private lives, careers, states of inebriation. Though she was very discreet in spite of what seemed like loose talk. She could rebuke you with an imperial SSH! if you encroached on taboo ground. Once I rashly mentioned a sexual aberration of an elderly Canadian (he liked to have nappies put on: but it was the *Canadian* element that struck me), and I was mortified at my lapse. Some of her best friends might have had these little eccentricities, but it was other more important things that mattered. It wasn't done, either, to go on too much about members' suicides – not gloomily, anyhow – it spoiled the moment.

IAN BOARD: The club was particularly busy between three p.m. and five-thirty p.m. The afternoon hours were always best to meet the most eccentric members, people who don't actually work, with Thursday afternoon the busiest time before the grander members, such as the Duke of Sutherland, left for the country.

DARREN COFFIELD: It was a rite of passage for many upper-class youths to spend a period of life slumming it around Soho. For these wannabe bohemians, the poverty was entirely self-inflicted. Being unemployable is hard work and adversity is an education; for an artist may gain inspiration from hustling in bars, but none from a desk job. Only the hardy could survive whilst the weak inevitably caved in and got a job.

BIG EDDI: Muriel had the ability to keep this group of disparate individuals in some degree of order as a family, and would look after various people in that respect. Alcoholics never remember people's names, so Muriel gave them names that would stick in her memory and create familiarity. Many members were known only by their nicknames. It was possible to drink there for years and be blissfully unaware of their real names and professions. The monikers made sense once you got to know the person – they were characters of club folklore. Such as 'Foreskin', a captain of industry; 'Twiggy', an international businessman of huge girth; 'Maid Marion', David Marrion; 'Minty', John Minton; 'Sylvie', David Sylvester; Francis Bacon's last muse, John Edwards, always referred to Francis as 'Eggs' as in 'eggs and bacon'.

MICHAEL HEATH: Because of my surname Heath, I became known as 'Hampstead'. There was also 'Stuttering Sara', 'Miss Whiplash', 'Black Sheep', 'Brian the Burglar', 'Mumsie', 'Mrs Sixpence', 'Miss Blowjob' and 'Miss Hitler'. One female member was known as 'Butter Legs' because they spread so easily. We were assigned names and roles as if in a Dickensian melodrama.

INDIAN AMY: I first went to the Colony in 1949. Muriel christened me 'Indian Amy' because I came from Bombay, although my real name was Cynthia Blythe. I used to go there every day of the week – I worked hard all day and got smashed every night. You never got stuck with one person, one was always being introduced to various people by Muriel, so your circle widened all the time. The most interesting people I ever met in my life were at the Colony. Other club owners would drop in from time to time, but Muriel never went to see them, she couldn't be bothered.

MURIEL: The trouble is if I go to someone else's club, I am liable to run into someone who owes me money. I don't mind having it out with someone in the Colony, but I don't like to embarrass them in someone else's place . . . It's a funny thing about people who give me dud cheques: they always say they do not know how it could have happened, they always blame the bank manager, that they had no idea that they did not have any money in their account . . . They may stay away for three months, but in the end they come back and pay up!

DANIEL FARSON: The club world is a shifting one. A club has its moment, and fades; people pass by or pass on; it's redecorated and loses its personality; another takes its place. Muriel is the exception – she continues . . .

MURIEL: John Braine [author of *Room at the Top*] was in here once and everyone teased him until he said, 'I've been insulted in your club.' – 'No room at the top for you here,' I said, 'Fuck off.'

MERILYN THOROLD: When I first went there, I was twenty-three and I thought, I can't believe I'm in this place with these poets and painters I admire so much. I didn't realise it existed. It was extraordinary. The conversation was so vital and witty. I was impressed not just by Noël Coward and E. M. Forster, but also by the poets who drank there too, like Louis MacNeice, George Barker, Paul Potts and David Wright. They were all painted by Patrick Swift, the 'poets' painter'. Observing Stephen Spender, Muriel said, 'I don't know why they call *her* Spender . . . *She* never puts her hand in her pocket.' Muriel always insisted on calling all of her male members 'her' or 'she', 'Mary' or 'Lottie'.

ALIX COLEMAN: Her members are hooked. Through the heavy club door, to be met, regardless of sex, with a chummy, adenoidal 'Hello Mary,' they find themselves greatly easy; there's an air of mild, fairly indifferent welcome about the place and a kind of liberating smut to Muriel's conversation. Its themes are repetitive and catchy . . . she don't care what she say, though others might.

DANIEL FARSON: None of them take themselves all that seriously – how could they with Muriel and Ian to demolish them? 'Look, she's got a new frock!' Muriel will cry at a member who arrives in a striking new suit, or to a well-known literary figure, 'Hello Kate, you're late. I'll give you a whack in a moment,' and turning to Ian, 'Look! She's wearing trousers today!'

FRANCIS BACON: . . . she dissolves the sexes so that they come together in a relaxed way to live out their hour's fantasy. That's happening all over now – it's called unisex, and she's been doing it for years. Her language has become very exaggerated and she turns on 'he and she', like 'Hot and Cold', until she doesn't know who 'he and she' are any more, and that vaporises the atmosphere for a start. She creates this state where people feel free to talk about themselves and their desires. I love her looks. I think she's extraordinary-looking. She has a very grand air about her. There's something there that has come from an ancient world – perhaps the Babylonian world. I've learnt ways of approach from Muriel. She made me understand how to attempt, at least, to enchant.

MAID MARION: Leonard Blackett replaced Francis as the club hostess, beaming at people with his long cigarette holder. Muriel nicknamed him 'Granny'. He was an old queen who'd been a captain in World War I and won the Military Cross for bravery at the Somme – Muriel said, 'She was a brave little soldier.' He was a small, quiet, impeccably dressed man who sat drinking every night in the Colony for twenty years, amidst all the mayhem around him, a real old-fashioned bachelor. 'They don't make queers like that any more,' said Ian.

MURIEL: I suppose poofs stood out much more then, although they didn't behave badly, no groping. Today chaps go on more queer than queers, but they're normal. Sometimes instead of getting pissed they get drugged – though not in my club. They wouldn't dare bring the stuff to the Colony. They've too much respect. It's the tone of the place, dear . . . and I have a very good eye for what's going on, pissed or sober.

GERALD McCANN: Muriel made them all behave. They wouldn't dare misbehave in her presence, she would hit them with her handbag. And to pep us all up, every so often she would give us a little yellow pill, after which the talking became rather feverish.

DAVID EDWARDS: The luxury of the club was that if you told a joke you would be thrown out. You had to survive on your own anecdotes and wit – Muriel and Ian were very strict on that.

MAID MARION: George Melly had a good sharp tongue, very witty. He wore very loud suits made from women's dress material and a big hat, and he really livened up the place. He used to come in when Mike McKenzie was on the piano.

BIG EDDI: Mike McKenzie played the piano in the club and was later the pianist at the Savoy. He was a very bright, small black man, from Guyana, handicapped with a withered leg. He came about because he took a one-week relief engagement, replacing the club's usual pianist, Yorke de Souza. Over time Muriel became more a friend than an employer. Colin MacInnes was best man at Mike's wedding in 1952 and Francis claimed that his favourite song was 'Strange Love', composed by Mike and his actress wife Liz. If Mike knew what songs you liked, he would play them as you came through the club door. Occasionally I would sing with him.

KENNY CLAYTON: The magic of Mike was the way distinguished artistes found it irresistible to get up and join him at the piano. If you were a club pianist, you were supposed to have musical numbers or theme tunes for individual members as they arrived. The actor Trevor Howard came in once and asked, 'Do you know "The Folks Who Live on the Hill"? It's my favourite song.' So, from then on, whenever he came into the club, Mike would play his favourite tune straight away. Francis Bacon's 'tune' was a jazz composition by Billy Strayhorn.

COLIN MACINNES: The greatest charmer is the pianist . . . He breaks off his current tune to play each new arrival in with a theme song he's chosen for them – either flattering, like 'You Go to My Head', or if he thinks they can take it, one loaded with innuendo.

GEORGE MELLY: When Mike left, we had a small, gay South African pianist, Todd Matshikiza. He was perfectly good, but people used to give him drinks and he couldn't hold them, so he'd wet himself and sit in a pool. So Muriel, being witty and quick, and him being a self-wetting South African, named him 'Victoria of Victoria Falls'. She had to sack him, not because of the peeing, but because he swore a lot when he was drunk. I said, 'But Muriel, you swear all the time.' – 'These words are all right from my pretty lips, but not from the pianist's. The carriage trade don't like it!' So poor Victoria of Victoria Falls went.

MURIEL: A man came barging in the door one day, shouting, 'Hands up I've got a gun!' Someone called the police while I kept him talking. Within five minutes the whole of Dean Street was blocked off. But when they searched the man, the only offensive weapon they could find on him was a pencil. I didn't press charges and later that night he came back and asked me if I would give him a job playing the piano for a pound a week.

FRANK NORMAN: Did he get the job?

MURIEL: What do you think?

DARREN COFFIELD: The next person to tinkle the ivories was Adam who played the piano in the evenings after college. For the first couple of months, he was so intimidated, he wouldn't leave his piano stool, even when bursting for a pee. He'd arrived at the Colony with some friends one Saturday night in the 1960s, intending to go on to an all-night film. But never made it . . .

ADAM: Nobody was at the piano and somehow, through a barrage of insults from Madam, I sat down and played. I thought maybe it was like a funny pub. Perhaps Muriel was desperate for something to hide the cigarette burns on the stool for she came over, thrust her half-full glass of champagne, covered with lipstick, into my hand and said: 'Put your bum down, Miss . . . and be my pianist from Monday nine o'clock.' I didn't really have much choice, did I? . . . I could hardly shut my eyes, let alone say anything. I couldn't believe that just because four-letter words were used instead of punctuation that everyone was in fact fantastically friendly. Now that I'm more at ease, what amuses me about people asking for tunes, which I never know anyway, is not that the person asks for the same tune every time he's there, but roughly once every five minutes.

GERALD MCCANN: One night Muriel said to Ian, 'I am not going to drink vodka, I am going to try that hash.' Someone had bought a big block of it for her birthday and Ian Board had it made into fairy cakes. So we were chatting and she ate a cake, then another with no apparent effect. Then she consumed a third . . . She slowly clambered down from her stool, steadied herself along the wall and went to the loo for at least half an hour. Eventually she came crawling back in slow motion and slithered, in reverse, back up on her perch and loudly proclaimed, 'I don't know, that hash doesn't do anything for me.' We were all on the floor in hysterics. She was totally stoned out of her mind but couldn't see it at all. Anyway her flirtation with hash didn't last long as she missed the swill of vodka round her tonsils.

DANIEL FARSON: But of course there are days when one opens the door jaunty with expectation to find that the magic of the soufflé has fallen – Muriel looking in front of her as if she is carved from stone, Ian exhausted: a couple of the duller members slumped on their stools while Adam plays 'The Party's Over' . . .

ADAM: I love Muriel saying, 'Hello me old mate' to someone who's just come through the door and then, while the guest is being signed in, turning to Ian and whispering all too audibly – 'What the fuck's her name?' But with people she knows, and there must be thousands of them, you always know where you are – you're either a good mate or you're not. I wish people who are quite obviously not would realise it sooner. I get so embarrassed when someone goes through those well-known rites of sycophantic sacrifice, self-sacrifice rather. There is no excuse for overstaying a patently wilting welcome.

DICK WHITTINGTON: Some Colony regulars were there strictly for their contributions to Muriel's purse, and it was noticeable that she could tolerate bores with a good cheque-signing wrist action. I recall one man who was violently anti-Semitic but welcomed by Muriel for his chequebook, which she demanded he produce whenever he caused her offence with some vile remark about Jews, niggers or queers. Since Muriel was a lesbian Jew, whose girlfriend Carmel was black, his tongue cost him dearly. This same man . . . once enthralled us by saying he had brought his new wife up to town from his country estate only once, and that was to be taught by his regular prostitute how to suck cock properly. We all hoped she was well paid for her tutelage for it must have been a pretty grim task.

DARREN COFFIELD: Muriel would milk the members who annoyed her. For example, during a conversation Charles Campbell was being picked on at the bar by a retired colonel, who began ranting at him for being a conscientious objector during the last war. Charlie tried to point out that he was only five when the war ended, but the apoplectic colonel was having none of it.

DANIEL FARSON: In the middle of a further tirade, the colonel was interrupted by Muriel who asked if he would contribute to her holiday in Mombasa. Obediently he paused and wrote out a cheque for £200 before continuing his abuse. When Charlie saw him the next day, the colonel was consumed with guilt. 'Do you think Miss M. will let me in?' he asked, which was rather preposterous considering his lavish donation to her hols.

DARREN COFFIELD: Muriel and Ian's annual holiday in Kenya was a necessary escape from the stresses of Soho. August was usually spent lounging by the pool, sipping the occasional beer and seeing nothing of the world outside. That is until one day they spotted the comedian Ronnie Corbett and his wife on the other side of the dining room. Ian wandered over and introduced himself, explaining that they had many mutual friends in common, such as Danny La Rue. From then on they became inseparable until the fateful evening when the Corbetts invited them to dinner at another hotel further along the coast.

DANIEL FARSON: 'Everything was *flambé*,' Ian recalls. They were placed in the grill-room near the window, which failed to open, and the temperature rose. 'They had those bloody *flambé* bananas and everyone was copying everyone else – the place was full of flames. Poor Muriel was trying to cool herself with the menu as a fan, but when the couple at the next table had flaming bananas too, she said, "I hope to fuck they choke you." Ronnie Corbett rose from his chair outraged. "If you are going to behave like that," he said, "I must leave," and stalked off to pay the bill. When he stalked back, he was met by the infuriating sight of the two tables joined together in animated conversation . . . and the grateful greeting from the young couple: "We haven't enjoyed ourselves so much since we came here!'" At which Mr Corbett's righteous indignation had no choice but to collapse. He joined them.

MAID MARION: A journalist asked a sunburnt Muriel if she had enjoyed her annual holiday to Kenya. 'How was Africa?' – 'Hot dear.' – 'Did you see any lions?' – 'If I want to see those,' replied Muriel, 'I usually take a taxi to Regents Park.'

DARREN COFFIELD: My favourite Muriel story is the one Dick Whittington told of when Muriel and Ian would go to the Mombasa Beach Hotel every August. On their third annual pilgrimage, 'the manager approached Muriel and asked her with due deference whether there was something wrong with the pool. Muriel fixed him with an obsidian stare and asked him what he meant exactly. He laughed nervously. Well, he could not help noticing that from time to time, she would take the few steps from her lounger to the pool before lowering herself slowly down the steps into the water, would stay there for a minute or two, then ascend and return to her cold beer. He paused awkwardly and crooked a quizzical eyebrow, begging for clarification. 'Don't be a cunt, dear. I only go in for a piss,' she explained magnanimously.

2

Send in the Clowns

DANIEL FARSON: Is there a common denominator that attracts such a motley crowd? A typical afternoon, and you might find Lady Rose McLaren; Allan Hall who is 'Atticus' of the *Sunday Times*; Desmond O'Donovan who sells TV networks in places like Mauritius and always looks wonderfully tanned and expensive in a smart blue suit; Lucian Freud . . . who sidles around the door for a Perrier water; . . . a hefty black girl who is plainly lesbian, judging by the stranglehold on her pretty companion; an ancient BBC radio producer asleep in a corner; myself asleep in another corner; Thea Porter who started the fashion in 'grannie, attic-type' dresses; . . . George Melly who has invited Muriel and Ian to join him on his TV chat show; Frank Norman who has written of Muriel that 'she is without doubt the most famous and best loved of all the club proprietors' and has just finished a play . . . loosely based on the club . . .

DARREN COFFIELD: It held the fascination of forbidden fruit. In this tiny one-room world, they could be found at four p.m.

on a sunny afternoon, curtains drawn, gossiping their lives away in a psychological pressure cooker. It became an impromptu performance space where Muriel was the ringmaster. Their feverish conversation and exuberance made the very room where they drank into a theatre. Some would recite poetry, others might burst into song but the star turns were always the club's 'clowns', and as we all know, some clowns are the stuff of nightmares.

KEITH HEWETT: Nina Hamnett would exchange anecdotes of her glory years for drinks. She was one of the truly great characters of her age, but one whose artistic talents were ultimately wasted by drink. By the time I met her in the Colony, she was living in penury – a monument to Fitzrovia's lost Bohemia, the area north of Oxford Street, which was all but gone post-war, bombed out and under redevelopment. Fitzrovia was a ghost of what it once had been. Young artists like Minton and Bacon would meet there and drift down to Soho where the bohemian crowd had relocated. Nina made appearances in Soho, but in her last years she was an unpredictable drunk who peed on the furniture. Such behaviour did not endear her to Muriel who nevertheless tolerated Nina as the 'Queen of Bohemia'.

SANDY FAWKES: I stumbled over Nina Hamnett . . . a famous beauty in the 1920s . . . She called the first volume of her autobiography *Laughing Torso*, but even at that age, I recognised there was nothing funny in an old woman lying in a pool of her own piss.

DARREN COFFIELD: She'd adopted a lifestyle considered outrageous – a heavy drinker, she was both bisexual and promiscuous. In her youth she modelled for Augustus John, and in

1912 travelled to Paris. She spent the next two decades flitting between both cities as an artist and model, meeting the entire avant-garde of both capitals. Modigliani painted her – she boasted that she had the best tits in Europe and would pull up her top to show them off. She was up for anything, including dancing naked on a table in a Montparnasse bar.

AUGUSTUS JOHN: She was the soul of generosity, as many a forlorn artist in Montparnasse in search of a drink, a meal and a doss-down could testify.

DARREN COFFIELD: When a young Bruce Bernard ran away from home, Nina took him in and fed him – 'She was very kind but I got bedbugs and left!' Often said to be neatly sick in her handbag, by this stage she was considered a cultural relic. A 1956 radio play featuring an unapologetic parody of her as an inept, talentless drunk was too much to bear. She jumped from her balcony and was impaled on the railings below, murmuring – 'Why won't they let me die?' She was visited in hospital by a distraught Lucian Freud who stared down in dismay at her shattered body. Her lingering death led to a coup in Bohemia with Muriel crowned 'Queen of Soho' and Francis Bacon superseding Augustus John as 'King'.

TOM DEAS: Life in the Colony thrived on frisson and whenever the club's green door clicked open, all heads would turn in expectation. If it were Francis, the room seemed to brighten in anticipation of an amusing afternoon. Francis rarely disappointed, and everyone suddenly raised their game a notch as they fed off his infectious enthusiasm – 'Look, do you want some champagne? Good. Well, you may not believe this, but . . .'

FRANCIS BACON: . . . the most *extraordinary* thing happened to me! I was in Westminster Bank yesterday and this stranger came up to me and asked if I knew the way to Harrods. Well, really! He could have thought of a better excuse for picking me up than *that* . . . As a matter of fact he was rather good-looking in a fascist sort of way, sunburnt, told me he was a colonel in the South African Army, and then he asked me for lunch.

FRANK NORMAN: The funny thing about [Francis] was that he wasn't by any manner or means the best-looking geezer in the world, in fact the truth is he was hideous, his teeth were like Gorgonzola cheese . . . and his mince pies were too close together, as though these slight disadvantages were not enough he was also queer, and only fancied rough trade which he picked up in the tougher pubs around the manor . . . mostly sailors and guardsmen, who loved him for the two quid he bunged them, and the booze which he poured down their throats . . . (usually the toughest one) . . . would most likely beat him up and roll him for his money and watch . . .

DARREN COFFIELD: A series of older lovers shaped Francis' life. He was introduced to the former fighter pilot, Peter Lacy, by Leonard Blackett at the Colony and for the first time fell totally in love – 'Being in love in that way . . . is like an illness.' Lacy was a former fighter pilot turned club pianist. He was also a sadomasochist with a comprehensive collection of rhino whips. After beating Francis with his frenzied foreplay, he would proceed to destroy as many of Francis' paintings as he could find. Lacy dominated Francis to the point where he found it impossible to paint – 'It was like that song, I couldn't live with him and I couldn't live without him.'

FORESKIN: Francis Bacon? Oh yes, he wasn't famous at the time – he was very anti-social and could completely blank people. I was sitting next to him one afternoon while he was going through his pockets – 'Here, you'd better have these.' They were scribbles and sketches. I thought, what would I want with that crap? And tore them up. Those scribbles are worth millions now.

GRAHAM MASON: Francis could charm people automatically. His magic, I don't understand how it worked or what it was, but it was. He just walked into a room and it lit up; it did happen, I assure you. You could have three or four people sitting in the Colony at three-thirty in the afternoon, a desultory chat – Francis would walk in and within ten minutes the place would be alive.

DARREN COFFIELD: He may have been making some of his most iconic paintings during this period, but money was often hard to come by. Both Daniel Farson and Charlie Campbell were offered a 'Pope' painting for £150. *Screaming Popes* – as the artist Elinor Bellingham-Smith called them – 'Popes Shouting on the Toilet', 'Popes with Toothache or Arse Ache' . . .

FRANK NORMAN: . . . [Francis] was a piss artist and he took great delight in turning his back on me whenever I went over to where he was standing, and when I spoke to him he would always without fail stare over my shoulder, or turn away when I was in the middle of a sentence . . . the reason for this was no other than the fact that I loved him. The more he ignored me the more I loved him . . . all of a sudden a lady came in (a lady being a bird who eats a banana sideways). She came straight over to where we were standing and showed out . . . Needless to say I was not invited to join the conversation that they struck up . . . Whenever I tried to chip in two pennyworth of dialogue he just glared over my shoulder and smiled at someone on the other side of the room. No matter how much he humiliated me I was still kinky about him . . . but then of course I am a terror for punishment.

MICHAEL HEATH: You couldn't go up and speak to Francis. You had to be introduced to him. Which Ian Board did many times because Francis would get so drunk he'd forget. Ian only did it to be malicious – he'd introduce me and say, 'Francis I want you to meet another artist, you'd get on so well together.' Francis was a terrifying man; he'd say, 'What do you do?' – 'I'm a cartoonist.' – 'Well, very important job that is. Chronicling life, putting it down on paper. *I salute you!* Of course, *I can't* paint or draw.' I would then edge away in case he blew up in my face. One day when Ian introduced me again for the umpteenth time, I went through the routine of telling him what I did for a living and he gave me his stock-in-trade response. As I turned away I overheard Francis ask Ian, 'Who was that cunt?'

RAY NATKIEL: Looking back on it all now, it seems like another world. Why did we all drink there? It was as if we were plucked in from the street by an unseen hand as we walked past. Around three-thirty in the afternoon, a shaft of light would come in and illuminate the bar and the thick smoky atmosphere, causing everything to develop a halo effect. It was a magical light where you could watch huge clouds of cigarette smoke dance across the room. Graham Mason could be found propping up the bar at three-thirty p.m. watching his cigarette smoke twirl around the room.

DARREN COFFIELD: Graham was friends with much of the artistic flotsam and jetsam that washed up in Soho. He enjoyed talking to Francis in the Colony because Francis was very funny, and Francis enjoyed talking to him until they had a furious row. Jeffrey Bernard once said to Graham, 'You know those fish in Richard's in Brewer Street, haddock particularly. You can tell if they're fresh by the eyes. Well, if you were a haddock I'd leave you on the slab.'

MAID MARION: Graham's one-liners were so dry they were hilarious. He was one of the great wits of the Colony alongside Muriel and Francis. Graham was originally from South Africa, was well-educated and had a very good job as a journalist, earning £20 a week, which was a fortune back then.

MISS WHIPLASH: He worked for TV news, viewing the news footage and taking out what was considered too harrowing for public broadcasting. The stuff they could broadcast was tiny compared to what they viewed – the footage was horrific. He worked with another Soho regular, Mike McNish, a talkative Scot. Their daily diet of horror transformed them both from sharp, witty, well-educated men into raging alcoholic nihilists who could see no reason or point to anything between the newsreels and the bar.

GEORGE MELLY: Dan Farson also had a sort of despair. It didn't kill him for a long time, but the fact is that at a certain point in the evening, he turned from being the very charming man he was, into a werewolf.

MICHAEL HEATH: If you met Dan in the morning, he would be charming – 'Oh, dear boy, how wonderful to see you, let me buy you a drink.' Then if you saw him in the evening, you soon became aware of his mood change – 'I hate you, you're disgusting, you can't draw! You're fucking rubbish!' Then the next morning he would have reverted back to his charming self – 'Oh, dear boy, how wonderful to see you, let me buy you a drink.' That always intrigued me. In the Charlie Chaplin film *City Lights*, a man is befriended by an alcoholic millionaire who insists on taking him drinking and then back to his huge mansion, showering him with money and presents. Then in the morning, the now sober millionaire denies any knowledge of him and gets the police round to throw him out.

ORLANDO CAMPBELL: I'm not sure if he had an innate sense of history, but Dan was right there with the central figures of the time, either photographing them for posterity or interviewing them. His job with *Picture Post* magazine introduced him to the bohemian world of 1950s Soho. He was later sacked from the magazine for a 'misadventure' with his boyfriend.

TOM DEAS: After that Dan moved to TV. He was one of the first investigative reporters for ITV television and became an overnight success. He was the first reporter to go on live TV without a clipboard and a list of questions to conduct a completely unscripted interview. This was unheard of in those days, questions were usually vetted and agreed by the interviewee beforehand. His pioneering approach made compelling television, taking an uncompromising, warts and all, look at contemporary issues. At the height of his fame, he was parodied on television by the comedian Benny Hill.

TWIGGY: The first time 'fuck' was ever said on television was when Farson was interviewing Caitlin Thomas, Dylan Thomas' widow. Farson had taken Caitlin up to Soho where they'd met Francis who got her absolutely rat-arsed. Caitlin started swearing live on national television. They had to pull the plug on the broadcast, which was a disaster. Entirely Francis' fault and done on purpose. It's a good illustration of Francis' relationship with Farson – he always said he couldn't stand the man, whereas Farson always said Francis was his best friend and tried to curry favour by finding men for him. They both shared a taste for rough trade.

KEITH HEWETT: He was generally known as 'Dan *Fat*-son' or 'Mind the Face'. He was a sadomasochist with a penchant for wearing ladies' lingerie. He especially liked sailors to beat him up, but because he was on television, he always said, 'Mind the face, mind the face!'

GERALDINE NORMAN: Dan used to stay with me from time to time; he'd come back drunk with some rough trade. Jeff Bernard explained to me that Dan would get down on his knees and bend over, holding up a picture of a sumptuous bosomy girl to get the rough trade really going. The last time he did this in my spare room and passed out. The rough trade went sneaking round to see what was worth pinching. Dan was arrested for picking up a boy in the Piccadilly public lavatories and sacked from television. He came from an affluent background and ploughed his entire inheritance into purchasing the Waterman's Arms pub and a very nice house in Limehouse by the River Thames where he lived with his boyfriend and, surprisingly, his boyfriend's girlfriend.

MAID MARION: Dan was not cut out for the pub trade and blamed his misfortune on the Colony accountant Fred Adams.

Fred was softly spoken and very overweight, with a huge nose, not the kind of character your heart would go out to immediately. He was on the committee of the Colony and known affectionately as 'Aunty Fred' because everyone told him their problems – the club's agony aunt. He was what you might call a late starter. One day he said, 'David, no one knows I'm gay, would you come out with me as a friend so people will know that I am gay.' We enjoyed each other's company but he liked to big himself up too much. He was the accountant for successful East End people like Thea Porter and Queenie Watts. When Dan bought the pub, he wanted to recreate the atmosphere of an old-time music hall, but it was never a success and he lost £30,000, a small fortune, which bankrupted him. One afternoon Dan came into the Colony yelling, *'You thieving bastard!'* Fred would look after the pub for him whilst he was away, but Dan had all his 'friends' running it; they were ripping him off. Fred went behind the bar to get things a bit even and say, 'I'm here now and I'll be watching you!' But the staff had it sewn up. Dan got taken in by a lot of people; he was a 'funny man' when he'd had a drink. You'd see him at the Kray twins' club, the Kentucky, but he wasn't particularly welcome there. He was pissed, swearing and slobbering all over the place. He loved himself for being a TV star. The twins didn't like swearing, especially in front of women. He was a brilliant man at times. It's funny how they just go downhill, isn't it?

DICK WHITTINGTON: Sometimes Dan would smother me with charm; at other times glare at me with a naked hatred that made me feel uncomfortable. After five years of this schizophrenic socialising, the mystery was decoded one afternoon in the Colony. Owl-eyed drunk he did an exaggerated double take, then slurred, 'Is it you, Dick, or that awful twin of yours I can't bear?'

TOM DEAS: Dan came from a long line of writers. His great-uncle, Bram Stoker, wrote *Dracula* and his father Negley Farson was a famous American author. Dan's bankruptcy forced him to move to Devon, where, between drunken bouts, he became a prolific writer. He'd get the Friday train up from Devon and wander into Soho. Being a television interviewer, he was a good conversationalist at the start of a session in the Colony. Then he'd hit the Golden Lion, a notorious gay pub, and from then on, it was mayhem – he'd be beaten up and robbed, have incomprehensible conversations nobody could understand, get drunk in pursuit of men (the more dubious the men the more he liked them) and would occasionally wander in with a black eye. Once the weekend was over, he'd head back home to Devon to dry out and write. One day I was with Dan in the Colony, and Francis Bacon wandered over: 'You call yourself a writer, do you?' – 'Yes.' – 'Your dad was a writer but not you!' And Francis went on and on until Dan eventually broke down and cried, grabbing at my arm, imploring me, 'Tell him he's wrong!' As if I could tell Francis Bacon he was wrong! Having got Dan in tears, Francis wandered back over to his champagne, happy that he'd upset somebody. He loved doing that. If he had it in for someone like Dan, he'd go on and on until he reduced them to tears.

JAMES BIRCH: Originally their relationship was the other way round. At the beginning Dan was quite important to Francis, interviewing him for TV – Dan was a household name and Francis was not. But he was such a sycophant that Francis couldn't stand it. One day Dan came through the door with some old cronies he wanted to impress: 'Oh, look some of my favourite people here – Francis, John, James . . .' Whereupon Francis said, 'Oh no, not you, Dan!' Poor Dan looked like a crestfallen schoolboy.

MOLLY PARKIN: Francis would bully Dan because Dan worshipped him; he was slavishly addicted to him. When Dan looked at Francis, he was like a puppy dog with adoration in his eyes. But you know, I have seen men kick a dog in the face. I'd say to Dan – 'Don't let Francis see you cry, he'll only get worse if you cry.' But as you know with alcohol, the mood can switch within seconds.

TWIGGY: Francis would walk around with his glass at half tilt and the champagne bottle at half tilt too, spilling it over the floor. He'd get through four bottles of champagne but gave most of it away, pouring it out generously with the Edwardian toast – 'Champagne for my real friends, real pain to my sham friends.' He was completely unpredictable, a lateral thinker, which permeated his paintings and conversation too. He'd occasionally wander out to the loo where he'd tip the contents of his own glass down the sink. He'd want everybody else to be merry, although he could be quite sober himself. There is a legendary image of Francis standing at the bar pouring champagne for Lucian Freud, Michael Andrews, Frank Auerbach and Tim Behrens; they were originally labelled 'Muriel's Boys' and then called the School of London by the painter Ron Kitaj.

DARREN COFFIELD: Dan Farson felt at that time the figurative artists in England were being ignored in favour of the fashionable abstract artists in America. Virtually unknown and isolated, this group of gifted artists came together through Muriel, and when asked by Dan why they did so, she replied, 'I think it's my charm, dear.'

TIM BEHRENS: The School of London never existed ... We were just a group of guys who got together in Wheeler's or the

Colony Room to drink . . . Lucian wasn't good and he knew himself he was a pedantic painter. I detested the way he painted . . . I always preferred Bacon, and especially Michael Andrews . . .

GERALDINE NORMAN: Michael Andrews had studied at the Slade, alongside Euan Uglow and Craigie Aitchison, and was a regular at the Colony. Once, Mike, Francis, my husband Frank and I all went and had dinner at Wheeler's. I had to produce a newspaper column for the next day and had no subject, so Frank said, 'Why don't you interview Mike and Francis about art and you've got a ready-made column?' They were very funny. Next morning the phone rang, it was Francis – 'I'm terribly worried. What's Geraldine going to say? Is it going to ruin me? Frank, can you bring a copy round so I can read it?' Mike was tall, slim, good-looking and had a nice sweet wife called June. A great friend of his was Jane Willoughby, who for years was one of Lucian Freud's lovers. Jane was the daughter of an earl and Mike would go to her home and paint the views. He was not interested in gambling and led a life not quite so down and out as the others.

IAN BOARD: Michael Andrews painted the club's mural, behind the piano. It's a copy of a Bonnard, oil on hessian, with about three million layers of nicotine on it. It took him a month to do whilst Muriel and I were on holiday in France. We used to close down the room to redecorate a bit – not too much, you don't ruin the atmosphere for a lick of paint.

KEITH HEWETT: Francis always stood by Muriel and there would be a circle around him. When the money rolled in, it was always champagne all round. But he could be offended and quite rightly so. We used to walk down Dean Street, pressed up either side of Francis, calling out, 'Bacon sandwich! Bacon sandwich anybody?' Francis didn't take to that too much. Another time we were drinking with Francis and the champagne bottle was empty. 'Where's the goose that laid the golden egg?' someone cried, 'Come on, goosey, my glass is empty!' Francis stopped his flow of money and quietly slipped away.

TWIGGY: Of course there were some who just wanted to drink for nothing, and Francis didn't seem to care; he was quite able to look after himself. Once in the Colony, there was a completely plastered guest sponging off Francis – 'Those fucking rubbish paintings of yours! Fucking popes and butchered meat, bloody disgusting.' And the same fellow had the gall to be drinking Francis' champagne – 'Call yourself a painter? You ought to be ashamed of yourself.' Francis listened carefully and smiled at the ranting figure, waiting for a pause. – 'Oh, I don't know, I think they're rather pretty.' This stopped his verbal assailant in their tracks. 'Any-*how*, 'owz about a-top-*up*?' asked Francis.

BRUCE BERNARD: I have to confess that I was one of those who took childish pleasure in imitating his enunciation, which we exaggerated as he often enjoyed doing himself, and which seemed essential to convey his full meaning and humour. Lying helplessly on the pavement, as he once did, and telling an interested policeman, 'I'm a very *fymous pynter*' is an anecdote completely lost unless the marvellously camp pronunciation of the word is conveyed.

DARREN COFFIELD: Francis was given a retrospective at the Tate in 1962. On the day of the opening, he received a telegram informing him that his lover Peter Lacy had died in Tangier. The night after his glittering reception, Francis went to the Colony for Lacy's wake. Dan had just returned from Paris and thought everyone was celebrating the success of Francis' exhibition. When Elinor Bellingham-Smith asked Dan if he'd heard the news, he replied, 'Yes, Francis must be overjoyed.' She slapped his face so hard that the noise caused Francis to turn round and gently steer Dan to the lavatory to explain that Lacy had died. That year, Michael Andrews immortalised the club in his painting, *Colony Room I*, capturing the club's golden age with Bacon and Freud.

JOHN HURT: This was Soho to me, this artistic community was so much more generous and so much more interesting than anything I'd known. But don't imagine because of all the stories I tell, it was just crazy dissipation. Of course we knew how to get drunk, but at the same time the intellectual vigour was extraordinary – feverish conversation.

DARREN COFFIELD: For some, Soho's Bohemia was an abominable sham whilst for others it was part of their schooling. The surrealist painter Edward Burra would visit on his 'London raids'. George Melly recalled he was 'a witty and malicious companion, speaking exclusively in "Mayfair cockney" who sounded like an Edwardian tart' and 'hated to discuss "Fart", as he called it'. Maybe this is where Francis acquired some of his affectations from?

GERALD McCANN: Jean Muir, the fashion designer, was very sweet. One day, she was perched on a stool, wearing a jacket with the belt very high up, and Francis was talking when suddenly his gaze went to the belt on Jean's coat – 'Why is that belt up there?' I said, 'Because she wanted it there, it's fashion.' – 'But it's ridiculous, it's up between her shoulder blades. What's it for? Is it the reins for riding her?' And he went on and on, and she was so upset by the whole thing because Francis was so vicious. Poor Jean, she shouldn't have taken it to heart, after all what did Francis know about fashion? I was walking down Savile Row once on my way to the club, and there was Francis and his sister, who was a very 'county' type of lady. She looked like a young Miss Marple, not at all the sort of sister you'd think he would have. I called out, 'What are you doing in Savile Row?' He said, 'Looking for a leather jacket.' I sent him to Loewe's of Bond Street, and he got himself that little leather bomber jacket that fitted him 'like a treat', as he put it. That and the black tie that Denis Wirth-Miller gave him, was about the extent of his excursion into fashion.

DAVID EDWARDS: Francis loved his clothes. He was very fashion-conscious and always immaculately dressed. One afternoon Francis walked in, annoyed and pulling his collar. – 'What's wrong, Francis?' – 'Fucking Harrods, I'm never going back there again.' He'd attended a special night for select clients and bought a lot of clothes, but when he got home he'd decided he didn't like any of them: 'I bought so many suits and shirts and threw the fucking lot in the dustbin.' You'd never seen the club empty so quickly. The next day everyone was up the club parading around in their new suits and shirts from Francis' dustbin.

GERALD McCANN: Francis loved my outfits and would remark, 'That's a lovely shade of pink, it's like ashes and roses.' I replied, 'Do you know Givenchy said that to me also,' to which Francis would murmur approvingly.

TWIGGY: Gerald McCann is a fashion designer who, he claims, originally discovered my namesake, the model Twiggy, back in the 1960s. He eventually moved to the USA and had a very successful career. He lived at the Algonquin Hotel – it's very elitist, you have to be proposed by a resident and vetted by the management. Gerald arranged for Francis and his new boy-friend George Dyer to stay there. They'd had a terrible row on the flight over and weren't talking to one another. Upon arrival, George went upstairs and left Francis to the hordes of journal-ists waiting for him in the lobby. After half an hour, Francis noticed out of the corner of his eye the hotel manager trying to attract his attention. 'Can't you see I am busy with the journal-ists?' cried Francis and ignored him. Eventually the manager had had enough, 'I'm sorry, Mr Bacon, I really must insist.' – 'Well, what is it then?' – 'I'm afraid Mr Dyer has been taken ill.' – 'Well? What's *wrong* with her?' – 'I'm afraid he's tried to kill himself,' to which Francis remarked, 'Well she would, wouldn't she, the spiteful bitch,' and turned back to the press.

DARREN COFFIELD: Legend has it they met in 1964 during George's attempted burglary of Francis' home. George was a petty criminal and heavy drinker who took obsessive care with his appearance. He soon became a Colony regular, confronting his daily hangover by drinking more. His rugged looks belied a soft, introverted personality. He was often the subject of Francis' pictures and, although he welcomed the attention the paintings brought, did not pretend to like them – 'All that money an' I fink they're reely 'orrible.' George eventually realised how dangerous their lifestyle had become. While in a clinic being treated for alcoholism, he wrote to Francis begging him to stay away from Soho, as it always seems to lead to disaster. Francis' earlier relationships had all been with older men, but now success made him the dominant personality.

JOHN HURT: I remember sitting with Francis at Muriel's and we were the only two people in there. He was reading the newspaper and I looked over and saw it was an article about Picasso. And Francis said, 'You know, when Pablo goes, I'll be number one.'

KEITH HEWETT: It wasn't always a foregone conclusion that Francis Bacon would succeed. In fact it was another Francis who frequented the club, Sir Francis Rose, who was widely tipped to succeed Picasso. Sir Francis was the last protégé of Gertrude Stein and provided an artistic link between the two great hostesses of the twentieth century.

DARREN COFFIELD: Gertrude Stein and Muriel Belcher had much in common. Both lesbians, they became gurus to those who gathered around them and acceptance into their circle was a sought-after stamp of approval. Francis Bacon was aware of Stein's salon from pre-war Paris, where regular guests included Matisse, Picasso, Hemingway and James Joyce. She met the twenty-two-year-old Sir Francis Rose at an exhibition in Paris and nurtured his career hoping he might become her next Picasso. Through her salon he met Cecil Beaton, who mentions Sir Francis in his *Diaries* as 'A man who causes such extra-ordinary violence around him. His life story is a long succession of suicides, killings, fatal accidents. In his wake he brings chaos.' Beaton noted that Sir Francis' nickname, 'Lord Chaos', was richly deserved.

Just as the two great hostesses had much in common, so did their favourite young artists. Like Bacon, Lord Chaos believed in creativity from chaos, saying: 'It is much easier to turn brilliant progressive ideas into chaos than dull and solid ones.' Born in 1909, they were exact contemporaries. Although Lord Chaos' art had no influence on Bacon, his lifestyle certainly did. He needed intense drama in his life in order to paint and engaged in increasingly destructive romantic relationships – dominating and weakening the mental state of a lover until they committed suicide. Like Bacon he also enjoyed becoming the victim, paying a sadistic ex-convict to beat him mercilessly. Both artists' creative paths ran in tandem with an increasingly desperate search for love – a gangster, a mentally disturbed former serviceman, and so on. As well as an unhealthy attraction to habitual criminals, they also shared an appetite for wayward muses – Francis had Henrietta Moraes and Lord Chaos, the dancing wild child, Isadora Duncan.

SIR FRANCIS ROSE: I painted [Isadora] in a studio that I had rented in the port of Villefranche . . . For this portrait she wore a large red shawl with a very long fringe that was later to be the instrument of her death [by becoming] entangled in the spokes of the wheel of the low sports car outside the Henri Plage.

DARREN COFFIELD: In his teens Lord Chaos met Jean Cocteau, who encouraged his artistic and sexual endeavours. Counting the artist Christopher Wood as one of his early conquests, he went on to have an affair with the Nazi leader Ernst Röhm, who Hitler later had killed on the Night of Long Knives. Fleeing for his life, Chaos sailed to the Far East on his huge yacht with his own personal zoo, which he was then forced to give away to escape the Japanese invasion of Peking.

KEITH HEWETT: Despite Gertrude Stein purchasing hundreds of his paintings and promoting him as the next Picasso, his artistic output was as erratic as his life. He threw his inherited wealth to the wind and by the end of the war, found himself washed up and penniless on the shores of Soho. He never became the next Picasso. It was Muriel's unshakeable belief in Francis Bacon that paid off, whilst Lord Chaos fell into obscurity despite publishing a memoir and appearing as 'Chaos' in Kenneth Anger's film, *Lucifer Rising*.

MISS WHIPLASH: The other person who rivalled Francis for Muriel's affection during the 1950s was Bobby Hunt. It would be difficult to overestimate Bobby's role in the Colony. He'd been a very early member, taking on the role of hat-check girl, and being paid in drinks for bringing in the right sort of drinker – those with money or wit, preferably both. John Minton first took Bobby to the club – he was a pupil of Minton's at Camberwell School of Art from the age of fourteen, along with other friends who became club stalwarts such as Owen 'Oska' Wood, Peter Dunbar (future husband of Marsh) and Pip Piper. I was made a member by Bobby and Pip. Muriel would greet me without much warmth and a dismissive 'take her down there, girl' to Bob, indicating the other end of the bar with a wave of her bejewelled hand. Bobby later told me my stammer upset her – very few people knew she'd had a stammer as a girl, and she hated to be reminded of it so I doubt I'd have been made a member if not introduced by Bob, since I never met anyone else there who stammered. I was often known there as 'Stuttering Sara', but never minded, since it was just another of the mildly offensive but affectionate nicknames that were ubiquitous in the club. Bob had the gift of the gab and he'd talk a mile a minute – an endless source of gossip and anecdotes;

he was a wonderful mimic. He'd known everyone in the art scene in the early 1950s, when his circle included Francis, Lucian Freud, The Two Roberts, Michael Ayrton, Rodrigo Moynihan and his first wife, Elinor Bellingham-Smith.

BOBBY HUNT: In 1955 Francis saved my life. I was working in a factory, trying to paint at the same time, and was very, very depressed. I even thought of suicide. I decided to pull myself together and walked from Lewisham to Piccadilly with my illustrations, when I heard a cry of '*Chérie!*' from a passing taxi and there was Francis. 'You look absolutely awful,' he told me, and gave me a five-pound note to go to Wheeler's 'for oysters to cheer yourself up'.

MISS WHIPLASH: Bobby's knowledge of the post-war British art scene was comprehensive and, in some quarters, respected. Francis dragged him off from the Colony one afternoon on a sudden whim to buy a Sickert. In Cork Street they'd examined a few, with Francis becoming ever more agitated as they reeled from one gallery to another, demanding that Bob advise him which to buy – 'Yes, but is it a GOOD Sickert?', then going on the turn, as he did, and flouncing off in a taxi, leaving Bob on the pavement.

DARREN COFFIELD: In the fifties Bobby bought a set of second-hand canvases to reuse, and discovered that one was a half-finished crucifixion by Francis Bacon (now valued at over £2 million). He told Francis who gave him £50 and demanded it back.

MISS WHIPLASH: Bobby had been very close to Francis in the late forties and fifties. They'd even lived in the forge at Groton in Suffolk at one point with The Two Roberts, all painting together in the studio – and his eye for Francis' work was keen. In the late nineties when the *Sunday Times* published a piece about a supposed portrait of Muriel on sale at Sotheby's, he was scathing – 'That's Nina Hamnett! It couldn't possibly be Muriel. Look at the proportions of the face – no matter how far Francis distorts a face he always keeps the proportions exactly correct. That's why they're always recognisable.' Sadly for Bob, his relationship with both Francis and Lucian deteriorated from the early days. Both had little respect for the practitioners of graphic arts for commercial purposes – and most of Johnny Minton's pupils followed him into illustration rather than sticking at painting. There may have been an element of personal rivalry too, in the sense that Bobby remained close to Muriel and was as much a son to her as Francis.

ISABEL RAWSTHORNE: Muriel showed her sense about people by recognising, long before he became famous, the exceptional qualities that were Francis' . . . She was genuinely pleased when any of her members had any success. When it came to the first night of *Blood Wedding* [which Isabel designed], she insisted on lending me her fox furs. Francis said, 'You must. It will please her so much.'

MAID MARION: Going to the Colony and meeting Muriel had changed Francis' life. Muriel also wasn't indifferent to the fact that her bet had paid off and Francis had become the most important living painter in Britain.

GERALD MCCANN: I went to the Colony with Francis' ward, Paul Danquah. I said 'Board & Belcher! It's like bed and breakfast.' Muriel said, 'She can have a pass and come here at will, nice boy.' After that we became friends. I met Lady Rose McLaren that night. She was a friend and patron of Francis' who had studied with Ballet Rambert and would do high kicks at the bar at the most inopportune moments during a conversation – much to Francis' amusement. A while later, Francis had an exhibition at Galerie Maeght in Paris, so a motley crew headed for Paris: Muriel, Aunty Fred, Lady Rose, Ian Board and myself. We arrived at Rue Cambon to a rather seedy, nice hotel with big brass beds and flowery wallpaper. We unpacked and went to the reception, a very smart gallery with Francis Bacon paintings everywhere. After a while, I looked for Muriel and eventually spotted her in the corner, sitting on a bench with this sort of seraphic smile on her face. I said, 'What are you so smug about?' – 'Just been sold for a lot of money, dear.' Her portrait had just been sold to the international financier Árpád Plesch, oh she was thrilled. As we were leaving I said, 'I think you had better sign the visitors' book.' It was lying open on the table and there was the most beautiful script handwriting by Eleanor Chaffe, the couturier. I said, 'Look, Eleanor Chaffe!' And Muriel went '*Huh!*', and right across the page in crabby writing she scrawled '*MURIEL BELCHER*', with ink blots.

GEORGE MELLY: Of course she adored it when her protégés became celebrated, but her attitude towards them remained the same. She was touched and flattered when she or the club appeared in their iconography. This could at times demonstrate her profound lack of physical vanity – to be immortalised by Francis Bacon demands a certain detachment.

GERALD MCCANN: Francis was busy courting clients so I was left to chaperone Muriel around Paris. There is a marvellous restaurant called the Bistro'k on Rue du Sergent Bauchat. A very chic restaurant. Muriel was in a mink coat with a very pink scarf tied under her chin with a vicious little knot. She looked like a very rich refugee. She tottered into the restaurant and sat down at a table by the door and said, 'This is very nice, dear.' She was tapping the table with those gothic hands of hers. Suddenly a magnum of champagne appeared and she said, 'This is very nice, dear, who's it from?' And the waiter said, 'It's from the proprietor.' – 'Bring him here!' she cried. The proprietor came from Birmingham, as did Muriel, and the two of them sat chatting, ensconced in deep Birmingham history. How it happened, I do not know to this day.

MARSH DUNBAR: Along with Muriel, the only other woman Francis Bacon claimed to love was the artist Isabel Rawsthorne who he painted many times – she was the lover and muse of Giacometti and her friends included Balthus and Derain, who also painted her.

DARREN COFFIELD: Like the photographer John Deakin and the painter Denis Wirth-Miller, Isabel has been diminished by her association with Francis, who promoted her as his muse and model rather than a creative force in her own right. She was an important part of the avant-garde, which at the time numbered just a few hundred people, including artists, collectors and dealers. Isabel and Francis shared a love of French literature and an abiding hatred of Henry Moore. Both heavy drinkers, they'd sometimes feign drunkenness when it suited them, and lost their partners to alcoholism. She was nicknamed 'Harpy' due to her shrieks of laughter and like Francis, became a close friend and confidante of Muriel. She married the composer Constant Lambert and for the 1951 Festival of Britain, designed the ballet *Tiresias*, which Lambert had been composing for many years. At its royal premiere in front of the Queen, it caused a scandal due to its gender-bending themes of sexual appetite. After reading the negative reviews of his 'masterpiece', Isabel's husband proceeded to drink himself to death in the short space of six short weeks.

MARSH DUNBAR: Isabel was sparkling. What a deeply wicked and naughty bird she was. As she got older she got more beautiful, damn her. She was one of the two women that Francis loved dearly. Francis and Muriel loved each other in a way I still don't understand to this day.

FRANCIS BACON: I don't believe in love really. It's marvellous if it happens. What is love?

DANIEL FARSON: Love is absolute, pure exhilaration, ecstasy of being alive in an extraordinary world.

FRANCIS BACON: I wouldn't have put it in those grandiose terms at all. I would have thought love was being decent from one person to another. God knows that's rare enough.

GRAHAM MASON: It was Francis who passed on to Jeffrey Bernard his philosophy of life that he was to adopt for the rest of his days – 'The only way you can possibly survive is to regard everything as being totally unimportant.' But Jeffrey also adopted a motto of his own with which Francis would have completely disagreed – 'There is no virtue in work for its own sake.' He never learned to work hard and play hard like Francis.

KEITH WATERHOUSE: . . . [Jeffrey] was introduced to Soho by his brother Bruce who was then at St Martin's School of Art. Finding himself in his element, he at once consolidated himself as a registered layabout. He worked at a variety of odd jobs – navvying, dishwashing, acting, scene-shifting, film cutting, boxing in a fairground, a spell in a coal mine even, and, disastrously, a stint as a barman . . .

BRUCE BERNARD: . . . [Jeffrey] got made a sort of hero of boozing and dissipation . . . Jeff pulled off this kind of dissipation in such style, with such panache. He was so funny and his mimicry was as good as Peter Sellers'. He's talked to Glaswegians in Glaswegian in a way that he'd be killed for if they found him out. He was amazing.

MAID MARION: I knew the Bernard brothers. All three were completely different in looks and personality. Oliver was a poet; Bruce I found rather dull, he was the bookish one; Jeffrey was boisterous, good-looking, always after the women. He drank to overcome his shyness and liked to gamble when drunk, often losing an entire week's wages in an hour.

DARREN COFFIELD: Jeff used to drink in the morning with Dylan Thomas, whom he considered 'a drunken little Welsh man who worked for the BBC . . . Hindsight,' remarked Jeff, 'is a wonderful thing.' He also recounted how as a young man he was first introduced to Francis Bacon by John Minton. Francis was wearing a new Savile Row suit, perched on top of a ladder, painting Minton's studio ceiling pure white, splattering himself with paint with complete indifference. When Jeff asked how he could ruin such expensive clothes, Francis laughed and said he threw them away like one of his one-liners. Minton himself personified the new post-war art set often remembered more for their louche lives – manic bingeing and promiscuity – than their art. Francis' muse Henrietta Law [Moraes] developed a crush on Minton, who in turn was in love with the actor Norman Bowler, who Henrietta then – was it out of spite? – proceeded to seduce.

JOHN MOYNIHAN: It caused quite an uproar in Soho and Chelsea at the time and the effect of the lover scorned was acute. Elinor [Bellingham-Smith] offered Johnny her Arpège-scented shoulder to weep on, which he constantly did at Muriel's. Minton's drinking escalated alarmingly after Norman's marriage to Henrietta.

DARREN COFFIELD: Minton had been very good to Francis at the beginning. Sharing a studio and introducing him to wealthy patrons. But their friendship steadily deteriorated into jealousy, with critics championing Francis' work over Minton's. At a lecture given by the critic David Sylvester, Minton rose to his feet and denounced Francis. Weeks later at the Colony, Minton again insulted Francis' paintings. In retribution Francis poured a bottle of champagne over Minton's head and massaged it into his scalp, repeating his mantra: 'Champagne for my real friends, real pain for my sham friends.' Deeply wounded, Minton found the public humiliation too much to bear.

MARSH DUNBAR: The boozing was non-stop. The wreckage from that time is terrible. Johnny Minton, the best man in the whole world, the kindest man you could ever meet, killed himself with sleeping pills at his home in Chelsea [in 1957]. He was driven to suicide by drink. He had been on a ferocious bender for several days when he asked Jeff to go buy a skull for him as prop for a play he was working on. Jeff must have known Johnny was at the end of his tether, yet he took the money and spent it on booze. It didn't seem a way to repay Johnny who'd been very generous to Jeff.

DARREN COFFIELD: Jeff's mother thought Minton was a philanthropist because he gave her son a daily allowance of ten shillings. 'She thought he was after my mind and not my beautiful body!' he gravelled.

IAN BOARD: John Minton said that the Bernards were the most bizarre family he'd ever known – 'They're all living in a fantasy world!' Jeffrey might have turned queer tricks for money in the early days. He never told the truth about his relationship with John Minton. Jay Landesman thought that Jeff might have been a little in the meat market – certainly Muriel referred to him as one of her beautiful hostesses. But he was only a prick teaser. He didn't come across for any of them. However, Jeffrey never lost his habit of fleecing homosexuals – Francis was always slipping him the odd £50 note saying, 'What will you do now, Jeffrey, now that your looks have gone?' But Jeff always denied that Francis had ever tried to seduce him.

TWIGGY: I was in the Colony one afternoon when Francis turned to Jeff: 'You know your problem, Jeff?' – 'No, Francis.' – 'You're not gay.' – 'Why, Francis?' – 'If you were gay you'd be a superstar by now.' – 'I know, Francis, but I was cunt-struck at the age of twelve.' The first time I met Jeff he offered to buy me a drink. I said, 'I'm a schoolboy, I can't buy you one back.' – 'This is Soho,' he said, 'when you've got money, you buy the drinks. When you don't, someone else buys them.'

JEFFREY BERNARD: The funny thing is I think there are a few people – I've usually been in some sort of trouble with women, drink or money – but a lot of people would oddly like to do the same things, but stick to nine to five. Commuting to work, they are probably killing themselves with British Rail coffee as I am with vodka.

DARREN COFFIELD: Jeff married four times and had lots of affairs. At one point even Marsh was smitten with Jeffrey: 'It really was like an illness. It wasn't even that he was a very good lover. I think it was because he was such a shit; he was a sod unless you did exactly what he wanted. We used to have rows about absolutely nothing. I don't know why, and it's really awful, but being a shit is irresistible.' Then Elizabeth Smart got Jeffrey his first job as a journalist, writing a column for *Queen* magazine, and Marsh found herself having to call the editor: 'I'm ringing for Jeff. He won't be doing the article. He's made another suicide attempt.' – 'Attempt?' barks the editor. 'Let me speak to the bugger: I'll give him a fucking foolproof method.'

SHAKESPEARE: In those days, people drank all day and because they were drunk, they felt they could say or do anything. But Jeffrey was in control, he was horrible when he was drunk. He was a misogynist. I admire him for writing that column every morning with a hangover – they all worked with a hangover. Francis painted in the mornings so he had the rest of the day to drink and gamble. It was a social cycle that took over your entire day. People would pitch up at the French at noon, lunch between one and three p.m., then off to Muriel's.

NORMAN BALON: I never liked Jeff in the early days – he was a layabout and a bum. He got his chance to come out from the wings through his mate Frank Norman. Jeffrey was heavily influenced by Frank and modelled his brusqueness on him.

GERALDINE NORMAN: I first met Frank Norman next to the ashtray in the Colony Room. It was one of those ashtrays on a stalk in the middle of the room and smokers tended to gather round it. I was out for the evening on a date with an American art dealer, Spencer Samuels. We also had with us an English art dealer, Barry Miller, and his girlfriend. Having got comfortably plastered, we went on to have dinner at the Dumpling Inn, a Chinese restaurant further down Dean Street. We settled down to a delicious dinner and in walked Frank with Francis Bacon and sat down at another table. Frank rolled over and said, 'Giza fag then?' So I produced a cigarette and gave it to him. Victor Lownes, who ran *Playboy*, was giving a party to celebrate the fact that he'd just bought a Francis Bacon from Barry Miller. So we were invited to the party and went round there. Lo and behold, Francis Bacon and Frank then arrived. I spent the rest of the evening sitting on a sofa with Frank, laughing my head off, and I never looked back. Soho was a constant inspiration for Frank's work. His first experience of Soho was sweeping out an illegal casino. Back then it was dirtier, more criminal and tremendous fun.

PAM HARDYMENT: Frank and Jeff were good mates and made a book together called *Soho Night and Day*. They both spent a year getting drunk in Soho for research purposes. It was the first advance Jeff ever received for a book and he lost it all in ten minutes, playing roulette. Frank was like a lovely uncle; we had a close relationship – I was brought up in the North and he grew up at the local orphanage, so we talked about the past a lot. He was one of my 'orphans' – I was writing a book about orphans at the time. There were a number who came to the club, it attracted outsiders.

DARREN COFFIELD: That's interesting, I always felt that the reason why the Colony had such longevity was that the club acted as an extended family for those who didn't fit elsewhere in society.

FORESKIN: That may be true, but Frank could also be a spiteful little shit. We used to tease him because he wore really pointy shoes. To be honest he was a bit of a tearaway; he thought he was unassailable. The sort of bloke you would normally avoid in a bar because he could become horrendous, just like Jeffrey Bernard and Dan Farson – they could turn nasty. There was an awful scene once when Frank had offended some gangster and there was a fight. Frank was screaming, 'Is he tooled up? Is he tooled up? Has he got a knife?' It was terrifying.

MAID MARION: Frank loved Muriel and wanted to write a musical about the Colony. One evening he was chatting away at the bar and Lady Rose McLaren came into the club, put her hand on his shoulder, and Frank almost jumped out of his skin – 'Don't ever fucking do that again. I thought it was the law.'

FRANK NORMAN: Some folk are allergic to cats' fur; others cannot bear to be in the same room as a bowl of roses. With me it's policemen. I simply cannot be doing with them, for they have the most dreadful effect on me: whenever I come into contact with one, I break out into a cold sweat, go very pale in the face and tremble.

DARREN COFFIELD: Frank had a subversive edge about him. He had a long, livid scar down one side of his face and looked like a bit of a gangster. His was a rags-to-riches story – he'd been a nobody, he'd had it rough. Joan Littlewood of the Theatre Workshop was a Colony regular. She staged all the original productions of Brendan Behan's work and made Frank Norman a household name with her musical adaption of his play *Fings Ain't Wot They Used T'Be*. Lionel Bart composed the songs. It was a great example of proletariat theatre – a cockney musical full of prostitutes and men in street gangs. It broke taboos and caught the popular imagination.

FRANK NORMAN: *Fings Ain't Wot They Used T'Be* opened at the Garrick Theatre on Thursday, 11th February 1960. It was a smash hit and ran for two years and one week, earning me an average of £200 a week. Without delay I acquired a red sports car and an insatiable appetite for Beluga caviar and Piper Heidsieck champagne.

GERALDINE NORMAN: At the start they were all very poor. Frank, Lucian Freud and the playwright Bernard Kops shared a squat in a bombed-out house in the early fifties. Bernard was always encouraging Frank to write down his anecdotes. Frank was a great raconteur and had marvellous stories about the Kray twins, life in prison and so on. Frank had been in prison several times and really didn't want to go back. He got a job delivering groceries and bought a second-hand typewriter on which he wrote his prison memoir *Bang to Rights*, which was a huge success. At one point Frank wanted to write down Francis Bacon's Soho life. I imagine it would be a natural thought, if you had any proclivity for writing, that you'd consider Francis an ideal subject. He'd take notes of what Francis was saying on the Colony Room toilet paper.

FRANK NORMAN: I felt like a spy. He spoke marvellously about Berlin in the 1920s, but things deteriorated to keeping my ears open, nipping into the lavatory to scribble notes on bits of toilet paper! In the morning I'd find all these screwed-up pieces of paper in my pocket scrawled in a barely legible hand with such choice remarks as – 'I have never had any love in the whole of my life – and what's more I don't want any. All I do is cast my rod into the sewers of despair and see what I come up with this time.' I was greatly relieved when the whole thing petered out.

KEITH HEWETT: But hardly a week went by in the 1950s without the Colony appearing in the *Evening Standard*'s gossip column, 'In London Last Night', written by John Moynihan, son of the artists Rodrigo and Elinor Bellingham-Smith. Rodrigo taught with Minton at the Royal College of Art, and gained fame for painting royalty. They were highly promiscuous and their circle of friends – Cyril Connolly, Colin MacInnes, Dylan Thomas, Sonia Orwell, Ruskin Spear, William Coldstream and David Sylvester – all socialised in the club: but of course, John Moynihan would never dare publish any of the real gossip.

DIANA MELLY: John Moynihan was my husband then, and Rodrigo Moynihan and Elinor Bellingham-Smith were my in-laws. They weren't very good parents to Johnny – they never showed him much love. Elinor was too needy and demanding, and Rodrigo was aloof and uncaring.

MAID MARION: Their private lives were kept out of the press – back then there wasn't the celebrity press like there is now. The members' privacy was guarded by Muriel. A friend once went up to a footballer and asked for his autograph. Muriel gave him a bollocking, 'This is a members' club. I don't expect my members to be asked for autographs; they come up here for the privacy.' If Francis rolled around drunk on the floor with another man, nobody cared. The club was supposed to be sacrosanct. What happened in the club stayed in the club and none of the journalists who drank there dared write about it. In the 1950s when gossip columns started appearing, Francis was a middle-aged man. The newspapers were more interested in rock 'n' roll and youth culture.

DARREN COFFIELD: In the early years, no one thought of pop music as anything more than a profitable gimmick. No one understood this was the advent of the teenage revolution. The first adult to realise this phenomenon was Colin MacInnes, whose book, *Absolute Beginners*, remains the most accurate exploration of the then uncharted territory of youth culture. He recognised its huge potential in the face of much disapproval. If Julian Maclaren-Ross recorded the life of 1940s London, then Colin MacInnes deftly depicted the London of the 1950s. When the prostitutes were banned from the streets, they were replaced by hordes of teenagers hanging about the fashionable coffee bars, who eventually became the new establishment.

MAID MARION: I didn't particularly like Colin MacInnes, he was a shit. He always had black boyfriends he'd parade around. Someone said, 'He likes black people so much, he actually offends them because he makes them blacker than they really are.' Which was a backhanded compliment.

MARTIN GREEN: What was always curious to me, with regard to Colin's relationship with West Indian [males], was that he had to adopt such a strange posture with them, denying our common humanity, let alone our linguistic and cultural heritage. I myself had a number of West Indian and black friends . . . whom I didn't look upon as other than friends but Colin was overly protective and paternal, almost like an officer mixing socially with other ranks . . . There was definitely a sexual edge . . .

DARREN COFFIELD: One of his West Indian boyfriends was arrested for nailing an interior decorator half-naked to a cross and tying him to a tree on Hampstead Heath. The bizarre case became a global news story. Was the crucifixion a sex game or a Black Magic ritual? No one knew. But it was interesting from a legal perspective as the accused was not allowed to use the fact the victim had asked to be nailed up as a defence. MacInnes operated in the twilight world of the insomniac, often arriving on a friend's doorstep after midnight, armed with a bottle of whisky and a West Indian boyfriend. The great-grandson of the Pre-Raphaelite painter Edward Burne-Jones, he studied art at Chelsea and was drawn to the Euston Road School of painting, becoming the art critic for the *Observer* newspaper. He didn't take Francis' artwork seriously and looked upon it as fashion, referring to him as 'the Norman Hartnell of the horror movement'.

IAN BOARD: Colin usually made a late appearance, always with a black boyfriend in tow, barking orders at them as they came in – 'Take your hat off, say good afternoon to Miss Belcher, sit over there – and don't smoke.' The rudeness to his black friends was astonishing and the extraordinary thing was that they obeyed him. He wouldn't have got away with that today. He appealed to Muriel's sense of humour. She enjoyed friction and he excelled in rudeness. 'Listen, Mister, just because we've met doesn't mean you're allowed to speak to me,' he would snarl, before moving on and leaving a lot of troubled water in his wake.

FIONA GREEN: At first Colin was gruff and prickly, but I soon learned that this was a defence mechanism, hiding his sensitive soul. He'd had a very difficult childhood and was astonished to see me cuddling my children, 'But they've done nothing to deserve it.' That told me a lot about how he was brought up and why he loathed his mother, the famous author Angela Thirkell.

GERALD McCANN: Colin was a bit of a bully, but if you attacked him head-on, he was quite a cowardly lion and became very nice – you just had to know how to handle him. We all hung out together in the Colony and in the summer, we'd all watch the tennis together. It was all very laid back, in a way. Then I met Tennessee Williams. He was very nice, it was before he went totally mad. He had this little moustache and sat on a stool. He was brought in by Colin and was extremely well behaved. I said, 'Do you know something? I have seen a great many plays but the one line I have always loved is: "I have always depended on the kindness of strangers." To which Tennessee replied, 'That's my best line. I don't know where it came from. It just came to me one day and I love it.' So that pleased him.

FORESKIN: Tennessee Williams was a bore. If you started talking about your profession or what you did for a living, some-one would shout out 'fucking boring'. There was an unwritten rule that people didn't talk of their success. Muriel frowned upon that. Everywhere else everyone talked about their future and their past to project an aura of success, but the Colony was always about the now, the absolute present moment. There was no need to impress anyone in Muriel's, your success became irrelevant in the wild abandon of a non-stop party.

GERALD McCANN: The Colony was totally asexual. No one cared about gender labels or what your orientation was – your sexuality was your own concern and sometimes the subject of learned debate. 'I think you should wear heels, dear, and a nice frock,' Muriel would say to some gentleman, 'and you'll feel happier in yourself.' She was marvellous at drawing people out – 'Haven't you got a nice cottage to go to, dearie?'

DARREN COFFIELD: Francis enjoyed wearing fishnet stockings under his trousers and experimented with dressing as a girl from an early age – until his father discovered the sixteen-year-old Francis dressed only in his wife's underwear and threw him out. Alan Haynes (a friend of Danny La Rue) was a famous female impersonator who frequented the Colony. He wowed audiences nightly with his drag act in his club, the Havajah, around the corner. There were also two transgender ladies who would come in the club quite a lot, drink lots of champagne and become incontinent all over the furniture.

MAID MARION: April Ashley was the first post-operative person to change gender in the UK. He had the snip, and his photo used to hang in the club. However, Vicky de Lambray I was surprised by. He was a very convincing female, slightly built with a very fine feminine face and voice. He'd been in jail for robbery, extortion and blackmail. He was an amazing character who always came in with £20 in loose change, which he'd put on the bar to drink. Those kinds of people could drink in the Colony because they felt safe there.

JAMES BIRCH: Vicky de Lambray was a transgender prostitute, who claimed to have given every member of the Royal Family a blow job, and subsequently went to jail for blackmail. He was paid a large sum of money by the Rothschilds after officially changing his name to theirs and putting a sign in the back of a kerb-crawling Rolls-Royce, stating: 'Vicky de Rothschild – Entertainer'. At that time, there was a tagline for an advert, for Wagon Wheel biscuits, which he liked – 'It's so big you have to grin to get it in.' He was murdered in suspicious circumstances, he knew too much. He had an address book full of dukes and coronets who were all doing drugs and he was threatening to release that. Quite a few members of the aristocracy frequented the club.

IAN BOARD: Princess Margaret liked it here. I didn't know who she was when she first came. What did I call her? 'Cunt,' I suppose . . . She came in with the photographer Baron, who was a great friend of ours. It was quite an occasion. I didn't treat her any differently because she was the Queen's sister. I treat everyone the same, on merit. After Princess Margaret left, Muriel quipped, 'If they joined together all the cocks she'd had, they'd make a handrail across the Alps.' Her husband Tony Armstrong-Jones came in later and photographed the club.

TOM DEAS: Nearly everybody who was anybody had been through the Colony at some point. But with the club being the club, nobody was going to be overawed by somebody famous.

MERILYN THOROLD: Olga Deterding came into the club. Muriel looked her up and down and said, 'She's not very pretty, is she?' Then someone whispered to Muriel, 'She's the richest woman in the world.' – 'Oh,' said Muriel. Then thinking about it for a bit – 'She's a very attractive woman that Miss Deterding!'

INDIAN AMY: Muriel was quite imperious. She had presence and demeanour. She was very intelligent and a psychologist par excellence. She could pick out all the rogues and con men that were there, she had a nose for them.

KEITH HEWETT: There was someone called 'The Black Widow', who dressed like a character played by Vivien Leigh, with a big black broad-brimmed hat, black dress down to her ankles, everything black. She was cadging money. You saw characters like The Two Roberts, well-known painters at the time. Robert MacBryde was a nuisance, he'd get very drunk and couldn't hold it very well. He was always rowing and shouting, such a contrast to Robert Colquhoun. They used to sit side by side. Colquhoun was tall, slim, suave and pleasant-looking, whereas MacBryde was rounder in body and face and much shorter. We really didn't take to MacBryde too much – he was the dominant one, noisy and aggressive. They sat on two stools at the end of the bar and felt like a permanent fixture. They shared a studio in a house off Kensington Church Street along with John Minton, and Jankel Adler – a cosmopolitan Polish Jew in his fifties who'd worked with Paul Klee at the Düsseldorf Academy before the Nazis denounced him as a degenerate. The Two Roberts referred to him as 'The Master'. He was very influential and introduced them to the work of Picasso. Unfortunately they both suffered from 'Sohoitis'. Colquhoun died of alcoholism, aged forty-eight, and MacBryde died four years later, dancing drunkenly down the road when a car struck him.

DARREN COFFIELD: Sometimes Muriel's unnerving sixth sense deserted her. The sight of the Marquess of Milford Haven, best man at Queen Elizabeth's wedding, sent Muriel berserk: "E's a copper! Get 'im out of 'ere!' – 'Muriel!' cried a distraught member, 'That happens to be the Marquis of Milford Haven!' – 'Don't talk shit! 'E's a copper! Get 'im out of 'ere!' Yet despite her lack of enthusiasm for pageantry or politics, Muriel knew many politicians, including Tom Driberg.

IAN BOARD: I adored Tom, he was a marvellous chap, queer as arseholes. He did a lot to save Soho when it was going through the corruption period with all those porn shops and sex cinemas. He survived thirty-four years as a Labour MP without his sexual exploits being reported; someone was protecting him.

DARREN COFFIELD: A few members would nowadays be condemned as sexual predators. Dan Farson recalled how, aged seventeen, he was sent by the Central Press Agency to cover Parliament, where he spent much of the time being chased up and down corridors by Tom Driberg. Yet despite such debauchery Driberg was never brought down by a scandal and was able to pursue young men in public lavatories until the end of his days. During a trip to Soviet Russia, he even found a 'cottage' in Moscow. His main interests were fellatio and politics, in that order. Muriel would say, 'Well, Tom was happy enough with Ronnie Kray's cock in his mouth.'

PAUL JOHNSON: At the Colony Room, Driberg often invited me back to his 'place', in order, he said, 'to discuss gnosticism'. –

'Oh, is that what you call it, Tom? No thanks!' His fondness for fellatio made him no respecter of persons. When he was Chairman of the Labour Party, he and Jim Callaghan, the Prime Minister, had to attend a Labour occasion in the North, involving a long car journey. They stopped to have a pee behind a hedge. Driberg, ever alert, exclaimed in delight, 'Ooh, I say! What a beautiful cock you have, Prime Minister! May I have a closer look?'

DARREN COFFIELD: The illegality of homosexuality meant that many people's identity put them in conflict with the state. For some, breaking the law in the name of love acquired a nobility. For others, the outrage it caused was an added pleasure. Francis Bacon certainly got a kick out of it, as did Driberg, whose memoir, *Ruling Passions*, shocked the public with its candid revelations of his cottaging and casual oral sex. Originally he was a journalist on the William Hickey gossip column in the *Daily Express*. Despite being both a communist and a homosexual, he received protection as an MI5 informer and was friends with the communist spies Guy Burgess and Donald Maclean, who were constantly drunk, both in and out of the Colony. Ian Board described Burgess as a creature from another world – 'larger than life, always drunk, always loud and always camp'. No one could have guessed they'd both become national hate figures. Maclean had become a regular at the Colony after his return from Cairo, where he'd been the head of the chancery at the British Embassy until his incessant drinking got him sent home in disgrace, the year before they defected to Moscow.

DOUGLAS SUTHERLAND: Donald Maclean, unlike his Cambridge acquaintance of almost twenty years earlier, Guy Burgess, was not a particularly convivial companion when in the process of getting seriously drunk. He was given to long periods of staring morosely into space, punctuated with moments of great volubility, while he aired his views on one subject or another with much thumping on the table, which sometimes degenerated into violent scenes. A lost afternoon at Muriel's was usually good for some diversion or another, which is hardly surprising in view of the extrovert nature of most of the members.

DARREN COFFIELD: The shockwaves sent through the establishment by Burgess and Maclean's betrayal also rippled through the Colony. Muriel and Francis knew them through their mutual friend, Brian Howard, who had originally introduced Francis to the Colony. The defection of Burgess and Maclean to Communist Russia fuelled a sharp upsurge in homophobia. It was rumoured that they spent their last night on British soil in the Colony. Homosexuality was now characterised as a dangerously peculiar hidden subculture and Guy Burgess became a symbol of its evils – blackmail, betrayal, corruption and communism. After their defection in 1951, prosecutions for homosexual activities rose sharply. The police began closely monitoring the Colony, warning Muriel when they felt homosexuals were becoming too prevalent in her club, to either 'tone it down' or be shut down. That other bohemian bastion, the Fitzroy Tavern, was later raided by police, who claimed to 'have seen many perverts . . . behaving in disgusting and disorderly manner'.

PAUL JOHNSON: Once, in Muriel's bar, which had only one loo used promiscuously by men and women, I found it locked when I tried the door, and a female voice within said prissily: 'It's occupied.' So I waited. Soon, Francis Bacon, drunk and bursting to pee, arrived. I said, 'There's a woman inside.' And he shouted: 'Come out of there, you bitch!' Then he began to kick the door. Nothing happened, so more kicking and shouting followed. Eventually the bolt was drawn back, the door opened and a beautiful woman emerged, nose in the air. It was Keeler. She did not look at us, but strode back to the bar. All she said was 'Men!' A lifetime of experience went with that one contemptuous word.

MAID MARION: Christine Keeler used to come up a lot. She didn't look as attractive in the flesh as she did in the photographs. She was a femme fatale figure who brought down the British government with the Profumo affair. She would never talk about anything of any interest. Stephen Ward, the poor man who was accused of being her pimp, also came to the club. He took his own life when the scandal broke. Some people refer to the Colony as a gay bar but it wasn't. There was a sexually liberated atmosphere in the club, but we didn't kiss and cuddle in public like they do nowadays. Muriel would tell them to 'keep it for the bedroom'. We never spoke Polari, the secret language between homosexuals, because there was no need. Muriel never used it, she was a quiet lesbian. Ian was gay but he would deny it and say – 'I'm not like you, I prefer women,' which was a lie. One night he picked up this young man who turned out to be a 'boy'. The boy says, 'I'm going home to tell my dad.' So the 'father' came to Ian's flat – 'You tried to interfere with my boy. I want some money otherwise I am going to the police.' Ian called Aunty Fred – 'What shall I do? If he goes to the police, I'll be ruined.' But Fred said, 'Just let it happen, say "fuck it". If he gets any money off you, it will never stop. You'll be paying them off forever. It's a set-up.'

DARREN COFFIELD: Homosexuals were often set up, framed or blackmailed and were seen as a soft touch by the establishment. Colony members Peter Wildeblood, Michael Pitt-Rivers and Lord Montagu had not sought their claim to fame. In 1954, they were jailed for homosexual sex. During the trial it appeared that the British establishment had framed them. The extensive coverage of the case and public outrage led to the decriminalisation of homosexuality in 1967, but Lord Montagu always denied the charge.

Yet despite all the set-ups, sex scandals and suicides amongst its members, the Colony was a matriarchy and Muriel forgave her children anything as long as they cherished and obeyed her. There was only one member whom she never forgave, and his name is now the stuff of legend . . .

3

Speakin' Deakin

IAN BOARD: John Deakin? He was a photographer who worked for *Vogue*. He was an extraordinary character – his bitchiness was wonderful, he had a really vicious tongue. He'd spend three days with Dan Farson, eating and drinking on the town, then he'd get sick of Dan, drop him, then go with Francis and fill him in with the gossip of who'd done what to who and who was sleeping with whom.

KEITH HEWETT: One evening in the French, Dan Farson could smell something strange was going to happen. There was this odd little man standing beside him – 'He looked like he had been rescued from a sea wreck and been fitted out by a generous crew. He clutched his overcoat like a Mandarin; it was covered in cigarette burns and wine stains as if he'd often fallen asleep in it.' The man was interested in Dan's camera so Dan told him he was about to join *Picture Post* magazine as a photographer, to which Deakin retorted, 'I am the star photographer of *Vogue*.'

BARRY HUMPHRIES: At Muriel's, John Deakin lurked in the shadows with his pitted, necrotic countenance and watery eyes. He was a photographer of some real talent, but relied on the munificence of Bacon, for whom he took clandestine pictures of corpulent men engaged in smudgy acts of torture and buggery – 'references' for Bacon's ghastly paintings, which reduced Deakin's snaps into blobs of placenta wrestling on billiard tables.

GERALD McCANN: John Deakin, I adored. He was tiny and smelly. You had to stand up-wind from him because he would wet himself and wear the same pants for days on end, so he and Sir Francis Rose were the two great stinkers. He was like a belligerent wasp and used to needle Francis Bacon. To listen to them both at the Colony was like something out of Jane Austen. 'You've never been south of Brighton!' Francis would say dismissively. 'I was at the yacht!' protested Deakin. 'No, you weren't at the yacht, you were at the quayside,' Francis replied haughtily. – 'No, I was, I *was.*' – 'You *may* have been on the gangplank, I'll give *you* that.' – 'Yes, I *was on the yacht.*' Then Francis said, 'Anyway I have a better bum than you,' and dropped his trousers. Everyone looked on in amazement.

DARREN COFFIELD: Deakin said Francis was 'an odd one, wonderfully tender and generous by nature, yet with a curious streak of cruelty, especially to his friends'. They naturally gravitated towards one another through their connection to the philanthropist Arthur Jeffries. In the 1930s, Deakin was Jeffries' boyfriend, and they travelled around the world together. The year before the Colony opened, Erica Brausen and Arthur Jeffries opened the Hanover Gallery in Mayfair. Erica ran the business, Arthur provided the financial support and Francis was one of their first artists.

DANIEL FARSON: I would meet John Deakin and Francis and we would laugh and laugh. They were the happiest years of my life.

FRANCIS BACON: John Deakin was a very interesting, amusing man who was brilliant, very irreverent and sarcastic. He wasn't a bon viveur, no, not at all. He liked drink but he needed drink more than anything else. He was rather remarkable in the sense that at two or three o'clock when he realised the drink was going in, he used to go home to disappear and go to sleep. He was extraordinary because he had great discipline that way. Muriel hated him.

DARREN COFFIELD: The Caves de France was where all the rejects from Muriel's, such as Nina Hamnett and The Two Roberts, would congregate. Maid Marion went there on a blind date with John Deakin. His friend Johnnie Quarrell, a good-looking docker, was having a fling with Dan Farson and had arranged for the Maid to come along with them.

MAID MARION: When I saw my date, I thought, Fucking ugly cunt, what do they think I am? A blind date? You'd have to be fucking blind to go with Deakin. He laughed and laughed at himself, but I didn't find him very funny so I had a laugh with my mate instead. Johnnie Quarrell used to nick stuff from them both as they got so drunk. He stole one of Deakin's pictures. Deakin would get absolutely out of it when he drank, very insulting, bitchy and quite difficult.

KEITH HEWETT: Deakin had plenty of enemies. He was as unreliable as Henrietta Moraes and got himself sacked twice from *Vogue*, which is no mean feat for a photographer. When his job for *Vogue* was under threat, the features editor suggested that he concentrated on portraits of artists.

HENRIETTA MORAES: He took a photo of Johnny [Minton] which I think is brilliant . . . He had a very good eye, but was an alcoholic, and that tends to get in the way.

DARREN COFFIELD: Though proud of his photography, he took little care of his work, which he would deface or discard at whim. His partially destroyed photographs lend his sitters a sense of the tragedy and chaos that belied Deakin's own self-destructive nature.

BRUCE BERNARD: Deakin could certainly seem a monster, but, while he inspired dread and loathing in some (including Noël Coward, Cecil Beaton and George Melly), he could also provoke affection in all kinds of people. More importantly, he was surely one of the best portrait photographers this century.

GEORGE MELLY: His portraits were a kind of magic, there's no other way of explaining it. Seeing behind the surface, you somehow got a very individual and accurate look at his subjects. The art critic John Russell wrote that Deakin 'rivalled Bacon in his ability to make a likeness in which truth came unwrapped and unpackaged'.

JOHN DEAKIN: Being fatally drawn to the human race, what I want to do when I photograph it is to make a revelation about it. So my sitters turn into victims. But I would like to add that it is only those with a daemon, however small and of whatever kind, whose faces lend themselves to be victimised at all. And the only complaints I have had from my victims have been from the bad ones, the vainies, the meanies.

BRUCE BERNARD: When I first met him [Francis], it was said that he would never allow his photograph to be taken. But soon after he allowed John Deakin to take the now famous mugshot *c*. 1950, and . . . After that the photographs seem to have come thick and fast.

HENRIETTA MORAES: I used to see Francis every day, drinking in Soho . . . Francis said, 'I'd like to paint you' . . . I said, 'Of course.' He said, 'Deakin can come and take some photos of you. I can't work from a live model because people are always so shocked and appalled by what I make of them' . . . Deakin came round . . . started taking these photographs . . . it seemed rather extreme . . . I didn't think Francis could possibly want to paint me in those attitudes . . . I saw Francis again about ten days later and Deakin turned up with these photographs. Francis took one look and said, 'Absolutely useless, they're all exactly the wrong angles.' And we had to do them all over again. Meanwhile, to amuse myself, I went to a really low drinking club full of sailors. Deakin was there, furtively flitting about with bits of paper, and so I went over to have a look and there were all these photos of me with no clothes on that he was selling to sailors . . . I was absolutely furious and yet I just couldn't really be angry because it was so funny.

GRAHAM MASON: Deakin was wonderfully funny, he said very sharp things indeed. He was a bugger, and it was a delight – he was terribly nice and gentle, and a dear friend. I worry about Dan Farson. He's invented this myth about Deakin being a misogynist and unspeakably vicious bitch, which ain't true. It's a peculiar thing but poofs in the 1960s didn't like women; it was really odd. A whole gang of bright poofs wouldn't have anything to do with women, but that changed by the end of the sixties. Francis was having them on, he didn't dislike women at all. He loved Muriel.

HENRIETTA MORAES: The pictures that finally got painted from Deakin's photographs . . . the nudes, I like but found more mysterious because there was one with a hypodermic syringe with three drops of blood on the bed. And I'd never really heard of anything like hypodermic syringes or serious drugs at that point. It later caught up with me . . . but that must have been something he'd just seen because it certainly did not exist in the flesh at all then.

DARREN COFFIELD: Although Francis used Deakin's photographs to paint Henrietta, he also, unusually, required her naked presence in his studio. Some models inspire artists by their looks, others with their personality. She was hypnotically warm and witty. Ruined by drink and drugs, this talented woman became known as a wild, thieving, foul-mouthed drunk, confessing – 'I pick up bad habits like iron filings.' However, the aura of danger – of walking on the precipice – helped the mood of Francis' paintings.

THEA PORTER: The first time I saw Henrietta Moraes at the Colony, I recognised her from Bacon's and Lucian Freud's paintings. She was sitting on the banquette below the window, and looked dark and powerful. I was wearing a turquoise ring from Aleppo that she admired; she said she had had a turquoise, but had lost it. Before I knew what had happened, she'd magicked the ring off my finger.

GERALD MCCANN: Part of the attraction of the Colony was that it was extremely difficult to get in. For example, one day this man arrived who was the chairman of a large bank, whose young protégé was a habitué of the club. Muriel looked around the door and said, 'Yes, Mary, what is it?' He replied gruffly, 'I'm here to meet Jonathan.' She said, 'Sit over there and be quiet.' Eventually Jonathan arrived and Muriel shrieked, 'She's over there waiting for you. Got a big handbag, have you, dear?' Muriel was wonderful. She'd set up a charity to raise money for Elmfield School, a place for disabled children, most of whom would die young. She was ruthless about getting money out of people for the school. Anyway, that evening the chairman of the bank had been sitting there watching various celebrities come and go and decided he wanted to be a member. So Jonathan came over and said, 'My boss would like to be a member, how much would that be?' Muriel chirped, 'Three thousand guineas.' The membership was then three guineas, but she made the bank chairman write out a cheque on the spot to Elmfield School. Muriel had found out that the X-ray machine the school so desperately needed cost £12,000.

IAN BOARD: When the thalidomide children were born, Dan made a documentary about them. When we saw it, we were appalled at the suffering of these deformed children. Muriel and I thought we should do something. So we asked Dan what we should do, and he said, 'Why don't you go and visit them.' So we went down one Sunday with boxes of chocolates, and it turned into an annual event where once a year we would throw a Christmas party for them. Various club members helped out – Victor Lownes would send Bunny Girls to hand out the presents.

ALIX COLEMAN: At Christmas they are given whatever they want . . . George Melly has played Father Christmas more times than he likes. Melly says he gets terribly hot and sweaty in his fancy dress, but wouldn't dream of refusing, summoned as he is by Muriel, 'the white witch of Dean Street'.

GEORGE MELLY: Muriel took it all very seriously. She took nothing else seriously except the treatment of these children, some of whom were nasty and always pinching me.

MAID MARION: The members gave their houses over to throw parties and raise money for the children. It was quite an expensive caper if your house got trashed. It would've been cheaper to pay them not to have the party and save yourself the cost of having to redecorate your house. Sandy Fawkes had a party.

DARREN COFFIELD: Sandy Fawkes had a lot of empathy for Muriel's charity since, like Frank Norman, she was also an orphan, abandoned as a baby next to the Grand Union Canal. As a teenager she went to Camberwell School of Art where her tutor John Minton introduced her to Soho. Minton was a trad jazz fan, and through him she met her future husband Wally Fawkes, the clarinettist and cartoonist who drew the cartoon strip 'Flook' in the *Daily Mail* – which often featured Muriel and the Colony.

KATE FAWKES: In the 1960s we would have Christmas parties in our house in Eton Avenue for Muriel's children's charity. My mum [Sandy] would help throw these parties. The first time, my brother, my sister and me were really excited that we were going to have this huge party. We saw all the golden chairs and tables of food being laid out. I remember seeing the coach arrive. No one had thought to prepare us for the initial shock of seeing these extremely deformed children. I am ashamed to say that as a seven-year-old, I was terrified and ran away and hid under the coats all day. No one realised I was missing until the evening when they discovered me still hiding under the coats, tearful, terrified, starving hungry and desperate for a pee. From then on we had these parties. Everyone came – Dan Farson, Jeffrey Bernard . . . once Frank Norman was so pissed and angry that he proceeded to punch his fist through every pane of glass that overlooked our garden. My sister wrote about the incident in her homework. At the next parents' evening, the teacher left open her schoolbook for my parents to peruse: 'Frank Norman came round our house at the weekend and smashed all the windows. There was blood everywhere.'

GERALD McCANN: I went to one of Muriel's fund-raising parties at George Melly's house. He greeted me at the door, wearing this Victorian hairdo with little curls and a very fetching number in taffeta with mittens, cigar and reticule – 'Hello boys, come in for a drink. The neighbours are complaining but we're doing it for charity.' In the far corner, the police were having neat sips of something lethal, whilst George wandered around looking perfectly at home in his green crinoline dress.

MAID MARION: Before the party at George Melly's, we all went round to Muriel's flat and got dressed up and did the make-up. Ian was dressed all in black – 'Like the Black Widow, darling,' Muriel said. I was wearing a very skimpy ballerina outfit. Everyone came dressed in drag or fancy dress except Muriel and Carmel who came as themselves. They were raising money for the children and had roulette and gaming tables upstairs – that was for their bit of fun and to make money. It was a lovely party. Later Muriel saw me stumbling about – 'Are you pissed, dear?' – 'No, it's these high heels.'

GRAHAM MASON: Muriel ended up hating Deakin very badly indeed. Because he made up a little gossip about her, and when Deakin gossiped he was wicked. Every Christmas, Muriel made a collection from her guests – gathered up money from her victims – for her children's charity. Deakin put it about Soho that Muriel was a total fraud and had pocketed all the money she raised for the children. It was a classic bit of Deakin bitchery, so she barred him from the club for life. Being barred is one thing, but when Deakin was dying of lung cancer, I said to Muriel, 'Listen, he's nearly dead for Christ's sake, can't he come back, just this once?' This was donkey's years after the great debacle. 'All right,' she said. So one Saturday afternoon I took him up there. He liked being in the room and had been there for hours in full swing. He was drinking red wine and when he left, Muriel calmly walked across the room, picked up his glass and smashed it in the sink. I was shocked. It exhibited an abiding hatred I thought she never had.

IAN BOARD: He was a monster. He really upset Muriel when he accused her of fiddling the books of the children's charity. *Oooh*, she had no time for him after *that*!

KEITH HEWETT: I knew John Deakin well, he was a war photographer – he could be very embarrassing and nasty. He had this habit of suddenly appearing in a pub, dashing up to you and kissing you unawares, fully on the lips. I wouldn't have said he had a caustic wit, but it was very sardonic and biting. He was rather short with an ugly, rubbery face, a bit scruffy and always slow at buying drinks. If you were out and about in Soho, you always bumped into him; he was a local fixture. He was a very good photographer and did a show of collages in a little shop on Museum Street. I had a look at that, and had much respect for his collages. But it was around that time that he turned to painting and I didn't have much respect for those. Maybe he gave up photography and turned to painting because he mixed with so many painters. It was typically perverse of him that he wanted to be considered a painter and rejected what he was good at. He could have gone on with *Vogue*, but his drinking and rudeness ruled him out of any success he might have had.

GRAHAM MASON: Francis, Deakin and myself would meet occasionally – Deakin bright and sparky in his baby-blue suit. He'd look at Francis and say, 'I suppose you've been daubing all morning again?' He so wanted to be a painter.

KEITH HEWETT: Maybe Deakin had an affinity with painters. His best photographs were of painters such as Lucian Freud who loved his wit. In Freud's portrait, Deakin looks sad. Francis worked only from photographs, whereas Lucian painted only from life.

HENRIETTA MORAES: Francis and Lucian, they couldn't be more different from each other. Lucian was small, dark and quiet, but was very talkative once he got in the studio; he'd rattle off Auden and long, complicated film plots. I'd sit there for twelve hours. He paints very, very, very slowly.

DANIEL FARSON: I once asked Lucian whether his sitters were his victims because of the look of pain on their faces – *they are all bored out of their skulls!* I originally owned Lucian's portrait of Deakin but was forced to sell it at Sotheby's to pay my debts to the wretched brewers who leased me the Waterman's Arms.

MARSH DUNBAR: Speaking of water . . . I used to go the Oasis baths to swim regularly. One afternoon I saw Deakin, he had an enormous bottle of tonic water, sitting there not swimming, in his baby-blue suit. I sat with him watching this man going up and down, up and down. He said, 'Marsh, would you like a drink?' I said, 'I don't like tonic.' He said, 'Don't be stupid, it's got gin in it.' So for a few weeks we did this and one day he saw a man he fancied rotten with artificial legs, swimming with shoes and socks drawn onto his plastic legs – going up and down, whilst we sat drinking gin.

DANIEL FARSON: When Deakin abandoned art as he had photography, Francis often came to his rescue by paying his rent and giving him money . . . which Deakin denied with tirades against Francis' meanness.

GRAHAM MASON: Dan Farson's view of Deakin is not accurate. Dan always portrays Deakin as a total shit but the only man John Deakin was really unkind to was David Archer.

DOM MORAES: Why nobody has ever written a biography of David is beyond me. He was a great man. He was tall and, when I met him, fiftyish and rather bald, with the flushed face of a drinker, and very kind, bespectacled eyes of that pale blue colour, which physiognomists have described as a mark of criminal tendencies. Archer walked with an awkward intensity of body, a Prussian stiffness, a bundle of newspapers always clamped under his left arm. He looked as though he were afraid he would explode.

DARREN COFFIELD: He came to Soho via a circuitous route, having moved his original Parton Street bookshop from Bloomsbury via Manchester to wartime Glasgow, by which time it had evolved into some kind of arts centre. Here he met The Two Roberts, Colquhoun and MacBryde. In 1956 he opened his last bookshop at 34 Greek Street behind the Palace Theatre. The shop sign read 'David Archer Bookseller Parton Press'. Germano Facetti designed the bookshop at a cost of £3,000, a huge sum in those days.

DOM MORAES: It was a beautiful establishment on two floors; besides the section which sold new books, it contained a library, a coffee shop and an art gallery where homeless poets sometimes slept. This bookshop became bankrupt very soon, due to its proprietor's habit of never accepting any money from his customers. Indeed he often gave them whatever was in the till, feeling they looked in need of a square meal.

PAUL POTTS: The actual physical way in which he gave money, was the most beautiful thing about him. It was as if he was conferring the order of merit on you, and all the honour was to you and not him. He really believed his function in life was to look after people who couldn't look after themselves, provided they had some talent.

DARREN COFFIELD: Archer attracted a large circle of bohemians – he was respected because he helped people. The very first exhibition at his bookshop's gallery was for his boyfriend John Deakin's photos of Paris. Deakin's young friend, Bruce Bernard, who'd decorated the shop, also helped to hang and look after the show. It was Deakin's first ever exhibition and was swiftly followed by a second one on Rome.

HENRIETTA MORAES: David Archer and his friend John Deakin were old friends of mine. I spent my early youth drinking in the same places as they did, and this bond, once forged, is impossible to overlook. Archer was a man the like of whom will not be seen again – gently born, eccentrically orientated, altruistically minded, hysterically tempered, kind, perceptive, a left-wing Fascist and patron saint of the forties and fifties poets – he had first published Dylan Thomas, George Barker, David Gascoyne, Sidney Graham and the very first novel by Graham Greene. His publishing house was called the Parton Press and it was entirely financed by David. He was so generous-minded that he let his authors own their own copyright . . . Of course he never managed to recoup any money. As soon as his authors became successful, which they invariably did, they would transfer to a bigger house with greater powers of distribution. Of course what David wanted was a literary salon in the style of Madame de Staël, and he got it. Colin Wilson, Christopher Logue, Colin MacInnes, Michael Hastings and many others, came in every day, drank endless cups of coffee and talked voraciously, but never bought a book.

DARREN COFFIELD: In the basement of the bookshop, was a coffee bar run by Francis' muse, Henrietta, who Bruce Bernard nicknamed 'Piss Off Darling'. There was a three-metre-high photo of Henrietta at the back of the coffee bar, which Deakin had printed on Facetti's instructions. David Archer meanwhile would publish the first collection of poems by Henrietta's future husband Dom.

HENRIETTA MORAES: One afternoon David and I were drinking in the Colony Room. 'Hello Cunty,' Muriel . . . greeted me as usual. We sat down on a banquette and David pulled some crumpled sheets of typescript from his pocket. 'I wish you'd read these poems,' he said, 'they're by a young Indian boy called Dom Moraes. I might want to publish them. What do you think?' I said I liked them and he seemed relieved and stuffed them back in his pocket.

DOM MORAES: . . . he offered to publish my first book of poems. I protested that he had not read any. 'But, my dear boy, I only ever read detective stories,' he said. 'I never read any of the poets I published. But I can smell a poet, if you see what I mean.' He then seemed to realise the possible implications of his remark. 'I don't mean that none of you ever bathe,' he added hastily, 'except Dylan [Thomas], you could certainly smell him, what?' For some reason he always talked like a Wodehouse character. But in July 1957, he published my first book, *A Beginning*. We had to distribute it by carrying it round the bookshops, some of whom grudgingly accepted a few copies on sale or return. But suddenly and unexpectedly, it started to get good reviews everywhere, from rather well-known poets. The bookshops started to order copies.

HENRIETTA MORAES: . . . it won the Hawthornden Prize, which hadn't been awarded for fourteen years . . . We had lunch at the Ritz with Lord David Cecil and L. P. Hartley . . . Mr Hartley pinched Dom's thighs and bottom, and we proceed-ed to a merry prize-giving, £100 and a party at Apollo [Place] afterwards. I remember Stephen Spender displaying his beautiful profile to great advantage . . . John Deakin tipsily photographing everything with aplomb and accuracy.

DARREN COFFIELD: By the 1960s, David Archer had exhausted his inheritance. Reduced to the role of Soho scrounger, he lamented, 'I used to sell copies of Dylan's *18 Poems* for three shillings and six pence each. Nowadays they fetch five hundred pounds. It makes me absolutely *furious!*' He'd gone from a relatively comfortable life to slumming it in a hostel with meths drinkers. His 'friends' had bled his finances dry and abandoned him. Merilyn Thorold was concerned he looked 'desperate and threadbare' in the Colony. When Merilyn asked Deakin to help with a fund she was raising for Archer, he told her, 'He can die in the gutter for all I care.' Archer now scraped a living selling lampshades in Selfridges. The ignominy of his change of circumstances took its toll. One chilly October evening in 1971, he climbed the stairs to the Colony one last time to say his goodbyes before retiring to his dosshouse. In the morning, the cleaners of the homeless men's hostel discovered him dead. By his bed were fifteen farewell letters thanking those few real friends who had tried to help him and an empty bottle of aspirin. The coroner's verdict was 'took his own life whilst the balance of his mind was disturbed' and listed his occupation as shop assistant. He'd died destitute and practically penniless although it was estimated that he gave away over £80,000 in his lifetime to impoverished poets and parasites alike.

MERILYN THOROLD: When I heard the Coroner's verdict, I was appalled that someone accused me of indirectly killing David when the money ran out. I was presented with a casket containing his ashes and received a final note from David. Inside with the note was a tiny sum of money, maybe £1.50 – his entire wealth at the time he died. His ashes sat in the casket in my drawing room for six months before I could arrange for him to be buried next to his parents at Castle Eaton. After the burial, the local vicar published a short piece about David for the parish magazine. The article came to the attention of the governor of a local school endowed by David's grandfather. The school had closed and the endowment was no longer needed. 'I'm sorry to learn of Mr Archer's death,' the governor wrote to me. 'We had been trying to contact him for some time to ask if he could make use of the money himself.'

DARREN COFFIELD: Maybe one of the reasons Muriel hated Deakin was because of his behaviour towards Archer. Certainly Dan Farson never forgave Deakin. In homage to Archer, he narrated a BBC radio programme about Archer's life of books and poetry, *A Gentleman of Soho*. The bookshop played an important role in many people's lives. It was there that Dan met his first 'Angry Young Man', Colin Wilson author of *The Outsider*. In 1956 he was the first person Dan interviewed for television, which helped launch his career. But Dan told me Deakin was jealous of his success, 'was treacherous to his friends . . . playing one off against the other' and that both he and Archer were 'constant victims'. In little more than a week after his former lover's suicide, Deakin was skipping off to Paris for Francis' exhibition.

IAN BOARD: We all went to Paris for the opening of Francis' exhibition at the Grand Palais in late October 1971. It was an explosive mix of people – myself, Muriel, Thea Porter, Rodrigo Moynihan and Deakin. It was a very important exhibition for Francis; it was to be opened by the President of France. We stayed in the Hôtel des Saints Pères, and the day before the show opened Francis' boyfriend, George Dyer, was found dead. Deakin was acting the clown – George's death had no effect on him at all. Francis had brought Deakin along to chaperone George, to keep him out of trouble and now he was dead. There was a great to-do and it was very hush-hush, you know!

It could have fucked up the whole exhibition – with more press on George's suicide than Francis' show.

MARSH DUNBAR: Deakin went to Paris although he was very ill at the time. He had a series of ailments, which Francis put down to his drinking. He was hospitalised and got better for a short while, but it was all downhill from there.

JOHN DEAKIN: I had been having treatment . . . but put it off until after the opening [in Paris] . . . now everything's under perfect control and much to Francis' annoyance had nothing to do with drink or, as the doc put it so delicately, my social life.

DARREN COFFIELD: When Deakin left hospital he was driven straight down to Brighton, where Francis had arranged for his convalescence in the Old Ship Hotel. He then toured various pubs and bumped into an old friend, with whom he drank in a club until the early hours. Bruce Bernard was the last person to speak to him. He phoned him at the hotel to ask how he was – 'He sounded weak and said he'd been drinking too much and was just waiting for some tea. It was the maid with the tea that discovered him dead in bed.'

FRANCIS BACON: I had to go down and identify the body and I thought, That's the last dirty trick he plays on me.

JEFFREY BERNARD: I said, 'Was it horrible, was it alarming to see someone that you've known for years, dead? How did you feel?' – 'It's the first time I've ever seen him with his mouth closed!' But of course Francis was obviously irked; that was a facetious typical Francis Bacon remark. I think Francis was very upset when Deakin died – everyone liked Deakin, except for me.

FRANCIS BACON: He was marvellously witty, yes. When we're dead we're no good. It's over, finished.

DARREN COFFIELD: The authorities told Francis that he needn't be next of kin after all. 'I know just what that means,' Francis fumed. 'He'll have a pauper's funeral and everyone in Soho will say I'm the meanest man in London.' – 'Oh no, we've been in touch with Mr Deakin's bank manager and there are more than sufficient funds to give him a good send-off.' Francis was amazed that Deakin had money all along, 'Of course, I did give him the proceeds of one of my paintings . . . they advertised for someone to claim it and discovered Deakin had a perfectly good brother!'

MARSH DUNBAR: Graham and I got stuck in a traffic jam and missed the funeral. When we arrived, they were burying him, filling in the hole and we said 'Stop!' And there was this little hole and he was down there somewhere, in a box. Oh, I miss him badly.

GRAHAM MASON: He left all his photographs and artworks to Francis. But Francis didn't know what to do with them and had no interest in keeping them. So he passed them on to Bruce Bernard who was always a fan of Deakin's photography. In 1984 Bruce organised an exhibition of Deakin's work at the Victoria & Albert Museum – *John Deakin: The Salvage of a Photographer*.

BRUCE BERNARD: The natural romantic inclinations of photography always need a corrective . . . Deakin . . . was really a member of photography's unhappiest minority whose members, while doubting its status as art, sometimes prove better than anyone else that there is no doubt about it.

FRANCIS BACON: I was very pleased that the Victoria & Albert Museum . . . arranged this exhibition of John Deakin's photographs – because his work is so little known when one thinks of all the well-known and famous names in photography – his portraits to me are the best since Nadar and Julia Margaret Cameron.

GRAHAM MASON: Deakin is now recognised as one of the outstanding photographers of the twentieth century. I sold the photo he took of Muriel recently, because I needed the money. He would have been so amused because he never had any money. Francis would bung him some, from time to time. He would be so amused to know how much I sold his photograph for . . .

MARSH DUNBAR: No, he wouldn't, he would be *furious*!

GRAHAM MASON: Fucking outraged! *Oooh*, he'd be cross.

4

Gamblers Eponymous

FRANK NORMAN: If you feel like gambling, I strongly recommend that you do not do it in Soho, for the dealers are professionals and so are the people you are playing against, and although you may not be actually cheated out of your money, the odds against you winning are very high indeed. Many a mug has lost every penny in his pocket and afterwards wondered how it happened.

TOM DEAS: One day Francis dropped his money in the club, a huge wad of notes, which I handed back to him and off he went gambling. An hour later he was back, asking Ian if he could lend him some money for the bus fare home. He'd been to Charlie Chester's casino and lost thousands within an hour.

FRANCIS BACON: I like the atmosphere of casinos . . . there's the excitement of winning or not winning, and the despair of people who have lost everything and all that goes on in a very concentrated space.

TWIGGY: Francis used to go to Charlie Chester's in Archer Street. Although one of Mayfair's exclusive casinos, the club itself was small and seedy with an old-world etiquette. The doorman, 'Mick the Hammer', was a former member of the Kray gang and would greet Francis with 'Hello, Sir Francis', and Francis would get all jittery about being called 'Sir'. It was the unofficial training school for croupiers. By the time we got there, Francis was normally drunk, which is what casinos prey on. He played roulette, which he said is 'the silliest game you can play because the odds are against you'.

DARREN COFFIELD: Francis' entire life was an optimistic gamble. He earned his money early on as a croupier at illegal gambling parties where he learned to count cards. However, Francis confessed to the artist Michael Wishart, 'nothing is more wonderful and refreshing than being completely cleaned out'. For that masochistic thrill, sometimes 'losing was better than winning'.

FORESKIN: In the 1950s, before English peasants invented the package tour, Francis, Muriel, Carmel and Ian used to holiday in casino towns in the South of France. In the evenings, Ian and Muriel watched Francis play roulette. It was in the days of currency restrictions, and they soon found themselves short of cash. So they decided to rob a rich friend who was staying nearby. While Ian stood lookout, Francis shinned up the drainpipe and robbed the apartment. Then they went to the casino to gamble their booty. Their luck changed and Francis began to win at the tables, but as he did so his face slowly turned a terrifying black – the boot polish he used as hair dye had melted in the heat. Having won their fares home, Francis shinned back up the drainpipe to replace the stolen money.

DARREN COFFIELD: When Francis left his first dealer Erica Brausen in 1958 to sign with Marlborough Fine Art, it was less of a career move than an attempt to settle a £5,000 gambling debt. Towards the end of his life when he was making so much money he didn't know what to do with it, his wins and losses were kept in ratio to what he was getting for his paintings. Despite his growing wealth, he never became a tax exile like so many of his contemporaries. Paying taxes in return for living in London was preferable to a loss of liberty.

MICHAEL HEATH: I used to see Francis early in the morning: he'd go to the gallery to collect £20,000 cash, put it in a paper bag and take it round to Charlie Chester's and gamble it away. We were in awe of that. They knew real criminals, the kind who would pull your fingernails out. If you'd bought a painting from Francis or Lucian and not paid, it was made quite clear to you that you were going to be in serious trouble – they knew people. They could crush people, and in a way I admired that because it was something I could never do. They would pick people up, buy them everything, spoil them, and then drop them and be quite cruel about it. They were doing things that were considered rather naughty.

GRAHAM MASON: Francis was attracted to underworld characters, who, like himself, enjoyed hanging out in clubs, drinking, gambling and being promiscuous. Francis loved taking risks, in art as in life. His lover George Dyer was poorly educated and worshipped Francis, much to his peril.

DARREN COFFIELD: Francis' money allowed George to attract hangers-on, who accompanied him on massive benders in the Colony. Quiet and composed when sober, George was uncontrollable when drunk. By 1971, Francis was trying to distance himself from George, who tried to gain Francis' attention by informing the police that Francis had drugs stashed in his house. The cannabis was stored in the base of an African statue given to Francis by the Kray twins. Francis knew the drugs were there, but feigned ignorance and blamed George for planting them. He claimed he couldn't smoke drugs because of his asthma – it made his head swell up and turn purple. Colony member Lord Goodman defended Francis in court and the newspapers had a field day.

MAID MARION: George was a fish out of water in the Colony. George must have had a drink problem before he met Francis. When he was sober he was a very smart, immaculately groomed man, but he couldn't cope with Francis' lifestyle. He never gave himself a chance to sober up properly; the alcohol was always in his system so he would get drunk really quickly and become incomprehensible. The only person who'd talk to him was Muriel. When I'd arrive she'd say to me, 'Thank God, that cunt ain't stopped going on and on. David, do something with George, get him out of here.' I used to have to take him somewhere else, but we had nothing in common and little to talk about. He must have known he was just being got out of the way. Francis had his big exhibition in Paris but George was unable to cope with it all – he went on a bender and brought a Venezuelan gigolo back to their hotel. Francis complained the man's feet stank and moved to another room. Next morning, George was found dead on the toilet.

MICHAEL HEATH: Francis is the strongest sexual figure of all time. He liked to be beaten up, he was a frightening man. The boyfriends he had were frightening too. He always wanted to find someone to dominate him – he should have gone straight and got married like I did, to a domineering wife.

MAID MARION: I met Francis' next muse John Edwards in 1972. There was a pub called the Crown & Anchor in Cross Street, Islington. I used to go every Wednesday for the talent competition and chat to my friend, the compère, Gay Travers, a female impersonator and pub entertainer. Gay was talking to John and he introduced me to him. John had a lot of charisma, he drew people to him. John took us to a club called the Paint Box, which is ironic when you consider he ended up with Francis Bacon. I introduced John to the Colony in '74 – John liked the club and Muriel nicknamed him 'Fuzzy' because of his hair. John was a barman, so Francis said, 'I'll come down and see your pub.' John ordered in lots of champagne but Francis didn't show. Next time John saw him at the Colony he gave him a bollocking, 'Why don't you turn up when you're supposed to, for this fucking champagne?'

DARREN COFFIELD: Francis enjoyed someone who had the courage to speak up to him like that. He found that very amusing and invited John to have lunch at Wheeler's, but John said he didn't like fish. So Francis bought him caviar. Then Francis took John gambling at Charlie Chester's, and when handed a membership form, John confessed he could neither read nor write. Francis said, 'God, that must be marvellous,' because he hated filling in forms.

MAID MARION: John was fascinated by Francis. They were like father and son but came from completely different backgrounds – Francis was well educated and travelled widely, while John was an East End barman at his brother's pub in Stratford, the Swan. John didn't read much – the poet Stephen Spender wrote to Francis, telling him how fortunate he was to meet someone who was so unaffected by everyday events, who you could just talk with. John was also a drinker, but unlike George Dyer who would get so absolutely pissed, John knew how to pace himself.

JOHN EDWARDS: Soon after I met Francis . . . he invited me to Reece Mews. 'People think I live grandly you know, but in fact I live in a dump.' By the time I'd climbed up the steep wooden stairs, guided by the rope banister, I could see he was right. 'You ain't 'alf lamping it a bit, Francis,' I thought to myself, I was shocked. He opened a bottle of champagne, probably vintage Krug, and I stayed the night. He slept on the couch, and I slept on the old circular bed. It was an odd bottle-green colour, with the headboard spattered with paint. The sofa, too, had paint stains all over it. We called its colour 'Belcher's Green' because it reminded him of his paintings of Muriel Belcher.

DARREN COFFIELD: Francis and John became inseparable. No matter how late Francis had been up drinking or gambling, he was always up at dawn to paint, usually with a hangover. John was the only person allowed to watch him work in his tiny, messy studio in Reece Mews, South Kensington. John appeared in Bacon's life shortly after he'd fallen out with Lucian Freud over Freud's 1974 Tate exhibition. Maybe he helped fill the void left by Freud?

MAID MARION: The true story is that John's brothers left London, and John said, 'I've got no one to look out for me now but I've still got Francis. I'm going to be with Francis.' So John employed a manager to run the Swan for him so he could go after Francis. It was all planned – he knew Francis fancied him; it was a shrewd move and why not? If it hadn't been John, it would have been someone else. I used to laugh with John and say, 'One thing they say about you is, "I bet he's hung like a horse. That's why Francis wants to be with him."' John said the rumours were untrue and laughed about it too.

DAVID EDWARDS: You'd read in the papers that the Edwards family mixed with gangsters – just because you're from the East End, the press like to portray you as a villain. Francis was madly in love with John; he was obsessed with him. If you walked into a bar and Francis was there without John, he'd be agitated. As soon as John appeared, he'd calm down. At the beginning John didn't quite understand what was happening, that he was Francis' muse.

MAID MARION: When John Edwards' dad saw Francis' painting, he said, 'I thought he said he loved him. Who's that? That's not my son! Fucking hell. Fucking awful.' He thought Francis was sinister and taking John over. John's mum, Beattie, said, 'Well, that's the way he paints people.' But as I said years ago – 'Muriel Belcher is Francis' *friend*? I wouldn't want a friend who paints a picture of me looking like she does.'

IAN BOARD: The only question about art John Edwards always asked Francis was, 'Why the fuck do you always paint me looking like a monkey?'

JOHN EDWARDS: We'd talk about everything. He was a beautiful man, you'd be hypnotised by him. He'd talk to you and you'd just want him to talk more . . . I think a lot of people misunderstood Francis. People got the impression of him as a bon vivant, the gambler, the drinker. That was part of it. But what people don't realise is that he was a very lonely and shy man. But I felt warm with him and I think he felt warm with me.

DARREN COFFIELD: John's sense of humour appealed to Francis. David Sylvester once asked condescendingly what type of wine John had served when he ran a pub in the East End. 'Vinegar', came the reply.

JOHN EDWARDS: . . . If people wanted to talk to Francis about art, he would use me as an excuse to deflect the conversation and widen it to something else – he'd say, 'Have you met John? He's a barman from the East End.'

DAVID EDWARDS: John and Francis' friendship was magical in a way, not sexual, although I think in the beginning, Francis would have liked it to be. It was a crush, and when that had gone, there was something on a much deeper level between them. If you saw them together, you could see their bond was strong. I went gambling a few times with Francis but I never liked Charlie Chester's. It was smoky, dingy – lots of Chinese in there gambling. Francis would give us all a pocketful of money to hold for him as we were going into the casino, 'Don't give it back to me. Even if I ask for it, don't give it back to me.' Ten minutes later it was, 'Give me that money back . . . Give it to me, *Give it to me!*' So it was pointless of him giving us the money in the first place really.

JOHN EDWARDS: . . . one night he won £15,000. I put some of it in his jacket and some in his trousers, so he wouldn't lose it.

The following morning, he phoned and asked if I had the money. I said no, I'd put it all in his pockets. We searched all over the flat and couldn't find it anywhere. And then a couple of days later, I came across it. He'd stuck it in a pair of old socks. He was so pleased, he gave me half of it.

DAVID EDWARDS: Francis gave John so much money that he had to carry it to the bank in a suitcase, and they had to shut the bank in the middle of the day to count it. Then the tax inspector decided to prosecute John for non-payment of tax after reading a newspaper article that John was Francis' model. At the end of the court case, the magistrate said, 'How do you intend paying it?' Francis immediately gets up – 'I'm paying it, how much do you want?' By this point the taxman was exasperated – 'You can't do that, it's Mr Edwards' liability not yours.' Francis, who never carried a chequebook and always had his cheques folded neatly in his top pocket, pulled one out with a flourish – 'I'm paying it. Don't tell me what I can and can't do.' And so Francis paid.

MAID MARION: Francis and John's relationship was not a one-way street – John looked after Francis too. Jeffrey Bernard resented the fact that Francis enjoyed John's company. He called him a 'bum boy', a male prostitute, which was untrue. There was a small television in the Colony, which they'd sometimes have on for the horse racing. Francis and Jeff would be glued to the television. Jeff was going to the betting office and asked Francis if he wanted him to place any bets. 'Yes, yes, on *this* horse.' Anyway, when Jeffrey came back, Francis asked what happened. 'Well, it lost.' John got up, went off round the betting office, came back and said, 'Sorry, that horse won. Give Francis the money.'

MARSH DUNBAR: Jeff would take bets for people – sometimes he'd think that a horse had no chance and would keep the money and not put it on with the bookie. He got into trouble if the horse won, because people would expect to be paid their winnings.

JEFFREY BERNARD: The only reason I've got any sort of name in this business is not because I'm good, but because I'm different . . . I was the first racing bloke ever to write about losing. Jay Landesman said that I wrote better about *loss* than anyone else. I don't mean loss of money, I mean generally: women, everything, health, you name it. I understand loss . . . I identify with it because I think life is fucking awful. The good day's the exception, not the rule.

DAVID EDWARDS: Francis gambled for escapism whereas Jeffrey gambled because he needed the money. Jeffrey always ran a gambling book on the coach to the Epsom Derby. He'd get quite nasty about it if you won and he had to pay out, 'Wait for your money . . . *wait for it!*' He was gambling with our money, losing it and couldn't pay us back at the end. Dear Jeffrey!

JEFFREY BERNARD: The most depressing remark I ever heard at Epsom . . . was by my bookmaker Victor Chandler. He greeted me once as I approached him . . . by turning around and saying . . . 'Here comes the lunch money.'

BOOKSHOP BILLY: The Derby was my one party of the year. I'd order the open-top bus to be outside Gerry's at six-thirty in the morning. The food and alcohol was all loaded and we'd leave by eight a.m. to get to Epsom and get parked as close to the finishing line as possible – it was a case of first come first served. We had a steel band onboard, and one of our guests asked if she could bring along her two friends who were vicars. One of the vicars was supposed to be meeting his bishop that day, and had to lie to get out of that – he'd told the bishop his elderly mother was ill and he had to go and stay with her, so he was very pleased to get out of that and come along with his 'friend' instead. We had a TV onboard to allow Jeff to take bets from Epsom and the other televised meetings, and watched the live broadcast building up to the races. Suddenly it showed they were coming onto our bus. The announcer said, 'There are many ways to come to the Derby . . . some with top hats . . . some with gypsies . . . but this is a nice way to travel and we are going onto the bus now.' Well, to their shock and amazement, the two fucking vicars were there, being broadcast live across the nation – including the one who is supposed to be at home holding his sick mother's hand. After the Derby we decided to go back to the Colony for a giggle, but the bus couldn't get round the corner at the Dog & Duck because of a signpost blocking our way. So we got off the bus, pulled the signpost out of the pavement and pulled round to the Colony. There was always a ladder hanging just inside the club doorway, so we placed it between the open-top bus and the first-floor window. Ian Board thought he was hallucinating when everyone suddenly began arriving mid-air, through the window.

MISS WHIPLASH: The Colony Room was classless, and functioned very much as a collection of overlapping groups. We all had our own chosen circle and it was possible to spend many years in that small room with people you knew only by name, or even just by sight. To belong, you only had to entertain, everyone had something to offer and appearances could be deceptive. Mick Tobin was known as an elderly and sometimes belligerent drunk who sold the *Evening Standard* at Leicester Square tube, but in his salad days he'd been a handsome ladies' man, painted by Lucian Freud with whom he shared a passion for punting on the horses. Sometimes he got lucky. I went up to the Colony to meet him on Derby Day in 1979, the year of Troy's win. Mick had a tip from W•••• •••••• himself, and slid out silently after the race to collect his winnings. The place was packed and we drank the club dry of champagne on Mick's winnings.

DARREN COFFIELD: Soho ran through Mick's veins; he was born and schooled there. After the war, he returned to the area and found a home in the Colony. Whenever he was homeless with nowhere to go, Ian Board let him stay in his flat. From the fifties onwards, Mick worked in the West End theatres, where he got his young friend Jeffrey Bernard a job as a flyman. He earned the nickname 'Covent Garden Mick' from his stint as a stage carpenter at the Royal Opera House. It was rumoured that people who stalled paying for Lucian Freud's paintings would be paid a friendly visit from an enforcer – Mick Tobin. He'd learned to box at school and spent several years in the Royal Navy, working as a stoker on destroyers. The intense physical work helped him become a contender for the Navy's middle-weight boxing championship. He was still capable of knocking out men half his age with a single punch well into his seventies.

BOOKSHOP BILLY: Mick would go round and have a word with anybody that upset Lucian. The story goes that Lucian, being a gambler, painted Mick to settle a debt with an Irish bookmaker that Lucian had fallen foul of. Lucian paid Mick for sitting for his portrait in Irish pounds from the Irish bookmaker. Mick was a bit wary and asked me if the Irish pounds were okay. I said, 'Of course they're legal currency.' Then he asked me to look after the money as he didn't want leave it 'under his mattress', so I put it in my safe. 'I'll try not to touch it,' he said. Well, he was in and out of the bookmakers after every race and it was all gone in no time at all.

FRANK AUERBACH: . . . [Lucian Freud] was a gambler far more reckless than Francis. He would get into debt with people like the Krays, which was not a healthy thing to do, and for many years he was nervous opening his door as to who might be outside. But he too must have had some sense of his own stature. Instead of selling one or two paintings cheaply, he pawned them, as Whistler had done, who also spent years in debt, and so when Lucian did finally make money, he was able to get those pictures back.

DARREN COFFIELD: In 1953 Lucian married the Guinness heiress Lady Caroline Blackwood; they became Colony regulars and eventually bought a house in Dean Street, Soho. They first met at Lady Rothermere's ball in 1949, which Francis had gatecrashed along with his new young friend Lucian. Later in the evening, Francis broke with royal protocol and booed Princess Margaret offstage. The humiliated princess fled and the stuffy ball descended into chaos. Caroline claimed that she had dinner with Francis nearly every night of her marriage to Lucian. They were a stunning Soho couple – young, beautiful and clever. But the intense socialising and heavy drinking took their toll on Caroline. She once asked Dan Farson, 'Have you ever driven with Lucian?' – 'Yes,' he replied, 'I was so terrified that when he stopped at a red light for once, I threw myself out.' – 'Exactly,' she agreed, 'that's what being married to him was like.'

BIG EDDI: I had a brief fling with Lucian and went gambling with him four times. Three out of those four times he crashed his car. The last time he crashed into a police car – he was the worst driver I've met in my entire life. He'd always say, 'You'd better get out and walk,' so I'd be left having to find my own way home by foot. Whenever I walked into the Colony, Lucian would wave his hand and shout – 'Give the lady a bottle of champagne.'

DARREN COFFIELD: Once, the painter Tim Behrens was leaving the Colony with Lucian when a man came up, greeting them with a disarming 'hello'. Lucian immediately headbutted the man and yelled, 'Run!' Once they'd shaken off their pursuer, a breathless Behrens asked Lucian how much he owed the man. 'Fourteen,' gasped Lucian. 'Pounds?' gulped Behrens. 'Thousand,' winced Lucian. Behrens had been taught by Lucian at the Slade and became close to him after he split from Caroline in 1956. They shared a flat for a time and hung out together in Soho, their 'school of ideas', where they'd play frenetic games of pinball in dingy cafés. For nine years Lucian was a father figure to the young Behrens who sat regularly for him up until 1964, when he was suddenly frozen out by Lucian and cut adrift.

MICHAEL CLARK: Muriel told me that Lucian once started a portrait of her, but the painting was never finished as the increasing number of sittings required became too demanding on her time. She summarised why she declined to continue, by saying to me, 'I couldn't be fucking bothered, dear!'

DARREN COFFIELD: Francis said that what was 'so awful about sitting for Lucian' was that he made you 'sit by the hour without moving an eyelash'. Initially they were very close. Lucian was a committed risk-taker, a passion he shared with Francis, under whose influence he began gambling. It was an all-or-nothing attitude that permeated throughout all levels of their lives. Together they represented Britain at the Venice Biennale in 1954. Francis, who obsessively painted countless portraits of Lucian, was the main reason for Lucian's frequent presence in the Colony. However, they had very different working patterns, with Lucian always leaving early in the evening to work throughout the night while Francis continued socialising until the early hours. Caroline blamed her husband's odd hours, sleeping all day and painting all night, along with his gambling and womanising, for the break-up of their marriage.

GERALD McCANN: Lucian was always broke and very sweet. I liked him. Then this girl appeared on the scene, an American. 'I hear you know everybody – painters, writers and poets,' she said, 'I'd love to meet some.' So I called up Lucian – 'How would you like to meet a rich American girl?' and told him to meet us at the Colony at three p.m. the next day. The following day the girl arrived, then Lucian. I went and got the drinks. After a while Lucian got up, wandered off and came back, and had another drink, then got up, wandered off again and came back. After the third time, I said, 'Have you got trouble with your waterworks?' – 'No, I have two horses running at Doncaster.' So that was the end of that romance.

PAM HARDYMENT: Lucian would just sit there and stare at me. He had that stare, as if he was staring deep into your soul, 'I like your eyes. I wondered if I could paint you?' – 'No thanks, I'm not sitting there for hours in some horrible studio being painted. It's not my thing, I don't stand still.' My family have berated me ever since. 'You could have been famous.' – 'Yes, and I could have been pregnant by him. I would have ended up sleeping with him like everyone else.'

DARREN COFFIELD: One night Ian announced loudly, 'I've been told by many women that Lucian is a great fuck. Why? Because he has a penis that curls round like a pig's tail.' I mentioned Ian's description of Lucian's penis over dinner with a doctor friend. He told me if it curled round like that, it meant the penis was broken – well, if true, it didn't seem to interfere with his love life.

MAID MARION: Lucian said to Francis, 'I think I'm gay,' to which Francis replied, 'With a tiny dick like that you can't be gay.' I found Lucian odd, intimidating. Francis was outgoing, but Lucian was difficult to talk to, he was so quiet. Muriel always called him 'Luce' and told me off for being so wary. I thought Francis and Lucian fell out over gambling, but apparently Francis was offered a knighthood twice and refused it, saying, 'I came into this world as Mr Bacon and I want to leave as Mr Bacon.' Lucian was looking forward to being honoured but didn't get it due to tax evasion. Then they just had this silly argument and didn't talk any more, and Lucian never came up to the club again after that.

IAN BOARD: There's one or two things I've observed about painters over the years. They are more jealous than musicians or poets. They are terribly jealous of each other. They give a pat

From the left: Ian Board, Carmel Stuart, David Archer and Nina Hamnett (seated).

Above: Ian Board, second from left. Muriel and Carmel, far right. Leonard Blackett, seated front row, 1950s.

Right: Frank, the barman, and Francis Bacon, *c.*1952.

Your hosts and hostess

Muriel Belcher, Ian Board and Carmel Stuart by Trog.

Right: Ian Board modelling, c.1950.

© Colony Room Archive

Below, from the left: Muriel Belcher, in blonde wig, Ronnie Kray, Joan Littlewood and actor James Booth.

© David Marrion

Muriel Belcher photographed for Francis Bacon by John Deakin.

Nina Hamnett leaving the Colony Room by Edward Wolfe (1897–1982). 11.5 x 8.5 inches, pen and ink. Whereabouts unknown.

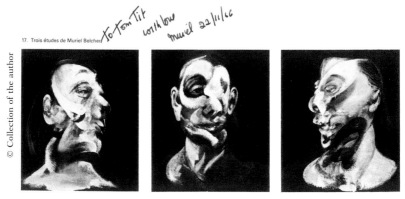

17. Trois études de Muriel Belcher

To Tom Tit with love muriel 22/11/66

Three Studies of Muriel Belcher from *Derriere le Miroir*, 1966, signed by Belcher.

Frank Norman outside the entrance to the Colony Room Club, Dean Street, Soho.

12 **Lying figure with hypodermic syringe** 1963

Oil on canvas
78 × 57 inches (198 × 145 cm.) illustrated in colour

Signed and torn page from an exhibition catalogue, featuring Francis Bacon's painting of Henrietta Moraes.

Henrietta Moraes photographed for Francis Bacon by John Deakin.

David Archer by John Deakin.

The 'Last Supper' photographed by John Deakin. *From the left:* Tim Behrens, Lucian Freud, Francis Bacon, Frank Auerbach and Michael Andrews in Wheeler's restaurant.

All good wishes to Billy, Daniel Farson

Daniel Farson: a werewolf in Soho.

on the back and say, 'I saw your show and liked it,' but what they really mean is, 'What a load of old rubbish.' They are jealous and lie a lot, but they are very loving, extremely generous and, on the whole, fantastically sympathetic. I love them.

JAMES BIRCH: Francis did not approve of Lucian's behaviour, which he considered to be the worst type of social climbing. Many years later when Lucian was having his retrospective at the Hayward Gallery, he called Francis to ask if he would please come to the opening. Having someone of Francis' stature there would consolidate his work. Francis was quite upset by the phone call, as Lucian had previously not spoken to him for many years.

DARREN COFFIELD: Lucian needed the patronage of the English aristocrats. His behaviour may have been due to a realisation that in a country as class-ridden as England, talent is not always enough. But Francis thought otherwise. He turned down the honours offered to him, 'Because in a sense it cordons you off from existence.'

Francis enjoyed the throng, travelling cheek by jowl on public transport, examining commuters' faces, fleeting glances of human heads distorting – twisting and bending out of shape in the reflections of the glass of a tube train. Once I was coming up to the escalators at South Kensington tube station, I could see the outline of a familiar figure ahead of me, pedaling away furiously with one foot in mid-air, trying to get on an escalator and repeatedly failing. It was Francis. I gently took him by the arm, helped him on and carried on my way without a further word. He didn't want to be chauffeured around, he liked the hustle of the street.

PAM HARDYMENT: He also loved an audience – the more packed the Colony was, the better. When the club was quieter, you could talk to him. When it was his birthday, we'd dance around the room and he'd have the look of a teenager on his face. He was at his own little party in the club and was very sweet – I never saw the nasty side of him, he loved women. He would talk to me about some cheap faux leather shoes he was wearing – 'Do you know I could sleep in these?' He liked talking to women about clothes in that gay way – 'I was taught as a child how to sew a button on.' So Francis got a needle and thread from Ian, and there was Francis saying, 'You see. I can do it!' And he sat there sewing a button back onto his jacket, wearing his plastic shoes. Then he'd say, 'Do you know I am the greatest living British artist?' – 'Yes, I know, but I've just come here for a drink,' I'd reply. 'Do you know there is no one to touch me? Not even that fucking Lucian Freud!'

JAMES BIRCH: Lucian was very competitive with Francis, even though they had not spoken to one another in years. Lucian would phone Dan Farson and do an interview with him as if in riposte to Francis. However, Francis could be just as bad and enjoyed playing weird psychological games with his friends. For example, I saw Francis and Denis Wirth-Miller walking up Dean Street to the Colony. Denis said, 'Look, Francis has invited you up for a drink, please abuse me.' – 'I can't abuse you.' – 'Please, just do it!' So we are sitting, Denis and I, on the banquette and Francis had his back to us at the bar. Denis kept nudging me. So I said loudly, 'Denis, you're a complete cunt.' Upon which Francis spun round and said, 'Yes, not only are you a cunt but you have always been a *complete cunt.*'

DARREN COFFIELD: When Francis became a Colony 'hostess' in 1948, Denis Wirth-Miller was one of the very first people he invited to come to the club. Francis and Denis loved Muriel's wit and archly camp humour, which they would often mimic when making a point in conversation. For Denis, who liked nothing better than drinking and arguing, the Colony was heaven, whilst for his partner Dickie Chopping, it was a 'hell-hole'. Francis and Denis' favourite party trick was a drunken argument culminating in a screaming match.

BIG EDDI: Muriel didn't mind people being at each other's throats as long as they didn't spill their drinks on her carpet. There could be terrible drunken arguments, but I don't know how real any of it was. The club was a performance space. They were being watched and were watching themselves in the mirrors. It was all an act really.

JAMES BIRCH: Dickie and Denis were really old friends of Francis. They were very discreet and were completely loyal to him. Francis expected that level of loyalty from people. Dickie was an illustrator and designed all the iconic dust jackets for Ian Fleming's James Bond novels. Francis introduced Dickie to George Orwell's widow, Sonia, who in turn introduced him to Ian Fleming. Denis was a painter who shared a studio with Francis Bacon in Wivenhoe, Suffolk, in the 1950s. They collaborated on some paintings that are now coming to light. He did a lot of the paint effects in Francis' paintings of the fifties. The hatched grass effect on the figures in the landscapes, baboons, etc., were all by Denis.

DARREN COFFIELD: Denis was an important part of Francis' life and that of the Colony. In the early years Denis could often be found at the bar vying for Francis' attention with Lucian Freud, who was to become a lifelong enemy, referring to Denis Wirth-Miller as 'Denis Worth-Nothing'.

JAMES BIRCH: I first met Francis with Dickie and Denis at the age of five. My parents rented a weekend cottage where these two artists lived. Francis was an odd-looking man. I remember him coming up to me and talking to me, and the smell of champagne on his breath made me flinch away from him. Denis was known as 'Nanny Worth-Millions' and was my babysitter, but somehow Francis got it into his head that Denis was my godfather.

DARREN COFFIELD: Denis enjoyed 'friction' and taunted David Sylvester in front of the writer Shena Mackay at the bar – 'Oh, and to think she used to be so pretty. What a shame!' This went on for a considerable amount of time until David lost his temper, punched Denis and busted his nose. Denis pranced around the club, laughing hysterically, spraying everyone with his blood. These mad little performances entertained the members as they whiled away the afternoon. Alcoholic amnesia was often cited the following day as an excuse for unpardonable behaviour. The members could be a treacherous bunch back-biting and bitching about each other's drunken behaviour whilst dreading to wave adieu to the Colony.

JEFFREY BERNARD: The only way you can give up drinking is to want to give it up and I don't want to. Alcoholics are terrible self-deceivers. I had two and a half years on the wagon once, because I did something ghastly, I hit a woman. We are great friends now, but sometimes I give her a sideways glance and think the mistake I made was not hitting her harder. Two and a half years on the wagon made me miserable, lonely, bad-tempered and melancholy. My wife later cited these things in the divorce.

BIG EDDI: Jeffrey was on the phone to his bookmaker and I said, 'Jeffrey, can you get out of the bloody way please!' and he just turned, hit me and fled. He stopped drinking for a few years after that out of remorse.

JEFFREY BERNARD: I'm not a shit. I'm a cunt . . . There's a great difference. A shit is intentionally nasty, and I've never been that. I've never deliberately caused a lot of misery. I'm not cruel. A cunt is a cunt by mistake – *it's accidental*.

MOLLY PARKIN: Towards closing time, Francis said to me, 'Let's have a change of scene now, Moll.' So we left the Colony and went down the road to the Golden Lion. It must have gone down in the gay annals that if you come to London and make your way to the Golden Lion, that's where you'll find your future. Francis always had huge wads of cash on him. So all these rent boys jumped up and came rushing towards him – 'Francis! Francis!' As they moved towards him, he took one of his wads of notes and threw it into the air like confetti, then another, then another. He kept throwing wads of notes into the air, watching the boys scrabble about, with glee.

IAN BOARD: The Golden Lion was one of the only two queer pubs in Soho. Francis and Deakin were regulars there. I always referred to it as 'The Meat Rack' and at closing time the police would regularly turn up with their 'meat wagon' to cart away the leftovers.

GERALD McCANN: After the Colony, sometimes Dan Farson would take me to a really seedy nightclub, which had bare electric light bulbs and dwarfs standing in a corner. It was very Hogarthian. Weird-looking people who only came out at night, generally after midnight – the graveyard shift.

IAN BOARD: We always closed the club at eleven p.m. prompt. I would call out last orders – 'Ladies and gentlemen, your very last orders *please*! Rush up, dash up, spend up, drink up and *fuck off*.' Muriel would call out to the stragglers, *'Don't you have lovely cottages to go to?'* The customers' handbags had been cleaned and rinsed dry by eleven p.m. We had got the best out of them and now they were someone else's problem. Muriel would have a cab waiting to take her home. And I might go and do a little light whoring at the weekend.

DAVID EDWARDS: In those days the West End was dead on a Sunday. Trading wasn't allowed and all the shops were shut, so Muriel, Ian, Dan, Francis and Carmel would all come to my pub in Stratford for a big lunch and a pub crawl. The fights would be horrendous because in those days everyone was terrified of not being there in case the others talked about them. Francis didn't want us left alone with Muriel, who didn't want us left alone with Francis; both petrified of one telling a story on the other. It was a love–hate relationship – they tried to maintain a hold over each other. For example, Francis would sell his paintings without Marlborough Fine Art knowing, to avoid paying them commission, but Muriel would know, so he would have to pay her off and then Muriel would have to pay off Melon Lips [Carmel] to keep *her* mouth shut. Muriel was a quiet lesbian. It took me a while to realise that friend of hers was her partner – she never sat next to Muriel, always two stools down the bar.

DARREN COFFIELD: Muriel was such an extraordinary character that it was inevitable someone should try and commit her to print. Allan [Alice] Hall undertook the task of writing a biography of Muriel and the club. This involved endless research drinking at the bar, but the stories were far too scandalous and libellous for publication in the sixties, so the project was shelved. Allan was another extraordinary Colony character – born in a Yorkshire mining village, at twenty-seven he became one of the youngest editors of a national newspaper, wrote the gossip column, Atticus, and in 1969 started one of Britain's first style sections at the *Sunday Times*. By the seventies, he became known for his wine column, 'Bacchus'.

DAVID EDWARDS: Allan then organised Muriel's sixty-eighth birthday party in the famous wine cellar at the Café Royal. It was the first time they'd ever used it for a function, so we had to have screens to hide what was being stored in the cellar. John Eliot was the cellar master at the Café Royal – he had his master's uniform on and a young chap with him to serve the wine. Muriel was born in 1908 and the party was in 1976, so Allan tried to get as much 1908 vintage as possible, but all he could get in the end are two bottles of port. But there are thirty people around this big table to celebrate Muriel's birthday, so John Eliot instructs his wine waiter to pour an inch of port into each glass; otherwise there won't be enough to go round. The young wine waiter goes around pouring the port. When he gets to Big Audrey, who is enormous and known as 'The Colonel', she grabs his hand and says, 'Pour, *you cunt*.' The young man is absolutely petrified, yanks his arm free and goes running off behind the screen to find John Eliot – 'Mr Eliot! I did as you said and this woman got hold of my hand and said, "Pour, you cunt."' John Eliot is aghast, 'You point her out to me, I'm not having people behaving like that!' So the boy points out Big Audrey. 'What did she say to you again?' – 'She said, "*Pour, you cunt!*"' – 'Well, don't argue with *her*, go and do what she says.' Everyone was scared of Big Audrey.

Allan hadn't told the guests they'd have to help pay for the party and that he needed the money. Eventually the Café Royal sued him and he had to ask his wife to bail him out. That was the beginning of the end of the marriage. He lived with his wife and three children at 40 Hill Street, behind the Dorchester, one of the most expensive houses in London – he went from having all that to having nothing. He came to stay with me for a weekend and didn't leave for ten years. It was a very expensive party.

IAN BOARD: After the weekend's proceedings, Muriel used to like a brandy or port in the morning for the little upset tummies and slight hangovers. When we lived in Clare Court on Judd Street (I was on the seventh floor and she was on the third), I'd collect her and we'd have a regular black cabbie waiting, called 'Ginger'. He'd pick us up for one and sixpence and take us to the club. Muriel, Carmel and I always ate lunch together but every so often, of a lunchtime, we would have to have a club committee meeting . . .

DAVID GENTLE: Committee meetings were generally held at the club at midday. They were quite informal and often followed by lunch at Wheeler's. Muriel or Ian would return to open the club around three p.m. In those days committee members included Allan Hall, Lady Rose McLaren, Thea Porter, Sandy Fawkes, Bruce Bernard and other well-known characters . . . I recall that Robert Carrier [the chef] attended on occasion. In practice the committee had little to do with the business of the club, but its activities typically included 'rubber stamping' new members – who in truth had to be approved by Muriel who ruled supreme – and discussing any event or gossip that involved the members.

MERILYN THOROLD: The name 'Colony Room Club' came from Muriel's partner Carmel. She was a black Jamaican, from the Colonies. They were a proper partnership. The trouble was Carmel did rather enjoy gambling and that caused stress.

DAVID EDWARDS: Carmel didn't have to work, she was kept by Muriel. She was always nicking money off everyone to go gambling at Charlie Chester's. Whenever Carmel used to go behind the bar, Muriel and Ian used to shout, 'Get away from that till!' She really was a compulsive gambler and her weakness was gaming tables. The three of them were as bad as each other. Once there was a £20 note that someone had dropped in the bar. Muriel finds it and puts it in her handbag. When she goes to the toilet, Carmel takes the note out of Muriel's handbag and puts it in her back pocket. Later, Ian takes the note out of Carmel's back pocket and puts it in his pocket. That's how it used to be, it would go round and round and round.

ISABEL RAWSTHORNE: Carmel, if she liked you, was fond of raising her skirt to show her streak of thick, long hair that went in a panel from navel to pubis.

INDIAN AMY: She never discussed her background. She was originally a club singer and had a marvellous sense of humour. When I first met Carmel, Muriel and Ian, they were very friendly, they had a lovely rapport. Ian adored Muriel and so did

Carmel. Then it went peculiar – a jealous friction got going, which turned into the Hundred Years' War.

MAID MARION: I became a go-between for the three of them when they refused to talk to one another. Muriel did love her and was quite open about being gay and having a black girlfriend. No one could blackmail her because everyone knew what was going on.

INDIAN AMY: The club got caught up in the Swinging Sixties and picked up the spirit of the age. But by the end of the sixties, Muriel was beginning to get ill. She had a major stroke and Francis put her into the London Clinic. It was the twentieth anniversary of the club and she tried to get up and skip out of the hospital. She had to be physically put back in bed. It all started from that major stroke – it led to a series of mini strokes, which dogged her for the rest of her life. Francis paid for Muriel and Carmel to go and recuperate in the West Indies, but it was no good, Muriel was slowly dying.

MAID MARION: I got a phone call when I was in the Swan one day in 1975. John's mum Beattie said, 'It's the Colony.' – 'For me?' It was Ian. 'Muriel's becoming more and more unwell and I need to be on the other side of the bar now. Will you come and work behind the bar?' I started straight away and was left to get on with running the club as Ian was often passed out on the banquette. I enjoyed it. Muriel knew he was light-fingered and put the trust in me. They were like a gang of thieves, no discrimination, they would rob Peter to pay Paul. Ian fancied all the ●●●●●●●●● brothers. Especially the one who stole Muriel's Elmfield School charity box from the bar. You have to be pretty low to do that, don't you?

DARREN COFFIELD: Money began to get tight when Muriel became ill. Aunty Fred sent out demands for unpaid bar bills. Frank Norman and Sandy Fawkes both vowed never to return over debts they said they were not liable for.

MAID MARION: Like Thea Porter, Sandy Fawkes enjoyed hanging out with Francis and drinking champagne. She was sent on assignment to the USA where she met this young man in a bar in Atlanta. She thought he was a cross between Robert Redford and Ryan O'Neal, so they had an affair and drove down the coast to Florida. He said his name was Daryl Golden, but really he was Paul Knowles who had murdered and raped over eighteen people, on a seven-month killing spree. Sandy always wondered what it was that stopped Knowles from murdering her, too. She wrote a book about it, *Killing Time*.

KATE FAWKES: In 1977 Sandy held the book launch for *Killing Time* in the Colony. It became a bestseller and the following year she went to Australia on a book tour. Upon her return Ian presented her with a bar bill for the period she had been away. Sandy disputed it, had a huge argument and never went back.

DARREN COFFIELD: Sandy started out as a research assistant alongside David Frost for Dan Farson's TV show. She was a familiar sight in Soho – with her huge fur hat plonked on her head, she'd match the men drink for drink. Dan Farson, Jeffrey Bernard and Graham Mason all enjoyed verbally sparring with Sandy, the clash of characters creating much hilarity. However, once she'd barred herself from the Colony, people always knew they could go 'upstairs' to escape her.

MAID MARION: Once Muriel was ill, Ian would get up to all sorts of things because he had no one to keep him in check. The Colony's handyman John Payne had a young girl up there on drugs 'doing things'. If the police had walked in, the club would have been closed down. All of a sudden the door opens, it's Muriel – 'So this is what goes on while I'm away!' You should have seen Ian's face. He didn't know what to say.

MICHAEL CLARK: From 1977 I was a frequent visitor to Muriel's flat. I was working on a series of portraits of her. She was propped up in bed and Ian was sat next to her chatting. He was reminding her of when she was telephoned from New York by the secretary of a collector who had just bought a portrait of her by Francis. The caller wanted to speak to 'Miss Belcher' to request some background information about the sitter for the new owner of the painting. Muriel's reply was, Yes of course, just have him send her two first-class return tickets to New York, via Jamaica, and she would gladly speak with him. The secretary said that the collector was a very generous man; however, she felt that on this occasion he would not be prepared to stretch that far. 'Could you tell me where he keeps the painting?' Muriel enquired. 'Oh yes, it hangs in his dining room.' – 'Well, please would you tell him from Miss Belcher, that the next time he looks at it, she hopes he fucking chokes.'

DIANA MELLY: Slowly over the years I came to dislike Muriel and her mercenary behaviour. It wasn't very nice for Carmel. People tolerated Carmel because she was Muriel's girlfriend. She was often ignored and belittled, and I look back on it now and think how she must have hated it all – I don't remember Muriel ever making anyone feel they should be nice to her. What really summed up the place for me was when my husband

George and I were leaving the club once – Francis Bacon gave George this big hug and turned to me, jabbing at me with his finger, and said, 'I've never quite seen the point of you!' And I thought, he's right, I don't have a point at Muriel's – I wasn't an artist or writer and I didn't bring in money by making lots of men buy me drinks at the bar. What was the point of me being in that club? And I think Carmel came to feel the same.

MAID MARION: After more than thirty years together, Carmel left Muriel and went back to Jamaica. It broke Muriel's heart – 'I'll never have her back.' – 'You will,' I said, 'I bet you a fiver she'll be back.' Ian hated Carmel because she left and he had to deal with the aftermath – 'All those nights I had to cope with my poor Muriel crying herself to sleep.'

MERILYN THOROLD: After two years, Carmel phoned Muriel from Jamaica and said, 'I want to come home,' to which Muriel replied, 'You are home, *Cunty*.'

MAID MARION: When she came back, Muriel got her a job at Neal's, Charlie Campbell's restaurant – working the till (in more ways than one). It took a while for her to get back into the flat with Muriel, but once she was in, that was it. It was love, they couldn't live without one another, and as Carmel said, 'No matter what Ian does, when I leave here I go to bed with Muriel, so I always win.' But Ian lost his temper with Muriel for taking her back and tried to push Muriel down the club stairs. After that Muriel didn't take any chances and had a banister rail fitted. Up until that point everything was going Ian's way; he stood to inherit the lot. There were so many arguments that Muriel disinherited him – 'He's such a silly boy, creating so much trouble about nothing.'

DARREN COFFIELD: Dickie Chopping went to visit Muriel and noted how 'frail and frightened' she looked, with 'one thumbnail between her teeth like a child'. Afterwards he went for lunch with Carmel, who told him she suspected Ian had been deliberately doping Muriel with drink and drugs, so her brain and body would deteriorate.

MAID MARION: She'd get confused and rely on Carmel to finish off stories and remember places for her. Ian told me that Muriel was leafing through a magazine and saw an advert for Cinzano. She lifted up the magazine to her face in an attempt to drink the picture. She literally tried to drink it off the page.

SHAKESPEARE: Merilyn Thorold was a wonderful woman who cared for those in Soho who were too poor or sick to help themselves, such as David Archer, Paul Potts and Muriel – who she nursed tirelessly on her deathbed. Merilyn said, 'You must come and see Muriel,' who by that stage was bedridden, very frail and sweet. It was as if Merilyn knew that these were important seminal moments in my life.

MERILYN THOROLD: Muriel thought one of the hospital doctors was a club member, Graham Mason. And when this doctor, who *did* look a bit like Graham Mason, used to go on his round, she'd say, 'We know who you are, Graham,' and give him a knowing wink. The doctor was terribly nice and would just say, 'Okay, Muriel!' They did this awful thing of trying to prolong her life – she was ill in such a lot of ways by then. I asked the nurse, 'Why are you doing this?' and she said, 'We don't do that sort of thing here,' meaning euthanasia. Muriel said, 'If only I could get to the window, I would jump.'

DANIEL FARSON: Would you commit suicide?

FRANCIS BACON: If I could do it properly and get a doctor to give me the right things. I've known people who have tried to commit suicide, they haven't succeeded and their brain has gone, they become vegetables. If you're going to commit suicide, you've got to just do it.

DANIEL FARSON: Don't you think it's an insult to life or is it the final accolade?

FRANCIS BACON: Don't talk bollocks, of course it's not an insult. What do you mean 'an insult to life'? Are you religious?

DANIEL FARSON: I have had friends kill themselves, John Minton and others. The next week I always think how they would have loved this or that. It seems to me such a waste. Hang on, hang on, then go out graciously.

FRANCIS BACON: But you're quite an old man, I'm a very old man; it doesn't matter, you just do yourself in. Why can't we get these cyanide pills the Germans had? They're the perfect thing, two minutes of agony then it's over.

DANIEL FARSON: But in the last moments of agony, you might think, Christ! I would like to paint that, that's the next painting and it's too late.

FRANCIS BACON: You either take it or not, the cyanide pill, you can't waffle over it.

MICHAEL CLARK: When Ian told Francis how ill Muriel was, he wept. It was the only time I ever saw Francis cry. Eventually I received a telegram from Ian, 'Muriel died in the night. Please come to West End.'

IAN BOARD: Muriel died on Halloween, 31 October 1979. The timing was perfect because we cremated her on Guy Fawkes Night. We had a bloody good wake after that, it went on for a week. Her funeral was at Golders Green Cemetery. Mike McKenzie played 'Send in the Clowns' and George Melly sang at the memorial service.

DANIEL FARSON: Jeff [Bernard] and I gave the addresses at her memorial service at St Paul's Church, Covent Garden, on Thursday, 29th November 1979. Deeply saddened, Francis took me to lunch at Wheeler's beforehand, where he helped me prune my address, which was too wordy. It is hard to avoid platitudes on such occasions, but I started by saying what I felt: 'I cannot imagine a finer opportunity than a service like this to give thanks, as we do now, for our great good luck in knowing Muriel Belcher who turned life into a marvellous party.'

SANDY FAWKES: It was George Melly who summed it up at her funeral. He said, 'I know this is a sad occasion, but I just want you all to imagine the look on St Peter's face when she arrives at the Pearly Gates, bangs on the door and shouts "Let me in, Clara!"'

ELIZABETH SMART: . . . we all went back to the club for sandwiches and free drinks and celebration of her great gifts. 'Because that's what she would have wanted,' said Carmel . . .

MERILYN THOROLD: When Muriel was dying in hospital, Carmel let Muriel's apartment to John Edwards and he wouldn't get out. Francis was so besotted by him, he didn't give Carmel the money for the apartment or tell John to leave. It was only £15,000, which to Francis was absolute peanuts. So there was a problem as Ian didn't have enough money to keep the club going and Carmel didn't have enough to buy a house in Jamaica. In the end, Ian bought the club from Carmel, with payments spread over a series of years. It all got rather bitter. I blame John and Francis who could have stopped it easily.

MAID MARION: John and Francis took some of Carmel's valuables from the flat before she went to Jamaica, to get their own back on her. Eventually Francis paid her off for the flat – in fact he had to pay her off twice because she went to Jamaica, squandered the money and came back again. Meanwhile, John had changed his name to John Edwards Belcher and was offered £20,000 by the landlord to buy back the lease on Muriel's apartment.

ELIZABETH SMART: 1980 without Muriel. It's a bleak thought for a motley lot of us . . . Genius is mysterious, specially when it works in an unlikely medium, bringing all the pains and disciplines of art to something touchingly ephemeral, when it could be done adequately with a lot less trouble. I think of one fashion editor, one wild window-designer, stripteasers, clowns and legendary singers and dancers. Most of all I think of Muriel, who managed to make running a club into an art form. All these enhancers of our bumpy stay on earth may be written about, and the compost from which they came discussed and analysed, but what they did can never be explained, and only the mystery remains as the generations come marching on.

Muriel will certainly turn up in many a memoir, but how can one recapture the magic, especially now that words seem to be getting obsolete? And the falsifying of the record – a false-faced facsimile of the real thing – pops up on television and radio and cinema and stage and in books, before you can say 'Obituary' . . . Why this gluttony for biography, when our lives are the briefest thing about us? It's a good story. But *it wasn't like that* . . . 'She was in fact a virgin,' said Carmel. And she never menstruated. Yet she was many people's mother figure, a nanny who dispensed rude words like soothing hot milk.

MICHAEL CLARK: After Muriel died, there was a state of interregnum at the club and a palpable sense of the presence of absence . . . Francis came in one afternoon. He was in an elated mood – 'I've just finished a painting, it's called *The Sphinx*. And the extraordinary thing about it is that it looks very much like Muriel.'

DARREN COFFIELD: A grieving Francis paid tribute to Muriel in the only way he knew how, he painted her. In the portrait, the sphinx and Muriel become one. Her fine-boned features and peerless gaze – from which no one could ever hide – now look out over the passing years in the National Museum of Modern Art, Tokyo. Muriel Belcher, one of the most formidable London characters of her day, infamous for her individual spirit and freedom of speech, painted as a timeless enigma.

FRANCIS BACON: I think of Muriel as a woman full of compassion but also someone who belongs to a very ancient world. A world before Christianity had dragged in its paraphernalia of petty morals and spite.

5

Ida Board: The Reign of Terror

IAN BOARD: I want to write my autobiography. I'd like to write a book about the Colony Room Club. I tell you why, because when I die an awful lot of idiots are going to try and write about this room. Just like those people who write books about Soho and know nothing about Soho whatsoever!

BRUNTON: Most serious drinking people in Soho know of the legend that is Ida Board – Ian David Archibold Board, known by his close friends simply as 'Ida'. An unsuitably effeminate name for such a frightening man. By this stage of his life, his nose was like a throbbing strawberry; it had grown out of all proportion due to years of alcohol abuse. He originally came from Devon and was very articulate, considering his poor education. Soho was his schooling and he listened to the radio to get the voice and accent right. When he was Muriel's barman, he kept his mouth shut and his ears and eyes open. He developed a sixth sense about people – he acquired that from Muriel.

IAN BOARD: Muriel taught me you're married to the business. You can be here from ten in the morning, to at least eleven at night. One is married to the job – I can't have a boyfriend full time, I can't have a *wife* full time. You can't do the job properly otherwise. I never had an education – I couldn't do a professional job like a doctor, oh no, but I simply love the idea of being married to this room. It's beautiful, I love it, absolutely adore it – I wouldn't mind dropping dead here. I love coming in here early when there is no one else here, just to sit and have a drink and a fag, and look around the place. I've got a little flat in Bloomsbury but it's just where I shave and shower. I eat very little; drink is my food, and vodka is my drink. As you may have realised, I am a bachelor – you can call me a homosexual if you like, although I don't practise any more because I'm married to this room. The reason I kept this room going was because of Muriel. Her capacious handbag now hangs from the ceiling near the window: it and this club is all I have left of her, and it is an object of some veneration. She used it for years. It has six different compartments in it – there was powder in one, dog biscuits in another. When she died, I went around to the flat and rescued it just in time from the dustbin. Every year I stick £20 in it for luck.

MICHAEL WOJAS: Ian never knew his real mother, she died when he was very young. He always felt like an outsider until he met Muriel. She became the mother he never knew, and the Colony the family he felt he never had.

IAN BOARD: The first thing I remember of my childhood is poverty. My mother died when I was four years old. I remember a little cottage in Clarence Place in Exeter. There were four cottages tied together with an outside lavatory. My mother was in a wheelchair and I was on the outside lavatory on a big square Victorian seat. I remember her putting me on it for a shit and I couldn't get off, so I shouted, 'Mum, Mum, I've finished. Will you come and wipe my bum?' And that's the only recollection I have of my mother.

When I went back years after, it was very difficult to find anything of the history of her, but she must have been a tough woman to cope with my father. He never mentioned her, never spoke of her, not a word. Never told me her name or anything about her. He was ignorant, my father. I never liked him. He wasn't an open person. He was a farm labourer. I suppose he thought I was a bit strange really, that I had ideas above my station. We lived as peasants and I loathed the idea of being there, it was ghastly. When my mother died, my father remarried, otherwise we would have gone to the workhouse. My stepmother was pregnant by another chap, so it was a marriage of convenience, like a public lavatory.

The Boards are very randy, they all have strings of children. I think I am the only poof in the family. There were seven full Boards, and one half Board. I felt I was an outsider, I felt unwanted. Can you imagine four boys sleeping together in one bed? And I was pissing the bed; I felt disgraced but there was nothing I could do about it. They'd wake me up in the middle of the night and make me go to the outside lavatory, which was freezing cold with no heat or light, and I wouldn't want to piss. I'd go back to bed, fall asleep and five minutes later, piss the bed and get beaten for that. The pissing attracted the bugs and the walls were crawling with these bugs, which I would squash and kill against the wall. Thinking back on it, I could design a wallpaper now with bugs on it, like Laura Ashley. It would make a wonderful design for pillowslips and sheets. My incontinence came in useful later, when I managed to avoid National Service in the Army by claiming I was a bedwetter, an hereditary affliction.

I was bored with school. I wanted to run away and at the first opportunity, I did. The circus was in town, and I had never seen a circus, so I played truant that day and ran away. When I was fourteen, I left school and did various odd jobs. I was a milkman and got caught fiddling the milk round. I could fiddle the cash, but not the books and that's how I got found out. Then I worked in a parachute factory, I don't know *what* I was doing there! Then I got into the hospitality business. I worked in a hotel restaurant, the Imperial Hotel in Exeter, as a waiter – and fell in love with an actress at the Theatre Royal Exeter, in the musical *Lilac Time*. I was hypnotised by her.

From Exeter, I worked my way to London – to escape. I went to London as a teenager with a Marks & Sparks bag and £10, and headed straight for Speakers' Corner where I picked up a man with whom I lived for some weeks. He introduced me to the famous Victor Silvy, the owner of one of the best restaurants in London, Le Jardin des Gourmets in Greek Street. While I was a waiter there, Victor fell madly in love with me. Muriel was a great friend of his and one day she came in to lunch with a group of friends. Without sounding too corny, I'm afraid all I can say is that our eyes met and everything clicked magically . . . [later] at a party upstairs in Victor's apartments, Muriel said to me: 'I've just opened a new club. Anytime you want a job, gel, you come along to me.' I said okay, and she opened here on December 15, 1948. And within six months I was behind the bar. We had a rapport, nothing sexual but very loving, which was marvellous for me at that age. A kind of loving that's indescribable.

MAID MARION: Ian became Muriel's barman, aged eighteen, and remained there, on and off, for the next forty-six years. Ian ran the club a bit more lax than Muriel. He still had the same people in, so it was the same club. He kept a house brick on the bar filled with Swan Vesta matches and smoked menthol cigarettes – he called them 'pansy fags' and claimed they made his sperm taste better. He was great fun until he'd had too much, then he was very insulting to people. He'd had a few good hidings and got barred from a lot of places.

GEORGE MELLY: Ian used to say when you came in, 'Hello, you stupid old cunt.' But one didn't take offence at this, it was rather affectionate. What he lacked was Muriel's wit. Ian would sometimes be reduced to incomprehensible swearing at people, 'Look at you, you great lump. Just take a look at yourself. You're a sad pathetic sight. For fuck's sake, pull yourself together . . . *Shut your cakehole, you boring dreary fart!*'

GERALD McCANN: Francis Bacon was quite wicked to Ian. One day he said, 'You know why Muriel chose you, don't you?' Ian asked, 'Why?', to which Francis retorted, 'You don't steal as much as the other ones!'

IAN BOARD: Muriel was everything to me. I've got very few friends. People think in this business you'd have hundreds of friends, but no. Acquaintances yes, friendship I think is a very limited thing. You can't have more than a handful or two.

TOM DEAS: When Ian first took over the perch he was often drunk, asleep on the banquettes. Maid Marion ran the bar brilliantly until one afternoon, roused by the ring of the till, Ian shot bolt upright and yelled – 'I knew you were nicking off me!'

The Maid exploded, 'Don't you ever accuse me of thieving off you in front of these people. *You do*, you thieve off the *fucking* lot of them!' and walked out. Then this lovely boy, Ben Trainin, son of Ian's friend Mumsie, became our emergency barman. Stuttering Sara, who'd had a fling with Lucian Freud, was on the prowl and Ian kept goading her – '*Go on Sara, give him one! – you could teach him a thing or two!*'

JIM MOORE: I was teaching at a school in Hornchurch when Mumsie came in as a supply teacher and we became friends. She brought me up to the Colony and made me swear to not mention her nickname in school – 'Imagine what it would do to my sex life!' She got her nickname from Ian because she'd repair his trousers, do his ironing, etc. Ian spent weekends with either Mumsie or Michael Clark because he hated being alone. He loved Mumsie fussing over him and cooking him pies – they were as thick as thieves those two. She was a total maverick. I was with Mumsie on the no. 8 bus on our way back from the Colony when a thought popped into my head – 'Mumsie, why do you think Stuttering Sara is so popular with men? Why does she have so many lovers?' Mumsie mused, 'Maybe she has a stuttering cunt.' Mumsie's son Ben worked behind the bar for a while. The last time I saw him, he came in from Berwick Street Market, saying, 'Do you want a banana?' He was flying on another level. He used amphetamines but it was never clear what killed him; he was so soft and lovely. Ben died in his sleep, aged twenty-nine, and it took the stuffing out of Mumsie.

DARREN COFFIELD: At times, the Colony was a theatre of cruelty. The club could take on the attributes of a cabaret about to teeter into a concentration camp or rather, in Ian's case, a concentration of camp. Ian's tantrums would lead members to bail out in fear of their lives. He was fearsome when he had his daily tantrum and lost a lot of members. If at times he was too abusive, it was the consequence of the job, sitting there for years listening to the chatter of genial guests who were more tedious than they realised.

ORLANDO CAMPBELL: Craigie Aitchison loved sitting in the club, observing. He was always amazed by Ian's behaviour. Watching Ian freak out on a customer was something of a revelation. 'Look! What's he going to do now?' Like driving past a car crash on a motorway and feeling hideously compelled to survey it in every detail. '*Look at him!* Oh my word!'

DICK WHITTINGTON: Ian had a great way with words, which, while repetitively profane, always struck their target. A small and inoffensive man, who'd never been there before, squeezed through the mob and asked Ian for a packet of peanuts. Ian gave him a withering glance, cranked the volume up and let him have it. 'Peanuts? Peanuts! You boring, dreary little cunt, this is the Colony Room Club not London Zoo. Fuck off!' The poor man disappeared down the stairs at a rate of knots, never to be seen again . . . At closing time, Ian would see the few remaining drunks on their way with the well-rehearsed shout – 'My name's Ian, Ian-David-Archibold, IDA! Ida-*fucking*-Board and I'm bored stiff with the sight of the lot of you, so *fuck off!*'

MRS SIXPENCE: Ian didn't like falseness – he'd seen them with their guard down and being their most honest whilst drunk. He also exploited a person's weaknesses and disliked those who thought too much of themselves. Lady Glory Cockburn came in and was being extremely pompous. When she heard Ian Board mutter an expletive, she turned to him and haughtily remarked, 'Do you mind not talking like that in front of a lady!' Ian smarted, '*Lady?* You common cunt, who are you?' – 'I am Lady Glory Cockburn of the port family!' – 'You're fucking wot?' Ian leapt off his perch and went over to the cupboard where he kept his membership files and began leafing through them. 'You're Lady *Wot?*' All of a sudden he found the page he wanted. 'Your name might *now* be Cockburn, but I remember your maiden name. Miss Mullings was your maiden name and you are a common tart. The only difference between you now and then is that you have acquired a title and elocution lessons!' – '*Ohh!*' she shrieked, and out she went.

BIG EDDI: Francis wasn't very keen on Ian. The reason Francis kept going after Muriel's death was because he felt it was his second home – he was so eccentric that in an ordinary pub he stood out like a beacon. I was naïve, in those days I didn't understand fame; there were just these interesting people who would drink in the club. Francis didn't like his ageing neck and so he always held his collar up, especially if he was contemplating something.

MAID MARION: He had a habit of pulling his collar whilst saying, 'Yes, *dar-ling.*' One day he came into the club, and there's Ian talking behind the bar, imitating Francis pulling at his collar, saying, 'Yes, *dar-ling.*' Francis said, 'Hey, are you impersonating me?' – 'No, I'm not. *You've been impersonating me for years!*' There was no love lost between them. Valerie Beston, his agent at Marlborough Fine Art, insisted Francis sign his bar bills before he left the club so no one could fiddle them, but not realising it gave Ian carte blanche to take what he wanted. The bills weren't signed for the amount, Francis just signed his name at the bottom. If it was £50 Ian would add '1' in front of it, to make it '£150'. That went on for years. Ian would go through people's bar bills to find out what he could add to them, to subsidise his own drinking. But as Francis said, 'I'd rather be in the hands of a competent crook than in the hands of an incompetent honest man.'

BOOKSHOP BILLY: When Ian went on the dry, he'd fill up a vodka bottle with water, so every time someone bought him a drink, they were paying for tap water. We put up with those kinds of things. When Francis was in, he'd order champagne by the bottle and at the end he'd pay. One day, he was ready to leave and said, 'How much do I owe you, dear?' And Ian said, 'Well, you've had six bottles, Francis,' so Francis reaches into his jacket pocket, holds out his hand and says, 'How come I've only got five corks, you cunt?'

MICHAEL WOJAS: I was aware of the games Francis played with people. Francis liked someone else to observe what he was doing to the person he was talking to, what he was saying and how he was saying it. He would take the piss out of people without them realising it and looking over to the bar to make sure I was clocking it. He especially enjoyed taking the piss out of Ian who'd retaliate and start a slanging match . . .

IAN BOARD: Fuck me, here come the scrubbers! I thought you were dead, dear!

FRANCIS BACON: Well, your life very much begins and ends in this joint, doesn't it?

IAN BOARD: How are you? Had a busy day? Yes, well, I've been busy doing a bit of whoring myself. You've left your make-up at the bar . . .

FRANCIS BACON: I'm not one of those 'made-up' old poofs.

IAN BOARD: Is he talking about art? What does he know about art? Is there an artist in the room?

DARREN COFFIELD: One night, Francis stood by the club door trying to leave for over half an hour. But every time he opened the door to leave, Ian fired another salvo at him and Francis was determined to have the last word. The tension in the room became electric. Then Ian exploded, '*GET OUT!* Call yourself a painter? You can't fucking paint. Take your boring friends with you and don't bother coming back.'

DI HALL: Francis couldn't bear me being a woman with my London accent. If I'd been a pretty boy, he'd have wanted to talk to me, but because I was a woman he put me down. I was chatting to John Edwards in the club when over wanders Francis – "Allo, who'll buy my violets?' (it was the Eliza Doolittle line from *My Fair Lady*), 'Who'll buy my Vi-O-Lets?' Upon hearing this, Ian went, 'How dare you speak to her like that. *HOW DARE YOU!*' – 'She's just a common . . .' retorted Francis. '*OUT!*' screamed Ian. 'Out? I'll never come back!' Francis fumed. '*You won't get paid for the champagne.*' – '*I don't fucking care. GET OUT!* She's a member. She has every right to be here. I'm not having you insult her.' So Ian threw Francis Bacon out of the club. John Edwards then turned to Ian, 'You can't do that to Francis.' – '*I SAID OUT! GET OUT!*' And Ian threw John Edwards out, too.

DAVID EDWARDS: Francis would always tell you that he hated Ian – 'I'm not going back to that club any more.' They had a love–hate relationship, but Francis would always go back, again and again. If you think about Francis and all the people he said he didn't like, he spent an awful lot of time with them. He always said he had to see Ian because he wanted to be with Muriel, but after Muriel died we all still went back there. What was the attraction of it? The grubbiness of the room? No, it was the unexpected people who came in – people with something to offer. There were no ordinary people there, only extra-ordinary people.

TOM DEAS: Ian was very handsome when he was young. Tyrone Power had an affair with Ian and fell head over heels in love with him. It was not accepted for a Hollywood star to be a homosexual back then, so Tyrone Power would stand on the other side of the road on Dean Street, heartbroken, hoping to catch a glance of Ian at the club window. He was infatuated.

IAN BOARD: I met Tyrone Power when I was very young and working as a servant for the film actress Florence Desmond. I met a lot of people there, including Elizabeth Taylor.

JAMES BIRCH: When Christine Keeler first went to the Colony in the 1960s, she thought Ian Board was the most handsome man she'd ever met and used to stalk him.

MARY SWAN: Ian lost his looks. He did terrible things to his face – he looked awful from sniffing amyl nitrate. Not many people knew he took poppers, but I knew the Irish sculptor who supplied him.

MICHAEL EDWARDS: I never saw Ian sniff amyl nitrate in the club – I saw him drink it! He downed it in one, then lit a fag afterwards and a huge fireball came out of his mouth.

DARREN COFFIELD: Ian was a heroic drinker who'd breakfast on brandy. If his drinking destroyed his youthful looks, it also shaped and nourished his enormous red nose. When Ian was told that he could have an operation to sever some blood vessels and return it back to normal, he said, 'Fuck it, it's part of my identity now. It's my trademark.'

JIM MOORE: One time we were going out from the club and Ian had some poppers on him. He dabbed the substance on his hands, then behind his ears like it was aftershave, and said, 'Come on, let's go!' Then he stumbled down the stairs because he was as high as a kite. Ian would regularly break his arms during drunken falls. It was a wonder he kept going; he'd often forget or lose things.

MICHAEL CLARK: The Colony Room 'Lost Property' repository was a green cupboard at the far end of the fireplace, past Daughter's favourite mirror, by the banquette where Lord Chaos once sat. It was where what was left that could not be drunk, eaten, smoked or spent, would reside – books, tapes, manuscripts, photographs, etc. Follow-up phone calls would be made, endeavouring to reunite property with the owners. Vacuuming the carpet one afternoon, a front tooth was found; it had been knocked out of a member's mouth the night before. It was returned later that afternoon. Once, stashed behind the piano, a large Harrods bag was found. The contents were revealed – surgical gloves, clamps, an assorted range of sex toys (dildos, plugs and beads), a shoulder-length brunette nylon wig, nurse's armband, riding crop, large tube of K-Y Jelly and a small brown pharmacy bottle with a screw-cap top containing a liquid. This particular liquid was available at the time on prescription, as Ian explained to me, 'for patients with angina'. Ian referred to this cache of left luggage as the 'hooker's hamper'. It was never claimed.

MISS WHIPLASH: The barman then was Michael Clark, now a distinguished artist in his own right, and heavily supported by Muriel, Ian and Francis. For all that the Colony Room had the reputation of being the lion's den, I always found it a benign place due to the kindness of whoever was behind the bar. In that sense my stammer protected me – they shielded me from predators and I could always chat with the barman if none of my particular friends were around. They had a genuine interest in the members and treated them as family.

MICHAEL CLARK: In many respects my painting career started there one Tuesday afternoon, late November 1977. I was on my way to the reading room of the British Museum and I saw a sign: 'The Colony Room Club, Members Only, First Floor'. I knew it as being a place where painters were accepted and painting was considered a serious occupation. At that time I had in fact given up painting, but I walked in off the street and met Muriel Belcher, Francis Bacon and Ian Board. And from that point onwards, I started to paint again. I think one of the most difficult things for a painter, apart from doing it, is to find a subject. When I met Muriel, Francis and Ian, I realised I had a subject as a painter.

THEA PORTER: Michael Clark was an art student when he wandered in. He'd heard that Bacon was always there. He stayed on and worked behind the bar on Saturdays. He was always talking about Rembrandt. He won second prize at the Royal Academy in 1981 with his portrait of Muriel in bed. It was, of course, her deathbed, and he has drawn her looking at us with brilliant feverish eyes.

IAN BOARD: Michael Clark did that portrait of Muriel. Francis loathes it – every time he comes in, he says to me, 'Why do you have that bloody thing up there? It's so awful.' I say, 'The only time I'm going to take that down is when you give me one of yours to put up there.'

JAMES BIRCH: One afternoon Michael Clark came in with David Bowie who enquired if he might have a cup of tea. 'Tea? Tea? No one ever asks for a cup of fucking *TEA!*' cried Ian. 'Did he say he didn't want a *drink*? You can be *barred*, sir!'

MICHAEL CLARK: Well, what happened was the National Portrait Gallery put on an exhibition called *The Portrait Now*, which included work of mine. The *Independent on Saturday* magazine dedicated five pages to the work, and within twenty-four hours of the article being published, it precipitated a telephone request for me to attend a meeting with someone. The venue was to be the Colony; however, for reasons of confidentiality, the meeting was scheduled for before the club was open. I had no idea whom I was going to meet. The door opened and in walked an attractive young woman who greeted me warmly, 'So pleased to meet you, Michael, I'm such a big fan of your work, as are David and Iman.' Walking to the window, she pulled back the curtain, announcing, 'They're here now!' The door opened and David Bowie and Iman walked in. I was slightly thrown by this. From the moment Bowie walked in, we fixed each other's gaze. Both of us could not help but smile and before he had the chance to say a word, I said, 'You probably don't remember the last time we saw each other? It was at the Hard Rock Café in Manchester in 1972.' Quick as a flash he replied, 'I'm always very appreciative of the Northern audiences.' He was interested in acquiring one of the portraits I'd done of Francis; however, I explained that Valerie Beston owned it, and it was unlikely that she'd want to part with it. So he suggested that I do a double portrait of himself and Iman. I pointed out that I was very slow in making work and that my paintings evolve like healing wounds. Some of my subjects had died before the work was completed. The conversation then carried on something like this:

MICHAEL CLARK: Can I get you a drink?

DAVID BOWIE: Let me get you one.

MICHAEL CLARK: No, let me do this one. What would you like?

DAVID BOWIE: Could I have a coffee, please?

IAN BOARD: I'm sorry, mate, we only serve alcohol. You could have an *orange juice*. Or a *Perrier*?

MICHAEL CLARK: That reminds me of something Ian once told me. There was a Frenchman sat in the far corner of the club, a guest of Francis. Someone asked if he would care for a drink. – 'Could I have a cup of tea, please?' at which the whole room burst into laughter. 'Here, Daughter,' Muriel said to Francis, 'who is the old cunt in the corner?' To which Francis replied, 'Well, his name is Henri Cartier-Bresson – they say he takes a very good snapshot.'

DAVID BOWIE: That reminds me of when we were shooting 'Ashes to Ashes'. Two workmen were standing by watching me, apparently in shot, so the production manager went over to ask them if they wouldn't mind moving. To which they replied – 'No.' – 'But we are shooting a video here, would you mind just moving please?' – 'No!' – 'Do you realise *who* that is?' – 'Yes, some cunt in a clown suit.'

DICK WHITTINGTON: One afternoon when the sun cut through the cigarette smoke like a cinema projector in that forever dark green room, there was a conversation about bisexuality, a hot topic because of Bowie's claims in this direction. Francis pulled a face in the mirror and adjusted the collar of his exquisite soft brown leather jacket. 'There's no such thing, dear, he's just queer like me.'

MAID MARION: After Michael Clark stopped helping, Ian boasted he had a wonderful new barman. 'That's good,' I replied. The next time I asked after the new barman, Ian drew himself up on his stool – 'Oh, that cunt left.' – 'Left?' – 'I trusted him to take the club's takings to the bank and haven't seen him since.' I said, 'Well, that's what you get when you treat people like that.' Ian burnt out a few barmen until he met his last and longest serving, Michael Wojas.

IAN BOARD: How did I first meet Michael Wojas? Do you know I can't remember. Michael will be able to answer that question.

MICHAEL WOJAS: Muriel died in 1979, fourteen months before I arrived. We met through an old mutual friend of yours, Mumsie. Her son Ben had done the job before me and I was her daughter Mimi's boyfriend . . .

IAN BOARD: Oh, get on with it for *God's* sake!

MICHAEL WOJAS: Well, from the first moment I was captivated by the room. It was something I'd never come across before in my life. And as it happened, Ian needed someone to work behind the bar.

IAN BOARD: What a sight he was when I first saw him, I tell ya! God, I wish I'd had a camera. He wandered in wearing one contact lens in one eye and a pair of spectacles with one lens in the other eye. It took me a while to realise what was so strange about him.

MICHAEL WOJAS: I had quite a sheltered upbringing, and was fascinated by the range of crazy extroverts here. Ian Board perhaps being the maddest. I'd never met anyone like Ian before. I was terrified. He used to call me every name under the sun. It took a bit of getting used to, the volley of abuse.

MAID MARION: I said to Michael, 'I don't know how you take it.' Ian enjoyed putting someone down, he got off on it. Michael was quiet and unassuming. A perfect yin to Ian's yang. I think one of the worst things was, Ian fancied Michael so much and just didn't know how to try it on.

MICHAEL WOJAS: Some people thought we were a couple. It didn't bother me. I found it amusing and Ian loved to play up to it. Because of my Polish heritage, Ian used to call me 'Pizda', which is Polish slang for cunt. Ian found it difficult running the club on his own and had been so dependent on Muriel. They'd a mother-and-son relationship, so he found the loss difficult to cope with. Ian's answer to Muriel dying – he was grieving really – was to drink himself senseless by early evening, go completely bananas over nothing and start smashing up all the glasses. I'd evacuate the club and get out of there, returning next lunchtime to a dishevelled Ian asking, 'What happened?' It didn't take me long to realise this was the place I wanted to stay, despite Ian – God knows how many times he fired me. I know every nook and cranny of the club because Ian would hide the club's takings every night when he was drunk. The next day we'd spend an hour trying to find them. You'd have to take a shelf off or dismantle the piano. He thought I was going to nick the money; it took him two years before he realised I was going to stay and trusted me. On the odd occasion I had a holiday, Ian would tell everyone I'd gone to prison. He had a great poker face – upon my return from 'holiday', club members would come up and congratulate me on being released from jail early, and Ian would just sit there smirking to himself.

RAY NATKIEL: Michael gradually took over all the day-to-day running of the club. He used to doctor Ian's drink and water it down. He did the same to Dan Farson – 'By now they can't tell the difference between water and gin.' He was looking after them, he did it out of care.

IAN BOARD: Mike Wojas saved my life after Muriel died. I really thought, What's happening? This is the end. Then he came along to help me here and absolutely saved the day.

BRUNTON: The club coped with all the changes in the area. It's not like the Groucho Club or Soho House – you don't go there to be seen, you go there not to be seen. It's a one-room bar where everything is on a personal basis. People either love that or loathe it. Some people you only take in once and they never want to go back! *It's unique!* Like Muriel, Ian used all the mirrors dotted around to see what was going on. If someone was in the lavatory for too long, he thought they were having sex and would be banging on the lavatory door, but I never saw anyone have sex up there, did you?

TOM DEAS: One afternoon, the Colony was like a cocktail party with lots of ladies in nice gowns. The restaurateur Peter Langan came in and got down on his knees in front of one lady, saying, 'I've always wanted to go down on you.' – 'How dare you!' She knocked him over and kicked him. Then Jay Landesman came over – 'You want to go down on someone, do you?' and pointed out a girl sitting under the television. Peter, who was sitting on the floor in his white suit, began to crawl on his hands and knees over to one of the ladies, sitting with a glass of champagne in her hand. He then proceeded to push his head up her skirt and perform cunnilingus. This was a bit strong even for the Colony – the conversation stopped and Peter just carried on. Eventually the conversation started again and everyone left him to it. The lady was sitting there quite happily and Ian went over, recharged her glass and poured the rest of the bottle of champagne over Peter.

MISS WHIPLASH: I'm sure Ian was goading Peter on. Some were cheering him on whilst others were clearly shocked. Then it stopped and he passed out and slept on the banquette for two hours while the party carried on around him. New arrivals were regaled with what had just happened. Even for the Colony it seemed a bit extreme. Peter, like a man mountain, was flat out horizontal, snoring. He eventually awoke and wanted another drink, but I did my best to dissuade him – 'Peter, don't you want something to eat?'

TWIGGY: Peter Langan was boring, sober. Half pissed, very funny. More than three-quarters pissed, a total pain in the arse. He was always trying to get Francis to hang paintings in his brasserie, but Francis declined. He knew that Peter got the restaurant capital back for the value of the paintings he was given. For many years it was decorated with David Hockney's artwork. There was a tabloid headline, 'THE MOST DISGUSTING DRUNK IN BRITAIN', with a picture of Peter, head-first, splayed out on the floor. What had happened was a female journalist came to the restaurant to do a feature on him and waited two and a half hours for Peter to come back from the Colony. When Peter finally arrives, his restaurant manager says, 'Your guest has given up waiting and is having dinner over there with friends.' So Peter wanders over to say 'bon appetit' and vomits all over her.

IAN BOARD: I've told Peter to piss off quite a few times. Usually when Peter comes in, he orders his bottle of champagne. If there's a bird here he fancies, I'll try to introduce him – not that I am procuring in any way. Then he'll fall asleep on the floor and I'll throw a coat over him and let him snooze. I just send the bar bill off to his accountant. Peter's behaviour is a natural part of his character – a great lump of Irish shit lying on the floor.

TWIGGY: There was one member who liked to be spanked. He'd come up to the club to be caned by Ian. One day he was in there, bending over, when I took the cane instead. I had a long run up from the far end of the room and gave him the most almighty whack. We never saw him again. You had to weigh up whom you could and couldn't take to the club. It was too peculiar for some people. For example, I had a friend over from the States, took him out for lunch and said, 'Right, I am going to take you to a place, I want you to understand it's not a gay club – the chap who runs it is gay and quite a lot of people there are camp.' He said, 'Oh, we have places like that in California.' I said, '*No*, I don't think you *do!*' I took him up there and for four and a half hours I don't think he said a word. He walked in and his jaw hit the floor. There was Molly Parkin with her tits out, being fondled by a seventeen-year-old black boxer, Peter Langan in a dirty white suit lying on the floor kicking his legs in the air and George Melly with a transvestite clarinettist jamming with Barney Bates. I bent down to Peter on the floor and said, 'I don't suppose there's any chance you can get me a table tonight for nine p.m.?' As the evening descended into serious drinking, Peter was shouting down the payphone, 'I don't care how you do it, give them Michael Caine's table.' By this time my American friend is completely rat-arsed. The next day we were both sitting in business class on the flight to Boston. He was hung over with huge baleful eyes. I said, 'I told you, you don't have clubs like that in California.'

IAN BOARD: I loathe saints, loathe flattery, loathe boring people who tell me jokes. I adore style and wit. Everyone here has some of it. I'm not here for the sake of my fucking health. But I'd rather be here in this little zoo than go to Regent's Park. Our new pianist, Barney Bates, has a passion for jazz, booze and abuse.

KENNY CLAYTON: The piano was covered in alcohol. Most pianists would shun it. The only other pianist, apart from myself, who could play it was Barney Bates. I don't think that piano had ever seen a tuner since 1948. You had to know where the dead keys were – it was like dental work; if you lose a few teeth, you still learn to get on without them. So I used to jump over them. My most memorable night playing up there was after Ian had taken over. He was at the bar doing a very good impression of Francis Bacon, then staggered towards me. He had a cigarette in one hand and a shot glass of amyl nitrate in the other. As he leaned over to the piano to request 'Send in the Clowns', his ash fell into the shot glass, which exploded in a huge ball of flames, *whoosh!*

GLENEAGLES: Ian developed this thing of Tuesday dance evenings and people would waltz around the room. Then someone started to imitate what it was like to be in a zoo and people began pretending they were monkeys. Michael Heath opened the door to be confronted by the sight of a load of people sitting and rolling around on the floor beating their chests and whooping like baboons. It reminded me of some of the imagery in Francis Bacon's paintings.

DARREN COFFIELD: Just like *Alice's Adventures in Wonderland*, the Colony was a place where time seemed immaterial. There were no clocks, because if there were, people would always be thinking about the train they've got to catch or their next appointment. The problem was you'd go for one drink and stay for hours. Suddenly five p.m. became ten p.m. – you couldn't look at your wristwatch without Ian berating you, 'Why are you looking at your watch? Are you bored? *You're bored!?* I am Ian-David-Archibold-*Bored!*'

DAVID EDWARDS: When Allan Hall was club chairman, he received a letter from Westminster Council saying they wanted to shut the club down as it was a 'rat-infested premises'. So Allan has to deal with the health inspectors when they come to the club. Allan warns Ian, 'Do not drink or do anything whilst the inspectors are here. Do not speak until you're spoken to.' So these inspectors are going around the club, demanding that this and that needs to be ripped out and changed, whilst Ian's sitting there biting his tongue, wanting to have a go at them. Allan manages to reach an agreement with the inspectors so that the club can continue operating subject to certain changes being made, so he's pleased and the council is placated. The inspector then turns to Ian and foolishly asks, 'Is there anything you want to say before we go?' – 'Yes, get your hideous teeth fixed, you horror.'

TWIGGY: The health inspector then sent a list two pages long, listing numerous faults with the club as he saw them. One of the remarks was that the club possessed the most disgusting carpet he had ever had the misfortune to come across in his entire career. To which Ian protested, 'But we don't drink off the carpet.'

BOOKSHOP BILLY: The carpet was so tacky after years of booze being spilt on it that if you stayed in the same position too long, your feet stuck to it. In fact you wiped your feet when you left the club, not vice versa. Reluctantly Ian ripped up the old carpet and replaced it with the cheapest he could find, so when you walked into the club, you were startled by a flash of bright green from wall to wall. Francis came in that afternoon and was horrified. Ian said, 'I told you, dear, we've been ordered to put in a new carpet.' Francis ordered a dozen bottles of champagne, shook them up, sprayed them over the carpet and said, 'Well, that's better.'

TOM DEAS: The ancient electrical wiring in the club was also a death trap. One day a spark came off the cable to the stereo, which turned into a flame racing along the wiring. Ian hopped off his perch, grabbed a fire extinguisher, aimed and fired. The next thing I knew was that the whole room was completely enveloped in white fog. We both leant out of the window, catching our breath. Eventually the fog dispersed and the entire green interior had turned white.

DARREN COFFIELD: The 1980s were very different – no internet, no social media. Even mobile phones were scarce. The only lifeline the outside world could throw to those adrift in a sea of alcohol, was a payphone at the back by the toilet and its extension, which sat on the bar next to Ian's perch. Whenever the phone rang, a chorus of members chimed anxiously – 'I'm not here!' Many were avoiding their responsibilities for the day, i.e. work, wives, husbands, families, etc. The one-sided conversations you could overhear with Ian on the phone could take on a surreal air of slapstick . . .

(The club phone rings on the bar next to Ian. The members chirp, 'I'm not here!' Ian momentarily surveys the room then picks up the receiver with a flourish.)
Yes . . .? What . . .? Who . . .?
(Coughs loudly.) Urrgh.
Okay . . . How are you . . .? Sorry . . .?
You're in hospital!
Are you dying . . .? What's the matter with *ya* . . .?
Oooooh! . . . two blood clots in your leg!

That sounds a bit 'dangereuse' – I speak French, you
know . . .

Oh, I'm sorry about that dear. You're being looked after
all right . . .?

Where are you . . .? – *Which* prison . . .? Well, hospital,
I mean . . .

Would you like me to come and visit you . . .?

Can't smoke! *CAN'T DRINK!* I should tell them to put
you to sleep . . .

Dying of boredom? There's nothing worse than *boredom*
really, is there . . . ?

Get out as soon as you can, get up here and have a
fucking good drink, mate.

(The pips on the phone begin to beep.) Your money's run
out, *you twot!* Look after yourself and see you soon.

*(Ian slams the phone down on the receiver and pronounces
gleefully to the entire room.)* He's dying, he's got clots
in his legs. Travelling up to his heart, with a bit of
luck. *(Laughter.)*

DAVID EDWARDS: Ian loved controlling everyone. There
was only one payphone in the club. He would listen in on
other people's phone calls on the extension. He was gathering
information on them.

DARREN COFFIELD: Sometimes the phone would ring and Ian
would break our conversation – 'Excuse me.' – pick up the
receiver and bark, 'What the fuck do you want? No, the cunt's
not here,' slam the phone back down, and say, 'You weren't in,
were you?' Over the years, the club only made one concession
to the march of progress. In the early days, there was one
communally shared lavatory halfway up the stairs, but the club

had one of its own installed at the back of the premises in the 1960s, replacing the cloakroom. Nowadays it has become fashionable to have unisex toilets, but the Colony always had one because it could only fit one closet on the premises. In those days the toilet area would occasionally act as a second bar and VIP area. Sometimes there was more action going on by the toilet than there was by the bar.

IAN BOARD: *La toilette!* Are we talking about toilets? A couple of years ago, the lavatory system, instead of going down through the plumbing, went up through the ceiling. I prefer the word 'lavatory'. Toilet, *twa-lette*, a 'khazi' in the army. A 'cottage', yes, with the odd queen in. The members here are all sorts – cottage queens, painters, doctors, lawyers, poets – a bit of everything, just like you'd find in a box of Liquorice Allsorts. The club isn't just for artists. A tremendous number of journalists and authors have drunk here, along with silly actors and actresses. They're never offstage, that lot, are they? Look at John Hurt, that twit. I hate him. I think I barred him actually – remember him? He did *The Elephant Man*. He's all right as a person really, but I think actors really do overact a lot of the time. One day he went on and on for about half an hour, boring the bloody arse off me – there's nothing more boring than a bore. So I said, 'Francis Bacon told me you're the most boring person in the world.' And he said, 'Oh no, Francis wouldn't say that about me!' I said, 'Well, he did,' and Francis happened to be just over there by the mirror, doing his hair. 'Look, go and ask him.' And he went over and said, 'Oh, Francis! Ian tells me you said that I am the biggest bore in the world.' Francis turns round, 'No, I didn't say that.' – 'No, I knew you wouldn't.' – 'No, what I did say, is you're the meanest cunt in the world because you never buy a drink.'

PHILIPPA CLARE: Many actors drank in the Colony – Tom Baker, Burt Kwouk, Denholm Elliott, Freddie Jones, Malcolm Tierney and Michael Elphick, etc. Michael was a lovely funny man. His character never changed when he was drunk. He was very gentle, sweet and cried at the drop of a hat. He cared for people; if someone was being given a hard time, he'd protect them. People in Soho looked after each other in their own funny way. If so-and-so hadn't been seen for a few days, someone would check up on them and make sure they were okay. They were proper friends, it wasn't just about drinking.

MISS WHIPLASH: There were random occasions when you'd encounter someone in the club who was legendarily famous, which could prove disappointing. I remember being pulled onto the lap of a very drunk older man who began to fondle my breasts. It was Trevor Howard. I've never been able to enjoy the film *Brief Encounter* in the same way since.

MICHAEL EDWARDS: 'Doctor Who' used to get to Soho about midday, stop at the deli, get fresh salmon and have it all prepared and laid out on the club bar for three p.m. . . . and if Jeffrey Bernard arrived after opening time, Tom Baker would tell him that he was late for work. I found Tom strange, women would fall at his feet but he never seemed very interested. He'd walk around Soho wearing his long trademark scarf and have a toothbrush sticking out of his top pocket to signal his availability. Tom Baker and Bill Mitchell were the two biggest voice-over artists at that time.

DANIEL CHADWICK: Bill was an American guy who dressed in black and looked like Johnny Cash. He did the deep, throaty macho voice-overs on ads for brands such as Heineken. He liked to play the big man, but was actually not that tall. One day Bill came into the Colony – 'Hi, Bill, how are you doing?' asks Michael. He replies throatily, 'I had a tough time last night – I was coming out of Ronnie Scott's, when two guys jumped me, brought me to the ground and tried to get my wallet. But I'm a karate man. So I rolled over, kicked the first one down, got the other one and chopped him down. Suddenly there was a taxi and I jumped in. The first guy came back, got me round the throat. Quick as a flash I slammed the door on his arm and cried, "Drive on!" I just escaped with my life.' – 'My God, that's awful! You'd better have a drink!' exclaimed Michael. The next day Michael is walking past Ronnie Scott's on his way to work, and sees the manager sweeping up outside – 'Hey, Michael! Your mate Bill was a bit drunk the other night. My two bouncers tried to help him into a taxi and he kept trying to fight them!'

PAM HARDYMENT: When my kids came up to the club, they were shaking with nervous excitement seeing Tom Baker at the bar wearing his long Doctor Who scarf and hat. He bellowed, 'Hello Ben! What would you like to drink?' Poor Ben nearly wet himself.

BOOKSHOP BILLY: Tom was a lovely, kind, good-hearted man, always up for a giggle and a laugh – he drank large gin and tonics with lots of ice from a pint jug. Everybody knew Tom; he was a cult figure, and always the centre of it because he is one of life's natural showmen. Saturday afternoons were always good because there weren't so many up there. At five-thirty we'd say, 'Put the telly on, Tom's on.' And Tom would be saying, 'Look, Francis, that's me on television.' Francis would reply, 'Oh, is it dear? Another bottle of champagne please.'

TOM DEAS: Tom Baker was one of Muriel's favourites, watching himself with exclamations of delight when he appeared on the box as Doctor Who after the Saturday racing. One afternoon I found myself standing at the bar talking to three blokes, all of them doctors – Tom Baker (Doctor Who), Bill Simpson (Doctor Finlay in *Doctor Finlay's Casebook*) and Neil Perrett (the Colony's medical doctor).

MISS WHIPLASH: The wit was what made it so exciting. They read widely. Tom, Francis, Jeffrey, John Hurt and Dan Farson – and they had good recall. They would be quoting to each other from a wide range of writers, and come out with great insights. You had to be as sharp as a tack to keep up; it was an education to be with them. It was quite terrifying at times as the conversation could be highbrow and you had to think fast. There was always a theatrical vibe to the club, which affected the way everyone talked, adding to the campery. This was even more the case when Tom Baker and John Hurt joined Bill Mitchell as the principal voice-over artists working in the Soho voice studios. All three would be in the Colony, often between studio sessions. You couldn't turn on the TV or radio in those days without hearing one of them. Tom was a witty companion and he and Jeff truly sparked one another off. Like Dan Farson and John Hurt, they had exceptionally good memories. Jeff was under sentence of death at the time if he didn't stop drinking, and was frequently in and out of hospital. One afternoon, having had a few in the club, Tom and I set off for the Whittington Hospital, where Jeff had once more been brought back from the brink and forbidden any more booze, ever. While we were sympathising with him, the hospital DJ came round saying, 'Is there a song you'd like me to play for your friend?' Quick as a flash, Tom said, 'Yes! Can you play him, "I'll Be Seeing You (In All the Old Familiar Places)".'

DARREN COFFIELD: People went to Soho in search of fun. When Will Self was introduced to the Colony by his friend Ben Trainin, Ian Board loathed him and called him a 'Ferret-eyed Fuck-pig'. Self declared some years later that he 'heard ideas and opinions expressed in the Colony that quickened the pulse of my own iconoclasm'. The other ferret-eyed fuck-pig, former heroin addict and writer who drank in the club was William Burroughs, author of *Naked Lunch*. Francis originally met him in Tangier, where his lover Peter Lacy played the piano at Dean's Bar, an expats' Colony Room. Burroughs' biographer Barry Miles told me, 'Bill [Burroughs] and Dean didn't get on', but Burroughs and Bacon enjoyed 'gossiping about mutual friends and what a horrible person Dean was and his terrible treatment of Peter Lacy . . . Bill very much liked Francis' paintings and probably – defying convention – asked him about them.' However, Burroughs denied there was any affinity in their work: 'Bacon and I are at opposite ends of the spectrum. He likes middle-aged truck drivers and I like young boys. He sneers at immortality and I think it is the one thing of importance . . . we are associated because of our morbid subject matter.' Francis found Burroughs amusing – he was very interested in writers and literature.

Sonia Orwell had a huge influence on Francis' literary tastes. He lived near her house in South Kensington, which Stephen Spender said was the closest thing London had to a literary salon: W. H. Auden, Iris Murdoch and Spender himself were all frequent visitors. Francis was fascinated by contemporary French literature and through Sonia's Parisian friendships met, among others, Georges Bataille and Michel Leiris.

HILARY SPURLING: Francis began a long dialogue in words and on canvas by asking Michel [Leiris] to write a catalogue preface for his show at the Hanover Gallery . . . 'Did I tell you we're all reading *L'Âge d'homme*?' wrote Sonia, passing on Bacon's request . . . 'It's agreed to be the book of our period by Francis and Lucian, who can talk of nothing else! Funny how painters read with such passion, when they're not in the habit of reading.'

DARREN COFFIELD: Nicknamed the 'Euston Road Muse', Sonia, under Cyril Connolly and Stephen Spender, became the indispensable kingpin of *Horizon* magazine. Julian Maclaren-Ross was among the authors she discovered. The magazine's backer, Peter Watson, was an early patron of Bacon and Freud. Sonia and Freud briefly became lovers and together with Bacon they formed a trio with wild drunken nights in Soho.

RODRIGO MOYNIHAN: . . . Sonia had a habit of taking things over with her flat shoes, finger rings and an Austrian Fräulein nature . . . you had to like her, even admire her. Men were besotted with her. She was a very presentable girl, very pretty with a strong puritanical streak.

DARREN COFFIELD: Sonia was Orwell's model for Julia, the heroine of *Nineteen Eighty-Four*. Although Sonia's vitality of spirit fed directly into his work, Orwell was dying. They'd both suffered disastrous relationships and needed the consolation they found in one another. 'He said he would get better if I married him,' she told Hilary Spurling, 'so you see, I had no choice.' The plan was for Orwell to stabilise his condition by travelling to a sanatorium in the Swiss Alps accompanied by Lucian Freud who'd help Sonia with lifting and carrying

Orwell. But four days before they were due to leave, Orwell died. Sonia never forgave herself for not being at his bedside (Freud had invited her out for a drink to cheer her up). She was forever racked with guilt.

HILARY SPURLING: When Francis Bacon's lover George Dyer killed himself . . . Sonia saw Francis through it with Michel Leiris . . . Francis painted George afterwards, writhing and vomiting in the bathroom of their hotel . . . Sonia spent evenings with him in London, drinking and going over what had happened. 'We talked about George and guilt for a very long time,' she wrote to Leiris, without specifying which George [Dyer or Orwell?], or whose guilt.

DARREN COFFIELD: Being the sole guardian of George Orwell's legacy was a heavy burden. Sonia became a target for those who jealously guarded literary criticism and publishing as a male preserve.

MISS WHIPLASH: In those days the French was known as 'The Publishers' Pub' – a central meeting place for designers, editors, illustrators and graphic artists, typographers, authors, picture researchers and small-scale publishers. Most of us liked to 'lunch', and we often used the Colony during the afternoon, where much networking was done. Names from that era include Barry Miller, Tony Matthews, Peter Owen, John Calder, Anthony Blond, Jay Landesman, Martin Heller of Orbis and Robert Adkinson of Thames & Hudson. The literary crowd hasn't had as much attention as the art crowd, but was just as numerous and influential.

I was taken up by Germano Facetti almost as soon as I arrived in Soho. The distinguished art director of Penguin

Books – tall, imperious, fierce, quick-witted and with rapier intelligence. It was instant cachet to be on his arm. He had no patience for fools and everyone raised their game when he was around. Germano was a leading graphic designer who, along with fellow Soho-ite Romek Marber, created the iconic covers for the Penguin series of crime novels, which led to the establishment of the 'Penguin grid'. He also put together the people who would become Pentagram, and rescued Bruce Bernard from digging holes in the road for a living. He gave Bruce a job as a picture researcher and taught him how to do it. Bruce later became picture editor at the *Sunday Times Magazine*.

DARREN COFFIELD: Germano and Bruce's relationship went a long way back. In 1956 Germano exhibited in Group One of the groundbreaking *This Is Tomorrow* show at the Whitechapel Gallery, which is credited with the birth of the 'Pop Art' movement. Later that year David Archer commissioned him to design his new bookshop on Greek Street. Bruce would help decorate the shop to Germano's design and hang the first Deakin exhibition.

MISS WHIPLASH: Germano was never at all comfortable in Muriel's; he always had the air of a shark trapped in a goldfish bowl. He'd survived two years in Mauthausen concentration camp – it became clear that his skills as an artist and his good looks had enabled him to survive while friends had died all around him, and he was forever prickly in the company of homosexuals and Germans. He was part of a large group of graphic designers, illustrators and art directors – Enzo Apicella; Harry Peccinotti; Dennis Bailey, art director of *Nova* magazine; Ken Grange and the Pentagram crowd; Ian Fleming; Dennis

Rolfe; Len Deighton; Pip Piper and Peter Dunbar, who all frequented the Colony.

SHAKESPEARE: Peter Dunbar was art director at the *Economist*. He employed Bobby Hunt to do cartoons and the two Barrys – Evans and Driscoll – to do the covers. Peter was really important in the Soho scene and was everywhere at the time. The two Barrys would hang out with the illustrator Owen 'Oska' Wood and Bobby Hunt. They were a quintet. They'd start at the French at noon, then go to Franco and Mario's trattoria, then off to Muriel's. They could afford to have long, boozy lunches since they were at the height of their careers. Barry Evans was doing illustrations for Consulate Cigarettes. Barry Driscoll was famous for wildlife illustration. Pip Piper worked under Peter for many years, and took over the mantle of art director at the *Economist* after Peter's death. He employed Peter's widow, Marsh, as a favour, which really helped her a lot.

JUPITER JOHN: Then there was 'Pickles', an editor for Quartet Books. Something of a Victorian character, he listened to classical music on a wind-up gramophone. I used to converse with him in a cod hybrid Shakespearian-Dickensian English. He was an honourable fellow, who once helped a drunken female barrister to her feet as she crawled on all fours out of the toilet and helped pull her knickers up. Giving him the unique reputation of being the only man in Soho to help pull up a woman's knickers, rather than trying to pull them down.

DARREN COFFIELD: Publishing wasn't as commercially driven as it is now, where often the accountant is the most important person. It was a gentleman's activity – they were usually either entrepreneurs or had family money. Publishing was run by men, whereas the editorial side was mainly run by women. It was very laid back.

SHAKESPEARE: Of all the publishers who drank in the club, none were quite as divisive as Jay Landesman, often referred to as the 'White Rabbit' because of his broad-brimmed hat, white gloves and two-tone shoes. He was a generous and marvellous man who helped many artists and poets, like Paul Potts. He'd swagger into the Colony with that American brashness that some English people loathe and plenty of wisecracks, which would get up Ian's nose.

PAM HARDYMENT: A friend of mine who was working for Jay said, 'You better come and meet this guy, his office is so pukka you have to see it.' So I met Jay, who took me to the Colony, and I thought, what an amazing place. He took me to the French, and said, 'Let's write some love songs on the sheets of the Eros Hotel,' which was just around the corner. I said, 'No, I think I'll come back to the office and look at your books.' So we did. I was totally drunk, threw up in a bucket and thought, I like this, I think I'll work for him. Jay Landesman was the most bohemian publisher in town. We just published books we wanted to do; it was money he could afford to lose. He could meet a guy at a bus stop and say, 'You're funny, write me a book.' Jay owned property around St Louis in the States, and his wife Fran was an heiress. Wherever Jay went, he was a cultural conduit for what was going on. Back in the States, he'd been part of the Beat Generation and friends with Jack Kerouac. I asked his wife if I could have an affair with him. She replied, 'Yes, but you have got to realise he won't leave me.' I said, 'That's fine, I don't want him to leave you, I want to have fun.'

The club became our second home as our offices were on Wardour Street. We were there constantly between 1977 and 1984. The first book we published was *By Grand Central Station I Sat Down and Wept* by Elizabeth Smart, which is now considered a literary masterpiece. It detailed her life with the poet George Barker – that was an artwork, that relationship, fraught with turmoil. Barker was a heavy drinker and Elizabeth took up the habit, which intensified when the two were together. The couple were involved in numerous fights. During one argument, she bit off part of his lip. George was a charmer, he could talk you into bed. I could see why she loved him – they were locked together, a complete symbiosis; they loved one another. Elizabeth was in the club a lot as she had a pied-à-terre on Peter Street. She was a bohemian, extremely sweet and smart; you didn't push over this old lady. She and Jay had spats about money because he didn't keep accounts like that; he'd just give people £50 here and there, not real publishing in that sense. She was very aggrieved. But we did publish her poetry book, *A Bonus*. There's definitely no money in poetry.

JAY LANDESMAN: By 1980 I had a collection of writers unsurpassed for eccentricity, who were no strangers to failure. A drinking session at the Colony Room with Dan Farson led to collaboration between a gullible publisher and successful author, which, on the surface, looked promising. [The politician] Jeremy Thorpe, Leader of the Liberal Party, had been front-page news for the better part of a year [accused of conspiracy to murder]. By the time of his trial, he was red hot. The idea of writing the story of what really went on while the retrial was in progress, and having it in the bookstores on the day the case went to the jury, held no terror for either of us. Farson was a fast writer, I was a fast publisher. When he outlined what he had in mind, I saw promotional potential, as well as another publishing first. [Farson] knew all the participants in the tragi-comedy well enough to write the inside story. Only no newspaper – not even a sleazy tabloid – would dare print it. In order to avoid libel, he'd tell the story from a dog's point of view, with all the dogs based on the real-life characters. He had a simple plot. Max Von Fleet, top dog in his district, has hopes of winning at Crufts. His chances are threatened by the arrival of a silly poodle called Maisie, who keeps barking her mouth off about an earlier liaison with the 'great dog', and its consequences lead to his trial. I was impressed – it was satire at its best. Unfortunately disaster struck when the jury returned a 'not guilty' verdict on the day the book was published . . . Farson and I were proud that we had broken fresh ground, but heartbroken that the jury's verdict had rendered the book dead on arrival.

PAM HARDYMENT: Then Jay published *High Life and Low Life*. He got the idea from meeting Jeffrey Bernard in the Colony – 'Hey, Jeff! I think your column in the *Spectator* would make a good book.' Jeffrey didn't care about the book; all he wanted was money and kept coming to the office, asking for it. Every time Jay saw Jeffrey, he gave him £10 in royalties. Jeff would complain, 'I want more money than this, you've sold hundreds of copies.' But we'd sold hardly any.

JAMES BIRCH: Jay Landesman proudly presented Ian Board with a personally signed copy of his autobiography *Rebel Without Applause*. Ian flicked through it, then ceremoniously ripped it into two – 'It's a pile of crap. All you do is name-drop,' and dropped it at Jay's feet.

DARREN COFFIELD: Many of the club's members were extra-ordinary eccentrics never destined to be famous but neverthe-less integral to the atmosphere. Elizabeth Smart once compiled a complete historic members' list for the Colony Room, now sadly lost. Some unfortunate members suffered from the local malaise 'Sohoitis'. It's a particularly virulent and contagious condition. One of the symptoms is drinking too much and talking about all the great 'works' you plan to create but never actually doing anything to achieve them. It really is a euphemism for the squandering of talent and youth.

PAM HARDYMENT: I believe in Sohoitis. I think we are all victims of it. I should have been a writer. Sohoitis is more dangerous than guns and knives. People come to Soho and never finish their manuscript, poetry, paintings or music because they become stuck in the bar. Like the poet Paul Potts, who was often passed out on the banquette by the lavatory, stinking to high heaven.

FIONA GREEN: Paul was a rare combination of man of the street and an eccentric member of the gentry, who'd lived on Jura with George Orwell in rural bliss . . . he shared the same publisher as Colin MacInnes and having fallen out at some point, they'd scream at the sight of one another across the bar, 'Fucking bastard!' Paul lived in real poverty – funded by well-wishers. The last time I saw him he was dressed like a character from *Playboy of the Western World*, with moleskin trousers, his flies undone and everything hanging out.

SHAKESPEARE: I couldn't go near Paul because he stank so much. But Merilyn Thorold could – she looked after him, she fed him, and took care of him. He looked sad and would just sit there until Merilyn came in to take him for something to eat.

JAY LANDESMAN: I was so fond of Paul Potts that I wanted to do something to revive his career. I let him know how much I regretted his not letting me do something for him, reminding him of what I had done for Elizabeth [Smart]. 'It's not too late, Jay, old boy,' he said, over the drink I'd just bought him. 'I have an idea that will make us both a lot of money. Let me edit an anthology of poems for you. I've got a great title: "Poems for Poor People".' In the old days he was tagged 'The People's Poet'. 'The only difference between me and a great artist is that I am not one,' he used to say. His enthusiasm for the project increased in direct ratio to the drinks I was buying. Before the afternoon was over, we had a golden handshake. His advance was possibly the lowest in publishing history – £5 and free Guinness . . . We both knew the book would never happen, but I enjoyed the liquid negotiations.

TOM DEAS: Potts' party trick was to soil himself on the banquettes. Graham Mason, who would occasionally lie down in the club to sleep off a vicious hangover, came in one afternoon unaware Potts had just been thrown out. He lay down to rest when he realised, to his horror, his head was where Potts had been sitting and suddenly jerked bolt upright, gagging on the stench.

DARREN COFFIELD: However, the most bizarre bohemian to inhabit post-war Soho was Gerald Wilde whose persecution complex led to him constantly being ejected from bars and wanting to fight the police. Diagnosed as a hopeless case of Sohoitis, the poet Tambimuttu (who originally coined the term) started a fund for 'Gerald Wilde the Mad Artist'. In Lucian Freud's eyes, Wilde was a great painter with a touch of genius. For Francis Bacon, Wilde was a 'dreadful bore' who banged on his door, demanding money for drink. Wilde boasted that Francis had ripped off his colours and became obsessive about these and other perceived slights and injustices. Eventually Wilde was identified as a dead tramp by the *Daily Express*, who had to issue an apology two days later with the headline, 'I'M FEELING VERY WELL SAYS "DEAD MAN"'.

TOM DEAS: Although Sohoitis is a terrible affliction, the club was conducive to those determined to make their mark. It may have been small but its reach was global and it indirectly led to one of the most important art exhibitions in post-war Europe. Not since Turner had a British artist been so honoured. Francis Bacon beat all other contemporary Western artists to be the first to exhibit behind the Iron Curtain. The news of Francis' Moscow exhibition provoked an outcry from the Prime Minister Margaret Thatcher – 'Not that dreadful man who paints those horrible pictures'.

In 1985, James Birch went to a rather posh party where he met a man who said, 'What are you doing?' James told him he was taking some artists to America. He said, 'Forget that, why don't you take them to the Soviet Union instead.' So he sent James to the Soviet section of UNESCO in Paris to meet a man called Klokov who said he would like to exhibit Warhol or Bacon in Moscow. So one afternoon upstairs in the Colony, James asked Francis if he'd like an exhibition in Moscow. Francis was delighted, as he'd always had a fascination with Russia.

FRANCIS BACON: It is a great honour to be invited to have an exhibition of paintings in Moscow. When I was young, I feel I was very much helped towards my painting after I saw Eisenstein's films *Strike* and *The Battleship Potemkin* by their remarkable visual imagery.

TOM DEAS: Marlborough Fine Art chose the pictures for the show. They had a difficult job trying to persuade wealthy Western collectors to lend pictures to their potential foe, Communist Russia. Francis helped finance the show, and James Birch did all the paperwork. It was considered a major coup that an exhibition of a 'decadent' Western artist could be put on behind the Iron Curtain during the Cold War.

DARREN COFFIELD: Francis wanted to take a train from Moscow to Leningrad to see the Hermitage. Daniel Farson gossiped that David Sylvester had said to Francis, 'Look, they'll know who you are and they'll want to kidnap you. They might even blow up the train.' However, David told me that Francis lost his enthusiasm for the Moscow show because many of his explicit pictures were excluded – 'His most important work in the Tate's permanent collection is his central panel of *The Buggers*. They censored it.' David always maintained that Francis didn't attend because of anything he had said, but because he was suffering from a severe bout of asthma. Francis had been looking forward to going to Russia; he was so desperate to go. He had been studying Russian for the previous six months to get a grasp of the language and even had his bags packed, but got put off by the Cold War paranoia – 'Everything had been closed up after 1917. It would have been fascinating to see the country.'

BRUCE BERNARD: . . . [The Russians] respond particularly well to what is heroic and direct in art, and Bacon's work is surely both. We all felt that the occasion had been a great and historic one, and regretted not being able to toast the artist in person.

TOM DEAS: John Edwards went to Russia as Francis' representative. When the exhibition opened, more than 400,000 Russians attended, dwarfing the queue for Lenin's tomb, and all 5,000 exhibition catalogues sold out. At the press conference, a British journalist piped up: 'Why does the Soviet Union allow an exhibition of a British homosexual artist when you sentence Russian homosexuals to five years in prison? Isn't it a crime to be a homosexual in the Soviet Union?' – 'We don't care about Francis Bacon's sexuality, only his art,' came the official response. The exhibition was a landmark event that marked a significant shift in censorship within the Soviet Union and became a symbol of Gorbachev's perestroika. After the exhibition, prices for a Bacon painting rose to over a million. When you think of all the Russian oligarchs who now buy Francis' paintings for record-breaking prices at auction, one wonders, Did they see the Moscow show in their youth? And would they believe that such an internationally historic event could be traced back to a tiny, shabby green room in Soho?

6

Crimes and Misdemeanours

DARREN COFFIELD: Francis Bacon said that if he hadn't been an artist, he would have made a marvellous criminal. His youth was spent living off petty theft and other people – he'd even been caught shoplifting in his favourite store, Harrods. Francis felt at home in Soho, an area associated with the underworld and petty crime. At one point he even had a minder known as 'Redhead Ginger'.

NORMAN BALON: Back then the villains didn't interfere with normal citizens; they didn't interfere with anyone except themselves. The only people who paid protection money were people who were doing something crooked – if you ran a legitimate business, you were able to appeal to the police every time.

IAN BOARD: The most basic London crime is protection. It involves a villain 'persuading' club owners to pay an agreed amount each week in return for not being 'troubled'. When a racketeer remarked, 'Busy little joint you have here, we must have a chat,' Muriel said, 'Piss off, we've got the police and press on our side.' He was found down the road three days later, hanging dead outside the French House. Those were the days of Jack 'Spot' Comer and Albert Dimes. They all liked to think of themselves as the Kings of Soho. Muriel was always known as 'The Queen'.

MAID MARION: Clubs were easy prey. Anyone who resisted their demands did not stay in business for long. Up until the Street Offences Act of 1959, there were hundreds of prostitutes roaming the Soho streets, jangling their keys and shouting, 'Short time, dearie?' Then, like Cinderella, at the stroke of midnight on the day the new law came into force, they disappeared. However, their clients did not – they still wander the streets of Soho in droves, looking for them.

DARREN COFFIELD: The ban led to an abundance of strip clubs, hostess bars and other outlets selling sex opening in Soho. Controlled by various villains, the police received huge bribes, paid in cash in the toilets of the Coach & Horses. Advertisements were put in shop windows with thinly disguised messages – 'Swedish chest for sale' – which caused much amusement to the passing public. Much of the prostitution in Soho was run by the Maltese mafia; they even had a brothel above the Colony. In the 1980s, a bunch of 'clippers' ran a racket at the top of Berwick Street Market. They'd get chatted up by men, demand payment up front for sex and tell them to go to the first floor, 41a Dean Street (the Colony), and wait for them. Once the punter had walked off, the women would immediately change their wigs and coats and go back on the street, waiting for the next mug. They had nothing to do with the club, but it was left to Ian to deal with the irate kerb crawlers and their bruised egos. Ian tried to explain it was a scam, but they'd demand to look around the club. Ian was sympathetic but made it clear it was best not to make a fuss; otherwise he'd have to call the police and they'd have to go home and explain to their wife why they were arrested in Soho looking for a girl.

IAN BOARD: Julian Ormsby-Gore, son of Lord Harlech, came charging up the stairs one day and said, 'Look after me, look after me, someone is chasing me.' We let him in and bolted the door; he looked terrified. His father, Lord Harlech, was then Ambassador to the United States. He was a scruffy git, but a lovely chap who'd get involved with very odd birds. Anyway, I called the police – 'We've got Julian Ormsby-Gore, son of the Ambassador to Washington here, in fear for his life.' The police blocked off the whole area – they were like flies round shit. But his pursuers had scarpered. Muriel said, 'It wouldn't have been such a bad thing if the crooks had got him and given the bastard a good wash.' Julian shot himself soon after, blew his brains out over some 'orrible little bird.

COLIN MacINNES: Not being, like the pub, a public house, the police in theory cannot go into a club without a warrant. But police officers do have a way of going where they want to, and from time to time they pay clubs a call. These officers grow less and less like their caricatures, and are increasingly difficult to spot. The legend is that, on the whole, 'The Law' is not hostile to the clubs – if only because they provide splendid fonts of information . . .

GEORGE MELLY: Most of the clubs back then were full of crooks and plainclothes policemen, which creates a rather gritty atmosphere. Muriel had none of that; the criminal fraternity were not part of Muriel's world. The Kray twins couldn't bear women using bad language. I think they would have been alarmed by the state of the language at Muriel's.

FRANK NORMAN: As a matter of fact, the London gangster is usually a very friendly fellow to meet. They are well-dressed, polite and very lavish with their ill-gotten gains. One might expect them to be coarse and foul-mouthed. This is rarely the case; on the contrary, in fact, they're liable to be more than a little naïve and puritanical. Many of them, for instance, would be greatly shocked if they heard anyone swear in front of a lady . . .

MAID MARION: Before his drunken foul mouth proved too much for them, Dan Farson used the Krays' Kentucky Club regularly – he liked the glamour surrounding gangsters. Francis knew the Krays from Esmeralda's Barn, their gambling club in Knightsbridge. Ronnie even visited Francis' studio once to deter him from suing a friend for payment over a painting. I went to Daniel Street School with the Kray twins and I was friends with Ronnie. On my first day at school, one of the twins came up to me and said, 'You're a twin, I'm a twin, how do you like being a twin?' The next time I saw them was in school assembly, saying their prayers. They had a good name then, they used to box for the school – two decent boys, they didn't go round bullying people. Later in life, I went out with Ronnie Kray, I was his boyfriend. Being with Ronnie gave me a reputation. My friend's mum said to him, 'Why are you going out with David? You know he's a gangster's moll?' It didn't bother me, there are worse things to be called. People obviously think, what's he doing with 'that'? But they wouldn't say anything, otherwise they'd get a fucking good hiding. One thing the Krays didn't stand for was being mocked.

TOM DEAS: Jeff Bernard often sailed close to the wind, once telling a chap at the Colony bar to stop being 'such a fucking bore'. He was shocked to discover that he had in fact insulted Ronnie Kray. Jeff said, 'It's a wonder he didn't blow my brains out.'

MAID MARION: The story about the twins and the Colony is a myth. They never went up to the Colony to extort money from Muriel, and she never told them to fuck off, because if she had, well . . . they had a reputation and Ronnie never liked being refused. Once I didn't want to go with Ronnie but he kept going on and on. I said, 'Ron, look I just came back from holiday and I'm with my brother. You're a twin, I'm a twin. I want to spend some time with my brother.' My brother said, 'Is he threatening you?' I didn't want my brother to stick his nose in, it would have been broken. Once you got involved with the twins, that was it. You were locked in and couldn't leave, you knew too much. There was a man called ●●●●, he was one of the gang. You saw him, then he disappeared and you never saw him again. Ginger Marks, he went, didn't he? They said he was propping up a flyover somewhere. Then there were rumours about Teddy Smith – he came up the Colony a lot – 'I'm creative now, David' – *Bang! Bang!* He was said to have had affairs with Ronnie and Tom Driberg. He disappeared the day after an argument with Ronnie in 1967.

DICK WHITTINGTON: We all have our Soho memories and mine are of the cast that came, and went, and died, old faces constantly being replaced by new. Soho . . . was such an exciting place, full of characters. How else to describe . . . Peter the Pornographer, Stephanie 'Steve' Storey, a pinstripe-besuited lesbian getaway driver, and the dapper and immaculately attired pornographer John Hawkesford who never did get over being called 'Rat of the Week' in the *News of the World*.

TOM DEAS: In those days there was a more relaxed feeling in Soho, less frenzied. 'Brian the Burglar' was very charming. He'd occasionally disappear for eighteen months at Her Majesty's pleasure. He once got put away for accidentally blowing up an entire post office instead of just the safe. Another time he was so drunk he blew open a post office safe on the wrong day, finding it empty. We were in the club, talking about going on a fishing holiday to Ireland. 'Oh, what kind of rod do you use?' enquired Brian. 'Hang on, I'll be back.' Off he went for half an hour and returned with a brand-new fishing rod in his hand, 'Will this do?'

MARY SWAN: Brian would take orders at Christmas time and go and nick them. He became a victim of his own success and would get blamed for all the burglaries in Soho and regularly get carted away. He became quite good friends with the police. He was drinking one day with this stranger who he'd just got chatting to. After a while he made his excuses and told the man he was going to the loo – but instead popped out and burgled the man's flat, came back and carried on drinking with him as if nothing had happened.

DARREN COFFIELD: Brian mentioned casually over the Colony bar that he'd 'done over' Margaret Thatcher's house in Chelsea and was astonished at the size of her insurance claim – 'I never nicked that much!' The famous confidence trickster, Charles da

Silva, often drank in the club and was much admired by Jeffrey Bernard. Da Silva had once sold a fictitious 'fishing fleet' from the Middle East to someone in Norway and even flogged 'rice fields' in Kuwait. He treated Jeffrey as his lucky mascot and would stuff fivers into Jeff's breast pocket after he'd completed a good con.

TOM DEAS: John McVicar, once the most wanted man in England, used to drink in the club – he was a pleasant chap. However, one afternoon, I walked into the club and suddenly this fierce-looking dwarf came up to me singing, 'Tom, Tom, the Piper's Son'. He grabbed my hands and danced round me like a demented pixie. I soon realised to my horror that it was the hitman 'Mad' Frankie Fraser. He might have looked like a pixie, but if someone said the wrong thing to him, they were in for it.

IAN BOARD: There were rumours circulating that Myra Hindley would come in on her day-release trips from prison, but I definitely wouldn't have allowed her in the club. Muriel used to bar people and I've kept up the tradition. If they're naughty boys, then I give them a rap over the knuckles and tell them to go home to their wives, girlfriends, boyfriends, trollops or whatever they've got, then have them back in a week or two. I've had to bar Jeffrey Bernard a few times. The only people who have been completely barred are those who got physical – we can't have physical violence up here. Then I have to jump off my perch and say, 'Right, on your way.' Then they are barred for life.

MICHAEL HEATH: The club at times was like being in a cell, depending on who you were drinking with. There were these two villains shouting about how they'd screwed this girl – 'I was fucking her like this and then I fucked her like that.' They were riling Ian, who suddenly exploded, 'I can't take it any more. I don't care who you fucked and where you've put it. Sling your hook and take your boring cocks with you. Here's your money back, now get out!' The two men stood up and said, 'You've made a big mistake.' I thought, God, they're going to kill him! – 'Fuck off, you boring cunts, talking about your dreary cocks, *get out!*' They got up and went to leave – 'You haven't heard the last of this.' Ian wasn't frightened of throwing people out; he kept people safe and would eject anyone who was trouble.

DICK WHITTINGTON: Ian was as brave as he could be nasty. I have seen him confront some very violent men and deny them entry to the club where others would have kowtowed. He knew that if other than the odd petty con man or pornographer got his foot in the door, then the Colony would be finished.

JOHN BAKER: One of Ian Board's pet hates was mobile phones. A recent invention, they were very expensive and large, like carrying a brick around with you. Woe betide anyone who had a mobile ringing on their person. He'd turn on them. Michael Wojas was good at cooling people off, but sometimes you could see that things were heading to a fight.

MICHAEL WOJAS: A guest came in and started using a mobile phone in the middle of the room. Ian said, 'You don't do that in here – no mobile phones. If you want to make a call, go and use the public phone box.' The man ignored Ian, who grabbed the mobile and chucked it across the room. The guy turns round and says, 'You think that's funny?', pulls out a carving knife and cuts the wire to the club telephone sitting on the bar, then holds the knife to Ian's throat, demanding an apology. Ian refused. He then wielded the knife at the members in the club, telling them to leave. There are times to be bolshie, and there are times to use kid gloves, and this was *serious shit*. He was totally off his face. Fortunately Ian kept him talking, trying to placate him. I was motioning to the leaving members to call the police. When the police arrived, an almighty fight broke out. It took four officers to get him out of the club and into a police car. He then took out a private prosecution against Ian for damage to his mobile phone. Ian received a summons to attend Wells Street Magistrates' Court to be prosecuted for criminal damage.

HAMISH MCALPINE: Dee Hammond, who ran Gerry's club, was a witness, but she refused to testify in court because the gangster, Scarlatti, got hold of her and said, 'Your club is in a basement and I'm going to roll a barrel of petrol down your stairs . . . lit.' Ian never spoke to Dee again after that. He saw it as a betrayal.

BLACK SHEEP: The defence lawyer retained by Ian was Ernle Money, a criminal barrister. Michael Wojas, Christopher Howse from the *Daily Telegraph* and a few others attended the hearing. Prosecution counsel opened the case against Ian for damaging his client's phone. What then transpired was pure theatre – Ian was dressed immaculately in a tweed suit designed by Thea Porter. He acted frail and weak. When he went into the witness box, he feigned that he could barely hear the prosecutor's questions and would Their Worships mind if he could sit down due to his poor health. Two journalists from *News of the World* were acting as witnesses for Scarlatti. Upon taking the oath, one was found to have antecedence (a criminal record), which indicated he was, at best, dishonest or, at worst, a convicted liar. He was dismissed as not being an acceptable witness. The other journalist entered the witness box and before taking the oath, offered up, voluntarily, his antecedence before being asked – he too had an extensive criminal record. The actual hearing was turning rapidly into something approaching a pantomime, which, given it was December, was appropriate. My only regret was that we had not taken in a tape recorder, because there was some wit, equal to that of Oscar Wilde's, expressed that afternoon.

MICHAEL WOJAS: Ernle Money was cross-examining Scarlatti in the witness box: 'Would you describe yourself a violent man, Mr Scarlatti?' – 'No, but in the East End I'm known as "Baby Face Scarlatti".' Because it was a private prosecution, Scarlatti could have his previous offences read out in court: carrying firearms, GBH, assaulting a police officer, etc. It was a long shopping list of offences – Ian realised he was saved and started blowing kisses to the prosecutor . . . Case dismissed!

DAVID SPITTLES: Soho still had a louche bohemian quality in the eighties before big business sanitised the place. Barry Fitzgerald first took me to the Colony. There were a lot of hangers-on and people who would never buy a drink, whereas Barry liked to splash it around and buy people drinks. Barry's father was a barrow boy on Rupert Street. When the first sex shop opened in Soho in the late fifties, Barry's father realised how much this shop was making next to his barrow, and decided to go into 'erotic literature'. Originally the pornographic bookshops were almost entirely in Soho. Norman Balon said the police used to charge the villains £500 to open a dirty bookshop, and then £100 a week to stop them from raiding them. All manner of books and films could be bought for a price. Lesbian, homosexual, bondage, rubber wear, punishment and so on. There was little call for 'straight gear'. It was Barry who got Peter Brunton the job with Janus, the spanking shop. Peter had just lost his job in film advertising. He was quite a character – one night I took a guest up to the club, who turned to Peter and said, 'It's a bit of a dive, isn't it?' – 'You've got to be joking, it's a complete shithole!'

IAN FREEMAN: The entire length of Wardour Street was all the film industry then – Paramount, Columbia, Warner Bros, Hammer were all there. The film industry shared Soho with the artists and villains. Peter Brunton introduced me to the Colony in the late 1970s. It was an eye-opener. It was different and a cut above the other clubs. Peter then worked in film advertising. He was the man responsible for bringing the cult film *Easy Rider* into the mainstream theatres and making it a huge financial success.

BRUNTON: My mother Nancy, who moved in theatrical circles, took a young starving Jeffrey Bernard under her wing, employing him as a dishwasher. Because of my very loud voice, Ian christened me 'Big Mouth' and my wife 'Miss Hitler'. I took in a friend one afternoon, and Francis Bacon was there with John Edwards at the end of the bar. – 'That's his lordship, isn't it?' I said, 'Leave Francis alone.' Unfortunately he couldn't resist the temptation and tapped Francis on the shoulder, 'Mr Bacon, Francis? *May* I call you Francis?', in an irritating way. Francis said, '*Yus*,' without even turning round. 'But, Francis, I would like to talk to you about a business proposition.' – '*Yus?*' – 'Francis, can you spare me five minutes? I have something that might really excite you.' With a resigned sigh, Francis eventually turns round. – 'I have this marvellous idea, as we all know your artwork is fantastic.' Francis gives him an incredulous look. – 'I would like to photograph all of your paintings and print them on the side of carrier bags.' Francis looked up and said, 'Cunt,' and turned back the other way.

MICHAEL HEATH: In the club there was always a whiff of an underlying violence, that something could happen at any moment. Francis would never let anyone buy him a drink. One of his grim pleasures was to pay and watch other people get drunk. He had to be in charge.

IAN BOARD: When they filmed the *South Bank Show* documentary here, they had to keep breaking the filming because Melvyn Bragg was getting so drunk trying to keep up with Francis. When he returned the next day, Francis did the same thing to him all over again.

MELVYN BRAGG: We met at nine in the morning in his studio . . . He had insisted we all drink the Bollinger he had lined up beside the sink, and at the restaurant we drank rough red wine. I had been on the wagon for a few weeks in Cumbria, working on a novel. This was an alcoholic waterfall. After the restaurant cleared, Francis and I pretended to have lunch and did the interview. We ate nothing but we drank on. We got very drunk. It showed. We slurred. Once or twice we all but stopped . . . We went on to Charlie Chester's gambling club next to some blurred drinking hellhole. At some time or other I found my way home, my liver leaping up to my ribs like a salmon . . . I saw what we had done a few days later. We were not entirely a pretty sight and there was plenty to laugh at, but what Francis said was true to the devil in him and I kept it in.

DAVID EDWARDS: It's never been spoken about before, but do you know Francis was petrified of the IRA because of his family connection with Ireland? He took the threat very seriously and was quite strict with John about not going to Ireland because he was terrified that he'd be kidnapped and ransomed. Francis always said, 'I grew up with an atmosphere of threat for a long time.'

DARREN COFFIELD: The memory of Ireland was problematic for Francis. After the Easter Rising, his grandmother had compromised the safety of the family by marrying the District Inspector of Police for County Kildare, one of the most dangerous and unpopular jobs in the whole country.

DAVID EDWARDS: Francis wanted to keep John out of danger and not be exploited. When John first met Francis, he asked John to throw a failed painting in the bin. But John didn't, he sold it to the infamous gallery owner, Robert Fraser, for £10,000, and Francis went ballistic. He was annoyed with Robert for taking advantage of John.

DARREN COFFIELD: Francis always referred to Robert Fraser as the 'Belgravia Pansy' in the Colony, just to irk him. Francis' abandoned paintings had started to be a problem. One unfinished painting found in a cellar sold at Sotheby's for £71,000. 'I can't tell you *why*,' fumed Francis, 'people are fools.' So Francis told John to cut up all of his discarded paintings into five-centimetre strips, horizontally and vertically, to completely destroy them and prevent them reaching the market. By this stage in his life, the value and fame of his artworks had far eclipsed his public persona as an artist.

BOOKSHOP BILLY: We were having lunch at a restaurant called Green's in St James's. Alongside the bar they had little cubicles, which you could dine in. My wife got up to go to the restroom, and on her return she said to me, 'Francis is in the restaurant with two women.' So I went over. He was with his dealer Valerie Beston and a buyer. He said, 'You will be up in the club later, won't you? I can't wait to get away from this fucking lot. All they want to talk about is painting all the fucking time.' At the lunch, the buyer asks Francis, 'How long does it take you to complete one of your paintings?' He's about to give her an answer, which was not the same as Valerie had told them. So Francis gets a big kick under the table from 'Valerie-at-the-Gallery'. There was Francis having to talk about his work when all he was really thinking was, Let's get up the club.

DAVID EDWARDS: Francis didn't take people to the Colony to do business. If Francis had to attend a formal event, he loved to arrive early and leave early. If it was one of his gallery openings and he was bored, he'd say, 'I have to go, I am having an asthma attack,' and off he'd go into the sunset.

JAMES BIRCH: Francis didn't act the celebrity. Everyone knew his name but not many people knew what he looked like, so he could walk down the street in anonymity. He was a cult figure who people would go and seek out in Soho. He didn't court publicity like the YBAs [Young British Artists]. I remember being in the back of a taxi with John Edwards, who was trying to impress the driver – 'Do you know who I am? I'm John Edwards, I'm a friend of Francis Bacon.' The taxi driver was uninterested – 'Yeah, all right, who is he?'

TWIGGY: There are a lot of anecdotes concerning taxis and Colony members. I would often help Ian Board find a taxi after closing – he'd stand on Dean Street, in his beret and scarf, swaying, whilst the taxis, who all knew him, would look the other way and drive by. So I developed a technique of ordering the taxi from the Groucho Club. I'd open the cab door and Ian would dash in, with the driver saying, 'Oh fuck!'

DARREN COFFIELD: Taking Ian to locations outside of the Colony was often fraught with challenges. He was invited by Lisa Stansfield to go and stay with her for the weekend. Ian caught the train to Manchester and found that he was in a compartment with a mother and screaming child, with the father inanely chatting away on his mobile. After half an hour, Ian told the mother he'd 'chuck the baby out of the window' if it didn't shut up, then grabbed the mobile off the man and threw it down the carriage. The man fled, retrieved his mobile phone and called ahead to the police to say there was a raving maniac loose on the train. When the train pulls in, Ian hobbles off with his walking stick, acting frail and innocent, straight into two waiting policemen.

LISA STANSFIELD: I arrived at the station – there was Ian on the platform between two policemen, so I walked up to them and said, 'What the fuck do you think you're doing? He's a little old man.' I knew how volatile he was. Fortunately the police recognised me immediately and they let Ian go.

MICHAEL DILLON: Ian was like a certain wine. He didn't travel well. The club was the only place he had complete control – it's the only life he had.

IAN BOARD: Soho is changing, it's getting so awful, but then London is so revolting now, disgusting – the traffic, the roads, the digging. Three years we have had digging up and down this fucking road. Drilling, *dril-ling*! They dig it up, fill it, dig it up again, fill it in again. Day after day, week after week, month after month. Is it supposed to give us some sort of pleasure? It's torture. I think I'd rather have gone to the Bastille and had my bloody head chopped off rather than go through the horror we get here. Really it is too much, *too much*! A lot of people are leaving London and going to the country. I go to Suffolk occasionally for weekends – the Edwards family live there, they're Londoners. I was there a few weeks ago sitting outside in the garden – I'd had a few vodka-*ettes*, very pleasant. The birds were twittering, I thought how wonderful it is here. Then Edwards came out and said, 'Those bloody birds have got to go!', gets his shotgun out and starts shooting. I said, 'You left the East End to come and find the peace and beauty of the countryside.' He said, 'I can't bear them.' I said, 'Move back to London with your bloody lorries and pollution.' I thought it was raving mad myself, that someone should start shooting those poor little birds. Now *pigeons*, I can't bear those bastards. Bloody *pigeons* and that's all because of that McDonald's muck! People actually eat it, you know. I tried it once and I thought, Why do people want to eat this? But they do! They queue up like at a concentration camp and pay fortunes to eat that muck. *Urrgh!* Then they chuck it all over the streets, which brings in those filthy fucking pigeons, shitting all over lovely buildings like my club.

DAVID EDWARDS: One Saturday, the Colony is as dead as a dodo. Ian and Francis are the only two in there. Francis has had enough of Ian and gives him some cash and tells him to 'fuck off and see Edwards in the country'. So Ian stops the first black cab he finds on Dean Street and says, 'Take me to Suffolk, you cunt.' An hour later we can hear a commotion out the back of the hotel – *'Cunt!'* The slamming of a black cab door and another voice bellowing, 'Never get in my bloody taxi again!' We can hear the devastation left in Ian's wake long before we see him. The bar is packed, but everyone is stopping to look at him. Ian strolls up to the barman, 'I want two bottles of champagne and a bucket of Guinness, *now!*' The barman politely says, 'Excuse me, what do you mean by a bucket of Guinness?' – 'I want a bucket of Guinness!' – 'We don't do Guinness by the bucket.' – 'Well, I want as much Guinness as you have and give it to all those fucking peasants over there!' From then on, it descended into chaos. They closed the bar and told everyone to leave. So we go down to Fred the farmer. He had a lovely house with a big roaring fire and all these wonderful glass goblets. We're all drinking happily when Ian says, 'I want a decent glass,' and throws his goblet of brandy into the fire, which goes *whoosh!* and bursts into flames. So now we have to leave Fred's. The next morning Fred arrives, unannounced, with a double-barrelled shotgun. 'Where is he?' – 'Fred, calm down, please . . .' – 'No one comes into my house and does what he did last night.' – 'No, Fred! *Please* . . .' He opens up his shotgun and shows me that the two cartridges are empty. – 'He needs to be taught a lesson.' There's no stopping him. So Ian's reclining in our drawing room on a chaise longue. Fred bursts in, *'You'll never do that to me again!'* And shoots Ian with both barrels. Point-blank. *BANG! BANG!* Ian just sat there, he didn't blink. I come running in. – 'What's happened?' – 'David, it's lucky he's such a bad shot. He could have killed me.'

MAID MARION: Often Ian's presence would be treated almost as a state visit to Suffolk. People would come to pay homage to

Ian, who'd act in a regal manner dispensing platitudes and comments. But you were always on a knife's edge because he was outrageous in any community. He didn't discriminate, he was abusive to everyone.

DAVID EDWARDS: That evening I threw everyone out to the village pub and they all came back earlier than usual. The next day at the pub, the barman said to me, 'You can stand there as long as you want; you're not going to be served in here again and you can take that lot with you.' I said, 'Whatever's the matter with you?' – 'Why don't you just take them away and *don't come back*.' – 'But I've done nothing wrong.' He pointed to Ian, trembling in anger, 'Last night that man over there came up to the bar, sneezing, picked up the bar towel, blew his nose on it, then laid it back down on the counter and put a glass on top of it.'

So next I take Ian to a friend's house for dinner. The following morning, Ian asks me, 'What was the name of that restaurant we went to last night? They've got some really good stuff in there,' and shows me his carrier bag full of silver, proper solid silver. 'We never went to a restaurant,' I said, 'we went to my friend's house and you've nicked all their silver!' That really did embarrass him. – 'There's only one way to get it back, we'll have to tell them the truth: "I'm so sorry we've got all your silver here. Ian thought he was in a restaurant where he has the habit of acquiring mementos."'

At the end of Ian's visit, we're both waiting for the train to take him back to London. We used to call it the 'Noddy Train' because it did a little circuit backwards and forwards to the mainline station. I'm standing there talking to Ian when the conductor appears and says, 'Excuse me, do you know this man? This train's not leaving until he gets off. We're not taking that man anywhere, not after what he called me!' So we go to the pub to wait for the next train. Ian orders some food. Suddenly there's the ping of a microwave – 'If you think I'm going to have any of that cancerous shit out of your *cunt-ing* microwave, you can stick it up your . . .' So now we're thrown out of the pub with nowhere to go. An hour later, the train comes back with the same train conductor as before – 'I'm not taking him!' So I end up driving him to Bury St Edmunds – 'There's a direct train to London, get on it.' He gets on the wrong train and goes halfway round England. The next day Ian rings me up and calls me every name under the sun.

MAID MARION: The countryside was never really Francis' favourite place as he suffered from asthma. But he would come up to Suffolk because John Edwards was there and Ian would often stay too. Every morning Ian would be sick. It was the citric acid in the orange juice he drank with his vodka, attacking the lining of his stomach. He'd say, 'I've got to have a "Vera Vomit" when I get up in the morning.' So John Edwards put cling film over the toilet pan. You can imagine the screams and expletives, can't you, as Ian's vomit ricocheted back on him?

JAMES BIRCH: John was always playing practical jokes on Ian. When Ian was going through a phase of wearing white jeans, John put brown shoe polish on Ian's perch, so that every time he stood up it looked like he had shitted himself. He would also stick signs to the back of Ian's jacket – 'I'M QUEER – KICK ME'.

DAVID EDWARDS: On another occasion, Ian had a broken arm, so John offers to wash his hair if he gets in the bath. Ian is unaware that John has bought some permanent red dye, so that when he says he is washing his hair, John is in fact dyeing it red – 'Keep your eyes closed in case the shampoo stings your eyes!' When Ian eventually opens his eyes, all he can see is red pouring everywhere from his head – 'You've cut my fucking throat, you've cut my fucking throat! *Get an ambulance!*' He thought he was bleeding to death. The next day I walk into the club to find Ian sitting in the middle of the floor on a bar stool, with a pair of scissors, cutting off all his red hair, which laid scattered all around him.

MRS SIXPENCE: Then Ian, to my amazement, invited us all to Sunday lunch. The table was laid with various bits of silverware he'd stolen from different restaurants and surprisingly it was a good, comprehensive Sunday lunch. We're all sitting around chatting when the conversation moves on to where we might go afterwards. Ian overhears this and takes offence, 'If you're fucking bored, you can fuck off.' – 'Ian, we are not bored.' – 'Fuck off *now*.' He picks up the table and throws its entire contents out of the window onto the street, four floors down. This might have been viewed, by any pedestrian, as attempted murder. A few minutes later there's a knock on the door – 'It's the police!'

MAID MARION: Ian would throw all sorts of things out of his apartment window. He even threw out his television in a fit of pique at the newsreader. He'd get so drunk he was open to being ripped off. He met one guy whom he liked to be tied up by. The young man would tell him to do this, do that, do the housework. Meanwhile he was casing the joint, getting to know where everything was. Ian was so pissed he fell for it. Once the man knew where all the valuables were, he tied Ian up one last time and robbed him.

DICK WHITTINGTON: I knew Ian better than most people, because in 1975 I ended up living with him, having emerged from a disastrous love affair on which I spent everything, including my house. I took a room in his chaotic flat in Clare Court, Judd Street, an experience that was frequently surreal. Ian in that period was still sexually active and partial to a spot of rough trade. This did not intrude on my life much, though occasionally I might push open the bathroom door of a morning to find some heavily tattooed man in leathers cleaning his teeth. After the first time I saw this, I made sure my sponge bag was kept in my bedroom, since I was pretty sure these one-night stands did not come with luggage. Ian was keen on sadomasochistic practices – he once nearly died when tied up and strangled by what might be called a shit that passed in the night – and sometimes my sleep would be interrupted by terrible shrieks and whip-cracks, never things I felt were for discussion the next day. The girls I brought back were fascinated by it all, and my own sex life was given certain new opportunities by their imaginative interpretations of what might be going on in the next bedroom.

I recall one night when coitus was interrupted by him crashing through my door with three chums. 'Oh, 'ello, mate, 'ow are yer?' He introduced us with an exaggerated wave, 'This is lovely Dickles.' He glared at our frozen pose. 'And that's one of his trollops. He's what we call normal.' One of his friends looked horrified. 'How horrid. How can you bear it under the same roof?' The third permanent member of our ménage was a cat called Thursday, a morose fat creature that did little except shit into a blue plastic baby bath kept for this purpose in the kitchen, an unpleasant insanitary touch since Ian rarely changed its litter and there was no way I was going near it. In order to cheer it up, Thursday was encouraged to inhale marijuana. This was achieved by blowing marijuana smoke into a paper bag and putting it over Thursday's head, a dangerous exercise since the brute would go berserk and rake Ian viciously with his claws as soon as the bag went on. He would hug the vile creature grimly. 'Hold on, mate, you'll be all right.' After a minute or so Thursday would visibly relax and the bag would be removed. If you've never seen a cat smile, this is how to do it.

JIM MOORE: Ian's flat was done up in the 1960s by Thea Porter. He had a beautiful amber mirror, gold fabric sofa – beautiful furnishings that had been fabulous but of course he'd trashed them over the years. There was a tiny studio kitchen covered in trellis, painted the same deep green as the Colony and covered with theatre posters. It must have originally been a very trendy-looking place. He had a real old-style American telephone in there and a fabulous collection of berets and perfume bottles that people had given him over the years. It was stylish but chaotic. He seldom ate there. Going back with him one night, there was nothing to eat apart from three cream crackers (the crumbs left on the ground), and half an onion with bite marks. I looked around and thought, My God! Ian had a friend who lived in the USA, Maxine, who used to come over and stay at his flat. Once he was cooking a chicken and turned it up to brown the skin and then forgot about it. Maxine arrived and they went off to the Colony, got as drunk as skunks and stayed all night. When they got back to the flat, it was boiling hot, with just a pile of ash in the cooker where the chicken had been.

DARREN COFFIELD: Ian gave his life to the Colony. His home life was nil. He'd go without food for days, then eat a cold tin of ravioli in the small hours. He drank brandy for breakfast, until his sixtieth birthday when he switched to vodka.

JIM MOORE: Ian lived on the third floor and would occasionally treat himself to a Chinese takeaway on his way home. He'd put his hand in the carton to eat, and then go along the walls, hand out, propping himself up on his way in his inebriated state from the building's entrance along the corridor into the lift, then out of the lift, along the third floor to his apartment door. So there would be a long, smeared trail of Chinese takeaway leading all the way through the building to his front door. The very next day when he'd sobered up, Ian would complain to the building's management about the communal areas – 'The fucking state of this place, *you don't keep it clean!*' One day he turned on all the taps in his flat and just left. His next-door neighbour, Mrs Ferrari, kept calling the club because the fire brigade had turned up and his flat was flooding the one below. Peter and I went with Ian and found the flat ankle-deep in water. Ian said, 'It must be a frozen pipe.' But the first thing he did was run around turning off the taps, so we knew full well what was going on: a fraudulent insurance claim. The people downstairs were furious. The fire brigade were tramping about the place, trying to siphon the water out. We sat on the sofa and Peter put his feet up, out of the water, onto the coffee table. Ian was talking to a fireman and, mid-sentence, turned around and said, 'Oi, you common cunt, get your feet back on the floor, it's not a trash joint!' He never missed a trick.

DARREN COFFIELD: One of Ian's lodgers was nicknamed 'Bunny' after her job for Playboy. Muriel would say to Bunny, 'What's that perfume, dear? Cat's piss?' It was Mumsie who fixed her up with Ian, and she found lodging there pretty grim.

He'd come home late and put on the soundtrack to *Cabaret*. It was always the same track and the record would always get stuck in its groove playing – 'Life is a cayy-beret old chi-ummm', on and on endlessly, whilst she was trying to sleep. Often she couldn't get out of her bedroom to go to work in the morning because Ian was lying unconscious in the corridor, blocking the door. He used to shout at her because she was so messy. He'd make plates and plates of sausage rolls in the oven and burn all his arms and scream at her, throwing the Hoover in her room.

BUNNY: The whole place stank of his aftershave. God knows what he wore – it really whiffed and was from Thea Porter, whom I also modelled for. She christened me 'Marvellously Vulgar'. She was good friends with Ian; she'd give him lots and lots of clothes and he'd walk around wearing these heavily embroidered chiffon shirts.

SHAKESPEARE: Thea Porter was very soft, very flaky and very elegant. Merilyn Thorold managed the shop for Thea, who was then a very important fashion designer. She was famous for her scarves, which Ian used to wear when he was out on the town.

JIM MOORE: She gave kaftans to Muriel and Ian, and many beautiful clothes with very beautiful detailing. Her flat was beautiful, full of lace and fabric, unusual pieces of furniture. Set into the wall was a dining area, all mirrored – ceiling, walls, table, etc., which was rather confusing when you'd been drinking. One day, walking past an antique shop, she remarked how beautiful the furniture in the window was and how similar it was to her own. When she got home she found her apartment completely empty – her boyfriend had fleeced her.

MAID MARION: Thea Porter sucked up to Muriel for Francis' exhibition in Paris – 'Oh, Muriel, you must come with me, I'll take you there.' She only did that to make sure she got a good seat next to Francis; that's all there was to it. I never saw Francis being overly friendly or affectionate to her; I just saw her as the 'Evil Little Dwarf'.

THEA PORTER: Muriel and Carmel had the largest, heaviest handbags in the world – I know, from having to carry them in Paris while Carmel helped Muriel down the stairs of a dykes' disco. This was when a large body of Colony members went over to Paris in 1977 for Francis Bacon's opening at Galerie Claude Bernard. It was a marvellous show, and some of us ended up at a bar near the Opéra, full of beefy, heavily lipsticked lorry drivers. This sort of group activity was discussed and carefully planned well in advance at the Colony . . .

MARY SWAN: Ian used to say, 'Behave yourself, Thea Porter!' She loved being reprimanded like a child. The Colony was her playground, she was a scream. Thea eventually fell victim to the rise of the sex industry in Soho. Princess Margaret, who used to visit Thea's studio in Greek Street, refused to come any more because the next-door shop had explicit sexual material in the window. In the end, what with the pornography and high rents, Thea gave up and left Soho altogether.

DAVID EDWARDS: Thea made a lot of money dressing Elizabeth Taylor and threw a party in a restaurant called Friends. She invited her accountant Aunty Fred, myself, Olga Deterding – 'the richest woman in the world' – and lots of aristocrats. It was an impressive line-up – the only person not invited was Ian. The night was going very well until there's a knock at the door –

it's Ian, pissed as a newt. He grabs a chair and pulls it right up between me and Olga – 'What the fuck are you all drinking? Brandy?' So Ian gets the waiter – 'I want six brandies and six ports and hurry up, you cunt.' So the waiter goes off and comes back with a tray full of drinks. 'What d'you call that, you ignorant cunt?' explodes Ian. – 'But, sir, you asked for six brandies and six ports.' – 'Bottles, *you cunt*, bottles!' screeches Ian. By this stage Olga is mortified and turns to Ian, 'Will you stop being so rude!' – 'Olga, dear, you might be the richest woman in the world but you're also the fucking ugliest.' Ian was outrageous. He took us out for dinner one night and we ended up having each course in a different restaurant because he kept getting us thrown out.

TWIGGY: Ian went into 'Cockroach' Wheeler's, sat down and the ashtray had about twelve cigarette stubs in it. So he tipped it on the floor and put the emptied ashtray back on the table. After we've all left Wheeler's and are sitting back in the Colony, the restaurant manager suddenly bursts in and goes ballistic, grabbing Ian's bag, which clangs and clatters with all the silver tableware he's just stolen, and empties it out on the bar. Eventually Ian was banned from Wheeler's for swearing so much that a large group of American tourists left, refusing to pay the bill. Ian was bemused – 'But I want to eat here!' – 'We can't eat here because you're bloody banned.' – '*Oh*, was it something I said?'

BOOKSHOP BILLY: Francis loved it at Wheeler's and they loved him too. When you went in, you had the oyster bar to the left and tables all around and at the back, beyond which was a cosy little room not many people knew about. It was private and it was a privilege to be there, because outside you had people queuing up waiting to be served. Francis was a big tipper – not to be flash – he just appreciated good service and his generosity was exceptional.

FRANK NORMAN: When I first began to go there, it was rather more a meeting place than a restaurant. Painters such as Francis Bacon and Lucian Freud, and writers such as Colin MacInnes and many others could be seen daily, sitting at the bar, drinking gallons of wine and eating dozens of oysters.

DARREN COFFIELD: Like Muriel at the Colony, Bernard Walsh at Wheeler's created a friendly atmosphere for artists. He'd allow Francis to run up a tab that would be settled once he'd sold a painting. Walsh would then send round a bottle of champagne in celebration and the whole cycle started again. Francis eventually gave Walsh a portrait of Lucian Freud in memory of the many splendid lunches he'd had there. Walsh commented, 'You have to look at it three ways to see it's Lucian. But it is recognisable.'

TWIGGY: People say that Francis couldn't draw, but I remember him drawing on a tablecloth in Wheeler's, saying, 'The problem with artists these days is they can't draw,' and he drew a perfect circle, freehand. I thought, wow! Not everyone was as besotted by Francis as we were. Sometimes other people in the restaurant were offended by our noise and chat. Once, sitting opposite a group of American tourists, Francis said, 'Tell me, Jeffrey, whom do you admire?' Jeff [Bernard] replied, 'Cyd Charisse, she was an American film star with long legs that men would dream about.' – 'Who do you admire, Francis?' – 'Well,' said Francis loudly for the benefit of the American tourists, 'I've always fancied Colonel Gaddafi.' This caused a great deal of consternation among the tourists. Francis went on, 'I was in *Paris* the other day, Jeffrey, and was waiting for an *aeroplane*. I got rather bored so I thought I *would* treat myself to a new watch to pass the time, a *Piaget*, a very pretty watch. Well, the next night I met a *sailor* without a bed for the night and took him home. There I was, lying on the bed like a vestal virgin, whilst my sailor was in the bathroom doing his ablutions, when I thought, He's not having my Piaget. So I took it and hid it under the bedside mat.' By now the entire restaurant had fallen silent, waiting to hear what happened next. 'And then the bathroom door opened and out came my sailor, bounding across to the bed. As he approached, I could hear this *dreadful squelch* as he crushed my pretty Piaget to pieces.' Pausing only for dramatic tension, he added, 'I suppose it was the most expensive *fuck* I've ever had.' Francis then paid the bill and strolled out of the restaurant.

DAVID EDWARDS: To arrive at the Colony in the company of Francis after lunch at Wheeler's was such a pleasure. Francis would pick up the lunch bill and pay with terrific style, always in cash, and then off to the Colony. There's a famous photograph of the Colony with Francis and the rest of us. When they took that photo, a film crew came with the biggest Polaroid camera in the world. The club was closed all day as they needed to take the camera to pieces to get it up the tiny Georgian staircase into the Colony. The photographs came out of the camera A1 size, so you can imagine the size of the machine. Because they were Polaroids, there were no negatives and each print was unique. We sat there all day on the condition that we could all drink as much champagne as we wanted. There were twelve of us there, and each person was meant to reflect a different aspect of London life – Thea Porter represented fashion; Mike McKenzie, music; Bruce Bernard, photography; Jeffrey Bernard, journalism; Tom Baker, acting; Francis Bacon, art; myself, antique dealing, etc. The camera crew made a clothes line going back to where the toilet was, so they could hang out the prints to dry. They finally finished photographing us at five p.m. Francis said, 'I want to buy a photograph, I want that one.' The photographer Neal Slavin was adamant, 'They're not for sale.' – 'But I want to buy that one.' Then Thea insisted she wanted one too. It wasn't long before this descended into a mini riot between the members and the camera crew. So I thought, How are we going to resolve this problem? There are twelve photographs hanging on the washing line by the toilet. I told Francis to keep arguing with them, so me and my brother John go out there, roll one up and throw it out of the toilet window, and come back in, where everyone is still arguing. The film crew then begin arguing amongst themselves, getting hysterical – 'Search the club, one of the prints has gone missing.' – 'No, you're mistaken, we've all been here all the time.' They then go back to arguing with one another and convince themselves there were only eleven prints to begin with. At the end of the day, the film crew felt so embarrassed they'd accused us of theft, they gave one of the prints to the club. Then I had to go downstairs to the Italian restaurant, where the toilets were, and climb out onto the roof to retrieve the photo we'd nicked.

PAM HARDYMENT: The famous club photo was great. But every time I was in deep conversation with Francis, John Edwards would interfere – 'You're not asking him for tickets to his exhibition, are you?' John made sure no one took advantage of Francis, but it was a bit excessive. He was like a black widow in the corner all the time.

TWIGGY: John was very street smart and extremely bright. Francis had a close circle of friends he would go to dinner with. I went to his home, Reece Mews, once. You had to go up a creaky wooden rickety staircase, where he showed me his studio. He made cups of tea in the most filthy cups I have ever seen, maybe they had been used for his paintbrushes. His abode felt intimate. He had a bath in his kitchen that was equally filthy. He always ate, but not very much – sparrow-like, picking at his food. Lunch could go on for hours. I mostly had supper with him, which was always quite early, around seven-thirty p.m. He rarely ate two courses.

JOHN EDWARDS: Francis was an excellent cook, he could have been a cook – he never ate a takeaway, he would always cook himself. He would phone me up at nine o'clock in the morning and we would have breakfast together. My nickname for Francis was 'Eggs' and we would often have eggs for breakfast. I would eat the yolk and Francis would eat the white part.

DAVID EDWARDS: Once Francis insisted we all went back to his house for lunch. When he opens his fridge, it's bare apart from a steak, a carrot and an onion. So Francis chops it up, puts it all in a pot and pours a magnum of Pétrus over it – to make a stew, from a magnum of Pétrus! As you can imagine there wasn't a drop of gravy left at the end. A few days later there were headlines about it in the newspaper. We knew it had to be one of us who had told, and we knew it was Ian because he was notorious for that – if there were any titbits, he would pass them on. Francis was so upset because the article made him look stupid. He did it as a prank but the newspaper made it sound like he was so rich he cooked with Pétrus every day.

DARREN COFFIELD: Ian always feigned a lack of interest in food but he counted the chef Simon Hopkinson of Bibendum, Peter Langan and Robert Carrier amongst his friends.

TOM DEAS: Robert Carrier and Ian would contradict one another and fought like cats and dogs but were the greatest of mates. Ian christened him 'Carrier Bag'. Robert was a lovely old queen, a pioneer of the celebrity chefs of today. He told me of an important lunch at Le Caprice with a media tycoon, who wanted to launch him and his cookbooks on American TV. Afterwards the tycoon asked him if he knew of anywhere to go for a digestif. So Robert took him to the Colony. But after he'd signed him in and looked around the club, he realised – 'I'd never seen it look so seedy . . . the tycoon fled and I haven't heard from him since!' Ian enjoyed deriding the things his members most cherished, or, in Robert's case, his recipes. Returning to the Colony after almost a decade, Robert minced out fuming – 'I haven't been here for ten years and I'm not coming back for another ten.' He was driven down the stairs by Ian's onslaught – 'And you stole all your recipes from Elizabeth David!'

DARREN COFFIELD: The food writer and cook Richard 'Dick' Whittington was handsome and witty, and moved effortlessly through the scene becoming friends with Francis, Jeffrey and Ian. He worked on a book with Alistair Little – a combination of Little's recipes from his restaurant in Frith Street and Whittington's own fierce love of straightforward cookery. The result was *Keep It Simple*, an instant hit in 1993. The title was credited to Ian Board, with whom Whittington had previously shared a flat.

DICK WHITTINGTON: . . . Ian might infrequently decide he was hungry and on just such an occasion after his drunken return from the Colony late one night, he taught me an important cookery lesson. There was some calves' liver in the fridge which he asked me to prepare with as little trickery as possible. 'Just show it a hot pan for a minute, dear,' he said, opening another bottle of brandy and lighting his sixtieth 'pansy fag' of the day, as he called menthol cigarettes. I, enthralled at the time by appearance on the plate and deglazed sauces of an intensity I would now find repellent, both overcooked the liver and presented it – artfully scattered with chopped chives – expecting an enthusiastic response. He took one look at it and threw it, plate and all, straight at the unopened window. There was a terrible crash and tinkling of glass . . . followed by a moment of silence. 'You cunt,' he gravelled, 'I said keep it fucking simple.'

7

Last Orders

SANDY FAWKES: The industriousness of the old school, who hand-stitched gloves, artificial flowers, made violins and boot lasts, was replaced by swish offices with every conceivable piece of advanced technology. The eighties had arrived . . . Inevitably, with the rise in rents and business rates, many cherished landmarks went under; Benoit Bulcke, the butchers; Parmigiani, the Italian store; the cigar shop that kept a gas flame on the counter and a gold cutter for its customers; all to be replaced by pop T-shirt shops, or something equally as useless.

DARREN COFFIELD: The nineteen-eighties is synonymous with the rule of Margaret Thatcher, whose photo was stuck to the old green water heater above the club's sink. The night Thatcher was re-elected Prime Minister, the pundits kept saying it was good for the ordinary people, to which the club chairman, Allan Hall, retorted, 'But what about the *extra*-ordinary people?' Despite three decades having elapsed, it was still possible to go to Soho in the 1980s and dip into the lifestyle of the fifties and sixties. The Colony offered a time-warp retreat with its anti-quated interior and exotic characters. Bacon, Belcher and Board were now legendary figures, and a new generation found their way to the Colony.

JOHN BAKER: I'd just seen Jeffrey Bernard on a television documentary and sought him out at the Coach & Horses. That afternoon I met Graham Mason and the following day he took me to the Colony. Graham was charming and had the most beautiful speaking voice I've ever heard. He was such a fascinating person to be around. He'd worked as a television journalist but I knew him in his later years when he worked for Bobby Hunt at the Robert Hunt Library, which specialised in military photographs. Its principal client was the *Economist*. Marsh Dunbar worked in the *Economist*'s art department and Graham and Marsh lived together. Long before Marsh met her late husband Peter Dunbar, she'd been married to Bobby, who'd never really fallen out of love with her. They were taken to the club as students of John Minton's and were very close. I know the Colony thing is not to tolerate bores, but Graham really didn't. He'd say, 'What are you talking to that cunt again for?' And that would be the start of the downfall of the afternoon.

Graham's day started with a can of lager before he left home, and a cup of what he'd call 'plastic' coffee – 'Mellow Bird's'. Then he'd go to the office to check the mail and shout down the phone for a few minutes – generally it was only for a few minutes, as he'd need to get to the Coach & Horses for eleven a.m., opening time. We'd stay in the pub until it closed at three p.m. Then we'd go to the Colony until five-thirty p.m. On the way back from the Colony, we'd stop at Gerry's off-licence to buy a litre and a half of vodka – the man behind the counter was forever showing Graham dirty pictures. After that we'd go back to the Coach & Horses. Graham had extra-ordinary stamina. I used to smoke in those days, but Graham was a proper eighty-a-day smoker which, in the end, did for him. Graham had various young assistants. He brought one with terrible acne into the Colony: 'You're a spotty little cunt, aren't you?' remarked Ian. The youth replied, 'What do you expect me to do about it?' Without hesitation, Ian quipped, 'I find a teaspoon of cum every morning does the trick.' Needless to say he never came back. However, one of his assistants Rupert Shrive went on to be a well-known artist.

RUPERT SHRIVE: Graham took painting very seriously. It was something he had enormous respect for and thought very mysterious. He knew a lot about it, and worked with Bruce Bernard on the bestselling book on van Gogh, *Vincent by Himself*. I painted Graham's portrait – he was very important in my formation as a painter. Graham would take his drink (a large tumbler of vodka and soda) from the Coach & Horses in his overcoat pocket and walk down the sunny side of Old Compton Street to the Colony. He'd go upstairs, take his glass tumbler out of his pocket, put it on the bar and Michael Wojas would refill it. He had the most extraordinary voice – even if a place was full, you could go to the loo and still hear him. His voice cut through everyone and everything. John Deakin was known for his quips and comments, and Graham was very fond of John so he used to repeat some of his best one-liners. Graham could be fierce and biting, but he could also be very kind and generous. He'd been a war reporter. It wasn't something he liked talking about – he'd witnessed a lot of summary executions in the Congo.

JOHN BAKER: Graham helped bring up all three of Marsh's sons. She and Graham went to live with Mumsie, for a while, because Graham had burnt down their Soho flat. The *Economist* had its print run on Thursdays so Marsh always had to go in early. They'd finish at about twelve-thirty p.m. when the first print run came off. Marsh would then go for what she called a 'haircut', a euphemism for an afternoon in Soho. Marsh was hilarious, she wasn't frightened of dressing up and had great style. She had an encyclopaedic knowledge of everyone who worked in the art world – she'd slept with nearly everybody.

GLENEAGLES: There was an expression, used by Marsh and Graham's generation – they would go and 'spend time in the country', meaning they were being sobered up and dried out. Marsh and Graham had both gone through it. Maybe with the passing of those great characters, the magnet of Soho is no longer there. But people would get to the point where, for self-preservation, they'd have to get away 'to the country'. Then, even years later, they'd get pulled back in by the siren's call. Marsh told me the magnet was too strong for her. I can feel it too. There's not a day that goes by when I don't miss those times. There are news items, sometimes a sentence in an obituary, that take me back there. I was one of the main libel lawyers for *Private Eye* and would frequent the Coach & Horses as they held their lunches there. There were local expressions: if you were in the Coach & Horses and said, 'I'm going round the corner', it meant you were off to the French, whilst 'I'm going upstairs' meant the Colony. The son of the editor of *Private Eye*, Fred Ingrams, took me to the Colony. For me, it was the elephants' graveyard. I felt I had graduated from the Coach to the Colony. For someone who had the potential for developing a serious drinking problem, it was heaven. I drank there with 'Tibbs' [Andrew Tiffin], the cartoonist. I poured a lot of money into the club, simply because I made a lot of money as a lawyer. When Ian's perch broke, I commissioned a new one from the designer Kathy Dalwood. Being a Scot named Glen and my profession, 'legal eagle', Ian christened me 'Gleneagles' after the famous golf course. Francis thought I was one of 'Thatcher's children' because I was young and doing rather well. He took me aside and asked me what I thought of Thatcher and her handbags. He loved the fact that she had such a strong personality. Strangely most of our chats were about politics.

DARREN COFFIELD: Francis frequently liked to discuss other people's day jobs. He was fascinated that John Baker was a policeman. Seeing dead and battered bodies interested him. One afternoon Bookshop Billy's wife arrived after a horse-riding accident, her face all bruised. Billy said, 'Look at this, Francis, Kim has a black eye.' – 'Ooh,' said Francis, 'oh, my dear! Look at those colours . . . Marvellous colours!' – 'Only an artist like Francis could look at the colours and not the wound,' said Billy.

TWIGGY: After the Colony we often had supper. Francis would say, 'Come on Twiggy, let's have fish and chips.' Which by that time was caviar and lobster. I'd insist on paying, as a lot of people would sponge off him. One time, Francis said, 'I sent you two tickets to the opening of my retrospective at the Tate Gallery.' – 'I know, Francis, they arrived this morning.' – 'Are you going to come?' – 'Probably not.' – 'But why?' – 'Francis, I really don't like your painting.' – 'That's perfectly fine. Neither do I, but there will be free champagne.'

DAVID EDWARDS: During his second retrospective at the Tate Gallery in 1985, Francis was lauded as the greatest British painter since Turner. One hundred and twenty-six of his paintings were exhibited, making it double the size of the exhibitions the Tate has today. He gave the Tate's caterers £30,000 extra himself, because he didn't like the wine and canapés they'd be serving. At the reception Francis was signing his exhibition catalogues, and Jeffrey Bernard was there right beside him, trying to borrow money from him.

BOOKSHOP BILLY: After the exhibition, John Edwards arranged for a group of friends to eat at Langan's Brasserie. Francis was going to join us later as he had to stay behind and shake hands with all the dignitaries. So the restaurant is closed, except for us guests who are still eating and drinking, when the waiter comes up and says, 'Excuse me, Mr Edwards, I am terribly sorry to trouble you' (you have to remember John is getting star treatment as the staff believe he is the one picking up the tab), 'I am very, very sorry but there is an old boy at the door. He says he is expected. What should I say?' Well, we all know who that old boy is, don't we? John is getting the VIP treatment inside, whilst the 'old boy' waiting at the door is the one footing the bill.

DARREN COFFIELD: Ian said that the rift between Francis and Freud culminated in Freud's refusal to loan Francis' painting of two men on a bed for his retrospective at the Tate. Francis couldn't understand Freud's refusal. Why was he so unfriendly? Francis got his revenge years later when he took Michael Wishart to see the Freud retrospective – 'Well, Lucian is extremely gifted, but I've never been interested in *expressionism.*' When Wishart informed Francis that Freud refused to see him because he said his *conversation* was so repetitious, Francis countered that he would no longer see Freud because his *work* was so repetitious.

Francis was at his zenith after his second retrospective and many young aspiring artists wanted to drink in the Colony. If you're going to drink somewhere, then why not go where the people you admire go? My new art-school friend, Joshua Compston, knew a well-heeled alcoholic. So there we were, propping up the bar aged eighteen, looking out for the club's most famous member. The year was 1988, and Francis Bacon's paintings were becoming the most expensive of any living artist in the world.

JOSHUA COMPSTON: Dressed like a piece of rough, already dirty, drunk on gin and desperation. Meet Francis Bacon . . . and curly haired, healthy-looking, rich commoner John Edwards, trying to keep his roots but being a millionaire. Rather funny . . . Bacon speaks loudly about the stupidity of my flowery patch on my linen trousers. Very disparaging about most art, very determined and cynical about his position as the painter of 'truth' (the way it is). Close to him lie champagne, Monte Carlo, stale and old rough boyfriends. Others are tolerated with a sickly smile . . . He'd rather not be there, though initially he was what is called quite polite! 'Champagne for your real friends, real pain for your sham friends.' I nearly drowned with champagne but I was there on some strange sufferance. Bacon is unhappy, bored and terrified of death. He recognises his position as being alone. All others are dead. A living modern master is rare.

DARREN COFFIELD: Joshua romanticised Francis. They say don't meet your heroes; well, that was certainly true in Josh's case. He's the art student in Dan Farson's biography, *The Gilded Gutter Life of Francis Bacon*, for whom Francis signs his book in the Colony. Francis was now a cult figure and his admirers became obsessed by him. Joshua would regularly go through Francis' bin in Reece Mews, hoping to find a slashed painting or some artistic pearl of interest. But all he found were letters from Marlborough Fine Art, saying that his plane tickets were booked for Monaco and the money wired to the casino. Joshua adored all those old Soho characters – he wanted to have that kind of reputation. Like Graham Mason, he was a divisive figure who people either adored or hated.

ZEBEDEE HELM: Ian Board, a man who liked to speak his mind and always called a spade a cunt, never appeared very pleased to see Joshua. Josh had dragged me up the rickety stairs, promising it would only be for one very quick drink. So I stood by the open window, puffing on a roll-up and looking down at the scumbags on the street below, while he and Ian shouted at each other. There were about six people in the place, muttering in corners, broken by sudden screams. Suddenly I noticed a change in atmosphere. The room started prickling, darting looks shot to and fro, and everyone was talking in louder voices. I looked round, and there, shuffling into the room like Gandhi in a shiny leather bomber jacket, was the tiny figure of Francis Bacon. Ever the opportunist, Josh was onto him like a pike. With a proprietorial hand over Bacon's shoulder, he ushered him towards me while ordering a bottle of champagne with the other hand. Before we knew it, we were drinking champagne with Francis Bacon. Several bottles later, we tumbled down the stairs into the dark Soho night. The next morning Josh woke up in a strange bed in a strange street without any underpants.

DARREN COFFIELD: Being a member started out as such innocent fun, but then, of course, there were the friendships that became drinking casualties. Some of the people I took there considered both myself and the club the personification of evil, vowing never to return. Others stayed the course.

CECILY BROWN: I quickly developed an addiction for the green walls, the rude banter and the promise of a possible glimpse of Francis Bacon. Ian Board I found terrifying, but luckily I was always with Darren, whom he adored, so I was saved the worst of his tongue.

DARREN COFFIELD: It was around this time that Cecily discovered that David Sylvester was her father. Francis had first met David in 1950. He had an insatiable appetite for food, sex, painting, football and cricket, although not necessarily in that order. Francis introduced David to the Colony and to Isabel Rawsthorne, who'd bring Giacometti to the club. The last occasion was during Giacometti's 1965 Tate retrospective, which David curated. But the Colony did not hold the same magnetism for David as it did for Francis. Over the years David began to loathe Ian Board and was perplexed as to why Cecily and I liked the place – 'I can't understand why you want to go to that club. I hate Ian Board . . . terrible man.' And so the years passed, the champagne flowed and a new generation washed up upon the shores of the Colony. One student I took asked Francis if he knew 'any good hangover cures?' Francis shot him a glance – 'Suicide,' he replied.

JAMES BIRCH: Francis asked an art student who her favourite artist was. 'Brancusi,' she replied. Francis lurched forward clutching his chest, 'Brancusi! Uurrgh!' She burst into tears.

TOM DEAS: Francis could be merciless to younger artists, who posed no threat whatsoever. A recent art-school graduate came in one afternoon to present the Club with his latest watercolour painting. This generous gesture was politely accepted by Ian until Francis arrived and his gaze fixed upon it. Smelling blood, the members in the room turned on the pretentious young artist and suddenly without warning Francis sprayed the painting with a bottle of champagne. The watercolour dissolved and dripped onto the floor, accompanied by a chorus of cheers, which drove the tearful art graduate from the club wailing, 'If I had done that to one of his, I would be up for criminal damage.' A few days later Francis told a snooping reporter, 'It's rubbish. I don't know anything about it.' Whilst Ian freely admitted he had encouraged it. When asked why he replied, 'Well . . . Sometimes these artists need a good kick up the arse.'

DARREN COFFIELD: Francis would always buy the drinks. He was very generous and had a healthy disregard for money. Sometimes literally so, letting it fall out of his pockets. He always carried £50 notes – he'd buy a bottle of champagne but never spend the change, half-stuffing it in his trouser pocket and often dropping it. Ten-pound notes littered the floor around his feet. Every time he ordered another bottle of champagne, he'd pay with a fresh £50 note. The money tantalisingly scattered around his feet seemed like a ploy to entrap potential prey or part of some strange mating ritual.

FRED INGRAMS: Everyone thinks that Bacon was drunk all the time, but he would disappear for months on end, working phenomenally hard. Then he'd get paid by Marlborough Fine Art and turn up with an entourage and a big wodge of cash on one of his legendary benders. By now he was the most famous painter in Britain alongside David Hockney, whom he hated and called the 'Liberace of the art world'.

DARREN COFFIELD: People mostly drank champagne or spirits in the club since the wine was like paint stripper. The tiny club's mini fridge only held about ten cans of beer, so all the cold ones would run out within a couple of hours of opening time. They were those tiny aeroplane-trolley-sized cans that tasted like fizzy gnat's piss. Mind you, the champagne wasn't that much better. Ian would gladly inform the uninitiated purchasers of the club's shampoo that unless they drank it regularly – day in, day out, as a matter of routine – it would be hideously common to drink champagne on their birthday. The year 1988 marked the club's fortieth anniversary and a huge party was organised to mark the occasion.

IAN BOARD: It's all going to be ruby red, dear – ruby red for the ruby anniversary. Michael and I will be dyeing our hair red for the evening. Michael Woods is decorating the club ruby too, and we'll be wearing special red outfits by Thea Porter to match.

KATE FAWKES: We all partied and went on holidays together. The 'family' relationships formed in the Colony also existed outside. To be the child of a Soho drinker was a great adventure but some were scarred by it – what we saw from an early age was imprinted on us. Some inherited the gene and went on to have addiction problems themselves; others like Suggs became great successes.

DARREN COFFIELD: Suggs' mum Eddi McPherson had been part of Soho since 1959. She started off as a jazz singer before working in various legendary clubs such as the Kismet (aka 'Death in the Afternoon') and Gerry's. She was a true force of nature. Never averse to shouting her mind, she could castrate a man at twenty paces with one lash of her tongue. She was known as 'Big Eddi' but no one dared say it to her face.

SANDY FAWKES: When she [Eddi] orders up her first bottle of pink champagne, her friends settle down for an amusing afternoon; those whom she dislikes slink out of the sight lines . . . Not for nothing is she nicknamed Eddi MacFierce One. As with many of the regulars before her, Eddi [brought] her offspring in . . . long before he attained the legal age to take alcohol. It did him no harm and he still returns 'home' for a glass or two whenever he's not touring as Suggs, lead singer with the band Madness.

DARREN COFFIELD: During Ian's reign, another generation began to emerge, many of whom were the children of key members – Joshua Bowler, son of Henrietta Moraes; Kathy Dalwood, daughter of Hubert; and Orlando Campbell, son of Charles.

ORLANDO CAMPBELL: I was first brought to the Colony in a carrycot and dumped on the banquette under the Michael Andrews mural. I must have been less than one year old, but already a regular. Muriel would put vodka on her thumb and shove it in my mouth when I was teething. I was seduced and doomed from then on. My father had been going to the club since he was eighteen and was good friends with Francis Bacon. He took us all during the school holidays where we met 'Sergeant Wilson' [John Le Mesurier] from *Dad's Army*. Muriel would tell Ian to open the till and give us £2, so we could go to the amusement arcade around the corner. At the age of eighteen, I was an art groupie and had grown up listening to stories about Bacon and Freud. So I decided to go and find the place. I remembered, it was green and up some stairs, but so were all the brothels. Eventually I got the right door and walked in. It was terrifying. – 'What the fuck do you want, dear?' I had never been called 'dear' in my life. 'I'm Charlie Campbell's son,' I said. – 'Charlie's boy. Well, why didn't you say so?' Ian's great, big, red, pockmarked nose lunged at me and his foul-smelling mouth gave me a big, wet kiss, with a tongue just to round the experience off.

On more than one occasion, I became homeless or was in-between flats and stayed at the Colony. But not by myself, Ian wouldn't let me, sensibly. All that stopped when one morning, I felt Ian's hand down my trousers, and being polite, I said nothing and moved a bit. It started again. I moved again. This went on and on, until I sat up and he went to the glass-cleaning sink – and repeatedly threw up until he'd had some brandy and coughed up what he called 'oysters' in his handkerchief. He then asked me if I wanted some orange juice. I said yes, and his shaking hand poured the juice followed by a huge vodka. I couldn't cope with the situation. Being an art groupie wasn't that glamorous after all. Eventually the Groucho Club opened next door. If anything it made the Colony even better because the club always closed at eleven p.m., and the Groucho at one a.m. Despite his moaning about it, Ian could be spotted there from time to time with some of the Colony's more well-heeled clientele, but not Lord Patrick Conyngham, who was banned on the opening night for peeing on a policeman's helmet from the first-floor window.

DANIEL FARSON: Being a lord is crucial to Patrick Conyngham – known in the gossip columns as Lord Matey – for without the handle, he could well be regarded as an outrageous exhibitionist rather than a colourful eccentric. He once heard that he was featured in *Tatler*, and phoned to see what had been written about him. Taking a deep breath, the journalist began, 'The *idea* of Patrick Conyngham is horrific: a philandering, rabble-rousing, excessive, more often than not to be found lying face down in a pool of vomit. The so-called poet . . .' – 'Hang on a minute,' interrupted Patrick aggressively, 'could you take out the "so-called"?' . . . He was reinstated by the Groucho on a pledge of good behaviour, but was promptly sick over a table of media members and barred again. On the third attempt he staggered in with a friend's dog, only to be stopped by the manager, a kind, tolerant man, who told him firmly: 'The dog is welcome, but you are not.'

DARREN COFFIELD: Ian knew the sound signature of each member's footsteps as they climbed the club stairs. I was chatting with him once when his ears pricked up like a gun dog. Nimbly dismounting his throne, he swung open the door and repeatedly slammed it on the potential customer, screeching 'fuck off'. The poor man yelped in agony at the onslaught of being crushed between the door frame and the repeatedly slamming door, and withdrew. Satisfied with having repelled his prey, Ian turned to me and said, 'That's Lord Patrick Conyngham, the "Underwater Poet" – I'm not having that cunt in here again!' It was Ian's complete disregard for status or rank that always endeared him to me.

ORLANDO CAMPBELL: There weren't that many young artists in the club during the eighties. It wasn't like in later years when Damien Hirst and the YBAs 'discovered' the club. There were still a lot of the old guard of painters around. I always thought it was very civilised to drink in the afternoon – while others were working in dreary offices, I was quaffing champagne with

Francis Bacon, Patrick Caulfield, Craigie Aitchison and a whole load of freaks and has-beens.

DARREN COFFIELD: The artist Chris Battye was often at the club dressed as a Teddy boy. His print of Francis and Ian Board leaving the Colony to go to Charlie Chester's hung in the club for many years as did Gavin Jones' double portrait of Ian Board and Michael Wojas. Fred Ingrams had a studio around the corner above the Coach & Horses. Francis bought a painting from him.

FRED INGRAMS: It became a big news item because Bacon didn't really buy art to look at; he was more famous for purchasing and destroying it. He was very complimentary about my artwork.

MICHAEL CLARK: It was very rare for Francis to talk about any contemporary work. I remember Francis talking to Robert Fraser in the club about how he wanted to make a film. Robert took out a handful of change and went to the payphone – 'You've got to make it, Francis, I'll call Frank Lloyd [of Marlborough Fine Art] now. How much do you need, one million? Two?' Then Francis came in one evening and said he had seen a most extraordinary film. He said it was called *Bad Timing* by Nicolas Roeg. It was very rare for Francis to talk about any contemporary work in such a way. He even references it in his notes for a triptych with a drawing that closely resembles his painting of Muriel as the Sphinx, signed off at the bottom, *Bad Timing*.

DARREN COFFIELD: Francis may have been ambivalent about contemporary art, but all around him a new generation of artists were springing up. Lord Patrick Conyngham, James

Moores, Daniel Chadwick and Marc Quinn were some of the 'bright young things' who revived the scene with their wild humour and drunken stunts. Marc was often in the Colony and was working as a croupier at the time. It never occurred to me that he was an artist until he cast his head in eight pints of his own blood, and exhibited it in a vertical refrigerator in a tiny London gallery. Unfortunately Marc didn't plan for the rise in room temperature when the exhibition filled up with people and his head began to melt.

DANIEL CHADWICK: Barry Flanagan was a friend of my mother's and Marc Quinn was my friend from school, so Marc got a job assisting Barry, and Barry took us to the Colony. He was a lovely funny man. In the 1970s, artists like Barry pretty much starved. But by the eighties there was a change. There was James Birch and Paul Conran of the Birch & Conran Gallery under the Colony, where Marc and I had our first taste of a new era in art. It was an amazing time – gallery openings and the Colony became a routine. There was this disparate group of people floating around who were to become key figures in the art scene, and what linked them was the Colony. I was an afternoon Colony person and you'd meet funny people in there and have lovely intimate conversations. Marc would drink harder and harder, faster and faster until he became uncon- scious. Mind you I did the same, too. They'd lean us up together, unconsciously propping each other up in our drunkenness. Marc was never horrible with drink, he was horrible without it!

JAMES MOORES: The first time Marc and I knocked on the door of the Colony, we felt we were trying to break into something, it was quite scary. 'Who are you cunts? Oh, Mrs Moores wants to come in, does she?' But there was also a warmth I found nowhere else in 'old' Soho. The most exciting thing about meeting Francis Bacon was the way he gave us his full attention – he seemed to hang on our every word, as if what we had to say was interesting and significant. As he was leaving, Francis said, 'Come along!' John Edwards spun round, grabbing my forelock in his hand and giving my head a sharp shove back into the club, saying as he pulled the door between us, 'Not you, matey.'

It was through the Colony that I met Bruce Bernard and was introduced to the photographs of John Deakin which he'd acquired after Deakin had died. Francis was worried what might become of Deakin's work and they went to his flat – just in time, as they found Deakin's family throwing all his stuff out on the street for the bin men, including all his boxes of photographs and the thousands of negatives. Bruce talked to the family, who were somewhat ashamed of Deakin's homosexuality. They said Bruce could take it all (there's a letter) so long as he took it right away. Francis and Bruce carried the boxes back to Bruce's flat where he kept them under his bed for many years. When I met Bruce in the Colony, he was looking to find a home for them. A number of people said I must buy them and Lucian Freud wanted the collection to be put in a safe place. So you see I didn't acquire the archive by any good judgement on my part, more I feel it was foisted upon me by some wiser people. It was only later in 1996, with the Deakin show at the National Portrait Gallery, that I really appreciated what I'd bought for a small amount to cover a few of Bruce's bills – it was immensely valuable. I felt I owed Bruce something as he'd have done so much better out of selling the archive at another time, but Bruce wanted the archive and Deakin's reputation cared for properly, so I repay him in that. Now we've gathered more material and explored it further. It seems that Bacon based a huge amount on Deakin's photographs.

DARREN COFFIELD: It's interesting that Francis paid homage to Deakin immediately after his death, and then dismissed him towards the end of his own life remarking, 'Deakin was . . . not a very good photographer. I only used him because he was there and needed the money.' Francis could be very fickle with his praise.

JAMES MOORES: Yes, definitely. Bacon was looking to his own reputation and degree of immortality towards the end, but the research into Deakin's oeuvre continues to feed Bacon's reputation and make him a stronger painter.

DARREN COFFIELD: Francis was now into his fourth decade of drinking at the Colony. However, new clubs were springing up. Across the road was Blacks, which managed to get hold of the Colony's membership list and tried to poach its members. A chap called Tom Bantock started the club after being banned from the Groucho for putting a lit cigarette in someone's pocket – which seems pretty mild behaviour to me. We once set light to an entire sofa in the Groucho. John Edwards and I had been sitting in the Colony, winding up Ian who threw us out. So we floated down to the Groucho, found an empty chesterfield and sat on it. John ordered more champagne from the waiter, and we sat there chatting away. He was laughing and gesticulating with a cigarette in his hand, the lit embers dropping everywhere. We were so deep in conversation that we didn't notice the sofa starting to smoulder. Moments later, the waiter reappears with a bottle of Laurent Perrier on a silver tray and duly announces,

'Mr Edwards, your sofa is on fire.' John was not at all fazed – 'Well, don't just stand there, pour the champagne over it!'

PHILIPPA CLARE: John and Francis? You just never knew where they'd pop up next. I was walking down the street one day when this arm came out of a doorway of a sex club and pulled me in. It was Francis. He said, 'Come in, we're having a video taken.' – 'Over my dead body!' I replied.

DARREN COFFIELD: Somehow the Colony still kept abreast of sex scandals before they came to light in the press. One lazy afternoon, a media mogul appeared with the journalist Simon Regan, a compellingly odd man in a cravat and crumpled velvet jacket. He was obsessed with injustice. 'If I had the chance,' he said, 'I would be a great repealer. Censorship laws, licensing, blasphemy, the Official Secrets Act – they would all be dumped. Then I'd disestablish the establishment.' Regan stood at the bar and announced that the Prime Minister John Major was having an affair. It beggared belief that anyone could find such a human specimen sexually attractive. Regan published the revelation in his magazine, *Scallywag*, but named the wrong woman as the mistress. Major sued for libel, employing the notorious libel lawyer Peter Carter-Ruck, whose name struck fear in the hearts of many. Regan received a phone call from this dreaded foe – 'Regan? Carter-Ruck.' – 'Carter-Ruck? I don't give a fuck!' quipped Regan, and slammed the receiver down on the libel lawyer. But Major won and Regan went to an early grave convinced that John Major was both an adulterer and a liar. Some years later, Major admitted to having an affair, not with his caterer, but with government minister Edwina Currie.

JIM MOORE: Sex scandals? Ian's parting shot to any pair of individuals leaving the club was, 'Off you go now and have a good fuck.' And I used to think, they're only going for the bus. There were a lot of people exaggerating their sexual prowess – a lot of gossip and supposition, sexually, which was what made it good fun as no one was really sure what was going on. When the AIDS epidemic began, all the publicans were scared. They were given the wrong information – it was thought it could be caught from using a dirty glass, so if Ian didn't like the look of someone, he'd smash their glass in the sink after they left.

DARREN COFFIELD: By the mid-eighties the AIDS virus was spreading misery and death. No one knew how to stop it and there was a lot of prejudice. People who'd contracted the virus risked being ostracised and persecuted by the wider community. Sitting in Mario's in Chelsea with John Edwards, Francis saw his favourite 'Belgravia pansy', Robert Fraser, looking blotchy and emaciated. 'It's AIDS,' commented Francis, voicing the fear of many. Four months later, Fraser was dead. Francis, John and Ian held a quiet wake for him in the Colony. Despite his dislike of 'gay militance', Francis signed a protest against the Thatcher government's Clause 28, which outlawed the discussion or acceptance of homosexuality within schools and colleges. Francis said, 'I don't go about shouting that I am gay, but AIDS has made it all the more worse, you know.' Since AIDS was then seen as a purely gay problem, the heterosexuals did not alter their behaviour and carried on regardless.

MARSH DUNBAR: There was an elderly squire from Yorkshire. He was an extremely important man and used to bring in this dolly bird. Muriel loved it – this silly little girl and this amazing major-type man. It went on for years.

GRAHAM MASON: – Remove that, he's still with us . . . I mean it! Turn that bloody recording thing off . . . you'll have litigation if you don't! You've totally given it away! *Ooohh* . . . since you've blown it, he married a smart lesbian friend of Muriel's who became his posh country wife. Their goings-on were manyfold.

DARREN COFFIELD: Some members led extraordinary double lives. Mr •••• would fly back from business trips to the USA and tell his wife he was on a later flight, days later, so he could have some playtime and lead his double life in Soho. For years his wife suspected nothing, until one day, when the flight he said he was on, crashed, killing all 180 passengers. Mr •••• had been partying in Soho and hadn't seen the news for days. You can imagine his wife's surprise when her chirpy dead husband rocked through the front door. It took some nimble thinking to talk himself out of that one.

IAN THE HAT: 'Foreskin' would come up and get agency girls. It was always a business trip that could be extended for a week or more – he'd fly back early and spend his time in Soho. He adored being around women. He maintained his double life for over half a century. But how he did it is still a mystery to me.

BOOKSHOP BILLY: One evening Foreskin was sitting at home with his wife, watching a documentary on Francis Bacon, featuring the Colony. His wife was aghast – 'Look at this! Look at all these horrible, horrible people, Peter!' – 'Yes dear.' He couldn't wait to get back there. Whenever he came to town, he went straight to the Colony.

FORESKIN: One night there were a lot of funny Northern accents and some odd bird wearing bovver boots and a beret.

After closing time I said, 'Let's go for a Chinese meal in Gerrard Street.' When I get quite drunk, I sing, and this girl in the beret was sitting opposite, and I remember hearing *her* sing and thinking, My God, girl, if you sung professionally, you'd probably make a bob or two. Three weeks later, I'm sitting at home with my daughter, watching *Top of the Pops*, and I thought, Fuck me – it's that bird with the beret! And I've been friends with Lisa Stansfield ever since.

JIM MOORE: Lisa would be in the club a lot with her partner Ian Devaney. She was very down to earth, unpretentious and funny. She'd hit the big time but it hadn't spoiled her in any way and Ian adored her like a daughter.

DARREN COFFIELD: Every December, a party was thrown to celebrate the anniversary of the club, during which the Colony would get so rammed that you wouldn't realise how drunk you were. Then as it emptied out after midnight, you'd realise you were too drunk to stand up – the only thing that had kept you vertical were all the other people packed around you like sardines. At this particular party, Lisa sang and a whole bunch of art students I'd brought with me, began a queue at the piano, clutching mistletoe, trying to procure a kiss from her. Ian was busy rushing past, ripping the mistletoe out of their hands. He loathed Christmas, the very mention of which was banned. He'd try and go on holiday far away from all the festive nonsense.

DI HALL: Ian said to me, 'That fucking Edwards is going to Barbados this Christmas without me.' So I said, 'Fuck them, you can come to my home in Goa.' So eventually I go home, thinking nothing more about it. The following morning I get a call from Ian – 'Hello mate, I've done it.' – 'Done what?' – 'I've booked it!' – 'Booked what?' – 'A flight to Goa!' I thought, Oh my God . . . I told him I was going to arrive on Christmas Day. – 'It's too expensive to fly then, I'll get there for the twenty-second.' Unfortunately I forgot I'd rented it out the week before. When I arrive in Goa, I see the tenant in the bar – 'Your friend Ian's arrived in a fur coat, which I'm sure is crawling with something, so I wouldn't let him stay.' Then I headed off and found Ian sitting outside my house, with his arms folded. 'Oh, hello Ian, I see you're sitting next to a hay bale.' – 'I know that, you silly cunt! *I've been sitting next to it for three days!*' Ian met a nice young Indian man who'd dress up in my saris and they'd do some dancing together. This became a regular occurrence. After the holiday, that young man wrote to Ian every week: 'You have taught me more than my uncle or father ever knew, thank you.' Ian would send him money and said it was the best holiday he ever had.

DARREN COFFIELD: The first week back after Christmas, I found Jeffrey Bernard holding court on the banquette by the window. Unusually Ian was sitting next to him, hanging on Jeff's every word. He was talking about a new government initiative to quell binge drinking by allowing children to accompany their parents to bars in an attempt to temper their attitude to alcohol. Jeffrey was apoplectic in his morose measured way – 'If it isn't hell enough having to drink every day in bars, without having to inflict it upon the children. The whole idea fills me with horror!' Poor Jeff was looking very frail. He had to be carried up the stairs to the Colony and back down again afterwards; he looked pretty ill. In fact he was looking distinctly *unwell* . . .

PHILIPPA CLARE: *Jeffrey Bernard is Unwell*? That refers to the *Spectator*'s habit of printing a one-line apology whenever Jeffrey was too drunk or hungover to meet the deadline for his column. Jeff is the only man I know who has made a living out of being an alcoholic. Keith Waterhouse said to Jeff he thought it would be great to make a play of his book, *Low Life*, and Jeff said he thought he was a 'complete cunt' as it was 'the most idiotic idea'. But Keith just went ahead and wrote the play anyway.

KEITH WATERHOUSE: . . . [Jeffrey] was a short sprint man – 600 words was his natural length. Within that limit the miniaturist produced some gems . . . But he had no need to beef up his column with anecdotes. Out of the raw materials of a blank and uneventful day, he could spin a 'suicide note in weekly instalments' . . . Jeffrey Bernard was not everyone's tipple. Some of those who disliked him complained that in the play I made him too endearing. If I did, that was how he chose to put himself over. But he had many unendearing characteristics. He could be boorish and dour, and was often unpardonably rude to those not quite big enough to take it. He would accept drinks from strangers and then tell them to piss off.

PETER O'TOOLE: Jeffrey and I go back to the late fifties, we were easy chums . . . The script appealed to me because Keith is an extraordinary dramatist. He'd written a beautifully tailored piece. I remember Noël Coward saying he could write dialogue by the yards, but it was plots that were difficult. So Keith had this extraordinary idea of taking a great deal of Jeffrey's dialogue, as he writes it in the *Spectator*, and incorporating it into a simple little playlet. It was vastly entertaining, for the material is excellent.

DARREN COFFIELD: Peter O'Toole took on the lead role and came to the Colony with Keith Waterhouse and the play's director, Ned Sherrin, for 'research'. They carried out various schoolboy pranks, such as dropping their trousers, and although his hell-raising days were behind him, O'Toole insisted on serving behind the bar. He knew the club from the days of Muriel, who came up with the legendary quip concerning his most famous role – 'If she was any prettier, they'd have to call her Florence of Arabia.'

FRANCES SLOWEY: The first night I went to the Colony was for the opening of *Jeffrey Bernard is Unwell*. Michael Wojas and I had been seeing each other seriously for a year by then. Ian's curiosity had got the better of him, and he asked Michael to invite his girlfriend so he could meet me. I was a nervous wreck, because I'd heard a lot about Ian. Michael came round the bar and introduced me to him. 'Oh Francis, Francis!' said Ian, 'meet Frances, Michael's girlfriend.' Francis Bacon whirled round looking so happy, 'What a coincidence, my name is Francis too!' He was so excited, it was like I'd made his day – 'Would you like a glass of champagne?' Then we left Maid Marion behind the bar and made our way to the premiere. When we arrived it was packed. The play had been going for a while when the actor playing Francis Bacon minced onstage wearing a beret and a smock.

TWIGGY: I was sitting next to Francis in the dress circle when he stood up in the middle of the audience and exploded – 'I don't paint in a fucking beret, you cunts, I paint in a Savile Row suit!', which brought the play to a complete halt. Peter O'Toole looked up from the stage, smiled for ten seconds, then carried on, knowing full well who'd caused the rumpus. Francis stormed out, followed by John Edwards. It took us an hour and a half to calm Francis down afterwards, he was livid. Then Ian Board caused a disturbance. He considered another of the anecdotes in the play inaccurate – the one where Bobby Hunt was going to a fancy-dress party and Muriel Belcher suggested he go as himself, 'a bald-headed cunt'. Ian shouted out, 'She never said that at all!'

IAN THE HAT: Every drinker in Soho had come to see the play, and by the interval they were desperate for a drink, even clambering over the seats. Someone got electrocuted – they spilt their drink on the lights, causing them to short circuit. The audience was ten or fifteen minutes late getting back in after the interval because of that. After the play we all decanted back to the Colony. Francis Bacon was there, still fuming at his portrayal.

PHILIPPA CLARE: When Peter took on the role of Jeff, he got Jeff's mannerisms really well because they hung out together. They didn't like sycophants – when Peter was playing Jeffrey, I sent him a telegram saying, 'Break a leg! And I'll come and be sycophantic afterwards.' The girl took down the message wrong and Peter received a telegram saying that I'd be 'sick and frantic' at the stage door afterwards. It was hilarious, and from that moment on we never called anyone sycophantic again, always 'sick and frantic'. No one believed the play was going to be the big hit that it was. Especially Jeff, he thought the whole idea was bonkers. I remember standing opposite the theatre and him saying, 'Look! My fucking name is in lights!' When it opened, *Jeffrey Bernard is Unwell* became the biggest hit after the musicals. It ran to ninety-eight per cent capacity houses.

JEFFREY BERNARD: I was somewhat childishly pleased at the fact that so many people who had predicted disaster would now have to eat their words. Even John Hurt, a friend of sorts, had dismissed it after having been originally offered the part by Keith, saying it might make a quite good radio play . . .

DARREN COFFIELD: I pitched up the afternoon after the play's London premiere to find Ian drunk and distraught on his perch, clutching his chest in an operatic manner – 'Muriel, my poor Muriel, they portrayed her as a common scrubber.' The mock grief and ham acting came as an unexpected reward, having missed the premiere itself. The play went on to run for a very long time. When Tom Conti took over the lead, he was taken up to the club by Keith Waterhouse. When asked what he'd like to drink, Tom Conti declared himself teetotal, so Ian christened him 'Tom Cunty'.

MICHAEL HEATH: Such was Jeffrey's vanity, he'd sit in the theatre bar during the performances, waiting for people to come out at the interval and buy him a drink. One night there was a new doorman who refused to let him in. 'Do you know who I am? I am Jeffrey Bernard!' The doorman waved him away – 'No, you're not! He's onstage.'

BOOKSHOP BILLY: For the first time in his life, Jeff had some money because Keith Waterhouse gave him a cut of the profits. One day, he was in the Vintage House off-licence in Old Compton Street and asked for a bottle of vodka and sixty cigarettes. 'Oh, I'm sorry, I've forgotten my credit card,' he said. – 'Sorry sir, there's nothing we can do.' – 'Don't you know who I am?' – 'Yes sir, that's why there's nothing we can do, sir.'

DARREN COFFIELD: The success of *Jeffrey Bernard is Unwell* made the Coach & Horses and the Colony familiar to a whole new audience. The outcome was that the Coach made a lot of money because it was full of people who had recently seen the play, asking, 'Has Jeff been in?', whilst the Colony was going through a fallow period. Although to the play's audience the club sounded glamorous, it was now being run on a shoestring and falling to pieces. Muriel's Jewish piano had lost its outer casing. The entire mechanism of the till was on show, making it look like a Heath Robinson invention. It had also stopped ringing up any prices higher than a pound, which meant if someone bought a largish round for, say £21, the till had to be laboriously rung twenty-one times –

Kerr-ching!
Kerr-ching! Kerr-ching!
Kerr-ching! Kerr-ching! Kerr-ching!
Kerr-ching! Kerr-ching! Kerr-ching! Kerr-ching!
Kerr-ching! Kerr-ching! Kerr-ching! Kerr-ching! Kerr-ching!
Kerr-ching! Kerr-ching! Kerr-ching! Kerr-ching! Kerr-ching! Kerr-ching!

MISS WHIPLASH: The club went through a phase when there were only about twenty members going night after night trying to keep it open: Tom Deas, Ray Natkiel, Ian the Hat and the other 'Ida Boys' who looked after Ian like sons. At that time Lisa Stansfield and her partner were a huge support to Ian, and provided some necessary glitter.

IAN THE HAT: A couple of years earlier in 1988, the licensing laws had changed, allowing pubs to open all day, which removed the main reason for having afternoon drinking clubs. There were three pegs behind the bar, which held the bar bills

'PAID', 'PENDING' and 'UNPAID'. The richest members were usually the worst at paying, although it would have been just loose change to them. 'Mary Poppins' used to come into the club. He was the son of P. L. Travers who wrote *Mary Poppins* and had never done a stroke of work in his life, just lived off the royalties. My God, he was boring. Ian and I fought over who was going to have to talk to him. Ian would just tell him to 'fuck off', so I got stuck with him. He was so tight Ian said, 'When he asks for a drink, make sure it's a double.'

MICHAEL WOJAS: Towards the end of 1990, the club's landlord, Mr Ibrahim, made an application to redevelop 41 Dean Street into offices. He came in one day and threatened to close the club. Ian gave him a volley of his best tongue lashes. The newspapers ran a piece on the incident. Mr Ibrahim complained: 'Why should I stand for it? They are drunk and rude and many of his members are homosexual.'

IAN BOARD: I phoned Lord Stuart of Findhorn. We've dispatched someone to stay with Lord Montagu for the weekend to bend his ear. We are not going to lose this club just because some cunt wants to turn us into offices.

MICHAEL WOJAS: Club member, Lord Montagu of Beaulieu, was head of English Heritage, so he came to our help. English Heritage were very good – they were looking for original architectural features and other angles to help us. The staircase was original – underneath the green-painted hardboard were the original banister rails. The eighteenth-century fireplace was still boarded up. We were trying to get it listed, but unfortunately there weren't enough original features. The building was built in 1730 and was the residence of a cabinetmaker called Thomas

Turner. A lot of journalists drank in the Colony, so we could always get articles written about the club. We even became a news item on the radio . . .

RADIO INTERVIEW

DISC JOCKEY: A Soho club is fighting plans to be turned into offices. The Colony Room Club in Soho's Dean Street has been a home from home for artists for more than forty years. Its members include luminaries such as Francis Bacon, Lucian Freud and *Lisa Stansfield*? Tonight an application from the landlord of 41 Dean Street comes before Westminster Council's planning committee. He wants to turn the building into offices. Ian Board runs the club and joins us on the line now. Good morning, Ian!

IAN BOARD: Morning to you!

DISC JOCKEY: The obvious solution would seem to be to move the club somewhere else. Why can't you do that?

IAN BOARD: If you were to give me three-quarters of a million pounds I think I could arrange it.

DISC JOCKEY: But wouldn't you lose something if you were to move the club?

IAN BOARD: Well, it would be impossible to replace it anywhere, even with three-quarters of a million pounds. You see, the room, after forty-two years, has its atmosphere and its absolute feeling. One can't buy that anywhere. Created in 1948, it is something that is there and must stay there. In all the bars and clubs I have been to in the world, there is nothing like it.

DISC JOCKEY: Of all the bars in the world it might be the best, but don't you accept Soho needs offices as well?

IAN BOARD: Soho's got enough offices. Last week I walked around, went up Wardour, down Dean Street, up Frith Street, and down Greek Street and along Old Compton Street, and saw over eighty signs that say 'To Let', 'To Rent', 'To Lease', whatever. And they have been stuck there, not for a week or two, nothing to do with this recession, they have been there for two years or more. They can't let offices not only in Soho but all over London, all over England, I should imagine.

DISC JOCKEY: Why should Westminster Council preserve an institution which is bound to attract the elitist label?

IAN BOARD: Why should they *wot*?

DISC JOCKEY: Why should they vote to preserve your club when it's bound to be labelled elitist? You have to be proposed and seconded by an existing member to join.

IAN BOARD: Of course, all clubs have that rule and regulation anyway.

DISC JOCKEY: Could I be in your club, Ian?

IAN BOARD: Well, you would have to be proposed and seconded. I'd have to size you up, I really don't know . . . That music you play, we don't play in the club.

DISC JOCKEY: On what criteria do you size people up for the club, then?

IAN BOARD: Behaviour, wit, charm, money . . .

DISC JOCKEY: Well, that rules me out, on all four counts!

DARREN COFFIELD: Our Colony was now threatened with extinction. I decided to avoid my art history lecture at the National Gallery and make a swerve for the three p.m. kick-off at the club. The place was quiet and still, the sunlight raking across the bar like a projector lamp. Ian was agitated and the air felt charged like the build-up to a thunderstorm. After my drink had been poured and slid along the bar, there was a pregnant pause, during which the door swung open and in stepped Francis Bacon, beaming so brightly his face lit up the room. He greeted Ian warmly and ordered champagne. During the ritualistic pouring of the champagne, Ian gyrated on his perch like an excited bird of prey in anticipation of a kill. Then in came the club's former pianist Mike McKenzie and his wife Liz. Francis was so overjoyed at seeing them, he threw the contents of his glass over the carpet whilst going to hug Liz. He ordered glasses for Mike and Liz and filled them.

Within half an hour, there was a small cast of the original fifties members standing around the piano. Then, without warning, the club fell deathly silent as Mike played the opening bars of 'Send in the Clowns' and Liz began to sing. As the song petered out, there was a long, charged silence; nobody dared speak, adrift in their memories of Muriel. Eventually Francis raised his glass: 'To Muriel.' It was an uncanny sight that made the hairs on the back of my neck stand up, an eerie sensation of another era and certainly the most fantastic afternoon of unabated nostalgia I ever witnessed in the club. Ian had called in the cavalry, or more appropriately in Francis' case, the artillery. If the landlord wanted a fight, then Ian was going for a full-blown war. Later, as Francis settled his bill, he stood by Ian's perch and pledged his allegiance, 'This club will not close, no matter what it takes. I will buy the entire building if necessary.' Upon hearing that, Ian clasped his hands together, as if in prayer, to give thanks.

MISS WHIPLASH: We gathered a petition of over a thousand signatures and wrote to Westminster Council. My letter explained how I had moved back to London, divorced, tried to rebuild my life, and how the Colony made that possible as there was a community to plug back into – a continuity was there – and how important it was not to lose that. Ian was so touched by my letter that Michael read it out to the club.

MAID MARION: A few people said to Ian, we'll buy you a larger premises, but Ian said, 'It won't work, I'm at home here. This is me.' The idea of moving the club elsewhere would not have worked. People often asked Ian why he didn't set up a club in New York and he said, 'There can only be one place and it has to be here.'

DARREN COFFIELD: The only time I ever saw Ian nervous was when we were congregating outside Westminster City Hall for the public hearing of the planning committee. A motley crew of around fifty, of the great, the good and the unwashed, caused havoc trying to get through security. The next obstacle was the lift – which we shoehorned ourselves into in smaller groups. The application to convert the club into offices was number seven on the evening's agenda, but when they saw how many we were, the committee swiftly moved it to number one.

MICHAEL WOJAS: Amidst the mayhem of jeering and cheering, the planning application was rejected, to a huge round of applause in the room, which shocked the chairman who remarked that they'd never had such a response to a planning application rejection before. Victorious we made our way back down, and had our group photo taken together, en masse, for the first and last time.

DARREN COFFIELD: And so our tiny Colony was saved, and its barfly existence buzzed on as usual. I was standing at the bar with Cecily Brown when in walked Dan Farson with Gilbert & George in tow. It was quite amusing to see the expression on Gilbert & George's faces – they were trying to be deadpan, but the confrontational claustrophobia of the club threw them. Ian knew Francis loathed Gilbert & George, so acted unimpressed. I had modelled for them and appeared alongside them in the press, so they came over and started chatting to me. 'I didn't realise you were members,' I said. 'No, we could never join a club,' replied George. Ian sat twitching on his perch, trying to stretch his neck, meerkat-like, so he could see over the heads of members to the very far end of the bar where I was in deep conversation with George. Dan was trying to order drinks but was on the verge of being incoherently drunk by this stage.

TOM DEAS: James Birch had organised a follow-up exhibition to his Francis Bacon Moscow show. This time it was Gilbert & George. Upon his return from Moscow, Dan regaled everyone in the Colony about how they got drunk and were fêted everywhere. Two hours later, James Birch came in and gave his account of their trip to Moscow, which was completely different from Dan's.

DARREN COFFIELD: Gilbert & George hired the whole Groucho Club one Sunday for the book launch of *Gilbert & George in Moscow*, which Dan Farson had written. It was a very interesting and exclusive party attended by many Colony habitués. Then some weeks later I was standing at the bar of the French waiting to be served. In front of me was Dan Farson blocking the bar with his huge girth and wearing the most enormous donkey jacket. Judging by his conversation with his young companion, they'd just both been ejected from the Colony by Ian. The rent boy remarked bitterly, 'The Colony will be so much nicer once Ian Board is dead.' Dan demurred, half agreeing, half trying to shut him up. Then, turning round with his drink, confronted me – 'Are you a pianist?' – 'No,' I said, 'and I don't write shit books on Gilbert & George either,' to which Dan replied, 'Touché!' and moved away.

They may have wished Ian Board dead, but little did they know none of them had long to live.

8

Death in Bohemia

MOLLY PARKIN: I was fighting to give up the drink and didn't set foot in Soho for ten years, except once when I was chairing a meeting for Alcoholics Anonymous on the fringes of Soho. I found myself outside the Colony. So I walked up and there was Ian sitting alone: 'Moll! I wouldn't have recognised you!' I had no make-up on and had put on a lot of weight. I looked like an exotic plant which had not been watered for a very long time. Ian became quite tearful at the sight of me. 'Moll, we've all been missing you. We thought we'd never see you again, why aren't you dressed up?' – 'You don't dress to go to AA, darling. Don't be upset, you know I wouldn't have lasted much longer if I'd continued drinking.' Ian said, 'I've thought of giving up but it would mean giving up this place and I couldn't have done that to Muriel. I promised her I'd keep it going. I hope something comes to change your life.' – 'I only lived to drink at the end, darling.' – 'But you were so funny and everybody loved you so much.' – 'The problem is I don't think I loved myself that much.' I couldn't go back. I had to keep away just to stay alive.

DARREN COFFIELD: The members' lifestyle was a form of existential suicide. After a heavy drinking session, those who lived in basement flats were prone to die in falls and the smokers were in even greater danger. A final cigarette in bed, after a ferocious bender, really could turn out to be their last. Several members' mattresses became impromptu funeral pyres as they went up in flames, such as Eva Johansen, who had become the Colony's resident wit after Muriel fell off her perch.

PHILIPPA CLARE: Eva was a copywriter. Like Dorothy Parker, she had a way with words, unbelievably dry and funny. A man came up and asked, 'Can you give me two pence? I need to phone a friend.' So she gave him four pence instead and said, 'Why don't you call *all* your real friends?' Upon entering the Colony, she'd remark, 'Ah, the sweet smell of failure.'

MISS WHIPLASH: Jeffrey Bernard had a strange effect on women and they'd become obsessed by him. The women he really liked were the ones he didn't fancy. His particular friend was Eva Johansen. They were two of a kind and were brilliant between twelve and six p.m., sparking off each other, and then turning into monsters. I was involved with John Hurt, and he and Jeffrey were good pals, which was difficult because Jeff was vile to me. Whilst John was off making *Midnight Express*, I discussed the problem with 'Evil Eva': 'Well, you know why, Sara, you haven't been to bed with him. Don't worry he can't get it up.' So I took the calculated risk of going home with Jeff, and he couldn't. After that he was lovely to me – result! Eva said, 'When it comes to Jeff and John, it's a case of "love me, love my dog", and, in this case, Jeff's the dog.' Eva was so funny, she was lethal. She lived like a man – we women who fitted into the Soho scene lived the way the men lived. She was sitting on the corner banquette, one day, handing out notes on the sexual prowess of all the men who came in the club. When John opened the door, she announced, 'And twelve out of ten for that one!', waving her cigarette holder in his direction. 'And how did you rate her?' I asked him. 'All I remember is a lot of leg waving,' he smiled.

MAID MARION: Eva was man-hungry, she'd fuck anything. She had about six dresses, all identical. She was eccentric, with shoulder-length hair and always looked a bit scruffy. She wanted me to marry her because she needed a British passport. Ian said, 'You're mad. If anything happens to her, you'll be landed with all her liabilities and debts.' One night she lit a cigarette in bed, fell asleep, and that was the end of her.

MISS WHIPLASH: We were all very shocked when she died. Such people weren't always easy to be around but they added hugely to the gaiety of Soho. There was no greater hellraiser than Peter Langan, who would wine and dine me around London's best restaurants, although Langan's propensity to fall asleep could be trying. He was unpredictable, amusing and very generous while demanding nothing in return. I dislike the portraits painted by lazy writers since his death, which depict him as some kind of drunken buffoon.

TWIGGY: One hot summer's evening, Peter came back from the Colony to his restaurant, picked up a chair, went to a rival restaurant and sat in the revolving doors, blocking anyone getting in or out, saying, 'Fuck off – they're closed.' He was a real character. I don't know whether he was pissed or not, but the tragedy was he tried to immolate his wife and ended up immolating himself. He doused her with petrol but she escaped through a window. He was badly burned; it took him six weeks to die.

DAVID EDWARDS: The people who shaped my life are all dead now. Fred Adams ('Aunty Fred'), the Colony's accountant, always told David Marrion that he'd leave him comfortably off in his will. So when Fred dies, everybody keeps asking David how much Fred left him. David says, 'Very comfortable, he's left me very comfortable.' He left David £500, so David went out and bought himself a new sofa – 'He left me very comfortable.'

DARREN COFFIELD: During the 1990s, so many members died that the landscape of the club irrevocably altered. The wakes of notable eccentrics, such as Vivian Stanshall of the Bonzo Dog Doo-Dah Band, were held in the club. But as one generation begins to die out, another 'discovers' Soho. Such was the way with the Colony. Most people my age were going to acid house raves in farmers' fields or clubs like Taboo. It was considered a bit old fogey-ish to go to a drinking club. But Joshua Compston engineered a situation where he was able to expand the club membership with people he thought were going to be of future importance: Tracey Emin, Gavin Turk, Langlands & Bell, etc.

DAMIEN HIRST: I tried to get in when I was a student because of the whole Bacon vibe, but I wasn't able to. The first time was after a private view with some friends and I felt completely at home. I got very close to Ian, bless him. He was great to me, like a grandma, and gave me advice. Bacon was around, but I never spoke to him. I had a lot of conversations with Ian about Bacon, what a sod he could be and what his good points were – he spoke about him as a friend. Ian Board talking about Bacon is better than anything you could ever read about him. I'd sometimes go in with my art dealer, Jay Jopling. Ian would just abuse him – 'You can fuck off! Who do you think you are, you great lanky streak of piss.' Jay could take me to all the posh restaurants I never used to be able to get into, but he couldn't get into the Colony.

SARAH LUCAS: Damien started hanging out there first. I suppose the initial attraction was Francis Bacon. Damien was very keen on Francis Bacon and getting in there. For Damien and Jay Jopling it made a lot of sense, in terms of getting their thing off the ground and selling work.

TOM DEAS: Before he became famous for doing the shark, Damien came up. The club was empty – just Ian, Michael Wojas and myself – when in wanders Damien with a portfolio. Ian said, 'What's that you got there?' Damien said, 'Oh, it's my artwork, would you like to have a look?' So Ian took the portfolio and leafed through it in stony-faced silence. You could see Damien was desperate for a reaction. Here were all his best ideas, which the art world was to fall upon, and there was Ian stony-faced. He shut the portfolio without saying a word, and looked up to the ceiling.

DANIEL FARSON: What do you think of the younger generation?

FRANCIS BACON: Rubbish . . . It's a kind of willed brutality, it doesn't really work.

DANIEL FARSON: You think it's overhyped?

FRANCIS BACON: The prices of paintings have become so ridiculous now. People have become obsessed by the money. They are haunted by it. They are not interested in art at all. Why should they be? Very few people are. They don't know the good from the bad. But they are influenced by the money. I long to see something new and exciting.

DANIEL FARSON: What about Gilbert & George?

FRANCIS BACON: Well, I don't really know about Gilbert & George; do you think they are any good?

DANIEL FARSON: I'm not sure.

FRANCIS BACON: Well, I'm certain! If they were any good, they would be exciting. What can one ask from art? Not any moral values, one asks for the excitement. And I don't find Gilbert & George exciting.

DANIEL FARSON: So what do *you* ask from art? You ask for excitement. What about pleasure? Do you leave some galleries feeling physically better?

FRANCIS BACON: Oh, shut up! You old thing, that's the way you always talk. Excitement is pleasure, isn't it?

DANIEL FARSON: Champagne rots the brain, Francis.

FRANCIS BACON: If you are excited by something, it gives you pleasure, doesn't it? Who cares a fuck about art! My painting has never been successful. They are extremely difficult. It's always been like that. I very occasionally sell something.

DANIEL FARSON: Did you know when you were in Muriel's in the fifties and unknown in the outside world, did you know you were going to become what is called the greatest painter of our time?

FRANCIS BACON: No. I've never heard such rubbish. I had no confidence in anything . . . I never went to an art school. But one day when I was about thirty, I saw an exhibition of Picasso's in Paris and thought I'll try and paint and that's how it started. The thing about life, is that after the age of thirty, there is a sense fundamentally about death. That's not looking towards despair, but a realisation that there is the grave coming up, closer and closer, closer and closer . . .

DARREN COFFIELD: Francis' answer to the prospect of death was more hard work and hedonism. In April 1992, against medical advice, he took a plane to Madrid to see his former lover. He fell ill on the flight and died alone in hospital of a heart attack. It was not so much a death as a disappearance. Just as he'd wanted. He managed to avoid the media circus that engulfs the death of a major figure – there was to be no memorial or place of pilgrimage. He'd told Ian Board: 'When I'm dead, put me in a plastic bag and throw me in the gutter.'

IAN THE HAT: Ian really loved Francis, so when I heard Francis had died, I popped up to the club to check that Ian was all right. Everyone just sat there in silence for about an hour.

TOM DEAS: We all gathered in the Colony, Francis' second home. As a tribute, Channel 4 cancelled its schedule and rebroadcast the famous *South Bank Show* documentary on Francis. There was a strange moment when you could see the triptych of John Edwards on the television screen at the same time as John was sitting under the television looking up at himself. It was dark in the club and the light from the television gave a wonderful seventeenth-century feel to the scene, like a Rembrandt painting.

IAN BOARD: At Francis' wake-cum-party, a new generation became evident. The fucking worms crawled out of their holes, but the extraordinary thing is that the younger generation came into full fucking bloom.

DARREN COFFIELD: Francis' death was a global news event. I was with Joshua Compston in our studio when it was announced in a newsflash on the radio. We shot each other a glance and headed to the Colony. There were thirty or so of us, including John Edwards, who sat by the TV. Every time he appeared on the documentary, Ian squawked 'Edwards', like a deranged parrot. The club appeared on the TV, with Francis at the bar and Ian taunting him. It seemed so bizarre to be sitting at the far end of the room, viewing both the programme and the club from the same angle as the documentary had been shot, with Francis on TV. Afterwards, John came and sat on my right and Joshua on my left. John told Ian he was now the last one left, so we all drank to Ian's health. The club was never the same again after that night.

JIM MOORE: You can't dispense with that human element. John Edwards pretended to be surprised that we were all there – but it was a family event, the Colony 'family'. Yes, there were famous people who walked through the door, but there were many *more* people who were not famous, who were the 'family', rich or poor, it didn't matter.

TWIGGY: The wonderful thing about Soho was when someone died, people just turned up; there was no official wake, it just happened. We treated death as an imposter, since no one had a lifestyle conducive to longevity. I arrived for the second day of Francis' wake. The Colony was absolutely rammed. Ian hoped they wouldn't make a fuss about Francis' funeral since his idea of a church service was to 'dispense with the normal ceremony and do something strange with an altar candle'. I was in gales of laughter.

DAVID EDWARDS: On the day Francis died, a friend rang me: 'David you've got to clear out the studio at Reece Mews, because that's the time people get burgled, when someone dies.' So I sent a van to clear out Francis' studio and bring all the pictures back to my home. I had a bedroom with thirteen Francis Bacon paintings in it. Can you imagine that? Few people knew where the paintings were for security reasons, but an article appeared in the *Sunday Times*, saying I was a gangster who'd nicked Francis Bacon's paintings and had them stored in my house. It was a nightmare scenario – we were sure it was Ian talking to the press. A week later, two vans pulled up outside my antique shop. They looked like villains but were in fact the police: 'We have information you're about to be burgled by some very nasty people who will hurt you.' They wanted to put us under police protection. I said, 'Is it just for me or my brother?' Then John rang me up saying, 'What did you give them my name for? I've got loads of police around here.' Francis gave John a copy of his will, long before he died. Both Jeff and Bruce Bernard thought they were going to get money, and when they found they weren't, we were completely ostracised.

MAID MARION: Ian was very upset that John had inherited all of Francis' wealth: 'You'd have thought Francis would leave *me* money in appreciation of what I introduced him to.' I thought, What rubbish. Francis knew it would set the cat among the pigeons leaving John his estate. The newspaper headline was 'EASTENDER LEFT 100 MILLION POUNDS', then it was sixty million, then it kept going down until it got to eleven million. I said to John, 'Poverty line, dear.'

MAGGIE SHEARER: The very last time I saw John, I ended up in a car park, doing lines of coke in his Bentley with the 'BOY 1' number plates. He was really pissed off – 'I've offered Francis' studio to the Tate but they don't want it.' So he donated it to the Hugh Lane Gallery in Dublin instead.

DAVID EDWARDS: Towards the end, John didn't answer Francis' calls. Francis rang me up a few days before he died as he'd just come out of hospital: 'Francis, are you okay?' – 'Yes, where's John? It's him I'm worried about.'

MAID MARION: Francis did not like John's boyfriend, which meant they saw less of one another. There were lots of silly rumours that Francis had hired a hitman to kill the boyfriend but none of them were true. I popped in the club one afternoon after Francis died to find it empty except for Ian and Graham (Mason) who were having a heated conversation. 'Everyone that ever got involved with Francis was emotionally scarred, died a hideous death or committed suicide,' barked Ian. 'But not John,' Graham gravelled, 'he loved John . . .' – 'You mark *my* words! Francis will get him from beyond the grave . . . he has the touch of *evil*.'

JIM MOORE: Ian thought that Francis' legacy was poisoned and that Francis only gave you something to see you off. Like when he bought John's boyfriend a car. He waited until the boyfriend had had too much to drink before giving him the keys to the car which he then crashed and was very badly hurt. Ian thought that Francis had done that deliberately. Ian said that Francis' money would kill John because 'He's never had to work for it, he doesn't know what to do with it and he won't take advice on how to look after it.'

DARREN COFFIELD: Somehow Ian had kept the club going with the classic characters for so many years. Now that he and Dan Farson were the last few of the original gang still drinking in the club, Ian wrote a new will and began contemplating his own mortality . . .

IAN BOARD: Friendship isn't easy to talk about. I wouldn't say I had any real friends now. The only true friends I ever had were Muriel Belcher and Francis Bacon – they're both dead now. Daniel Farson has never been a friend of mine in the ordinary use of the word, but he has been important to me in many other ways.

DANIEL FARSON: We have always had a warm relationship punctuated by frequent arguments and personal attacks . . . But as Francis Bacon once said, 'If you can't be rude to your friends, who can you be rude to?'

IAN BOARD: It's just like trench warfare in here when we don't get on, and other members often get caught in the crossfire. We know exactly what we're doing, and, more often than not, if someone is misguided enough to intervene, we may round on them. Then they really will have something to tell their grandchildren.

All the viciousness is soon forgotten though, and we can forgive each other anything over a drink – we're like the Ugly Sisters.

DANIEL FARSON: I've dedicated my book, *Soho in the Fifties*, to Ian and the Colony, because they've remained a constant and secure feature throughout my life, just like the Himalayas . . . Those like myself, who have known Ian for many years, are aware that the cruel posturing conceals a character with genuine compassion, affection and sympathy for those about whom he cares. He is not quite the shit he looks.

MICHAEL WOJAS: The private Ian was very different from the public Ian – he was very sensitive and kind to many people. But that side of him does not get told.

JOHN BAKER: The Colony's resident doctor, Neil Perrett, was one of the worst doctors in the world – albeit a lovely bloke. He was a great fan of the joke that an alcoholic was someone who drinks more than their doctor and he'd never met one. Members afflicted with VD would approach him to carry out impromptu medical consultations in the club's toilet. John Deakin and Dan Farson were regular patients.

JIM MOORE: I took Ian to see Neil in April 1994, two months before he died. He'd been complaining about a fluttering sensation in his chest. At the end of the appointment, he came out and insisted we all go to the pub with Neil. I think it was then that he was told he didn't have long to live.

MICHAEL WOJAS: Ian took the attitude that he'd never take a day off work, even if he had to crawl in. It took me two months to persuade him to have a week off. When I went around to see him, he was very weak, but refused to get an ambulance as he was worried what the neighbours might think. So I took him in a black cab. At the hospital he was diagnosed with lung cancer. Ian had made me his next of kin and refused to have any cancer treatment. I visited him every morning, then Ian would look at his watch and say, 'It's two-thirty, go and open the club, Michael.'

JIM MOORE: The hospital facilities were basic, so the club members brought Ian food and medical supplies. He had a continuous flow of visitors. It was the day of Gay Pride when I visited him. Ian was lying stretched out, seemingly unconscious, and a small lady was sitting beside him. She whispered to me in very hushed tones, 'I've been here for a couple of hours and he's not moved much in that time. I've brought some smoked salmon and a newspaper for him. I'm going now . . .' So I sat down and read the newspaper. After two minutes, one of Ian's eyes pops open – 'Has she gone, dear?' – 'Yes.' – 'Thank fuck for that! Throw that fucking muck in the bin and don't let her come back.' We had a little chat and he said, 'Off you go now to your poofs' rally.'

RAY NATKIEL: The lady in the next bed had very few visitors, so whenever Ian was sent flowers, he told the nurse, 'Give them to that cunt in the next bed. She'll love them.' And of course she loved it, sitting in a bed completely festooned like a florist's shop.

DAVID EDWARDS: It was awful because it was an open ward and in the next bed was a woman, dying. Her husband was holding her hand under the bedsheet. Ian turned to me and said, 'You see what I have to put up with here? He's fingering his wife under the bedsheets.' – 'No, he's not Ian.' The lack of privacy where everyone was dying was shocking, so to change the conversation, I said, 'Ian would you like a drink?' So David Marrion goes off and comes back with a big bottle of vodka and some mixers. David asks, 'Who's paying for this?' Ian pulls the oxygen mask off his face and says, 'Edwards can pay, he's fucking rich.' I replied, 'Ian, darling, where you're going, you won't need any money, you pay for it.' That made him laugh and he paid for it – it was the last drink he ever bought.

BLACK SHEEP: On the Sunday I arrived at Ian's bedside at about eight a.m., he was on the bedcovers, asleep, legs bare since it was turning into a hot day. I thought he was sleeping off the alcohol from the previous evening. Eventually Stephen Pickles came into the ward and we both sat on either side of Ian.

STEPHEN PICKLES: Ian's breathing sounded its effortful rhythmic rasp as I sat beside the bed. His nose, always a red-veined ornament of prodigious proportions, seemed to have grown larger, like a huge pitted strawberry on the verge of exploding. He was sweating profusely, so I took a flannel from a nearby dish, and after moistening it with tap water, gently mopped his shining brow, which was burningly hot, so it seemed. I did this for a while, and all was quiet and calm, when suddenly he thrust his head and shoulders forward, opened his bright glaring eyes and snarled 'fuck off' at some spectral presence at the foot of the bed, two words so frequently uttered from his perch at the Colony Room door. Then he sank back into a limp swoon, and everything was as quiet as before. I gently continued to dab his forehead now and then when, quite unexpectedly, he once again opened his piercing eyes, which gleamed like glass beads, and poked out his tongue with rude defiance, keeping it there for a brief pointed moment, then fell into dozing stillness. This extraordinary act reminded me of the camp strolling player in the film *Death in Venice*, who sticks out his tongue at von Aschenbach with such triumphant contempt.

MICHAEL WOJAS: The day before, on the Saturday, Ian wanted all the visitors to have a drink around his bed to celebrate Muriel's birthday. I'd told him her birthday wasn't until the next day, but he'd told me to shut up. The next morning, I got a phone call to say get down the hospital quickly as he was dying. It was as if he had decided to die on Muriel's birthday. It was very strange – when Ian died and the blood drained from him, his famous nose shrank back to normal. I took the vodka bottle from his bedside cabinet and made the sign of the cross over him with the contents. Ian's funeral was at Golders Green. There weren't many people there and someone remarked that they'd never seen all of them in broad daylight before. Allan Hall gave the eulogy.

ALLAN HALL: What is one to say, knowing that kind words at a funeral were an offence to Ian – hypocritical bollocks, as he would say. His sentiment was that if it wasn't worth saying in the subject's lifetime, it shouldn't be said at all . . . it was not his habit to speak behind anybody's back. If Ian had anything to say about you, he wanted you there so that he could derive his full demonic pleasure from it. Nor will it be seen as flattery if I remark on Ian's uncommon command of abusive language. No one I have ever known was able to sustain invective for so long, employing such an economy of vocabulary. His facility for constructing a whole day's conversation using no more than, say, twenty words, all offensive, was an impressive achievement.

Certain men of imposing stature have seemed destined for immortality. Ian was not amongst them – and yet the memory of him is ineradicable. I have said we laughed and laughed with him – and are we not going to continue to retell those scandalous stories and laugh again?

RAY NATKIEL: At the end of the eulogy, Allan declared, 'You are now publicly friends of Ian Board.' As the coffin was about to go, Michael Wojas put a glass of vodka on it. 'Won't that explode?' I asked. 'I shouldn't worry about that, there's a whole bottle in the coffin.' As the coffin slid in, I could swear a puff of smoke came out of it.

BLACK SHEEP: Some days later, a memorial service was held for Ian at 'The Actors' Church', St Paul's in Covent Garden. Every living member of the Colony Room Club was for the first time gathered in one place, albeit in a church. But not one photograph of the assembled members was taken as a historical record.

MICHAEL WOJAS: The church was jam-packed, standing-room only. People said, 'How did you manage to pack out that church for a Soho drunk?' I followed the formula of Muriel's memorial service – one hymn, 'Jerusalem'; Mike McKenzie played 'Send in the Clowns' on the piano and Lisa Stansfield sang it.

TWIGGY: I was sitting next to Eddi reading the order of service for Ian's memorial. It said that Peter F•••••• was going to give the eulogy. I thought who is that? I have never heard of that name before in my life. Then when he stood up, to my surprise it was the man I had drank with all those years, known by all and sundry simply as 'Foreskin'.

FORESKIN: There are many wonderful memories of Ian. We would have various escapades drinking around town. One particular Sunday, I was staying with Ian and we went to his local pub, where we met two blokes who worked at the Palace Theatre. We were having a conversation about what on earth one does on a Sunday, when one of these blokes said, 'There's a place on Tottenham Court Road, we could go up there for a drink.' When we got to this place, everything in it was red – front door, stairs, ceiling, carpet, furniture, all red, and in the corner was a little red bar. There were four people in there, two males and two very attractive females. I remember thinking, this could be interesting. At about midnight, I said to Ian, 'We've got to go, they've run out of vodka.' And Ian went ballistic at the man behind the bar. 'But I'm having a good time! How dare you! What sort of fucking place do you call this?' I managed to get Ian halfway down the stairs before he said, 'Hang on a minute,' and ran back up for another go, 'What sort of place do you call this? Come to *my* place, the Colony Room Club, 41a Dean Street, and see how to run a fucking club properly, *YOU CUNT!*' The next morning, we went back to the same pub and those two blokes were there again. I said, 'That was an interesting place you took us to last night. What kind of club was that?' – 'That's not a club,' they said, 'it's their home – I only met them on Friday and they said you must come over for a drink sometime.'

DARREN COFFIELD: When the memorial service drew to an end, the great and the not-so-good shuffled out of the church, where there was a plate collection made for a worthy cause. Outside the church in the accusing daylight, the club members mingled in decreasing circles, dozens of them looking strangely pale in the sunlight. It felt unsettling to see so many familiar faces in the large expanse outside the church, as opposed to being squeezed inside the tiny green club. It added an unexpected agoraphobic twinge to the occasion.

MICHAEL WOJAS: Ian wanted me to chuck his ashes out over Dean Street. So I thought if I tipped them through the club's air extractor, they'd be blown out all over the diners eating in the restaurant below, since Ian loathed the place. So I phoned the club's solicitor and asked if there were any laws about scattering human remains on a public highway. He said I could only do it if I didn't tell anyone and Ian would have hated that.

IAN THE HAT: Ian did ask me if I'd consider working with Michael once he'd gone. So when he passed away, I was given the opportunity to go in and become Michael's barman, with him on the perch. I did think long and hard about it. It was potentially a life-changing experience and not necessarily for the better. I turned it down for the sake of my health.

FRANCES SLOWEY: Daniel Farson came up from Devon to lend his support to Mike and have a few drinks. Then we saw him again a few days later, half dressed with a black eye – he'd lost his tie, could hardly stand up, and his wallet had been stolen. Poor Dan, typical Dan. Mike came in for a lot of abuse from the 'old guard' saying things like, 'Oh, it'll never be the same again.' They were really bitching at him. There were some nasty, nasty people coming in and gloating in a ghoulish manner. Mike was in a bad way, and the club wouldn't have functioned without me. I was his backup.

JIM MOORE: Michael showed me Ian's will. Michael Wojas was one beneficiary and the other was Michael Clark, who'd been very helpful to Ian after Muriel's death. Ian was passionate about Michael's art and thought he could be the next Freud. But a furious argument occurred one night between them. Ian took down his portrait by Michael Clark from the club wall, tore it up and even banned his name from being mentioned. Michael Wojas and I had spoken about whether to ask Michael and Sue Clark to come to the hospital to see Ian. Finally Ian relented and said, 'Do what you want,' and they visited Ian in hospital.

FRANCES SLOWEY: Michael and Sue Clark were at the bedside with myself and Mike when Ian died. They were still close. In a sense, Ian got what he wanted – Michael Clark got the insurance money and Mike got the club. I have no doubt in my mind that Ian always intended Mike to run the club, that was a given – Muriel left the club to her barman Ian, who in turn was going to leave it to his barman Mike Wojas. Maybe he intended Michael Clark should get all his insurance money but Mike was livid about it. He was convinced that half the money was for the club.

JIM MOORE: There was pressure put on Michael Clark to share the bequest with Michael Wojas but, understandably, he refused and became persona non grata. Michael Clark came up to the club, pulled down his portraits of Muriel and Francis from the club walls, never to return.

RAY NATKIEL: I knew Michael Wojas needed our support, but some of the other members were ambivalent. After his dispute with Michael Clark over Ian's insurance, we arrived at the club to find Michael Wojas blind drunk and distressed – 'Clear out the club, everybody out!' – and we said, 'We can't leave you like this.' So we decided to lock up the club, put him in a taxi and look after the takings until the next day. We found a cab driver who knew him, because no one else would take him in that state. Ian's death hit Michael Wojas a lot harder than he showed – he'd looked after Ian for over a decade; he must have even wiped his arse at some point.

PAM HARDYMENT: Michael knew more than he ever said about anything. The club was run on a shoestring – they didn't make much money. When Ian died his entire life savings were £6,000, which is a pittance when you think of all the money that went over the bar. I worked behind the bar for a year, long after Ian died. If someone offered me a drink, I'd keep it as a tip. I had to drop it into my handbag – if it went into the till, I'd never get it out.

MICHAEL WOJAS: It's the only club of its kind left in Soho with the old afternoon drinking licence. All the other clubs around here are open until at least one a.m., but Ian always said, 'You've had the best out of them by eleven p.m. They're pissed and they're broke. Let someone else cope with them.' I'm the proprietor, bar manager, lavatory attendant, psychiatric counsellor, odd-job man and accountant – there certainly isn't anything I haven't done.

DARREN COFFIELD: Michael did a marvellous job in getting the club up and running and thriving again after Ian had almost run it into the ground. The club had been in financial difficulties for years and Ian had wanted to sell the Michael Andrews mural to raise cash, but Michael Wojas talked him out of it. Going home one night, a man came running across the road, pulling out a Stanley knife – 'Give me your wallet!' – and slashed Michael's face, which left him with a very long scar down the left-hand side. He claimed criminal injury compensation for the attack and received £10,000, some of which he gave over to the club to pay off Carmel and keep it going.

DAMIEN HIRST: I remember saying everything's going to be okay to Michael after Ian died, but I couldn't see any way of bringing the club into the present . . . It was like a mortuary in there.

JIM MOORE: Without Ian the club felt empty and much of the humour had gone. Ian died of lung cancer and Mumsie of the liver. Everybody thought it would have been the other way round, as Mumsie always had a fag in her mouth. Ian used to say, 'You can hear her getting off the train at Euston with all that wheezing and coughing.' When Mumsie went into hospital, she wrote in pink pen on a yellow Post-it note: 'GREAT PAIN NEED HELP', and never spoke again. The staff started the morphine treatment. Life support was kept on until her sister could get there, to be switched off at precisely nine p.m. on Saturday evening.

BLACK SHEEP: That night, a few of us assembled in the club in order that we might drink to Mumsie. A few minutes to nine, we all stood up and embraced each other. Then the phone rang. The news came through from Mumsie's very good friend, Jim Moore.

IAN THE HAT: Foreskin hired a luxury coach for Mumsie's funeral in Crewe. We met in the Colony at seven a.m. The first thing we did was toast Mumsie. Finally we staggered out and climbed aboard with every alcoholic drink known to man. The driver said there was no drinking or smoking allowed on the coach, which everyone ignored. We'd not even left Soho before the driver crashed the coach. Later we stopped off at an off-licence by a motorway service station, I don't think they'd taken so much money in their life. We cleared the shop of all its booze and bought absolutely nothing to eat.

JIM MOORE: Because Mumsie always had sweets in her hand-bag, the coffin lid was decorated with sherbet lemons, jelly babies and a large heart of dolly mixtures. Mumsie's daughter found a female priest for the funeral and explained that her mother was an eccentric funky lady, so the priest arrived at the funeral in a short skirt and snakeskin boots, unbelievable in 1996.

TWIGGY: Crematoriums and funeral parlours can be awful, but this place was full and not just Colony people – all the consti-tuents, if you like, of Mumsie were there, actors, musicians, a huge mix. Ray Natkiel stepped forward with a bottle of vodka which he poured over the coffin as it was lowered into the grave. It was priceless.

BLACK SHEEP: The return home was like an expedition on a scale equal to trying to reach the North Pole . . . At a motorway service station near Birmingham, I distinctly remember people looking at us assembled in the foyer of the service station, laughing, crying, singing, smoking and generally acting beyond redemption . . . a wagonload of lunatics on their way to the asylum.

TOM DEAS: The lifestyle of the members was taking its toll. Jeffrey Bernard stopped coming to the club when he lost his foot due to diabetes and couldn't get up the stairs. He had achieved fame for being 'unwell' and had seen off many doctors, who warned that his lifestyle would kill him, some of whom went to their graves long before Jeffrey.

JEFFREY BERNARD: I don't like doctors and I think they don't like me because I tend to make them feel redundant. I don't like the way they stand at the foot of my bed in white coats and play God. Mind you, I have been married to women who stand at the foot of the bed, wearing nightdresses, who think they're gods as well.

GERALDINE NORMAN: My husband Frank was devoted to Jeff and I was pretty devoted too. Jeff came to Frank's funeral with me; he was jolly nice to me in those days – I was very conscious that Jeff was the closest friend he'd had. I was living here and lonely, so I invited Jeff to have a bed-sitting room in Frank's old office. I thought, like everybody else, that Jeff was dying, and I hadn't anything to do with my life – it was all ashes – so why didn't I devote myself to seeing that Jeff had a comfortable death? Which many women have thought . . . and then the bugger went on living. I imagined that I'd be making Jeff exquisite little meals and taking them to the bedside of this poor pathetic guy. In fact he was a Cordon Bleu chef, so we had some jolly dinner parties. One of his best friends, Eva Johansen, stayed over once and claimed to have met Frank's ghost, which I was extremely jealous of.

I was always rather shy of Jeff. We got on very well for the first few years, but we never really 'played' together. I wasn't at the stage of life when I wanted to go on benders, so we lived rather separate lives here. I think he would be absolute hell to live with if you were in love with him. I put up with it for so long because I really did come out of Frank dying with the feeling that there was absolutely nothing left that I wanted out of life, a complete crash. So I really didn't mind if Jeff set light to the sofa, or was passed out on the kitchen floor when I came in, in the middle of oceans of washing-up. The danger with Jeff was that he often passed out with a lit cigarette – once he burned my sitting room down. The reason that I finally asked Jeff to leave was not because of his terrifying domestic habits, but I couldn't bear living with his intense unhappiness – it's difficult enough dealing with one's own life. He hated himself, he was frightened of dying. He had to drink to get himself out of that depression. His high point was about eleven a.m. in the morning – whenever he'd had a second double vodka – through to about three p.m., when he was charming, wonderful company, very funny, then he went down into the slough of despond again.

Then one day, whilst Jeff was in Tenerife, I opened his bank statement by mistake and discovered that he had £13,500 in his current account. That made it easier to harden my heart. If he wanted, he could afford a suite at the Ritz. I was going away and he'd said he wouldn't move till I came back. I returned to find the sink completely piled with washing-up, slices of bread and marmalade on the floor, and he'd gone. Along with the vodka and fresh oranges. I laughed and then had this idea that I'd write about it for the *Spectator*.

DARREN COFFIELD: Jeff was incensed when Geraldine submitted her article. He stopped its publication by protesting that it breached his financial privacy. The news that Jeff was financially well off electrified Soho – 'All this time I've been conned,' said one friend, off whom Jeff regularly cadged money. Jeff showed Geraldine's article to everyone, with the amount of money in his account edited out.

JEFFREY BERNARD: Yes, I am still vain, you can't get rid of that. If I were standing in front of a firing squad, I'd say, 'Hang on, let me brush my hair first,' in case there was a photographer standing next to the rifles . . . I've always been drawn to the things I was told not to do. Drink, sex. God! How I have loved sex and racing. They're against the rules and that's why I like them. I never liked anything that was good for me, like All-Bran and fresh air. I like the things that kill me. I don't mind dying, I just don't like the idea of being dead – I'm gregarious.

PHILIPPA CLARE: Jeff getting ill and having to go to hospital became a running joke. In the pub outside the Middlesex Hospital, we overheard this doctor saying, 'I have a patient who's a miracle man . . . A miracle man! He has pancreatitis, diabetes, he's an alcoholic and yet he's getting better.' And we said, 'Yep, that's Jeff!' When Jeff had his leg taken off, Peter O'Toole brought him a Walkman, because he knew he loved Mozart. Jeff took one look at the gift and said, 'Why are you buying me a fucking *Walk-man*? I've only got one leg!'

NORMAN BALON: In the end, he just got worn down by it all. Jeff phoned the hospital to ask what would happen if he didn't go in for his daily dialysis. They said he'd die. So he stopped going – it was suicide. People gathered around his bed at home the evening he died, and had a party round the bed.

PHILIPPA CLARE: I said to him, 'Come on, pull yourself together and I'll take you to the Chelsea Arts Club for lunch tomorrow.' But he said, 'I've had it. It's enough now.' And he lay there on my chest and died. Jeff's funeral was hilarious. We were at the crematorium and Peter O'Toole suddenly disappeared and came back – 'Come on, follow me, this is too good!' And he took me round the back, to where the last person had just gone through, a turf accountant, and Peter showed me this great horse he'd found made entirely of flowers.

MARSH DUNBAR: Jeff's funeral was packed by ex-wives, lovers and old friends. Most of us had to introduce ourselves. My dear, they lined the walls and sat on the aisle of the chapel. God, apart from Mozart and Beethoven, was not mentioned. Jeff's last laugh was when we came out of the place – *it pissed down!* – all the cars were at least two minutes' walk away . . . let alone the only pub. But being the gentle soul he was, it only lasted five minutes.

PHILIPPA CLARE: After the funeral, with Jeff's ashes over my shoulder, we took him one last time around Soho: the French, the Coach & Horses and the Colony. Peter O'Toole thought it was fantastic, as he'd never had so many free drinks in his entire life.

DARREN COFFIELD: Jeffrey had stopped being unwell on 4 September 1997, aged sixty-five. The man who was London's most disreputable wit, had finally succumbed to one of the many illnesses that had plagued his life. Jeffrey now joined those Soho legends – Brendan Behan, Frank Norman, Dylan Thomas and Francis Bacon – whom people boasted they'd known far better than they actually had. No one was more surprised by this than Dan Farson who, after Jeff, was the last man standing.

BLACK SHEEP: Dan stormed into the Colony and had obviously been drinking heavily. At length, he sat down on the banquette, above which was the television. Michael Wojas told Dan to shut up and then turned on the television. A programme on Channel 4 about art commenced. The presenter was a well-groomed person, speaking in a clear, educated voice about Gilbert & George. We could not believe that this person, talking with such confidence and undoubted authority, was the same red-faced person sitting on the bench below, his shirt hanging out and vomit on his jacket, and in the throes of hiccups, drink spilling out of his glass.

FRED INGRAMS: The trouble with Dan was he always got everything wrong because he got so pissed. Jeff Koons was in town, having an exhibition at Anthony d'Offay, so Dan arranges to meet him for a newspaper interview at the Colony. It was such a weird thing to have Koons in the tiny club. At the time, he was married to an Italian porn star (Cicciolina), and came in saying, 'I have a wife – she doesn't speak English and I don't speak Italian.' He then produced an obscenely fat roll of banknotes and announced, 'Anthony has given me some money for entertaining whilst I am in London.' At which point every single person in the club emptied their glass, and the day descended into a monumental session of drinking Jeff Koons' money. In the midst of all this, Dan was trying to interview him for his newspaper article. The next morning I got a call from Dan saying, 'Can you remember anything Jeff Koons said?' I said, 'No, I don't remember anything.' Dan winced, 'I don't remember anything either!' He wrote a whole newspaper article on Jeff Koons, which he'd completely made up.

JIM MOORE: A friend was in a play called *The Homosexual* with Lucian Freud's muse, Leigh Bowery. Dan really wanted to meet Leigh and said, 'I'll be back and we'll go in a little while together.' I was quite relieved he'd gone because he was really drunk. Then when he came back up the stairs, I disappeared into the club toilet for a minute and then shot out of the door and was off. I arrived just as the play started, a small intimate event. About ten minutes into the performance, I could hear this really drunken voice outside, booming, 'Where is he? Where is he? Jim Moore! He's in here somewhere, and he's got my *fucking* ticket . . . *There he is* . . . I can see him!' Dan came staggering down into the performance space, coughed very loudly and his trousers fell down to his knees. It was hilarious. The actors built it into the act, with Leigh standing there, ad-libbing with these dildos in his hands.

DANIEL FARSON: I met Damien Hirst at the 1992 Turner Prize dinner in the Tate Gallery. After chatting amiably, a cloud crossed his ragamuffin face and he asked who I was. He recoiled: 'Not that nasty man who writes those horrible things about me?' As I had just described him as a taxidermist trying to emulate a pop star, this was unanswerable . . . But he hurried away and cried when he lost the prize.

DAMIEN HIRST: I was really shocked when I told my mum that I'd met Dan Farson because she said, 'Not thee Dan Farson!' I was like, 'What do you mean "Not *thee* Dan Farson?"' She said, '*Ohhh God*, he had this big TV programme in the 1960s, he was a household name.' I said, 'Oooh, get off! What, *that bloke*? Babbling like a complete alcoholic?' I thought, it must be a different Dan Farson.

BRUNTON: The only time I remember Dan being clear and lucid about anything, was when he was due to interview Damien Hirst but I'd never heard of him. I overheard the interview – it was peculiar – and Dan was rattled by this new talent. It lasted for over two hours and then Damien left. Immediately Dan came over to me and said, 'Did you understand one fucking word of that? I didn't. What was he talking about?'

DAMIEN HIRST: I felt sorry for Dan after Bacon's death. Dan must have been really shocked that he was the last one left, because he was like a little kid who idolised all these other people.

DARREN COFFIELD: Dan knew that he could make a lot of money from writing a biography on Francis. Frank Norman had tried, then Bruce Bernard. *About Francis Bacon* was intended to be a scrapbook – an illustrated book with some personal comments by Bruce himself. Francis was initially enthusiastic about the project until he read some of Bruce's comments about his pictures, which led to him insisting on the removal of any mention of his former lover Eric Hall or any artwork by him before 1944. Bruce was upset and said that Francis would deny anything that did not suit his public image – 'Never heard of him. Never met him. What he says is lies.' Like an Orwellian act of doublethink, Francis wanted to erase, dominate and control his past. Bruce complained that his 'marvellous good humour of past decades had greatly diminished, and he was defiantly defensive about his work . . . He had also alienated his few good painter friends . . .'

JAMES BIRCH: Francis demanded that his portrait of John Edwards be put on the front cover. Bruce disagreed because he disliked John. So Francis contacted his lawyers and had the book stopped. Even now, long after Francis' death, it cannot be published because of the legal injunction placed on it. Bruce was being pig-headed. Francis saw John as a surrogate son; he was always trying to promote John. He would tell people what a great photographer John was and we'd all go 'Wot!?' Then Dan tried to write Francis' biography, but Francis paid him £10,000 not to do it. However, Dan was quite sly, and kept gathering information on Francis in the meantime. That's how he managed to publish the biography so quickly after Francis' death. In *The Gilded Gutter Life of Francis Bacon*, Dan wrote about Francis' life as opposed to his artwork, that's what made it so fascinating.

DARREN COFFIELD: Dan's legacy is all his wonderful photographs and writings about Soho and its inhabitants. He gave his last public performance opening the Soho Village Fete in the summer of 1997.

DANIEL FARSON: I have loved Soho passionately since I drifted into the French House at the age of twenty-two. Now at the age of seventy, I certainly stagger in, but if not, certainly stagger out. In the post-war gloom of Britain – God, it was gloomy – Soho was a light, sometimes a red light. Here there were no rules, no conventions of sexuality, class, money or age that divided the rest of Britain. To be young and different in the regions of Britain was hell. But in Soho it was heaven because you could be that, of all things, yourself. Francis Bacon told me he went to the Colony Room to lose his inhibitions. Which was rather odd as he was the least inhibited man I have ever known.

It has always been the genius of Soho to swing with the punches, to absorb and welcome the outsider, while retaining its unique personality. People today complain that Soho is not what it was, 'but is, never was' as Ian Board used to say. People complain that the characters have gone. Well, of course they have, many of them are dead. Francis Bacon has been succeeded by Damien Hirst, and I like to think of Muriel and Ian knocking it back in that great afternoon club in the sky with Muriel telling St Peter, 'Come on girl, hurry up with the drinks.' Soho is still gloriously eccentric. Do you know how Soho got its name? From the hunting cry of the Duke of Monmouth as he called his hounds to pursue hares across the fields, which are now Soho Square. The hunt is still on . . . So join me in echoing the 'tally-ho' cry of Soho –

So-ho,
So-ho!
So-HO!

JOHN BEASLEY: The last time Dan and I happened upon each other, the Colony was unusually quiet, and we sat more or less alone at the bar for many hours. That night he was in a gentle and reflective mood, quite probably because he knew his end was nigh and showed me lumps on his neck to prove it.

Dan told me he hated his drunken self. One incident particularly played on his mind. He'd spent an evening in a hotel bar in Switzerland with a newly married couple. They'd had such a good time, swapping jokes and anecdotes right up until the booze seriously hit Dan's brain. Then he became a monster – aggressive, insulting and unbearable. The sorrow in his eyes and voice as he told that story was tragic. The next morning, he'd woken up cringing in horror at the gratuitous cruelty he'd inflicted on his innocent companions. And yet, without missing a beat, his whole tone changed as he began to reflect on the wider role of alcohol in his life. Without it, he suggested, he'd never have reached his full potential since, for all the harm it had done him, booze had given him opportunities he'd never otherwise have exploited.

I liked Dan a lot that evening, he was sweet and vulnerable. He recalled how his father Negley had been a foreign correspondent in Berlin during the 1936 Olympic Games. Negley took Dan to an event where the two of them stood in a receiving line for Hitler. The Führer paused and patted the nine-year-old Dan on the top of his little blond head, complimenting his father on producing such a fine example of the Aryan race. Hitler, said Dan, had been wrong about everything, including that. I know everyone in the world is, according to the theory of six degrees of separation, close to everyone else. But one away from Hitler? That, like Dan, is unforgettable.

LESLEY LEWIS: Daniel Farson died on 27 November 1997. His funeral was held in his home village of Appledore in Devon. I arranged his memorial with Michael Wojas at St Paul's, Covent Garden. Lisa Stansfield sang 'Stardust', accompanied by Kenny Clayton on the piano. George Melly and Timothy Spall gave the addresses. George was just about to deliver his eulogy when a band outside in the piazza began playing 'What Shall We Do with the Drunken Sailor'. The timing was uncanny – Dan was the ultimate drunken sailor.

GEORGE MELLY: Well, the last time I was in this building, it was Ian Board's goodbye. Dan was in the congregation, looking rather thin. Dan was a very complicated figure; you see there were two of him – there was Dr Dan Jekyll most of the day, and then there was Mr Dan Hyde who came about seven o'clock every evening. When he wrote his autobiography, he said he regretted every night he turned into this sort of werewolf because 'I've lost many friends.' When I reviewed the book, I said, He hasn't lost me and never will, simply because I avoid him in the evening.

But Dan was also amazingly disciplined. He was up early to write – how he did it I do not know . . . His best books will live because they are remarkable. *Soho in the Fifties* is a wonderful evocation of that dodgy time. He also wrote the best book to date on Francis Bacon, *The Gilded Gutter Life*. It's not the most profound book, but it was certainly the Francis Bacon we knew in the Colony Room Club rather than that figure struggling with emotion and paint in his disgusting studio in Kensington.

TIMOTHY SPALL: I always had this romance about Soho. Dan was the best person I could have met because he really was 'it'. He managed to explain the inexplicable romantic notion you get for the place. I loved the drama of Soho and Dan, and the two affections grew together. I was really proud that this seminal character was a mate of mine. One night he took me to a pub called the City of Quebec. He said, 'This is where I pick up people.' I thought this is a real hellraiser . . . A couple of days later, I got a letter, apologising. He was worried about jeopardising our friendship which was preposterous as I'd had a fantastic evening. He said he'd left a present for me behind the bar at the French to say sorry. He'd left me this – a silver-topped walking cane inscribed: 'Presented to Bram Stoker Esquire by the crew of USS *Chicago*'. Which is a gift of such beauty. Not only was this, the author of *Dracula*, Bram Stoker's cane, but this ship is where the actor Henry Irving and he would go to a drinking club. I said, 'I can't accept this Dan, it's too generous.' He said, 'Have it, I'd only sell it, you keep it.' That was such a touching present. If there was a fire in my house, the only thing I'd go back for, apart from my wife and children, would be that cane.

9

Fings Ain't Wot They Used T'Be

DARREN COFFIELD: By the time of Daniel Farson's death in 1997, the club came to epitomise a bygone era. The once unknown Francis Bacon, who had acted as 'hostess' for Muriel in 1948, was now, along with the equally unheard-of Colony Room Club, the subject of a feature film, *Love is the Devil*. Derek Jacobi played Francis Bacon; Tilda Swinton, Muriel Belcher; and Daniel Craig (the future James Bond), Francis' lover George Dyer. Daniel Farson worked as an advisor on the film – it was to be his last project.

JOHN MAYBURY: My general subject matter is dysfunctional artists, fucked-up people who have great depth creatively, and use alcohol as a bridge to get to that creativity. What's strange about all the people I've encountered along the way, is that there is a kind of ladder – a family tree – that connects all of us, which has been passed down through generations. I am a Londoner, all my life I've been hanging around London. I've met people of all ages and there's a strange currency – which is passing the baton, moving information on, and it's up to you to step up and take the baton from those people, and share the information again.

HAMISH MCALPINE: John Maybury's reappearance at the club in the nineties coincided with that of the YBAs. There was this influx of bright new innovative artists, and being very witty and funny, John fell into the spirit of the Colony.

JOHN MAYBURY: As a young man I thought I had seen it all, when the artist Michael Wishart dragged me up the grimy staircase on Dean Street. Pushing open a door, which released clouds of billowing smoke, I found myself bathed in the deeply unflattering absinthe-green glow of the Colony Room. As an art student in my first year of studies, I immediately recognised the poisonous, waxy face of one of my great heroes. It wasn't William Burroughs, or a coke-addled David Bowie, but the greatest living painter, Francis Bacon. Beady-eyed, paralytically drunk, but supremely alert, Bacon eyed me up before I was melodramatically distracted by the hostess of the Colony Room, the sphinx-like Muriel Belcher. Unbeknown to me, Miss B. was in the final stages of a ravaging tsunami of cancer, yet her London 'gutter poise' lent her the hauteur of a diamond expert appraising a dodgy fake. Cut to 1990-something, and the BBC asked me to make a movie about Francis Bacon. I immediately refused. But then I read *The Gilded Gutter Life of Francis Bacon*. Far more interesting and more true than the serious memoirs by Michael Peppiatt or David Sylvester, it actually deals with the visceral qualities of who Francis Bacon was . . . Daniel Farson's memoir does celebrate a very honest story about the gutter life. Quoting the super cliché of Oscar Wilde, there's something very magical and beautiful about

London – the best people lie in the gutter and do look up at the stars. I remembered my student days and my adoration of the sequence of paintings Francis had produced of George Dyer. Having lost my lover to a death invoked by an excess of pharmaceuticals – I felt that, somewhere between my own experiences and the reality of Bacon's life, a story was there to be told.

MICHAEL WOJAS: John spent three years interviewing Francis' friends, fighting for a script that made the art establishment feel sick. Dan said that Francis didn't want his life story told until he was dead, although he did once send him a joke telegram suggesting several titles. One of these was 'Gilded Gutter Life'. So this became the title of Dan's biography, to which the BBC had bought the rights in 1995.

JOHN MAYBURY: I hung out with Dan, generally getting very, very drunk. In the summer of '96, I was in the club almost every other day, listening to these people's amazing stories. A thousand different Francis Bacons emerged, and of course everybody thought they were the expert.

DARREN COFFIELD: John's decision, instigated by the BBC, to rely so heavily on what Dan had told him and put the love affair with Dyer at the centre of the film, annoyed those who saw themselves as the gatekeepers of Francis' flame. Michael Peppiatt described it as 'a lurid, almost tabloid, exploitation of Francis Bacon and his work'. The Arts Council said the script was 'prurient'. 'There is a lot more to us than our love lives, isn't there?' said Lord Gowrie, chairman of the Arts Council, named in the press as the man behind the effort to stop its lottery funding. Sex, drugs, suicide, homosexuality and sadomasochism – it would be impossible to make any kind of film of Bacon's life without these. John Maybury felt his opponents wanted to sanitise Francis – 'Bacon of all people would have hated censorship.' The Arts Council then tried to dilute the film by demanding that the words 'cunt' and 'cunty' be removed from the script in order to be eligible for funding. And then to make matters worse, the film's main star pulled out of the project.

JOHN MAYBURY: Malcolm McDowell was my first choice because I love [Lindsay Anderson's] *If . . .* and I love *A Clockwork Orange*. When I was trying to think who could play Bacon, what excited me was the idea that if you fused the anarchist student [from *If . . .*] with [*Clockwork's*] Alex the 'droog', the grown-up version of Bacon is a sort of 'ultra-violent hoo-ray'.

DARREN COFFIELD: Derek Jacobi was drafted in as a last-minute replacement. His performance had a weird effect on some of the Colony regulars whom John Maybury had recruited as film extras.

JOHN MAYBURY: When Derek walked onto the Colony Room set, Sandy Fawkes burst into tears, rushed up and threw her arms around him, crying, 'Francis, Francis, how can you be here?'

DARREN COFFIELD: Sandy didn't need to dress up for the film. As a former fashion editor, her wardrobe was full of beautiful clothes from the 1970s. She habitually wore a fur hat which some unkind people said resembled a dead cat stuck on her head. On the first day of filming the Colony Room scenes, Tilda Swinton sat and talked with Sandy, to learn more about Muriel and her character.

MICHAEL WOJAS: Because the club is so small, it was impossible to get a camera crew inside, so it was reproduced in every detail as a very convincing film set – even the members couldn't spot the difference. I was happy to work on making the film, but others were less than helpful – John had a huge problem in securing the use of any of Francis' paintings in the film. Marlborough Fine Art, which then controlled the estate for John Edwards, refused to cooperate, so the production designer Alan MacDonald made copies of Francis' paintings without any figures in them. Then in another twist, David Sylvester denied John the use of any of Francis' words, as quoted in his famous book of interviews.

JOHN MAYBURY: I think the BBC made a big mistake at the time that they bought the rights to Daniel Farson's book and set the project in motion. If I'd been in control of that situation, I'd have contacted the Bacon Estate and David Sylvester first, because I think those people should have been on board if at all possible. It was a case of the film and TV world not understanding the art world.

MICHAEL WOJAS: The film is the story of Francis' eight-year love affair with George Dyer, whose destruction is observed by a group of Francis' friends, among them Henrietta Moraes, Muriel Belcher and Isabel Rawsthorne. Dan admired the casting of Tilda Swinton. He said that Muriel was very beautiful when she was young and looked like Hedy Lamarr. Dan's involvement in the film upset several of Francis' friends, one of whom, on hearing Dan had died of cancer, said, 'Oh, good'. Furious at the petty-mindedness of the 'art world intellectuals', John dedicated *Love is the Devil* to Dan – 'The film,' he said, 'is my revenge.'

JOHN MAYBURY: I thought, well, if I'm going to have extras playing painters, writers and artists, why don't I just wheel in some real painters, writers and artists? And I was really lucky because everyone was so gung-ho about it.

TRACEY EMIN: It was actually very difficult being just an extra. When we see the film in twenty years' time, we won't be looking at someone playing the part of a seventies bohemian person, we'll actually see Sarah Lucas in the scene at the French House and say, 'Oh, that's so-and-so' – in a way it's got a double amount of history in it.

LESLEY LEWIS: I thought it was a stroke of genius making the Colony regulars extras in the film. That way they couldn't be mean about it.

MICHAEL WOJAS: Lucian Freud said he 'found nothing in it that,' he recalled, 'in words or actions, any memories of the people whose names are used for the parts'.

DARREN COFFIELD: It may not have met with Freud's approval, but the film was embraced by the Colony. By the time of its release in September 1998, the club was entering its fifth decade. The interior was festooned with golden ornaments and set pieces commissioned from Michael and Eileen Woods, featuring Muriel and Ian floating above the bar as cherubs, flanking a huge illuminated number '50'. That year Michael Wojas also commissioned a film documentary of the club, which involved shining TV lights into crannies where no light had shone for fifty years – zooming in on dying fag butts and pickled noses. A Colony summer garden party was held, where it rained all day and Kathy Dalwood streaked naked for £100.

TOM DEAS: They also filmed the fiftieth anniversary exhibition of Colony Room artists. Michael had invited members who were both professional and amateurs to be in the show, which he co-organised with James Birch. And not without some controversy – as some members took exception to a photograph of Francis Bacon's dead body on a mortuary slab.

LESLEY LEWIS: When Francis died in Spain, people took the piss out of me for sending someone along with flowers – 'Oh, he wouldn't have wanted flowers. He wanted to be stuck in a bin bag,' they said. Some photographs were taken of his corpse – they were a bit morbid I suppose. The next thing I know is that Shakespeare is exhibiting these pictures on the wall. They should never have been let out, they weren't for public consumption. I thought I was the only one who had them as I was given them by the photographer. I wasn't very happy about what happened.

SHAKESPEARE: I was working as picture editor on Sandy Fawkes' book on the French House, and going through the archive, when this mortuary photograph of Francis on the slab fell out. I took down the agency's and photographer's details on the back, bought the copyright and made the artwork.

MICHAEL WOJAS: It was quite an undertaking to put together the fiftieth anniversary exhibition, coping with thirty-four artists and their egos in one show. As the sculptor Hubert Dalwood designed the club ashtray for the twenty-fifth anniversary, I thought it would be nice to commission his daughter Kathy to design one for the fiftieth.

DAMIEN HIRST: The great advantage Michael has got over other people in the art world, is that he gets artists to agree to things when they are drunk in his bar.

MICHAEL WOJAS: Damien was like Francis in his sheer enthusiasm and ebullience. His spot painting is behind the bar – I love it. At the moment it's wrapped in cling film with the caption 'NOT WORTH A FUCKING PENNY'. Other times I put it in bubble wrap. Damien couldn't think of what to put in the fiftieth anniversary exhibition. So we just sat in the Colony all night drinking. Suddenly at six in the morning, Damien had a eureka moment – 'I've got it. Three ducks going up a wall.' It was supposed to be a parody of the flying china ducks you used to see on living-room walls in the 1950s. – 'Okay, but what are you going to call it?' – 'Up, up and away,' he laughed.

DARREN COFFIELD: Tom Deas, a book designer, created a witty invitation card for the show in the shape of a green circular plaque of the type often seen on historic buildings around London. At the opening, Michael emptied Ian Board's ashes from his urn into the life-size bronze bust of Ian by Kate Braine, the idea being that, even in death, he could sit overlooking the bar. The show was widely reported in the national press, putting the Colony to the fore once again.

ORLANDO CAMPBELL: Michael was brilliant at running the club after Ian died. He completely rejuvenated the place and got in all the big names of the nineties. He put on events, which appealed more to the younger generation of artists, and got rid of all the empty champagne bottles, which Ian had strategically placed around the club.

Day in, day out, dealing with cunts all the time and being nice to people, whilst hungover from the day before, takes a lot of energy and stamina. Someone once asked me if I'd be able to do it. I said, 'No way! I'd be dead within a month.' I would often use the rear exit of the club. This involved climbing out of the back window next to the club's payphone, and walking precariously across the rooftops to the first floor of the Groucho Club. If you got the wrong window, you climbed directly into the bar, which looked strange and drew too much attention. If you got the right window, you'd end up in the passageway. Eventually Michael began to get very angry about it, so we had to start using the stairs.

SALLY DUNBAR: Michael had a no-frills approach. When the uninitiated enquired about the wine list, he replied tartly, 'Red and white.' Another victim asked if he might have a slice of lemon with his gin and tonic? – 'We don't serve food here.' A guest once asked for a Bloody Mary, so Michael rummaged around the back of the fridge, where he found an old, mouldy carton of tomato juice. Wiping the mould off the spout, he served the woman who then exclaimed it was the tastiest she'd ever had and promptly ordered another one. Michael loved that story.

LESLEY LEWIS: Then he got that beautiful girl, Claire de Jong, to work behind the bar. But the really foul-mouthed members became too embarrassed by their bad behaviour in front of her. So instead of attracting customers he actually ended up losing business over this beautiful blonde.

JUPITER JOHN: One Christmas I found myself at the bar surrounded by a group of old embittered men, all shouting and snarling at each other. It was pitifully cold. Michael was behind the bar and I thought maybe he doesn't turn up the heating because this lot are roaring flames at each other. One of the men was shouting, 'Oh, it's you, you cunt. I was rather hoping you'd fall down the fucking stairs and break your fucking neck.' – 'Break my neck? I'll throw you down them, and crack your fucking skull open if you don't shut up, you old cunt.' As I stood there, mulling on the meaningless of life, with icicles forming on my shrivelled heart, you could be forgiven for thinking that the angry howlers were patients in the security wing of a mental hospital. Then all at once, the whole room went silent. They all turned around and looked at me as one. And the loudest of the lot said, 'I like the cut of your jib . . . do you fancy some champagne?' And that was very much the Colony. Sudden, unexpected reversals of mood and fortune, one way or the other.

DARREN COFFIELD: In the late nineties, absinthe, a potentially lethal drink (banned in several countries) and enjoyed by nineteenth-century artists such as van Gogh, began to appear in the UK. Michael invited the importers to the Colony for a tasting event. Within an hour they became so stupefied consuming their own product that they were crawling around the club on all fours, completely paralytic. The members soon aped their example.

GERALDINE BLAKE: Michael was the most unique person I have ever met. I learnt to be generous from Michael because he was so giving with his time and energy. He was very quiet in the way he did that – an amazing understanding of human nature. There were always people wanting to be counselled by him, and each night when the club closed, there'd always be someone asking for his advice. He was the draw for me; it wasn't the club or its history. Muriel and Ian were legendary for their rudeness and sharp tongue, but Michael didn't seem to be any of those things.

MICHAEL WOJAS: I prefer only to get involved when it's necessary, with the minimum of restrictions and constraints on people. My aim is to bring together people without force or insistence. Ian always wanted to have things centred on him, and this hindered interaction between people.

SALLY DUNBAR: Michael was very friendly, self-effacing and mild-mannered. He was thrust into the limelight and it didn't suit his personality at all. He didn't like to hold forth and be the constant centre of attention.

IAN THE HAT: The Colony had always been run by the force of the personality on that stool by the door. And if, for some reason, the proprietor wasn't on that stool, there'd be a power vacuum, and someone would try and take advantage. I watched people itching to get on the perch. Some would jump on and sit on it whilst Ian went to the loo.

DARREN COFFIELD: Michael had this nervous habit of rocking backwards and forwards, which made him appear uncomfortable on the perch. It wasn't his style – he preferred walking around, working the room. But Michael's ending of the 'proprietor on the perch' scenario unwittingly led to a change in the nature of the club as the members no longer lived in fear of being chided for their behaviour.

BIG EDDI: He didn't have the personality to sit on the stool by the door as Muriel and Ian had done before him. Being greeted at the door by the club proprietor was part of the performance, and how the Colony had been run for years. That all died out when Michael took over – the club slowly changed from being a place where members acted as entertainers, to being a place where people came expecting to be entertained.

MICHAEL WOJAS: Outwardly the club doesn't appear to change, that's the magic. I think it's important for people to have clubs where they're just not anonymous – they're part of the family of the club, where everybody helps each other. The place engenders generosity of spirit. Time is the most precious commodity – finding people who are prepared to give you their time, not their money, is hard. It's like the old bartering system. If people can't pay their membership, they give me a picture, or do a job for me.

DARREN COFFIELD: A lot of people, who'd stopped drinking in the club during Ian's reign, returned to the fold under Michael's more benign dictatorship. The most notable being Bruce Bernard, who walked in unannounced, halted abruptly in the middle of the room and slowly looked around the walls, reminiscing and taking it all in. Michael told me he'd seen that look before on old returning members, and knew immediately that Bruce was dying. Bruce returned the original wooden Colony sign, which had been stolen some years earlier from the staircase. He could be seen regularly propping up the bar for the rest of that year, before passing away in 2000. Michael's duty of care ran beyond the four walls of the club – he'd visit elderly housebound members like Marsh Dunbar and Graham Mason, taking carrier bags of wine and other goodies round to their flat in the Isle of Dogs, where they still liked to keep a well-stocked fridge . . .

Group photo to mark the twenty-fifth anniversary of the Colony Room Club, 1972. *Front row, from the left*: Thea Porter, Jean Muir, Anthony Blond, Earl Cawdor. *Second row*: Isabel Rawsthorne, Alan Haynes, Hubert Dalwood, Lady Rose McLaren. *Third row*: Lord May, Muriel Belcher, Peter Jones, Robert Carrier, Annie Ross, Denis Vance, Tom Driberg MP. *Back row*: Ian Board, Adam, the pianist, Ian Winchester, Francis Bacon.

Above: One afternoon in the Colony, a local sex shop owner asked Francis Bacon to help paint his windows black to circumvent the new obscenity laws. Afterwards Bacon held an impromptu street party outside the shop to celebrate his latest artwork. *Clockwise:* Clare Rimmer, Catherine Shakespeare Lane, Michael Dillon, Ian Board, Francis Bacon, John Edwards, Will Self, unidentified figure, Allan Hall.

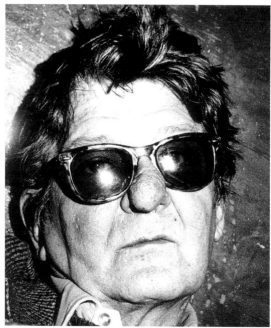

Left: The Reign of Terror: Ian Board surveys his prey.

Members of the Colony Room Club photographed by Neal Slavin for his book, *Britons*.
Back row, from the left: Michael Wojas, Tom Baker, Bruce Bernard, Liz McKenzie,
Michael Clark, Allan Hall. Muriel Belcher's handbag hangs in front of the window.
Middle row: Mike McKenzie, Francis Bacon, Ian Board, John Edwards, John McEwan.
Front row: Thea Porter [on the floor], Jeffrey Bernard, David Edwards.

Peter O'Toole working behind the bar of the Colony.

Peter O'Toole, Jeffrey Bernard, Keith Waterhouse.

Jeff Koons.

Andrew Campbell, Gavin Jones, Ian Devaney and Lisa Stansfield.

Left: Tilda Swinton as Muriel Belcher and Tallulah as Ian Board on the set of the feature film, *Love is the Devil.*

Colony 50th Anniversary group photo. *Sitting on the floor, from the left:* Michael Wojas and Jenny Mortimer. *Front row:* George Melly, Ray Natkiel, Foreskin, Andrew Campbell. *Middle row:* James Birch, Marc Quinn, Damien Hirst, Chris Battye, Clem Crosby, Francis Fry, Merilyn Thorold, Mick Tobin. *Back row:* Claire de Jong, Arif Djan, Frances Slowey, Tom Deas, Stephen Pickles, Catherine Shakespeare Lane, Michael Heath, Hamish McAlpine.

Poster advertising Colony Room 'Performance Bar Art', 1999.

Cerith Wyn Evans, Stefan Kalmar and Michael Clark (choreographer).

Sarah Lucas and Damien Hirst.

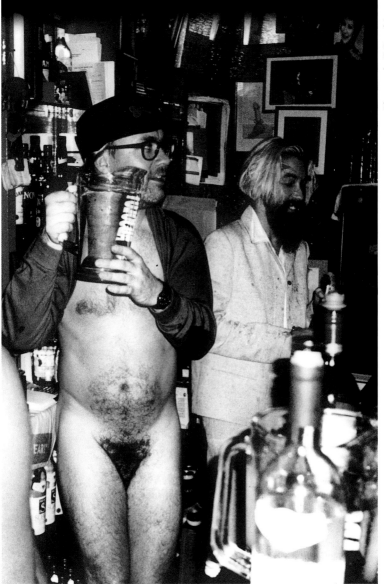

Performance Bar Art: Damien Hirst and Mia Norman.

Left: Daniel Craig and
Heike Makatsch.

A blurred hellhole. *From the left:* Twiggy; Tom Deas, book designer; Jenny Mulherin, publisher; Andrew McKie, obituarist; Ray Roberts, photographer and picture editor for the *Sun*; Michael Wojas; Ray Natkiel, *Economist*.

Above: Dick Bradsell
and Michael Wojas.

© Amelia Troubridge

Left: Sebastian
Horsley, a dandy in
the underworld.

© Pascal Latra

Michael Wojas, 1956–2010.

GRAHAM MASON: I've got one of the old Colony Room fridges.

MARSH DUNBAR: How many fridges have we got, for God's sake?

GRAHAM MASON: Five.

MARSH DUNBAR: You've got a thing about fridges, haven't you?

GRAHAM MASON: Yeah, Michael Wojas sent me a postcard once saying: 'Dear fridge fetishists . . .'

DARREN COFFIELD: Marsh died in 2001 and Graham exactly a year later. Graham's obituary, like those of many Soho characters, was written by the journalist and Colony habitué Christopher Howse, and is considered an exemplary example of that particular literary strand.

DAVID EDWARDS: Muriel would have been amazed at how long the club carried on after her death. By the time Michael took over, many of the classic club characters had died, so it became a different club then . . .

AMANDA HARRIS: I was underwhelmed by the Colony at first but I was intrigued by the barman who was polishing glasses intently and blatantly sizing up my character to see if it was appropriate. The barman Michael offered me his flat while I looked for somewhere to live – I was going through a divorce and effectively homeless. I accepted even though I didn't know him, the club or anyone in it at this point. But it felt like the right thing to do. I thought that instant support, that family feeling of helping each other – a community of care – was one of the most powerful distinguishers of the Colony. Another thing was how inventive the place was. Not just inventive by trade, but the atmosphere that was created some nights with the right mix of members was a heady form of performance art.

JOHN MAYBURY: Over the years Michael became more than a friend. He was a confidant, advisor and, had I had my way, a bit on the side. That brilliant Polish maverick managed to maintain not only the spirit of Muriel Belcher and Ian Board, but to bring the club into the twenty-first century with insane performance bar nights.

HAMISH McALPINE: At the 'performance bar' nights, the most unlikely and impossible people worked behind the bar together. It was a kind of an art world 'in-joke'. They helped revitalise the place.

SARAH LUCAS: I'd been in a couple of times with Damien. I hadn't been going very long when I volunteered to come and work there one afternoon a week. And so then I got to know all the old members who were there in the afternoons, which was interesting.

MICHAEL WOJAS: We had guest bar staff every Tuesday for a year in 1999. Word got round that Sarah Lucas was working at the Colony, and a whole new membership base developed from that. The performance bar nights were an amazing scam. All the artists worked for nothing, and we had loads of people in. Damien Hirst did it, Tracey Emin, Suggs, Jay Jopling, Daniel Craig, Sam Taylor-Wood – even Kate Moss had a go, but that was an impromptu one.

DARREN COFFIELD: The performance nights aroused the interest of Olympus, who donated cameras to photograph the great, the good and the insufferable. It was the most photographed the club had ever been in its fifty-year history.

HAMISH MCALPINE: Then the club became a YBA stronghold in Soho – because it was not easy to get in, the Colony had a cache for the YBAs, like breaking into the establishment, except that it was the bastion of anti-establishment art.

SARAH LUCAS: Like a lot of these things, people start going and everyone thinks that must be interesting. A lot of them didn't like it. It still stayed very much the Colony and not like other private clubs, because you could only get so many people in there. Unfortunately I can't remember the memorable nights because I was far too pissed.

TRACEY EMIN: I did have qualms about being a member. There were certain questions I wanted the answers to. Like, could Michael get some decent wine in? If there was no one in the club, would it be possible for me to use my mobile phone? Could I drink water and abstain from alcohol?

DARREN COFFIELD: David Sylvester defined traditional culture as 'wine culture' and pop culture as 'coke culture'. Well, the YBAs were 'narcotic culture'. Michael was more accommodating than Ian and played to the YBAs' whims. Michael came to my birthday party that year and wanted my advice about entering the entire club and its contents as an artwork for the Turner Prize. I remember thinking it was a daft idea but now, in retrospect, it seems ahead of its time.

MILLIE LAWS: When the YBAs came, there were lots of late-night lock-ins. There are loads of stories, like me and Sarah Lucas getting our tits out at the bar. One night I swapped clothes with Jay Jopling. We went into the toilet, and I came out in his suit and he came out in my white long dress. The next day, Jay's secretary phoned Michael – 'You know those photos that you took last night, what are you going to do with them?' Michael said, 'What do you mean? I'm not going to give them to the press!' That was the beauty of the Colony: what happened in that room stayed in that room. People knew it wouldn't be reported. It was a naughty room – there were all sorts of 'adventures' going on in the corners.

JAMES MOORES: The Colony became much more 'pop-starry' when Damien Hirst and Sarah Lucas started coming to the club. We were all thinking, How can Damien and Sarah be pop stars? The absurdity of it was funny, but it became glamorous and began to attract interest from all quarters.

DARREN COFFIELD: Michael Wojas was now firmly part of the art world party scene, and the drink and drugs were starting to dominate his life. Whereas before he would abstain from alcohol and tobacco at weekends, he was now partying seven days a week, and enjoying a taste of the limelight. Michael's new friends led to the break-up of his engagement to his long-term girlfriend, Frances Slowey, who, knowing Michael's heroin problem in his youth, had been trying to keep him on an even keel and away from Class A drugs. His appearances at the Colony became erratic as he was often elsewhere attending an event. Whereas Muriel and Ian lived and breathed the Colony, Michael was finding it stifling and wanted to spread his wings.

GERALD MCCANN: We used to go to the Colony to be lazy and have fun. People now are too venal. We liked money, but liked it to happen by accident or by nefarious means. Before, they were artists, now they're just cash merchants. My philosophy in life is to take a stand, take a risk. These people want it before they have done it, they cheat also – they don't give *themselves*, they give you a cute quickie. It's like a 'knee-trembler' of art, there's no love in it. The advent of television has taken away a lot of socialising – people would come out and congregate in pubs, making a home from home. They don't stay out like they used to: it has stifled creativity – people's minds would be preoccupied creatively and not be distracted by television. It has done a lot of damage to the salon. Vivienne Westwood thought she could do it, but I don't think Vivienne should ever run a salon. The private clubs you have now, what are they? They have bully boys on the door, staff come in and are fired two weeks later, a chef who thinks he is God . . . they're losing their style here. Whoever thought up 'Cool Britannia' should've been whipped to death. Dreadful thing.

DARREN COFFIELD: Michael had a new girlfriend called Pascal Latra who was keen on singing in the club. She sowed the seed in Michael's mind that they should run special musical events. The artist Paul Fryer would also often belt out a number or two – Tom Jones' 'Delilah' was a particular favourite. So Michael began putting on music events once a month on a Sunday called *Showtime*, and compèred by Phil Dirtbox.

HILARY PENN: Michael got annoyed with Dirtbox: that there were more musicians than guests – since the musicians got free drinks all night, it meant the bar takings were down. So Michael took over the guest list of performers. There was an entrance fee to get in, and it would go on until the early morning. There were some horrific performers who Michael had to pull the plug on.

SUGGS: Myself, Joe Strummer, Ian Dury and a lot of other musicians enjoyed drinking at the Colony. Sometimes we picked up new material at the bar. Michael had built up this idea of having music, so we made this TV show from the Colony, called *Suggs in Soho* – which was a bit mad as once the camera crew installed themselves in the club, there was no room for anyone else or the band. I was interviewing all sorts of people at the bar, and Michael kept filling my glass up with vodka, so you could see my deterioration by the end of the programme.

GUY RIPLEY: One day Joe Strummer got a phone call from the BBC asking him to appear on a radio programme for Bob Dylan's sixtieth birthday the next morning and play one of his songs. Later on, sitting in the club, Joe said, 'Fuck, I've just realised I don't know how to play any Dylan songs!' So Joe goes to Denmark Street, wanders into a music shop and asks to borrow a guitar, then wanders back via a record shop with Bob Dylan's greatest hits. So we end up sitting down in the club with a ghetto blaster playing bits of 'Blowin' in the Wind', while I helped him work out the musical chords – I played and Joe wrote them down. Only then did the realisation hit me – 'I'm teaching *my hero*, Joe Strummer, how to play Bob Dylan. If only my school friends could see this!' Michael let me sleep over that night in the club. In the morning, the barman Matt Cogger came in whilst I was asleep, picked up my phone and changed his name in it to '*Daily Telegraph*'. He then sent me a text message saying: 'Can you please contact the office urgently about an incident in the club last night.' I wake up, read the text and say, 'Fucking hell, Matt, I've got to call the *Telegraph* and tell them how I taught Joe Strummer to play Bob Dylan!' Then I noticed Matt's body shaking with his head out of the club's window – he was laughing so much, he couldn't keep a straight face.

DARREN COFFIELD: Numerous other musical mavericks such as Genesis P. Orridge and Shane McGowan also liked drinking in the club – its track record of attracting musical rebels went back to the club's very beginnings. One notable rebel was Isabel Rawsthorne's second husband, the composer Constant Lambert, who was irresistibly drawn to self-destruction. When his lover, the artist Christopher Wood (after whom he named his son, 'Kit'), fell under a train in 1930, he married Kit's mother and began an affair with Margot Fonteyn. Then, after Constant had drunk himself to death in 1951, Isabel suddenly found herself a young widow with a stepson who was a complete carbon copy of Constant. Hedonistic, promiscuous and easily bored – Kit had a strong rebellious streak, once complaining to his father, 'Daddy I like music that is short and loud and drinks that are long and fizzy.' A remark which belies the two things which fuelled his adult life, one helping him make a fortune and the other helping to kill him. Unfortunately Kit is remembered more for his debauched antics than for his actual contribution to pop music. He founded the first successful independent record label (Track Records) and revolutionised the course of popular taste as the manager of the rock group the Who.

KIT LAMBERT: Just to succeed in life is banal to the point of failure. The purpose of success is to have something substantial to wreck. And the ultimate triumph is to create a magnificent disaster.

DARREN COFFIELD: It was this simple philosophy of Kit's that gave the Who their anarchic stage act culminating in self-destruction. Smashing up your instruments at the end of every performance was a very expensive habit. Kit was often on the Colony's payphone, doing business or having arguments. Once, after a furious argument on the phone, Kit wanted to send a telegram full of expletives but the local post office refused to send it. Not to be deterred Kit jumped a flight to Greece and sent it from there.

MICHAEL CLARK: Kit Lambert used to spend a long time on the payphone. He smoked a lot and the ashtray was full of long cigarette ends, stubbed out well before they reached the filter. One evening Kit told me that Isabel Rawsthorne was his step-mother and had the biggest tits in London – wearing a large coat, she would conceal him underneath them, smuggling him in and out as a schoolboy to see X-rated films, and give him alcohol and cigarettes. On one occasion, she took him to see an exhibition where he saw a man crying. 'Why is that man crying?' he asked her. She explained to him that he was the artist and that he was crying because none of his work had sold. It was Francis Bacon. 'You should paint Francis,' Kit said to me, 'I'm thinking of taking on some painters, I used to be involved in pop music – there were two people I was interested in, and each of them only needed £30 a week, a record player and rent for a bedsit. One was called David Bowie and the other was called Marc Bolan but I didn't have the money at the time.' Kit took a small black Smythson's address book and, starting at the back, fanned through the blue pages with his thumb – 'I'll put you under "P" for "Painter".' As he reached midway through the P's, he slowed down and I glimpsed one of the entries – 'P' for 'Pleasure' – a bath-house address in Amsterdam.

DARREN COFFIELD: Bitchy, camp and forever joking about his sexual activities, Kit was a natural fit at Muriel's. But unfortunately for Kit, the music industry sobered up and became less amused by his antics. A publicity stunt, to promote a record, involved sending radio DJs a pill in a plastic envelope with a label attached, stating: 'Take this pill and it will change your life.' Unable to resist, the DJs consumed it, a very powerful laxative, which took them off air and into the lavatory for a week. On another occasion he insisted on taking the director of a large record company out to lunch. The director waved at his desk – 'I can't go now. Look at all that paperwork.' Not easily dissuaded, Kit slung the papers out of the window. Like other members before him, Kit began to be seen as increasingly unreliable and eccentric, until one night, drunkenly climbing the staircase to bed, he toppled and fell to the bottom, landing on his head. He died two days later, in hospital, aged forty-five, just two weeks younger than his father at the time of his death, a tragedy which typified the brilliant but bitterly short lives of many of the Colony's more rebellious talents.

SALLY DUNBAR: Michael Wojas was a closet rocker, with his studded shirts that the designer Pam Hogg made for him. On music nights, you could barely move in there. No one was paid to perform, but there was such a queue that sometimes it was difficult for people to get on the list. The Blockheads, Chas Smash, Paul Weller, Sebastian Horsley, all sorts of people performed there.

JUPITER JOHN: Sally Dunbar was ever welcoming, and when you are new to a place, that counts for a lot. Always have good memories of Sally who had more of sunshine about her than a full moon, which is how I'd describe most of the clientele – the full moon regulars. Different people would get up and play and sometimes there'd be a free slot. One night I said to Sally that I'd like to be booked in sometime, meaning two or three songs. The next time I played I did my three songs, and then as nobody else came forward, did a couple more. Later on, Michael congratulated me on the set, and gave me a hefty amount for my trouble, along with the cab fare home – this was on top of getting a free bar tab. I'd been booked in for a full set and not realised, Michael was very fair in paying, and generous to me and others with his time. Another music night descended into chaos. Michael kept twiddling with the amplifier and mic – there was a rattling sound coming from somewhere and he was determined to resolve it whilst stoned out of his head. The guitar distorted as I was playing and then the mic cut out. Finally Wojas pulled the plug on me, saying, 'You fucked that one up, what a load of fucking shit!' At that moment Sally produced the culprit . . . a forgotten tambourine.

SHAKESPEARE: Michael's reign took more of a music slant than a visual-art slant. I used to find myself sitting next to a guy I was told was from a band called Blur, but I never knew who they were, so it never impressed me.

DARREN COFFIELD: Blur's Alex James, the actor Keith Allen and Damien Hirst all hung out together. They were following in the footsteps of hellraisers like Richard Burton, Peter O'Toole and Richard Harris, except that they were always getting involved in drunken pranks which made them more akin to the Three Stooges.

ALICE HARTER: The *Showtime* nights were quite mad, with the European spoon-playing champion followed by someone singing falsetto on the piano. It was noisy and varied – anyone could come and perform and it was always packed. Alabama 3 drank and played in the club. They'd become well known due to their song being the theme tune for the TV series *The Sopranos*. I was managing the Magic Numbers, so I asked Michael if I could put them on and that led to them being signed and becoming the band of the summer, with a hit record played everywhere. Michael supported me, gave me the keys to the club and let me shoot music videos in there. Once he did a whole weekend of music and performance to raise money for Jake McLellan, his former barman, who had cancer – and that turned into a Colony music festival at the club.

DARREN COFFIELD: *Showtime* attracted a different crowd on the whole. You didn't have to be a member, you paid on the door, which meant that the club lost its exclusivity and became popular with a whole new crowd. The club was again riding high in terms of attracting famous actors, musicians and artists. One night, the dancer Wayne Sleep kept cocking his leg right up onto the bar whilst explaining to me how he lived in Francis Bacon's former studio in Kensington. I kept slowly edging my drink along the bar to safety, away from his jubilant high kicks. The following night, Damien Hirst arrived with the Hollywood icon Dennis Hopper, of *Easy Rider* fame. Hopper had had a reputation for his debauched drink- and drug-fuelled lifestyle; however, by this stage of his life he'd cleaned up his act and was teetotal. He stood in the middle of the room like a stupefied zombie. After a long pause and without uttering a word, he raised a camera to his glassy eye and began very slowly and deliberately recording the club in every detail like a forensic photographer at a murder scene. Michael was taken aback and deflated by the deathly silent star. As Damien went to leave the club with Hopper, Michael pulled him up by the door – 'Damien, do me a favour?' – 'Yes, Michael, what is it?' – 'Please don't bring any more of my heroes up the club.'

LISA STANSFIELD: I think Michael was really underrated. It was cruel the way that some people treated him. The old school of the Colony really thought that Michael was taking it for granted, and changing it into something it shouldn't have been. Whereas I thought that things have to move on, so that it's got the life again to be a vibrant, beautiful thing.

MICHAEL WOJAS: This club is not run for personal gain. It's very hard to find anyone nowadays who doesn't just think of themselves first and who'd commit themselves to this. The emphasis on the 'I' not the 'We'. I always put myself out for other people, often to the detriment of myself. At the end of the day, if it doesn't feel right in here, people will go somewhere else. As it is, people often drop in on their way to the theatre, then tear up their tickets and say, 'Sod it! I'd rather stay in here all evening.'

DARREN COFFIELD: Kenny Clayton played the piano every Friday evening in 2001. It created a wonderful mood, with everyone joining in and singing along, like the old days. Another Colony art exhibition was held. Michael, tongue in cheek, named the show *2001: A Space Oddity*. It included a lot of YBAs who had recently become members. The Colony was now being repopulated by a very different, younger generation, as the old guard were fading out. After inheriting Francis Bacon's estate, John Edwards' appearances in the Colony rapidly dwindled.

DAVID EDWARDS: John went to Florida to get away from the press after Francis died. The newspapers said that Francis left his estate to someone who was illiterate, but John wasn't illiterate, he was lazy. Someone who's illiterate doesn't buy the daily papers. He was exceedingly streetwise, he could read people and would play on it to test them. He would ask people to write a cheque out – if you put the wrong number on it, he knew straight away. I've never taken a drug in my life, it got the better of Michael Wojas and I saw what it did to my brother John. He became paranoid at the end, suspicious of everyone and their motives. I remember being in New York with him and a man was following us. 'John, who is that?' – 'My bodyguard.' – 'What the fuck do you want a bodyguard for?' I said, 'You're John Edwards, no one cares who you are.'

MAID MARION: Eventually John and his partner Phil the Till settled in Thailand. In 1999 John brought a court case against Marlborough Fine Art for exploiting Francis and his artwork. In 2002 when John realised he was ill, he settled the case out of court. John had had a cough for a long time and I started to think he was doing it deliberately to get attention at times. It became so frequent I told him to go and see a doctor about it.

DAVID EDWARDS: The phone rang in the middle of the night – it was John. I can't remember what we talked about and then came the bombshell halfway through: 'David, I'm dying. I've got cancer.' It seemed like an eternity before I could answer. I knew when John told me, he was also giving me the task of telling people what had happened. John always called me the '*News of the World*' because I couldn't keep a secret. The first person I rang was David Marrion to come over. The following morning David and I caught the train to London. John opened the door to Reece Mews and we greeted one another in the same way that we'd always done except that there was no eye contact, which seemed to give us both strength. It was a strange lunch. It was agreed that our mum should be told before the newspapers got hold of it – 'BACON HEIR HAS CANCER'. It also became clear that John wanted to spend the rest of his short life living – life couldn't have been that good for him, but there was one consolation, that being David Marrion. He was back there like the old days at John's side, being his hands, voice and strength.

MAID MARION: John wanted me to look after him because he said I was the only one who'd never asked him for anything, so I flew out to Thailand. John was riddled with cancer. He was on a lot of medication and his mind would wander. It was a huge responsibility for me to administer all the drugs to him and I also had to wheel him everywhere. It was hard work and John hated being in a wheelchair, so the situation became heated and led to arguments. He kept wanting to go out and I had to say, 'Look, I'm worn out, I can't take you out tonight.' – 'You're no good, I'm going to get a younger friend.' – 'Good, you get your younger friend, I'm going home.' – 'You can't leave.' – 'Yes, I can. You watch me.' – 'Don't leave . . . *don't let him leave*. I don't want a younger friend. *I want you.*' I was intending to look after him to the bitter end but the stress of it all began to take its toll. John noticed I was getting too thin. Then a few days later a consultant came by – she'd been sent to look at me. She told me I'd done all I could and needed to take care of myself and go home. I called Brian Clarke and he caught the next flight over to replace me. Towards the end when John was lying in bed with Brian at his bedside, he turned his head to the door and said, 'Do you know what would be wonderful? If that door opened now and The Maid walked in.'

DAVID EDWARDS: Like Francis Bacon, John's wish was to be cremated immediately. So many people wanted to attend John's memorial that I hired a coach to take everyone from Suffolk to London. After the service we went to the Harrington club in South Kensington. John left £50,000 behind for magnums of champagne to be served at his wake. However, something didn't feel right – I felt we were in the wrong place and we really should be at the Colony, so we all filed back on the coach and decamped to Dean Street. How the coach got down the tiny street I don't know – it parked right outside the club, blocked the road, and we all went upstairs where Michael Wojas was waiting by the bar.

DARREN COFFIELD: Everyone in the club was shocked by John dying so young. Such an untimely death inevitably makes people re-evaluate their own lives. Michael Wojas began to look towards the future.

MICHAEL WOJAS: To mark the fifty-fifth anniversary of the Colony Room Club, I held an exhibition and auction at the Elms Lesters Painting Rooms, Soho. The purpose was to secure the long-term future of the club. The proceeds were to be used to set up a Colony Room trust fund with appointed trustees. The trust would then release money to the club for such things as rent review costs, refurbishments and various club projects.

TOM DEAS: The auctioneer was also a member who worked at Sotheby's. The auction was chaotic and ran out of time. I remember that Tracey Emin helped out on the podium during the bidding and a Damien Hirst butterfly painting was sold.

MICHAEL WOJAS: I try and keep my ideas and options open, raise the profile of the club and encourage new members to come in. I am open to change, open to new people. A new generation of artists now frequent the club who I suppose are the equivalent of Francis, Lucian and Frank Auerbach in the 1950s – the YBAs . . . and I want to keep the momentum going.

MAID MARION: Michael's idea of moving the Colony to new premises wasn't new – John Edwards at one time wanted to get bigger premises for the club. But Ian wouldn't have it. Perhaps he thought that if it expanded he wouldn't be able to manage it, I don't know. Groucho's opened next door, then Blacks. John said quite a few times that the Colony should get bigger premises. However, Ian loved it there, it was his home from home.

MICHAEL WOJAS: I've had some conversations with some new wealthy members about expanding. I would like to enlarge it somehow, I have considered moving it, but that would be a shame because the room as it is, is magical. If we took everything from the room and moved it somewhere else, it wouldn't be the same, but let's see how it goes. I'm open to ideas but not anything that will mess it up.

Since the club opened in 1948, the walls have soaked up so much of what has gone on here. Muriel was the black sheep of her family. Her inclination was towards people who were also apart from the norm, people who didn't conform in some way. The club was also a home to a large number of immigrants from the Caribbean and Africa. Like-minded people could socialise here free from the prejudices of mainstream society. The membership were all outsiders, people without a family and who were looking for one.

I am an outsider, too. I was born in 1956 to Polish immigrants and brought up in a confined Polish community in England. So coming to the Colony was like walking into the bar in *Star Wars*. I'd never met such an eclectic group of people. Of course now it's become my life, it would be impossible to do it otherwise. There's not much time for a life outside the club; it's a vocation, it's not like a nine-to-five, Monday-to-Friday job. My years of running the club have been absolute heaven and absolute hell – in equal measure – fifty-fifty. But obviously all the good times outweigh the times I feel I can't cope with it any more. The club has always been a family. It's a front room with a bar in it, where everybody helps each other. I know if I was ever in trouble the family of the club would come and help me . . .

10

No Post-Mortems

SALLY DUNBAR: No matter what drama happened in the club, the next day Michael's attitude was 'no post-mortems', which I thought was a brilliant concept. Every drinker has been in that situation, where they don't want to remember what they did the night before, let alone have someone else remind them.

DARREN COFFIELD: Every party must come to an end and, after there being a continuous daily party on the premises of 41a Dean Street for fifty-nine years, the delayed hangover was bound to be raw and extremely painful. The year 2008 didn't bode well, with the much-loved YBA Angus Fairhurst hanging himself at a beauty spot that March. Whether this made Michael Wojas re-evaluate the direction of his own life is a matter of conjecture, but he stated his intention to close down the club ten days after Angus' suicide. Michael announced that he'd agreed with the club's landlord, Mr Ibrahim, to extend the lease until the Colony's sixtieth anniversary in December 2008. A letter was sent out announcing his decision, ratified by the club's committee – which came as an unexpected shock to all the members, many of whom began to rally round and fight to save the club, only to find that the 'proprietor' didn't necessarily want to. Thus began the early symptoms of the inevitable violent hangover and ignominious end to London's longest-surviving perpetual party.

Colony Room Club
41 Dean St, London, WC1D 4PY

9th April 2008

Dear Member,

An Extraordinary General Meeting of the Colony Room Club Committee was held on 28th March to assess the current state of affairs regarding the Club premises and lease.

The Club has always had a seven yearly renewable lease, with the lessee being respectively Muriel Belcher, Ian Board and Michael Wojas. The current lease ended on 25th March 2008, and the landlord has applied to court for the lease to be terminated on 11th July 2008 (the discrepancy is due to him being late with his application). His reason is that he wishes to carry out a complete internal and external structural overhaul of the premises which is long overdue.

We have taken legal advice which suggests that the landlord has a strong case and that even if we managed to successfully contest this in court, the legal costs incurred are likely to be prohibitively expensive. A successful action on our part is likely to result in an immediate demand for a large rent increase, increasing the expense of this course of action. Another issue that we need to consider is that Michael has indicated that the Club, in its current premises, has reached the limit of its financial viability (i.e. the space is not large enough to run a sustainable business), and with every new legislation that restricts the activities we can offer to members (e.g. live music), there is less scope for our revenue to keep pace with growing costs (i.e. rates, rent and utility charges).

We therefore need to consider finding a new home for the Colony Room. We are now actively exploring the potential for a move to new premises.

We have also considered whether we might attempt to raise the money to buy the whole building. Whilst we are interested in exploring whether this is feasible, we need to bear in mind that the landlord has made it clear that he does not wish to sell the freehold.

The good news is that Michael has met directly with the landlord and negotiated an agreement (without prejudice) to extend the lease to the end of December 2008. This means that the Club could continue to celebrate its 60th year through to the anniversary on the 15th December, and then vacate the premises by the end of the year.

Michael has also decided that, after 27 years, it is time for him to move on. It's a remarkable achievement that he has kept the Club going, in the original room, for so long. He is no longer prepared to use all his energy fighting a cause where the odds are so heavily stacked against him. Therefore this seems the natural time for him to start a new chapter in his life and whilst we are extremely sad to see him go, the Committee fully understands and supports his decision to do so.

The Committee will be meeting again at the end of April. We need to know what the members think about these options, and what support members may be willing or able to offer. Please get in touch with us with your feedback, ideas or thoughts. You can contact us by:

- Emailing the Committee at colonycommittee@yahoo.co.uk
- Leaving a letter for the Committee behind the bar
- Speaking to any Committee member when we are in the Club

We look forward to hearing from you and will keep you informed throughout this year about any action to be taken.

Yours sincerely

Geraldine Blake, Clem Crosby, Derek Cross, Justin Mortimer, Sally Dunbar, Clancy Gebler Davies, James Birch, Jenny Mortimer and Amanda Harris
(The Colony Room Club Committee)

DAVID SPITTLES: Unlike other clubs, the Colony wasn't a 'business'. Money-making wasn't the main reason for the club – it ticked over. You acquired a certain status to be there. Just as Ian rode the wave of Bacon's reputation, Michael did the same with Hirst. But in the dynamic of its success lay the club's destruction: being part of the Colony had been like being in on a secret, which all changed when the YBAs discovered the club – overexposure in the press ruined it. On the back of them were a lot of wannabes who turned up and diluted the place.

CHRIS BATTYE: The people got very destructive towards the end. There were new people who really didn't fit in and people became pitted against one another – you just knew at the end that it had got out of control. Michael found it difficult to say no – he certainly didn't set out to destroy the Colony.

DARREN COFFIELD: The traditional afternoon drinking culture had died out along with those who'd practised the noble art. This was Tony Blair's Britain of 'Cool Britannia', where the YBAs had arrived amid a blizzard of cocaine. Drugs began to predominate the scene. Since drug dealers don't tend to accept credit cards, people would spend all their cash on drugs and then run up credit at the Colony bar. There was one guy, M•••••• ••••••, who knocked Michael for a £2,500 bar tab. Quite a few people took advantage of Michael's good nature and fleeced him.

SALLY DUNBAR: I was horrified like everyone else when I heard the club was going to shut. We were all shocked. There wasn't just one reason to close the club but many. Michael felt he didn't have the money and the energy to fight on for another lease. Also the club was falling apart and needed a lot of reno-vation work – everything kept going wrong and it hadn't been rewired since it opened. Then there were other nails in the coffin like the smoking ban. Soho was changing and people were being squeezed out. The landlord had left the two floors above the Colony vacant to reinforce the idea that the club was obstructing him from being able to let the rest of the premises. He was determined to get Michael out at any cost. Michael thought there'd be a huge expensive court case and he'd lose.

DAVID GENTLE: Over the years there were litigation disputes with the landlord who wanted to redevelop the property, despite a vociferous 'Save the Colony' campaign in 1990. In about 1998 my firm acted for Michael when he applied for a court order from Central London County Court for a new lease in his name under the provisions of the Landlord and Tenant Act 1954. During that trial Michael Wojas' title to the lease was challenged by the landlord but accepted by the court. From 2005 onwards, the club began to get into financial difficulty and on several occasions Michael was late in paying the rent, which resulted in the landlord bringing county court proceedings. This, together with the landlord's expressed intention to refurbish and redevelop the premises at the end of the lease, was likely, in my view, to prejudice Michael's right to renewal under the Landlord and Tenant Act 1954. The lease was due to expire on 11 July 2008 and, as anticipated, the landlord sought possession. This would have had to be decided by the court, but Michael was not in a financial position to finance further litigation.

SALLY DUNBAR: There was that famous quote that they never tolerated bores in the club? Well, there really were a lot of bores in the club in the last couple of years – Michael felt the quality of membership and the people who drank in Soho was on the wane.

DARREN COFFIELD: Soho's Bohemia had been on the wane since the seventies. By the nineties, with property prices on the rise and Westminster Council's campaign to sanitise Soho, people sought out pastures new. Just as Bohemia had migrated, post-war, from Fitzrovia to Soho, it now moved from Soho to Shoreditch, then a poor dilapidated area. Colony member Joshua Compston led the way in the creation of the Shoreditch art scene of the 1990s. Reminiscent of David Archer's bookshop, Joshua set up Factual Nonsense, a project space in a former Victorian furniture factory in Shoreditch where he began to nurture an artists' salon in the East End. All that Joshua had he gave to art – he was a heroic catalyst. He reached the wider public with bizarre street happenings, such as *The Fete Worse than Death* in 1993, in which many future art stars participated, including Damien Hirst dressed as a clown, selling his first spin paintings for a pound each. The second *Fete* in 1994 attracted 4,000 visitors and was the pivotal event that turned round the fortunes of a forgotten backwater of London.

GARY HUME: We went mad in a fantastic, anarchic dark celebration of just being there. It became very apparent that that area was our home. But weirdly, dead on that moment when Joshua recognised what was happening, it was completely going to change.

DARREN COFFIELD: Joshua's death in 1996, aged twenty-five, made it apparent that the area had become the new Bohemia. His funeral was attended by hundreds of mourners including many leading figures of the London art scene. His coffin was painted by Gary Hume and Gavin Turk and carried through the streets of Shoreditch by a procession of mourners, a jazz band and mounted riot police. After his funeral at Christ Church, Spitalfields, many mourners migrated to the Golden Heart pub a few streets away. It was the first time artists like Gary Hume had ever been there. Run by Sandra and Dennis Esquilant, it gradually became the social fulcrum of the arts in the new East End Bohemia. As the Colony had been known affectionately as 'Muriel's', the Golden Heart became known as 'Sandra's'. Shoreditch and Spitalfields became the new playground for another generation of bohemians and rich kids 'slumming it'. One afternoon in 2003, I overheard a young artist stood at the Colony bar, lamenting, 'Everyone drinks at Sandra's now. The Golden Heart is the place to be.' Michael gave the interloper a withering look. 'Don't worry, they'll be back,' he remarked. But they never really did come back – slowly the Bohemia of Soho declined as the Bohemia of the East End grew.

MICHAEL WOJAS: My only real goal is to send people away happier than when they came in. The drink helps. But it is, today, so difficult. Paperwork and petty laws. It takes great skill to make Soho *not* Soho, but they're doing a hell of a job.

LESLEY LEWIS: The village atmosphere in the community has deteriorated as the people who work here in Soho can't afford to live here any more. The social housing was redeveloped and the people pushed out. The trades are diminishing in the area – when I first came here, there were three butchers and a fishmonger, now there are none.

DARREN COFFIELD: It was in nineteenth-century Paris that the bohemian template was shaped, with Henri Murger writing a series of stories about down-at-heel artists and writers, *Scènes de la Vie de Bohème*, which Puccini later turned into the opera. Amorality, freedom of spirit and dissolute behaviour were the marks of the bohemian. At one time in Soho it was all there – drink, sexual licence, spontaneity and an artistic impulse to reject bourgeois sensibilities. This was exemplified by the experience of walking down a Soho street with Lucian Freud, who liked throwing pennies at the heads of unsuspecting pedestrians as a way of bringing them to a higher level of consciousness. The 1960s led to a social revolution where hedonism became commodified. Slowly the cafés where people had sat all day, penniless and killing time, were replaced by expensive brasseries. Disregard for money and convention was eventually usurped by the new values of chic hipsters, heralded by a millennial puritanism that saw the once clutched bottle of alcohol replaced by the mobile phone. Networking and PR became as important for artists as their artwork, but social media a bohemian doth not make.

DAVID HAYLES: My friend said he'd got a gig in this really cool place called the Colony Room doing these cabaret nights. I thought, I've got to see this. Inevitably it had been taken over by this new crowd who obviously thought this was the place to be, a bit like going to the French House – absolutely rammed. As there are less and less of these places, they become more and more crowded. It was full of these overenthusiastic people, using the piano – dreadful. The regulars were crushed up against the walls thinking who allowed this lot in? Just awful. The whole point was it was a hideaway for when the pubs were closed. You know how there was one toilet? I couldn't get in – queues of people, all doing cocaine in the cubicle. The cliché is that Soho is not what it used to be, but really that was the end of it. You don't have that louche lifestyle now – it used to be the case that you get your work done, then have a good old drink up in the afternoon. Now you grab your baguette and espresso and take them back to your work desk.

MICHAEL WOJAS: I find that the calibre of members has slowly fallen, in line with the general dumbing down of society as a whole. I make members of people I would have turned away ten years ago, simply to survive.

DARREN COFFIELD: Like a species bordering on extinction, the last of the bohemians congregated in the Colony, bitching, arguing and loving in a fog of cigarette smoke. The club was now like an unfinished bottle of champagne found in an old cupboard with all the sparkle gone. It had slowly been allowed to slide over a period of years. One could witness people stand-ing around, nursing a lukewarm bottle of Becks, watching a football match on TV, just like in any ordinary high street pub. The signing-in book for visitors had disappeared, and the bar staff, who now worked in shifts throughout the day, didn't know who many of the members were. It was obvious that Michael's heart, for whatever reason, was no longer in it.

MICHAEL WOJAS: Having seen parallels between Ian's tenure and mine, I realise that Ian chose to stay and die running the club, convincing himself that he was fulfilling a promise to Muriel, but not fulfilling himself. Whilst my brain and energy are intact, it would be criminal not to try and use them. Not that I suddenly think I am a genius, but what is the point of everything I have learnt from the Colony if I can't use it? All my creativity is locked up, staying in the room . . . And eventually to the grave, thinking what if I had . . . ?

DARREN COFFIELD: All the proprietors of the Colony were killed by their work environment. It was certainly taking its toll on Michael. Muriel had Ian to rely on, and Ian in turn was helped by Michael. But after Ian died Michael had no one to shoulder the burden. When I ran the bar for a day after Ian's death, you could have counted all the people that had ever worked there on one pair of hands – it had a cachet to say you had worked there. Whereas by the end of Michael's reign, dozens of people had worked there. Michael had a large turn-over of staff but no single dedicated full-time person to share the responsibility for it, as he'd done for Ian.

SALLY DUNBAR: No, and it would have been a huge undertaking – people like Michael took a lot of looking after. It would have been a full-time job as well as having to act as his psychiatrist and social worker. I ran the club for Michael whilst he was on holiday once, and it was so late by the time I'd cleared up after everyone left, that there seemed little point in going home, so I slept on the banquette cushions. But you weren't on your own at night, no way – you felt you could see the ghosts going round the mirrors. There was so much atmosphere and energy of good times being had. All those people that came through that place.

IAN THE HAT: It was a legendary space. It was almost a cult, what with Francis Bacon's paintings about despair and Jeffrey Bernard's 'Low Life' column. It's only now people are dead you find out there was a dark side to it all.

IAN FREEMAN: I'd never take my friends there – they might become a member and ruin it for me. Many people wouldn't admit it but they were enamoured with being part of the bohemian crowd. You could go to Tramp and Annabel's, but they were just a load of rich twits. When you went to the Colony you saw proper people. They may have been drunks but they were *talented* drunks. Towards the end Michael misused the club for his own purposes. It was not pleasant to visit and several of us stopped going.

ALYSON HUNTER: It was not inevitable that the club had to close. The rent was cheap and the people loyal. Some of the older members approached me to ask Michael to stop taking drugs and allowing 'druggies' in the club, otherwise they'd stop coming. They were the heads of big companies and pillars of the establishment – they didn't want to run the risk of being in a club that might be raided over drugs.

DARREN COFFIELD: I was disturbed by the rumours rippling out far and wide, way beyond the shores of Soho. I waited for the right moment and took Michael aside discreetly first thing one afternoon when the club opened. 'Some people are gener-ating some seriously damaging gossip,' I said. 'Michael, you're the licensee running a famous club. Can't you tone it down?' Michael's attitude was, What's it got to do with them, and that the gossipers were 'all a bunch of hypocrites'. My interven-tion irritated him. I found out after his demise that Abigail Lane and Sarah Lucas had also tried to have a friendly word, to no avail.

ALYSON HUNTER: Certain drugs suck you into thinking, these people are my friends; I take drugs with them, of course they can come into the club. Drugs have their own psychosis and that's what happened to Michael. Gradually the nicest people lose themselves in their addictions.

DARREN COFFIELD: Most of the members were addicted to one thing or another, but I felt things were changing for the worse when Michael put a steel door and intercom at the bottom of the staircase. If you think of all the criminality that went on in Soho throughout the fifties, sixties and seventies, Ian had never resorted to those measures to shut out the outside world. It completely changed the feel of the club, having to ring a bell and be buzzed into the building.

ALICE HARTER: The steel door was put in to get round the smoking ban. Johnny Borel from Razorlight was quoted in the press saying that his favourite bar was the Colony because you could still smoke there after the smoking ban. That caused Michael a lot of problems with the authorities. I asked Michael about it and he said he didn't even know who Johnny Borel was!

DARREN COFFIELD: Michael then tried to ban smoking in the club and removed all the ashtrays, but the members ignored him and carried on regardless, migrating to the toilet lobby area, which became a de facto Salon des Defumés.

DANIEL CHADWICK: Michael was a very quiet, sweet person, genuinely nice. The problem was that you must never have a drug problem when you work behind a bar. It's fine being addicted to alcohol if you're a barman, it rather suits the atmosphere.

DARREN COFFIELD: Next door, there was a nice homeless man who lived in a sleeping bag for many years outside the Groucho Club, nicknamed 'Outside Dave'. He knew all the local hustlers and would source substances for Michael and many famous people who drank in Groucho's and the Colony. He had dirt on everyone and threatened to write his memoirs because he needed the money. At this point, all the eminent people who'd used his 'services' had a whip round and found him a nice flat in another part of town in return for keeping quiet.

HAMISH MCALPINE: Heroin was being bought and sold. Sebastian Horsley, who like Michael was a heroin user, became the local dandy with his stove hat and impeccable suits. When he wasn't in the Colony, he was working at home across the road on his autobiography *Dandy in the Underworld*.

JUPITER JOHN: Some people didn't understand Sebastian, but I saw him from another perspective – he became the living embodiment of a Georgian performer. There was something of the minstrel in him in that he would wander here and there, forever ready with some witty remark. He was not beyond laughing at himself. One night he recited a poem he'd written about death when a chorus of 'Always Look on the Bright Side of Life' broke out. He joined in with the laughter. Sebastian had a charismatic, translucent essence. We both hated the summer and loved the winter. His favourite month was November. Sebastian was a lost little boy – beneath the peacock bravado, there was a very vulnerable, gentle and sensitive being. One time when I was standing outside with my girlfriend, Sebastian walked by and I asked him where he was going – 'I'm going to a brothel. D'you care to join me?' – 'Oh, thank you, Sebastian, but I'm with my girlfriend, that's her standing over there.' – 'That's all right, tell her she's welcome to join us.'

HAMISH MCALPINE: Paraphrasing a tag line for a famous brand of cereal, Sebastian said, 'You know what Michael Wojas' problem is? *Smack, Crack* and *Pot!*'

GUY RIPLEY: I spent a whole night with Michael discussing his financial problems and when the morning finally came, I went round to Damien Hirst's. He was now teetotal but still had the good manners to offer me a cold beer at nine in the morning. – 'Can I have a word with you about Michael? He badly needs a helping hand.' Damien said, 'I'm not paying his drugs money but I'll pay for him to go into rehab.' Michael was furious with me as he'd expected me to go round to Damien's and have a business conversation about the club's future and not say, 'Michael's lost the plot.' Then Michael started wearing a T-shirt bearing the slogan: 'REHAB IS FOR QUITTERS'.

TOM DEAS: Ian Board taught Michael all he knew, not only how to run the bar, but also how to manage people. Somehow over the years Michael forgot everything Ian had taught him. Muriel and Ian would never have allowed drugs on the premises as they knew the dire consequences if it took root, but Michael thought he knew better.

DARREN COFFIELD: Since his death, Michael has been portrayed in the press as a drug addict often found slumped on the club toilet, which is far from the truth. In the final years of the club, Michael rarely went home – he slept in the club, he couldn't escape it. He'd wake up with the stale smells, the rotten toilet and wash in the club's stained sink. Living like that must affect your mental state surely? It's not a pleasant existence, is it?

ALICE HARTER: No, Michael had dedicated his entire life to the club and it was a thankless task. He was drinking quite heavily and there was no retirement fund. He had a lot of insight which not everyone else had. Michael didn't want to pass on the club, he considered it a burden.

SALLY DUNBAR: Some of the members fought to keep the club going without Michael, but he wasn't replaceable in that way – he had a photographic memory and could remember people and places effortlessly. He knew who the members were, their likes and dislikes, what they drank, their profession, their parents' profession, etc., etc. – a huge reservoir of knowledge that died with him.

GERALDINE BLAKE: When the club's lease came up for renewal, Michael realised he had come to a crossroads and decided he had had enough. Michael had been trapped in that room for twenty-seven years and could see it was going to kill him. It wasn't the kind of job where you retired, you died on the job. The person who Michael wanted to take over the club said, 'no way!' so Michael felt the club was no longer viable and wanted to close it and get on with the rest of his life. He thought he'd get the support of his members but instead he got a lot of abuse and accused of stealing money and art from the club.

DAVID GENTLE: The club contained a number of works of art and paraphernalia donated over the years. As far I'm aware, there was never an issue as to whom these works might belong and I had the impression that they were either loaned to the club or had been donated to either Muriel or Ian . . . Ian was certainly aware that the mural had value, and, on more than one occasion, discussed selling it, although Michael Wojas, who increasingly became the business voice of the club, discouraged it and the mural remained until 2008 . . . I was subsequently informed by June Andrews, Michael Andrews' widow, that when Michael Andrews was a student at the Slade and a regular attendee at the club, he was short of money, and one summer in the 1950s, Muriel paid him to decorate the club. He decided of his own volition that the back wall was bare and painted the mural without any instructions from Muriel, and intended it as a gift to her. Muriel was delighted. There had been a suggestion that the mural was donated to pay a bar bill, but that was strongly refuted by June Andrews.

TWIGGY: Bollocks. The mural was given to the club in lieu of a bar bill. The canvas was originally for a lady from Yorkshire to decorate her tea house but it was too big. There's an affidavit from Ian Dunlop, who was present when Michael Andrews was hanging it. Furthermore, there are minutes, under Meakin's chairmanship, describing it as a valuable asset of the club, tentatively valued at £100,000.

DARREN COFFIELD: The story as Ian Board recounted it to me was that in 1957 Michael Andrews redecorated the club from cream to Buckingham Green with his students from the Slade. He then installed a mural based on a painting by Bonnard, which was originally commissioned for the visitors' tea room at Ebberston Hall, North Yorkshire, by Margaret Fenton. Her sister Juliet was Michael's girlfriend at the time. One member, who was a conservator at the National Gallery, asked Ian if he could clean the mural and Ian reluctantly agreed. The conservator arrived armed with chemicals and cotton buds, which he used painstakingly to gently lift the years of grime and nicotine from the delicate painted surface. Then, after a couple of hours of this tedium (and several brandies), Ian plugged in the club's vacuum cleaner and rigorously hoovered the entire painting whilst the conservator recoiled in horror.

CLANCY GEBLER DAVIES: I was the only person on the committee who voted against selling off the mural because I knew we had absolutely zero chance of arguing that the interior of the club was worth preserving once it had been removed. The committee got blamed for a lot of what went on towards the end, but no matter what we said, Michael would just go ahead and do what he liked. In reality the committee was toothless – we fought hard on many points – so much so that my invitation to committee meetings was 'forgotten' on a number of occasions.

DAVID EDWARDS: There was nothing new with Michael wanting to sell off the art. Ian was always selling stuff from the club whenever he was short of money. He'd often get things copied, sell the original and put the copy back in the frame. The only difference between Ian and Michael was that Ian did everything discreetly while Michael made it into a huge public event.

DARREN COFFIELD: Michael had organised a sale of many of the club's artworks and furnishings through a London auction house to raise some cash. The Colony Room art auction marked the point where the battle lines were drawn for civil war within the club's family. Michael claimed that all the artworks belonged to him, but many members refuted this and threatened legal action. Accusations abounded that the club's assets were being stripped to fuel Michael's drug habit, whilst others countered that Michael deserved the money since, after a quarter of a century working there, he had no retirement fund. Sebastian Horsley said he'd donated his artwork to the club and demanded it taken out of the auction. Upon hearing this, Michael flew into a rage and stormed out of the club across the road to Sebastian's home, hammering on the door.

SEBASTIAN HORSLEY: You are a completely corrupt cunt, Wojas. You know full well that I sold a painting in lieu of membership. You gave me back my expenses and you used the rest for your drug habit, you fucking useless junkie. Usually the powerful behave like gangsters and the powerless behave like prostitutes. You are unique – power corrupts but powerlessness corrupts even more. Goodbye and goodnight. *Fuck you, Crack Head*.

DARREN COFFIELD: With the threat of legal action, many of the artworks did not reach their full market value and were sold too cheaply, the Michael Andrews mural being an obvious example. However, the rebel members succeeded in freezing the proceeds of the auction through the threat of legal injunction and accused Michael of taking a bribe from the landlord to hand back the lease. The club's solicitor, David Gentle, strongly refutes that a bribe was ever offered, much less taken.

TWIGGY: The problems really began to start after the club's then chairman, Michael Meakin, died. He was a solicitor and old friend of Muriel's and Ian's, who made sure everything was run properly. Once he'd died, the club began to slide – Michael Wojas was cashing cheques to himself for large amounts. He'd developed a very expensive drug habit, which was being entirely funded by the club. The club was a viable business, but couldn't afford Michael's drug habit and it all became very chaotic.

WILLIAM CORBETT: The annual membership fees should have covered the bills. But Michael obviously spent that on other things – that's why he started selling off the club's possessions.

CLIFFORD SLAPPER: Michael interpreted gifts of artworks, donated by Hirst and others, to have been given to him, as assets of the lease that he owned, rather than to the club and its members – but it was hard for many of us to understand how the artworks were his.

TWIGGY: Forget the artworks for a moment – I roughly estimate that in the last years of the club, at least £200,000 disappeared from the bank account. One, a cheque for £50,000, falsely countersigned.

IAN FREEMAN: The committee member who was supposed to countersign the cheques developed Alzheimer's. Michael forged her signature on the cheques to withdraw money from the club bank account. When we found out, we threatened NatWest with legal action, which they settled out of court.

WILLIAM CORBETT: The club went down for very little money. It wouldn't have cost much to save it. If you think of all the YBAs who drank there and did well out of their association with the place, they could've bought the place and saved it.

TWIGGY: Michael became quite nihilistic towards the end. He seemed to think he was the club, whereas I always thought the club was made by its members. I wanted Daniel Thorold to take over from Michael – he'd been going there since he was a baby with his mother Merilyn, who'd been on the club's committee, Daniel had also managed El Vino's bar in Fleet Street. The idea was to pay off Michael, giving him what he would've got from the landlord for surrendering the club's lease. The club had been going for so long it was bigger than any one person.

DAVID GENTLE: I was in the club one evening and was approached by Michael Peel ['Twiggy'] who explained that he and some other members were anxious to keep the club running at 41 Dean Street. I told Twiggy that there was a right and wrong way of dealing with this, and he should contact me in office hours. I subsequently advised that the only practical way to deal with the landlord was to confront him with a fait accompli by assigning the lease to members of the club who could afford to litigate, as both the 'Licence to Assign' and the 'Notice to Terminate' would be contested. It was suggested that Ian Devaney and Hamish McAlpine would assume that role. It would at least have given the club an arguable case to present to the landlord. In order to achieve this, I prepared a draft agreement on Michael's behalf, assigning his interest in the lease and in the club. This was submitted to the solicitor acting for Hamish and Ian.

HAMISH MCALPINE: As soon as I heard Michael intended to close the club, I started a campaign to find out what was going on and save it. But Michael wouldn't give us any information. None of us knew that by that stage Michael had handed the lease back. It was not in Michael's remit to do that – it was a viable business. So the whole time we were mounting a campaign to save the club, it was in fact a fait accompli and the deal had already been done. I believe Michael sold the lease back to the landlord to pay off his drug debts. He had no authority to do that and that's why Michael kept it a secret.

SHAKESPEARE: When something can't function any more, then it should end rather than turn into some ghastly parody. So when Michael told me he wanted to close the club, I was resigned to it straight away because there was no one left to take over. Traditionally it had been handed down from barman to barman, and he could never find a barman to take it over.

TOM DEAS: The Colony's last barman, Dick Bradsell, was great. It was difficult to fit in there, if anything he was overqualified – a legend in the bar world, a quirky character with a kindly, curt manner; he was the godfather of the cocktail revival and turned it into a fine art. He instinctively knew how to blend and pair tastes, the way a master parfumier knows how to make a scent.

DARREN COFFIELD: Dick trained up the bar staff at the Groucho, and at the Atlantic Bar & Grill, they even named a bar after him – Dick's Bar. A number of his concoctions became modern classics, in particular the Espresso Martini, invented for a supermodel who wanted to be both woken up and intoxicated – an icy espresso shaken with sugar syrup, a double vodka and Kahlúa. It coursed through the body like rocket fuel and became an instant classic.

WILLIAM CORBETT: Dick fitted in so well because he wasn't pretentious. He had a cult following and was a centrifugal force on the party scene. He brought a lot of people to the Colony. He was wasted there, in a way, because they didn't do cocktails! But he was a people person and loved the eccentricities of the members.

TOM DEAS: Didier Avignon designed some new drinking glasses for the club. Each had a derogatory term etched on the front in small capital letters. Dick always served the glasses back to front with the text facing towards the bar, so the recipient had no idea what was written on their glass until they picked it up and turned around, drink in hand, for all to see. Dick dispensed the labels as he saw fit – Peter Brunton was a 'FUCKING BORE', another was a 'KNOB JOCKEY', someone else was an 'ARSE' and so on . . .

DARREN COFFIELD: Dick said that of all the bars where he had worked, his favourite was the Colony, where shaking cocktails was actively discouraged – 'Michael hated me making cocktails so much, he used to hide my equipment.' Dick often had to improvise and use his fingers to strain the drink. One of the most intellectually luxurious of London's pleasures was whiling away an hour in the sole company of Dick at three p.m. before the club began to get busy. We'd discuss everything from poetry to Dungeons & Dragons (a game he was obsessed by), *Star Trek* and serial killers, as he scientifically sliced an entire carrier bag full of lemons and limes, purchased at his own expense. This used to make Michael twitch with vague irritation as he strongly disapproved of Dick serving food in the drinks.

HILARY PENN: Dick and Michael ended up having a fruit war. Michael demanded Dick stop the fruit as it was fucking up the dishwasher. Then the members complained they wanted the fruit back, so Dick had to resort to smuggling in lemons and limes like contraband. Patti Smith came up one afternoon with a member – 'Yeah, Patti, this is the Colony Room Club. Dick, make us two of your special cocktails!' Michael shot Dick a glance as if to say, 'YOU DARE!' So Dick made them a vodka, Campari and grapefruit juice. Meanwhile, a mix tape was playing on the music system when unexpectedly one of Patti Smith's songs came on, and everyone suddenly became quiet and sat in awkward silence. Without a word, Patti suddenly got up and strode out, followed by the member who later returned – 'Patti couldn't drink your cocktail because of her medication – she can't take grapefruit – you didn't throw those drinks away, did you?'

DARREN COFFIELD: The news that Michael was intending to close the club stung Dick who muttered, 'It wouldn't happen if Michael Meakin was alive.' Dick was however fiercely loyal to Michael, who had employed him when he was in dire straits and others in his profession had turned their backs on him. Regrettably the club could not be handed down to Dick for legal reasons.

SHAKESPEARE: Do you remember the banana incident? Hamish McAlpine put his head around the club's door and kept chanting, 'Michael must die! Michael must die!' Dick picked up a banana and threw it at Hamish's head – 'Get out of here, you fucking monkey!'

DARREN COFFIELD: A group of members formed a shadow committee to take on the club's official committee. There were now two distinct camps within the club accusing one another of various crimes ranging from libel and slander to gross negligence, financial embezzlement and wholesale deception.

DAVID GENTLE: The subsequent campaign run by the shadow committee divided the club into those members who supported Michael and those who thought him to be the devil.

SEBASTIAN HORSLEY: Things are going from bad to worse at the Colony. Here's the summary: the members of the Colony want to save the club. The Colony committee led by Michael

Wojas do not. The club is being completely mismanaged. There is no transparency or consulting of the members.

DARREN COFFIELD: Many members felt torn between their friendship with Michael on the one hand, and the preservation of the club on the other. The problem was that, although Muriel, Ian and Michael referred to themselves as the 'proprietor', they were in actual fact the 'club secretary'. The reason was that the change in the 1964 Licensing Act lost the afternoon drinking clubs their three p.m. to eleven p.m. licence and put them on pub hours. Those that relied on afternoon trade were driven out of business. The police began victimising club owners and were given powers to raid and search premises without a warrant. A whole range of punitive fines were put in place to ratchet up the pressure – £900 fines for selling drinks to non-members. Muriel had to pretend to serve food in order to obtain a 'Supper Licence', which allowed for alcohol consumption. Lord Goodman then helped Muriel continue to serve alcohol in the afternoon by reneging her proprietorship and passing 'ownership' of the club to its members and delegating the management of the club to a club committee. Muriel then became the club secretary but naturally carried on as if she were the proprietor and her word was law. Ian and Michael followed in her footsteps. The club committee was mere window dressing. The whole idea of the club being beholden to its rules of governance only ever came about in the last year of its existence as a mechanism for trying to keep it open. Until then AGMs and club rules were only ever paid lip service.

MICHAEL WOJAS: I've saved the club three times. I'm not being a cunt, despite what the shadow committee says. Unless things change, we can't go on, not here.

TWIGGY: It is Michael Wojas' duty as Club Secretary to act in accordance with the rules of the club and he has patently not done so. To this end, I and many others do not believe that Michael has acted in the best interests of the club. We wrote to Michael twice in a friendly tone, asking for a General Meeting so that members could find out about the club's future.

MICHAEL WOJAS: Nothing 'friendly' and not enough members' names to demand an extraordinary general meeting of the club.

TWIGGY: We asked for a meeting in accordance with club rules . . . to get some answers. Those who regularly use the club will be able to judge for themselves if they think there has been a fall in attendance due the current dispute over the club's future.

MICHAEL WOJAS: One would have to be deaf, dumb and blind not to notice a drop in takings of forty per cent.

TWIGGY: Michael is alone in poisoning the atmosphere of the club. His initial response to the letter, asking for the club to be saved, signed by ninety-five members and friends, was to post childish notices in the club and endeavour to drive out the people who had signed it. He then decided to call off perfectly reasonable negotiations to assign the club's lease – following our discovery that payment of the rent had not been made. All the information about the club's finances is known only by Michael. It is our understanding that no accounts have been done for some while . . . The rent on the club is only £12,750 a year plus VAT. Yet by his own admission he does not collect membership fees from many members. What Michael describes as the poor financial state of the club could have been alleviated if he had collected this income regularly . . .

MICHAEL WOJAS: This one is a CLASSIC and deserves a few lines! By my own admission, I am happy to trade off membership dues in exchange for members providing services for the club (e.g. various jobs, equipment, admin work, etc. . . .). Also I have put memberships on hold if a member comes and explains their financial difficulties, a practice passed down from Muriel and Ian, with the expectation that it would only be necessary for a year or possibly two. However, as an example, let us look at Member 1735 – 'Twiggy' – 'payments made from 2000 to 2007 equals *Nil* . . .' – extreme poverty was cited each year when the fees were requested – '. . . payment made in 2008 equals £100 . . .' – but only in April, presumably in order to lead this futile campaign as a paid-up member.

TWIGGY: Michael says that people wanting to save the Colony could well end up being responsible for its premature closure! This would also have an effect on negotiating a lease for any new premises. The cynical among us might well interpret this as Michael sowing first the seeds of a get-out clause – 'couldn't find new premises through the fault of the members etc., etc.' . . .

MICHAEL WOJAS: Oh yes, that would be it, twenty-seven years carefully working out a get-out clause, only to be rumbled by the self-appointed 'Brain of Britain'.

TWIGGY: Michael seems to see the sixty-plus members who were signatories to the request for a General Meeting as some kind of malign body bent on acting in direct opposition to him . . .

The upshot is that Michael, in his capacity as Club Secretary, has no intention of calling a meeting, despite the fact that the refusal to do so is in opposition to the club's rules and statutory obligations . . .

MICHAEL WOJAS: Blah, blah, blah.

TWIGGY: The club belongs to its members and consequently the members also have the right to be consulted in regard to any disposal of the club's assets. I do not apologise for endeavouring to keep the Colony Room Club going in its current and much loved home. *Save the Colony Room Club!*

MICHAEL WOJAS: The nerve of the man! . . . The shadow committee talked to the press, who wrote that the club faced 'extinction at the hands of the man in whose care it was entrusted'. How about – 'who refreshed and reinvigorated the club throughout the nineties, fighting off a previous plan to develop the building and dragging it into the twenty-first century as a vibrant entity, after finally managing to settle a ten-year-long negotiation on the lease'?

DAVID GENTLE: By this time Michael was worn out, very unwell and being openly accused of various things including the astonishing and defamatory allegation that he had taken a backhander from the landlord to forfeit the lease.

SEBASTIAN HORSLEY: Michael, I've left you a message saying sorry and I am sorry. I don't want to fall out with you. I probably got involved in something I shouldn't have. And I blabbed my mouth off without thinking. Forgive me. I just care about the club. And I can't bear the idea that it is going to close. I love what you have created there more than you will ever know. Anyway, I'm sorry. If you can't fall out with your friends who can you fall out with? Anyway, can we forget it and be friends again?

HILARY PENN: Michael saw the shadow committee as a knife in the back. Of course there were a lot of good intentions but also a lot of malice as well. Michael really loved Sebastian, but fell out with him over the shadow committee, and Michael started shouting, 'Judas! Judas!' whenever he saw Sebastian in the street.

SEBASTIAN HORSLEY: Don't you fucking 'Judas' me, you cunt. Judas stabbed Jesus in the back. A true friend always stabs you in the front. It is you who are stabbing all your members in the back. I love you. But I love the Colony more.

DARREN COFFIELD: The shadow committee contacted English Heritage in an attempt to save the club. It finally came down to a choice where they would either place a preservation order and save the Colony or a Victorian prison. They chose the prison. We shouldn't have been too surprised – after all, the Tate Gallery turned down the studio of Britain's greatest twentieth-century painter, Francis Bacon, when offered. It was eventually shipped to Dublin where it was appreciated. If the Colony had been in Paris, it would have been lauded as a 'living' national treasure and its 'proprietors' festooned with plaudits. But the club was in Britain, and fell prey to a zealous homophobic landlord and the inertia of the bureaucrats who litter the art establishment. The threatened closure attracted a lot of media coverage and featured on the BBC's flagship news programme, *Newsnight*.

DAVID GENTLE: Michael was treated in an appalling way both before and after the club closed in December 2008. The proceeds of sale of the art, in the region of £30,000, mostly made up from the sale of the mural to June Andrews, were frozen in the hands of the auctioneers. Michael got back the unsold art, which belonged to him, but the proceeds of the auction were lost in the legal costs incurred by the shadow committee in the court proceedings, forcing an Annual General Meeting.

DAVID EDWARDS: David Marrion received a letter out of the blue from Michael asking him to attend the AGM to be elected as the club's new chairman. We were both walking down Dean Street on our way to the meeting when all we could see was this large mob in front of us, gathered outside the club, spilling out over the road. We forced our way through to the street door, where we were told by a bouncer that it was 'members only'. I explained that we were in fact life members and had been invited by Michael Wojas.

MAID MARION: Michael shouted down – 'Is that the Maid? Let him in.' There, sitting on the landing toilet was Michael with a large bottle of vodka, obviously out of it. He seemed very agitated and nervous. He said he'd be up in a bit, so we carried on up to the club.

DAVID EDWARDS: The place was heaving and we worked our way to the bar only to be told – 'This is a dry bar, no alcohol is being served during the AGM.' So I asked for two tonics and made my way back down to the landing toilet – 'Can I have that bottle of vodka please, Michael?'

MAID MARION: We didn't stay long. It was awful – the people who were supposed to be Michael's friends had turned on him. They were trying to hijack the club.

DARREN COFFIELD: The members had to file in one by one, some, such as Sebastian Horsley, were not allowed in whilst other non-members were, at Michael's discretion. Once inside the powder keg of a club, they were handed out voting forms listing the five existing members of the committee seeking re-election and the seven members of the shadow committee wanting to replace them. Michael took the microphone and spoke for half an hour – a long diatribe about how the 'Save the Colony' campaign was not helping matters. When asked why he had introduced postal votes into the election process, he replied that he had the right to alter the rules as he saw fit. He was then forced to admit that only the five current members of the committee were listed on the postal votes. The room erupted in a roar of protest that the election was rigged and Hamish McAlpine led a chant of 'Mugabe!' A vote of no confidence in the existing committee was proposed but Michael refused to let it be carried. When asked about his previous promise to open the club's accounts to scrutiny Michael refused. He was then asked what his own intentions were for the future of the club but declined to comment. Then over the top of the catcalling and infighting Michael read out his poem to the baying mob:

I DON'T CARE IF YOU'RE A WANKER
I DON'T CARE IF YOU'RE A CUNT
I DON'T CARE IF YOU'RE A MORON
AND YOU DON'T KNOW WHAT YOU WANT
WHEN WILL YOU UNDERSTAND YOU'VE KILLED
THE THING YOU LOVE?

IT'S TIME TO MAKE A STAND AND TELL YOU TO *FUCK OFF!*

Immediately after the meeting, Michael sent a text message to all the members. It simply read:

Congratulations. You have just lost your club.

HILARY PENN: The following Monday, 15 December, Michael threw a party celebrating the sixtieth anniversary of the club. That Friday, 19 December, was the members' final night in the club. Hamish proposed a toast: 'To Michael Wojas for fucking the club up!' Dick got out a water pistol and shot at him. Michael spent the night sitting on the landing toilet because he couldn't cope with seeing everybody. Then the next day Michael held a private party where he sang Alex Harvey songs. It went on until all the booze ran out. The last bottle was Ricard. It was a major piss-up, like a wake. Dick smashed Peter Brunton's photo on the mantelpiece – it was the only thing broken at the party, despite rumours that Michael had smashed up the club. Eventually it was just Michael, Sally Dunbar and myself at four in the morning. Michael didn't speak in the cab home and said little for the next few days. He had a dartboard at home with Twiggy's face on it, which he threw darts at. On Christmas Day he came to stay at my place, and then on the 28th he went back into the club with some friends who helped him load the contents into vans – I've no idea where they went. He didn't go back to Soho or ever mention the club again. Then he cut all connections with me without ever explaining why, which was devastating. I became a target for abuse because the members thought I was still Michael's girlfriend. It was very painful. I was put in an impossible position – people were verbally attacking me for what Michael had done, but by then I was no longer seeing him. I didn't want to admit that our relationship had fallen apart because his enemies would have relished it. Eddi McPherson was particularly vile – 'He never loved you. He just used you to spy on the shadow committee.'

HAMISH MCALPINE: Michael Wojas then had a 'Smash Up the Club' party for his junkie friends – a wrecking party with sledgehammers – they literally smashed the club to pieces.

DARREN COFFIELD: A few months after the club had closed, I went with a small group of people, including Black Sheep, Kathy Dalwood, Sebastian Horsley, Laurence Lynch and Peter Brunton, to a planning meeting at Westminster City Hall to appeal against the landlord applying for change of use of the building. Although the Colony had shut, there had been a club at 41 Dean St since 1915 and it seemed worth preserving its use for another generation. They screened some photos of the Colony's interior, the sight of which made me sick in the pit of my stomach. The interior had been wrecked and stripped of all its former glory. It was a dead shell with some vestiges of the green woodwork standing like hacked vegetation, a few of the red terracotta tiles on the floor acting as a demarcation line where the bar, frequented by the great and not so good, had once been. All the glass shelving and copious fitted mirrors had been smashed out. I thought it was a vindictive reprisal from a frustrated and bitter landlord who had finally seized back his property. It never occurred to me that Michael might have had a hand in it all; it was so completely out of character.

FRANCES SLOWEY: Unfortunately, addictions change people and never for the better. I knew Michael since I was fourteen and he was eighteen – he was a friend of my then boyfriend. Mike studied chemistry at Nottingham then went to Cambridge for a job at a chemical factory that only lasted a week before he decided he wasn't going to become a chemist. We had a wonderful time in 1977 – me, Michael and some other friends got a transit van and went all over the countryside to festivals. It was like a 'five go mad in the countryside'.

Michael was very fond of his mother and father. They were captured by the Russians in the Second World War and walked from Siberia to Cairo to escape the Soviet labour camps. Then they fought at the infamous Battle of Monte Cassino. They obviously had a lot of stamina to survive, and maybe that's where Michael got it from – it took a lot, going behind the same bar in that tiny room day after day, year after year. After the war, his dad had a job delivering fruit and vegetables. One of his customers was the serial killer Mr Christie, of 10 Rillington Place, who he remembered as a 'nice quiet man'. His dad liked to gamble but was kind to Michael and Michael adored him.

By the time Michael took over the Colony from Ian, we were engaged to be married and drinking too much. Then Michael began to socialise more with the 'new' club members who were into hard drugs, and coming home later and later. If you run a bar, you really need to get the rest to start over the next day, but he wasn't getting back until six a.m. I'd have to get up early to clean the club, then run it for the afternoon until Michael turned up. His new 'friends' basically turned him against me and liked to portray me as the nagging wife. They were just using him. The more I said to Mike, This has got to stop, the more I was made out to be a nag by his drug buddies. I couldn't cope with it.

We know alcohol changes people but the drugs had a devastating effect. Michael always self-medicated; he was very disciplined and for years he controlled it, but there is a fine line between genius and insanity, like with his nervous affliction of rocking backwards and forwards. To sleep he had to have the radio on so he could focus on that rather than what was going on in his head. He had the most brilliant brain, he definitely had autistic leanings, a savant quality about him. All the time I'd known him he'd taken drugs, but at weekends he wouldn't drink, smoke or talk as he'd had enough of that at the club. Once we split up, he got heavily into drugs and then swapped the smack for crack. Sometime after, I went to rehab, got clean and gave up drinking. Damien Hirst offered to pay for Michael to go to rehab, and although it was risky for me, I said to Michael I'd be happy to run the Colony for six months while he got clean. I begged him, but he wouldn't – 'I don't want that on my medical records!' Whether it was drug paranoia I don't know; it seemed such a strange thing to say.

GERALDINE BLAKE: The week after Michael called last orders for the final time at the Colony, he stopped drinking and smoking. But it was way too late as far as his health was concerned. He had big plans for all the things he wanted to do – he would have been the only proprietor to have had a life after the Colony, and that's why he wanted to leave earlier than Muriel and Ian, whilst he was still alive.

FRANCES SLOWEY: It was so sad in the end, after the Colony closed. I used to visit him in his flat in Vauxhall. He was completely broke and didn't have two pennies to rub together. There was a nice man down the road who ran a café and if there was any food left, instead of scraping it in the bin, he'd bring it round for Michael. He was extremely ill. He became very annoyed with his consultant who said, by the state of his liver, it looked like he'd been 'mainlining' drugs. Michael was very indignant – 'I've never injected drugs in my life! How can he say that?' And I thought, because of how you've been caning it. I went to visit him in hospital the afternoon he'd been told he had liver cancer. Unfortunately his sister Tina, who he was very close to, was also diagnosed with cancer, which hit Michael hard. She died a couple of weeks before Michael. He was too ill to attend the funeral and was really in a bad place. I tried to cuddle him, but it was so hard because he was just skin and bones. You'd think a cuddle might hurt him, he was so emaciated.

TOM DEAS: I saw Michael on the Monday before he died. He was in good spirits, reading some fact sheets on his condition, and was very optimistic. But once they told him he wasn't going to get a liver transplant, he went rapidly downhill and lost the will to live. He was dead within the week.

FRANCES SLOWEY: Towards the end of his life when he was clean from drugs and alcohol, he could see clearly and had time to reflect. He was full of regret for things that had happened but what can you do? An addiction is an addiction. When he took over the club, he was fully aware of the commitment – he'd seen what running the club had done to Ian and knew the consequences. It's a way of life, running a drinking club. It's a vocation like being a priest, a calling. It was bloody hard work, it was relentless, it never stopped. He was a psychiatrist, counsellor, banker and good friend to so many people; a good man, a lovely man, with such a good brain and a good heart. It's a pity more people don't remember him for that.

DARREN COFFIELD: After twenty-seven years of service, Michael Wojas closed the Colony Room Club on 19 December 2008. He survived the club by eighteen months and died on 6 June 2010. He was fifty-three years old.

Afterword

If you, O honest, not inhuman reader, ever find your way into Bohemia, my best wish for you is a club, a company of fellows as jolly as yourself, a good, cosy room . . . of whatever talk, of poetry, of romance, of pictures, sounds sweetest to your ears.

– Arthur Ransome, *Bohemia in London* (1907)

Writing the biography of a vanished world once populated by many of my friends has been problematic. If the Colony Room was the jewel of bohemian Soho, then Muriel, Francis and Ian formed the prism through which I viewed the club and its multi-faceted relationships radiating outwards. There is no direct or correct way to view the Colony; it was so diverse that one could easily write an entire book focusing on the performers or even just the literary types who drank there. But as Ian Board would say, 'Why spoil a good story for the sake of accuracy?' That's Soho personified.

Strangely, although it evaporated long ago, people still travel to Soho in search of Bohemia, their heads more full of poetry than sense. Sadly the Colony Room has been converted into an apartment and the Soho characters supplanted by a social media-obsessed generation who'd rather message a stranger on the other side of the world than converse with the person standing next to them at the bar.

Bohemia was a borderless country where big hopes were often matched by short purses, and penury was a small price for the freedom of living outside convention. The inhabitants of Bohemia tended to have untidy lives and even untidier deaths. Our numbers may be dwindling but the Colony lives on in our hearts – as a club, it is no longer a building, nor a location: the Colony Room exists in the energy of its surviving members, and so long as we spread the spirit of the Colony, a refuge for life's natural reprobates and rebels, it shall live on.

Down with the duds
Abhor the bores
Prick pomposity
Loathe all labels
Vivre la différence!
Vivre la Colony!

Acknowledgements

First, I would like to pay homage to the many friends and members who have died during the course of making this book: Tom Deas, Michael Peel (Twiggy), Eddi McPherson, Ray Natkiel, Matt Cogger, Dick Bradsell and lastly, Keith Hewett, whose anecdotes and insights into 1950s Soho were both unexpected and wonderful.

I would like to thank Derek Cross for his typographical advice; Clive Jennings and Isolde Nash for their editorial insight; David Marrion for his archive of Colony material; John Baker, Philippa Clare, Michael Clark, Tom Deas, Craig Easton, David Edmunds, David Edwards, Kate Fawkes, Wally Fawkes, Michael Heath, Pascal Latra, Geraldine Norman, Catherine Shakespeare Lane, Neal Slavin, Amelia Troubridge, and James Moores and Jane Rankin-Reid of the John Deakin archive for permission to reproduce their artwork and photographic material.

I am indebted to everyone who agreed to be interviewed and helped with the creation of this book. Those who went above and beyond the call of duty include: Norman Balon, John Beasley, James Birch, Charlotte Black, Geraldine Blake, Tyrel Broadbent, Alisdair Deas, Ian Devaney, Laura Fishman, Di Hall, Amanda Harris, Alyson Hunter, Millie Laws, Stephen Lees, Maria Lennon, Laurence Lynch, Hamish McAlpine, Jim Moore, Sophie Parkin, Hilary Penn, Glen Reynolds, Frances Slowey, Lisa Stansfield, Ken Thomson, Sara Waterson, Clare Wright and Zinovy Zinik.

Lastly, I am grateful to my daughter Kira, whose marvellous humour helped me through difficult times; the birth of my son Orlando, which spurred me on to create the book I had spent years planning in my head; and the unstinting support of my wife Ewa, without which I could never have completed it.

Credits

—•—

Tales from the Colony Room: Foreword by Barry Humphries (copyright © Barry Humphries, 2019); *Soho in the Fifties* (copyright © Daniel Farson, 1987) and *Never a Normal Man: An Autobiography* by Daniel Farson (copyright © Daniel Farson, 1997), reproduced by kind permission of A. M. Heath & Co Ltd; *The Girl from the Fiction Department* by Hilary Spurling (copyright © Hilary Spurling, 2002) reproduced by kind permission of David Higham Associates; *The Guntz* (copyright © Frank Norman, 1962), *Soho Night and Day* (copyright © Frank Norman, 1966) and *Norman's London* (copyright © Frank Norman, 1969) reproduced by kind permission of Geraldine Norman; *Jaywalking* (copyright © Jay Landesman, 1992) reproduced by kind permission of Cosmo Landesman; John Edwards, copyright © The Estate of Francis Bacon, all rights reserved; Dom Moraes (copyright © Routledge, 2004); *Henrietta* by Henrietta Moraes (copyright © Henrietta Moraes, 1994) published by Hamish Hamilton; 'High Priestess of Camp' (copyright © Elizabeth Smart, 1980) reproduced

Biographies of Contributors

—————

ADAM Adam Stevenson, Colony's pianist *c.* 1972–1974. Lives in Morocco.

AUERBACH, FRANK British artist and Colony regular during the 1950s, with Bacon, Freud, Behrens and Michael Andrews (School of London).

BACON, FRANCIS (1909–1992) aka 'Daughter', British artist known for his paintings of screaming popes and crucifixions. He became an enigmatic cult figure among a group of artists later known as the School of London.

BAKER, JOHN aka 'Graham's [Mason's] policeman', a former police detective from Birmingham.

BALON, NORMAN London's rudest pub landlord at the Coach & Horses, Soho, 1943–2006.

BATTYE, CHRIS British artist known for his Teddy boy suits and paintings of the Colony.

BEASLEY, JOHN Transitioned from being a prosperous businessman to a poor artist at the Colony during the 1990s.

BEHRENS, TIM (1937–2017) British artist and Colony habitué with Bacon, Freud, Auerbach and Michael Andrews (School of London).

BELCHER, MURIEL (1908–1979) aka 'Mother', founder and proprietor of the Colony Room Club, 41a Dean Street, Soho, London; the subject of several paintings by Bacon and an influential figure in London's post-war art scene.

BERNARD, BRUCE (1928–2000) Brother of Jeffrey and Oliver Bernard; a picture editor and writer who photographed many influential artists including Bacon and Freud.

BERNARD, JEFFREY (1932–1997) Brother of Bruce and Oliver Bernard; known for his weekly column 'Low Life' in the *Spectator* magazine, recording the louche bohemia of London's Soho.

BIG EDDI (1939–2018) Edwina McPherson, jazz singer and mother of Suggs (lead singer of Madness); she worked at Gerry's club and the Kismet.

BIRCH, JAMES Art dealer, curator, author and partner at Birch & Conran Fine Art, Soho, and a Colony committee member.

BLACK SHEEP Stephen Lees, contract lawyer and author.

BLAKE, GERALDINE Charity director and former Colony committee member.

BOARD, IAN (1929–1994) Ian David Archibold Board, aka 'Ida' (after Muriel's mother, Ida Belcher); Colony's barman from the age of 18, then club 'proprietor' from 1979 until his death aged 63.

BOOKSHOP BILLY Billy O'Connor, publisher and well-known Soho figure who appears in both Tom Baker's and Norman Balon's autobiographies.

BOWIE, DAVID (1947–2016) Musician, songwriter, artist, actor and fashion icon.

BRAGG, MELVYN Author and broadcaster.

BROWN, CECILY British artist and the daughter of the art critic David Sylvester and author Shena Mackay.

BRUNTON, PETER (1943–2010) aka 'Big Mouth', worked in film advertising and then the Soho sex shop Janus, which specialised in spanking equipment.

BUNNY A furtive creature burrowed in deepest London.

CAMPBELL, ORLANDO Son of Charlie Campbell; ran the Crucial Gallery and two private drinking clubs – the Globe, Notting Hill and Green Street, Mayfair.

CHADWICK, DANIEL British sculptor and inventor.

CLARE, PHILIPPA Manager for musicians and actors. Her friends and lovers included Jeffrey Bernard, Michael Elphick, John Hurt and Peter O'Toole. Her father was a war hero and MI6 agent who also frequented the Colony.

CLARK, MICHAEL British artist; many Colony members became subjects for his artworks, which can be found in collections around the world.

CLAYTON, KENNY British music producer, conductor and pianist who worked with Shirley Bassey, Petula Clark, Matt Monro and Sacha Distel.

COFFIELD, DARREN British artist, author and bibliophile.

COLEMAN, ALIX (1925–2008) Feminist, fashion expert and prolific journalist for *Sunday Express*, *Sunday Times*, *Guardian*, *TV Times*, *Nova* and *Queen*; married Woodrow Wyatt and met her second husband, film critic John Coleman (1927–2001), at the Colony whilst lodging with Isabel Rawsthorne.

COMPSTON, JOSHUA (1970–1996) British artist and curator; his gallery, Factual Nonsense, became associated with the YBA generation.

CORBETT, WILLIAM British photographer and author of *Behind the Green Door* and *Gerry-Go-Round*.

DEAKIN, JOHN (1912–1972) British photographer and member of Bacon's Soho circle; a chronic alcoholic who died in obscurity.

DEAS, TOM (1933–2018) Scottish artist and designer who created many of the Colony's invitations and ephemera, and became a club 'fixture', perched on a stool in a pale suit, nursing a gin and tonic.

DILLON, MICHAEL Former member of the Colony committee, now the proprietor of Gerry's club, Soho.

DUNBAR, MARSH (1931–2001) Born Yvonne Marsh, she frequented the Colony from 1949 with Bobby Hunt; later married Hunt's friend, Peter Dunbar, and had three children.

DUNBAR, SALLY Writer and voiceover artist who served on the Colony committee.

EDWARDS, DAVID Brother of John and Michael Edwards; a former publican and antique dealer, he lives in Suffolk with his partner John Tanner.

EDWARDS, JOHN (1949–2003) Brother of David and Michael Edwards; a former publican, from 1974 he became Bacon's muse and heir.

EDWARDS, MICHAEL Brother of John and David Edwards; a former publican.

EMIN, TRACEY British artist, famous for her 'unmade bed'; part of the YBA generation.

FARSON, DANIEL (1927–1997) British writer, photographer and broadcaster who became a household name in the early days of commercial television.

FAWKES, KATE Daughter of Wally and Sandy Fawkes; now a writer/producer.

FAWKES, SANDY (1929–2005) Journalist and author of the bestseller *Killing Time*.

FORESKIN A character of club folklore. His home life as a respectable pillar of his local community was in sharp contrast to his Soho life as a fun-loving, insatiable womaniser of considerable wit. Somehow, despite the laws of physics, the two worlds never collided.

FREEMAN, IAN Honorary charity Treasurer and Trustee of the Royal Variety Charity and nephew of the impresario Lew Grade.

GEBLER DAVIES, CLANCY British photographer whose father, Stan, was an author and Colony habitué.

GENTLE, DAVID The club's solicitor 1968–2008; responsible for drawing up the last wills and testaments for Muriel Belcher, Ian Board and Michael Wojas.

GLENEAGLES Glen Reynolds, author and former libel lawyer for *Private Eye* magazine.

GREEN, FIONA British artist, wife of Martin Green; their home was the last refuge of Fitzrovian bohemianism; visitors included Paul Potts, Colin MacInnes, Thabo Mbeki and Harry Diamond.

GREEN, MARTIN (1932–2015) Poet, publisher and husband of Fiona Green who came to Soho as an army conscript with his friend John Moynihan and worked in David Archer's bookshop.

HALL, ALLAN (1929–2001) Journalist, gossip columnist and newspaper editor who invented the annual Beaujolais Nouveau race.

HALL, DI Daughter of a fishmonger who became part of the Soho scene after the collapse of her marriage in the 1980s.

HARDYMENT, PAM Book editor, author and former lover of Jay Landesman.

HARRIS, AMANDA British actor and member of the Royal Shakespeare Company. She received an Olivier Award in 2004.

HARTER, ALICE Music promoter and manager who participated in the *Showtime* events at the Colony.

HAYLES, DAVID Author and friend of Joshua Compston.

HEATH, MICHAEL British cartoonist and illustrator; his work has appeared in numerous publications including the *Spectator*, the *Sunday Times* and *Private Eye*.

HELM, ZEBEDEE British artist and friend of Joshua Compston.

HEWETT, KEITH (1928–2016) Studied at the Borough Art School under David Bomberg; worked on set and production design in theatre and television; head of art at three London secondary schools.

HIRST, DAMIEN British artist famous for his 'Shark' sculpture; part of the YBA generation.

HORSLEY, SEBASTIAN (1962–2010) British artist, author and Soho dandy.

HUME, GARY British artist; part of the YBA generation.

HUMPHRIES, BARRY Australian comedian, actor, artist and author; famous for his alter ego, Dame Edna Everage.

HUNT, BOBBY (1929–2007) Art instructor at the University of Cambridge, picture researcher, jazz musician, cartoonist and owner of the Robert Hunt Picture Library.

HUNTER, ALYSON New Zealand artist; her work is in numerous collections worldwide.

HURT, JOHN (1940–2017) British actor nicknamed 'The Naked Civil Elephant Man' by Jeffrey Bernard. He appeared in 129 films, including *The Naked Civil Servant* and *The Elephant Man*.

IAN THE HAT Ian Richards, former barman at the Coach & Horses and the Colony; now head of Crisis at Christmas for Crisis UK, the charity for the homeless.

INDIAN AMY (deceased) Cynthia Blythe, born in Bombay, British colonial India, where her parents owned a tea plantation. She was an air hostess for TWA (Trans-World Airlines) in the days when air travel was exclusive and glamorous. She was arrested for smuggling gold ingots under her coat whilst boarding a Constellation plane bound for India in 1951.

INGRAMS, FRED British artist who had a studio above the Coach & Horses, Soho, in the 1980s.

JOHN, AUGUSTUS (1878–1961) British artist who superseded John Singer Sargent as Britain's most fashionable painter; said to have sired over a hundred children.

JOHNSON, PAUL Journalist and author of over 40 books.

JUPITER JOHN Jack Moon, musician, diarist and television writer.

LAMBERT, KIT (1935–1981) British record producer and manager of the rock group the Who.

LANDESMAN, JAY (1919–2011) Publisher, writer, nightclub proprietor and father of Cosmo Landesman.

LAWS, MILLIE Reflexologist and former Colony bartender.

LEWIS, LESLEY Proprietor of the French House, Soho.

LUCAS, SARAH British artist; part of the YBA generation.

MACINNES, COLIN (1914–1976) British journalist and author who depicted youth and black immigrant culture during the 1950s in his novels.

McALPINE, HAMISH British businessman and film producer.

McCANN, GERALD (1931–2019) British fashion designer and Francis Bacon's favourite 'frock-maker'.

McLAREN, LADY ROSE (1919–2005) British aristocrat who trained as a ballet dancer and made her debut at Sadlers Wells in 1937. After the death of her husband in 1953, she became friends with Muriel Belcher and Francis Bacon.

MAID MARION David Marrion, born in the East End of London and attended school with the Kray twins. He spent many years running bars including the Colony.

MASON, GRAHAM (1942–2002) South African journalist, posted to London as a foreign correspondent in 1964. He eventually worked for ITN until discovered drunk under his desk one day.

MAYBURY, JOHN British filmmaker. In 2005 he was listed in the top 100 most influential gay people in Britain.

MELLY, DIANA Author and former model; wife of Michael H. St George Ashe, John Moynihan and second wife of George Melly.

MELLY, GEORGE (1926–2007) English jazz singer, critic, broadcaster and writer. He scripted a satirical newspaper strip 'Flook', illustrated by 'Trog' (Wally Fawkes), which often featured the Colony.

MISS WHIPLASH Sara Waterson, worked in publishing; her lovers include Lucian Freud, John Hurt and Germano Facetti.

MOORE, JIM Former schoolteacher now living in Kuala Lumpur, dealing in oriental antiquities.

MOORES, JAMES Owner of the John Deakin archive and founder of A Foundation.

MORAES, DOM (1938–2004) Indian writer, poet and third husband of Henrietta Moraes.

MORAES, HENRIETTA (1931–1999) Born Audrey Wendy Abbot, aka 'Hen', the muse for many artists including Lucian Freud, Francis Bacon and John Minton. Married to Michael Law, Norman Bowler and Dom Moraes. Infamous for her hedonistic lifestyle, she died leaving few possessions and a large pile of unpaid bills.

MOYNIHAN, JOHN (1932–2012) Journalist, author and son of Rodrigo Moynihan and Elinor Bellingham-Smith.

MOYNIHAN, RODRIGO (1910–1990) British artist and key figure in London's post-war art scene.

MRS SIXPENCE John Tanner, interior designer and partner of David Edwards.

NATKIEL, RAY (1942–2018) British artist; short, thin and wiry with a long, flowing black beard, he was often referred to as 'Rasputin Ray' as he chain-smoked his way through 40 Gitanes a day, working at the *Economist*.

NORMAN, FRANK (1930–1980) Former convict and author whose prison memoir *Bang to Rights* was a huge literary success; his play *Fings Ain't Wot They Used T'Be* won an *Evening Standard* Award for Best Musical in 1960. Married to Geraldine Norman.

NORMAN, GERALDINE Journalist, author and advisor to the Director of the State Hermitage Museum, Russia.

O'TOOLE, PETER (1932–2013) British-Irish actor who achieved fame in the film *Lawrence of Arabia*.

PARKIN, MOLLY British artist, novelist and journalist, infamous for her sex-ploits in the world of art and fashion until she joined Alcoholics Anonymous in 1987.

PENN, HILARY Manager at the French House, Soho.

PICKLES, STEPHEN Lecturer in English at Hertford College, Oxford; former Editorial Director of Quartet Books.

PORTER, THEA (1927–2000) British fashion designer whose customers included Lauren Bacall, Elizabeth Taylor, Mick Jagger and Princess Margaret.

POTTS, PAUL (1911–1990) British poet and friend of George Orwell, of whom he wrote a memoir, *Don Quixote on a Bicycle*. Potts lived in poverty and died from a fire in his bedroom.

RAWSTHORNE, ISABEL (1912–1992) British artist, designer, model and muse. Her bohemian friends included Picasso, Epstein, Derain, Giacometti and Bacon. Married the journalist Sefton Delmer, and the composers Constant Lambert and Alan Rawsthorne.

RIPLEY, GUY Songwriter and former barman at the Colony.

ROSE, SIR FRANCIS (1909–1979) aka 'Lord Chaos', artist, author and illustrator; a once important figure who has faded into obscurity; last protégé of Gertrude Stein who promoted him as the next Picasso.

SHAKESPEARE Catherine Shakespeare Lane, British artist, archaeologist and theatrical photographer.

SHEARER, MAGGIE aka 'Polish Maggie', friend of the Edwards family.

SHRIVE, RUPERT British artist who worked with Graham Mason at the Robert Hunt Picture Library and had a studio above the Coach & Horses, Soho.

SLAPPER, CLIFFORD Musician and composer.

SLOWEY, FRANCES Former fiancée of Michael Wojas; her years working in the Colony gave her a good grounding for her current occupation as a carer for people with mental health issues.

SMART, ELIZABETH (1913–1986) Canadian poet and author who had a turbulent relationship with the poet George Barker.

SPALL, TIMOTHY British actor who became a household name in the TV series *Auf Wiedersehen, Pet*.

SPITTLES, DAVID British journalist.

SPURLING, HILARY Award-winning author and friend of Sonia Orwell.

STANSFIELD, LISA British singer, songwriter and actress.

SUGGS Graham McPherson, son of Big Eddi; British singer-songwriter and musician who came to prominence as the lead singer of the ska band Madness.

SUTHERLAND, DOUGLAS (1919–1995) British author and journalist; his *Portrait of a Decade*, featuring many of the colourful characters of 1950s London, centred on the Colony.

SWAN, MARY Worked in publishing; moved to Chelsea with her four children in 1965, where her neighbour took her to lunch with Bobby Hunt who introduced her to the Colony.

THOROLD, MERILYN (1935–1999) Colony regular from the mid-1950s. After her divorce in 1963, she worked for the fashion designer Thea Porter. She remained good friends with Carmel Stuart after Muriel died. In later years she became a photographer and travelled extensively. She was a club committee member until her death, aged 64.

TWIGGY (1952–2018) Michael Peel met Muriel Belcher only once: 'Hello, you fat cunt, who are you? Twiggy?' Consequently the moniker stuck, the anonymity of which suited his career selling high-value computers to major banks.

WATERHOUSE, KEITH (1929–2009) British novelist and journalist. The film of his 1959 book, *Billy Liar*, was nominated for six BAFTA awards, including Best Screenplay.

WHITTINGTON, RICHARD (1948–2011) aka 'Dick', food critic and writer, renowned for his curse-laden, invective-strewn, expletive-ridden tirades – a monstrous skill he acquired as Ian Board's lodger during the 1970s.

WOJAS, MICHAEL (1956–2010) Barman at the Colony Room Club 1981–1994 and the last 'proprietor' 1994–2008. He died eighteen months after the club closed, aged 53.

Notes

The principal source for writing this book was the collection of over thirty interview tapes with club members handed down to me by Michael Wojas. Using these as the nucleus, I then carried out numerous other interviews with surviving members to complete the biography. I have also used my own recollections of conversations and events during my membership, the most important of which are cited below. If a member is deceased and no historic interview survives, I have referred to their published biography. All the material in this book has been edited for clarity, brevity and lucidity with minimal changes to standardise punctuation made silently, so the reader is not distracted.

INTRODUCTION

xv   These ghastly English laws: Andrew Sinclair, *Francis Bacon: His Life and Violent Times* (London: Sinclair-Stevenson, 1993), p. 248
xviii I remember Dylan Thomas: recounted by Ian Board

SOHO INTRO

xxiv I knew Soho: Francis Bacon interview, Colony Room audio recording

xxv Soho has always changed: Sandy Fawkes, *The French* (London: Lewis & Botham, 1993), p. 52

xxv The years immediately after the war: Douglas Sutherland, *Portrait of a Decade: London Life 1945–1955* (London: Harrap, 1988), p. 67

xxvi When I first knew Soho: Bacon interview, Colony Room audio recording

xxvi Soho, like anywhere else: Frank Norman and Jeffrey Bernard, *Soho Night and Day* (London: Secker & Warburg, 1966), p. 92

xxvi Sex has always been: Daniel Farson's opening speech, Soho Village Fete, 1997

xxvii Why did I fall in love with Soho: Jeffrey Bernard radio interview, Classic FM, *c.* 1989

xxvii My London is Soho: Frank Norman, *Norman's London* (London: Secker & Warburg, 1969), p. 248

CHAPTER I: MURIEL'S

1 In Soho alone: Norman, *Norman's London*, p. 186

2 Clubland is a place: Norman and Bernard, *Soho Night and Day*, pp. 98–99

7 To open a members' club: Colin MacInnes, 'At Mabel's', *Encounter*, May 1957

8 As a woman alone: Daniel Farson, 'The Calumny Room', *Harpers & Queen*, December 1988, p. 272

8 'Members only': Daniel Farson, '"Open Your Bead Bag, Lottie!"', *Club International*, December 1974, 3:12, pp. 9, 10, 91

10 Muriel had an arrogant nose: Fawkes, *The French*, p. 32

10 What makes her difficult: Daniel Farson, *Soho in the Fifties* (London: Michael Joseph, 1987), p. 44

11 I had one nice brother: Farson, '"Open Your Bead Bag, Lottie!"', p. 10

12 The members were theatrical: Farson, '"Open Your Bead Bag, Lottie!"', p. 10

12 She fell in love with a poof: Farson, '"Open Your Bead Bag, Lottie!"', p. 10

13 I don't disapprove of much: Alix Coleman, 'Muriel, Olwen and Elizabeth', *Nova*, December 1969, p. 62

13 Her Jewishness was important: Elizabeth Smart, 'The High Priestess of Camp', *Harpers & Queen*, January 1980

13 Muriel's wit came from: Richard Whittington, *Colony Room Club 50th Anniversary Exhibition Catalogue*, A22 Projects, London, 1988

13 Language is effective: Coleman, 'Muriel, Olwen and Elizabeth', p. 62

14 She could be incredibly kind: *Salvage of a Soho Photographer: The Life and Unsteady Times of John Deakin*, Analogue for Channel 4, 26 March 1991

17 It's like a tank: Farson, '"Open Your Bead Bag, Lottie!"', p. 10

17 When [Francis] first came here: Anne Sharpley, 'Laughs up at Muriel's', *Evening Standard*, 17 January 1973, p. 13

18 You came to the Colony: Francis Bacon and Daniel Farson interview, Colony Room audio recording

18 It had a strange entrance: Bacon and Farson interview, Colony Room audio recording

20 They can't be so clever: Sharpley, 'Laughs up at Muriel's', p. 13

20 'Muriel Belcher. Muriel Belcher!': Farson, '"Open Your Bead Bag, Lottie!"', p. 9

21 Credit, according to: MacInnes, 'At Mabel's'

21 Muriel Belcher has her areas: Coleman, 'Muriel, Olwen and Elizabeth', p. 62

23 Club owners are various: MacInnes, 'At Mabel's'

23 I can listen to three: Coleman, 'Muriel, Olwen and Elizabeth', p. 62

23 I remember, once, wavering: Smart, 'The High Priestess of Camp'

24 I have yet to meet: Norman, *Norman's London*, p. 187

24 Muriel is the only person: Farson, '"Open Your Bead Bag, Lottie!"', p. 9

25 the Colony also was a kind of: Smart, 'The High Priestess of Camp'

27 The trouble is if I go: Norman, *Norman's London*, p. 188

27 The club world is a shifting one: Daniel Farson, 'Full House', *Queen*, November 1969, p. 108

27 John Braine: Coleman, 'Muriel, Olwen and Elizabeth', p. 62

28 Her members are hooked: Coleman, 'Muriel, Olwen and Elizabeth', p. 62

28 None of them take themselves: Farson, '"Open Your Bead Bag, Lottie!"', p. 25

28 she dissolves the sexes: Coleman, 'Muriel, Olwen and Elizabeth', p. 62

29 I suppose poofs: Coleman, 'Muriel, Olwen and Elizabeth', p. 62

30 The greatest charmer: MacInnes, 'At Mabel's'

31 A man came barging in: Norman, *Norman's London*, p. 189

31 Nobody was at the piano: Farson, '"Open Your Bead Bag, Lottie!"', p. 18

32 But of course there are days: ibid.

33 I love Muriel saying: ibid.

33 Some Colony regulars: Whittington, *Colony Room Club 50th Anniversary Exhibition*

34 In the middle of a further tirade: Farson, '"Open Your Bead Bag, Lottie!"', p. 18

34 Everything was flambé: Farson, ibid.

CHAPTER 2: SEND IN THE CLOWNS

37 Is there a common denominator: Farson, "'Open Your Bead Bag, Lottie!'", p. 18

38 I stumbled over Nina Hamnett: Fawkes, *The French*, p. 16

39 She was the soul of generosity: Augustus John, *Finishing Touches* (London: Jonathan Cape, 1964), p. 109

40 the most extraordinary thing: Daniel Farson, *Never a Normal Man: An Autobiography* (London: HarperCollins, 1997), p. 116

40 Being in love in that way: conversation at Colony Room bar

40 The funny thing about [Francis]: Frank Norman, *The Guntz*, (London: Pan Books Ltd, 1965), p. 126

41 [Francis] was a piss artist: ibid., pp. 126–7

43 You know those fish: Christopher Howse, 'Jeffrey Bernard' (obituary), *Independent*, 6 April 1997

46 Sometimes Dan would: Whittington, *Colony Room Club 50th Anniversary Exhibition*

48 The School of London never existed: 'Timothy Behrens' (obituary), *The Times*, 18 February 2017

50 I have to confess: Bruce Bernard, *12 Photographs of Francis Bacon* (London: British Council, 1999)

51 This was Soho to me: John Hurt interviewed by James Naughtie, *Today Programme*, BBC Radio 4, 18 November 2015

51 a witty and malicious companion: George Melly, *Slowing Down* (London: Penguin 2006), p. 104

53 All that money an' I fink: Michael Peppiatt, *Anatomy of an Enigma*, (London: Weidenfeld & Nicholson, 1996), p. 214

54 I remember sitting: John Hurt, *Today Programme*

55 It is much easier: Sir Francis Rose, *Saying Life: The Memoirs of Sir Francis Rose* (London: Cassell, 1961)

55 I painted [Isadora]: ibid.

57 In 1955 Francis saved my life: Daniel Farson, *The Gilded Gutter Life of Francis Bacon* (London: Century, 1993), p. 63

58 Muriel showed her sense: Isabel Rawsthorne, *Memoirs*, private collection, London

61 I don't believe in love really: Bacon and Farson interview, Colony Room audio recording

62 [Jeffrey] was introduced to Soho: Keith Waterhouse, 'Last Orders for Jeffrey Bernard', *Daily Telegraph*, 13 September 1997

62 [Jeffrey] got made a sort of hero: Graham Lord, *Just the One: The Wives and Times of Jeffrey Bernard* (London: Sinclair-Stevenson, 1992), p. 137

63 It caused quite an uproar: John Moynihan, *Restless Lives: The Bohemian World of Rodrigo and Elinor Moynihan* (Bristol: Sansom & Co. 2002), p. 167

65 The funny thing is: Jeffrey Bernard radio interview, Classic FM

65 It really was like an illness: Lord, *Just the One*, p. 108

65 I'm ringing for Jeff: ibid., p. 130

67 Some folk are allergic: Norman, *Norman's London*, p. 157

68 Fings Ain't Wot They Used T'Be: ibid., p. 203

69 I felt like a spy: Farson, *Soho in the Fifties*, p. 39

71 What was always curious to me: Martin Green, 'Colin MacInnes: an awkward guest', *London Magazine*, October 1999, p. 39

71 the Norman Hartnell: Peppiatt, *Anatomy of an Enigma*, notes section, chapter 9

76 'E's a copper!: Sutherland, *Portrait of a Decade*, p. 213

76 'Well Tom was happy: Sophie Parkin, *The Colony Room Club 1948–2008: A history of bohemian Soho* (London: Palmtree, 2012), p. 105

76 At the Colony Room: Paul Johnson, *Brief Lives* (London: Hutchinson, 2010), p. 100

77 Donald Maclean, unlike: Sutherland, *Portrait of a Decade*, p. 213

78 have seen many perverts: Sally Fiber, *The Fitzroy*, (London: Sally Fiber, 2014), p. 93

78 Once, in Muriel's bar: Johnson, *Brief Lives*, p. 152

CHAPTER 3: SPEAKIN' DEAKIN

82 an odd one: Robin Muir, *A Maverick Eye: The Street Photography of John Deakin* (London: Thames & Hudson, 2002), pp. 12–13

83 I would meet John Deakin: conversation at Colony Room bar

83 John Deakin was: Bacon interview, Colony Room audio recording

84 He took a photo of Johnny: Patrick Cooney, 'The Queen of Soho', *Guardian Weekend*, 22 August 1998, p. 22

84 Deakin could certainly seem a monster: Bruce Bernard, 'Fearless Exposures', *Independent Magazine*, 23 March 1991

84 Being fatally drawn: Farson, *Never a Normal Man*, p. 114

85 When I first met him [Francis]: Bernard, *12 Photographs of Francis Bacon*

85 I used to see Francis every day: *Salvage of a Soho Photographer*, Analogue for Channel 4

86 The pictures that finally got painted: ibid.

86 The first time I saw Henrietta: Thea Porter, 'Muriel's Academy', *Harpers & Queen*, November 1982, p. 222

88 At Christmas they are: Coleman, 'Muriel, Olwen and Elizabeth', p. 62

91 Francis and Lucian, they couldn't be: Cooney, 'The Queen of Soho', p. 22

91 I once asked Lucian: conversation at Colony Room bar

92 When Deakin abandoned art: conversation at Colony Room bar

92 Why nobody has ever written: Amitava Kumar (ed.), *Away: The Indian Writer as Expatriate* (New York, London: Routledge, 2003), p. 207

93 It was a beautiful establishment: ibid.

93 The actual physical way: *Paul Potts: A Gentleman of Soho*, BBC Radio 3, 14 July 1974

94 David Archer and his friend: Henrietta Moraes, *Henrietta* (London: Penguin, 1995), pp. 40–41

94 One afternoon David and I: ibid., p. 43

95 he offered to publish: Kumar, *Away: The Indian Writer*, pp. 207–8

95 it won the Hawthornden Prize: Moraes, *Henrietta*, p. 55

96 I used to sell copies: Robert Fraser, *The Chameleon Poet: A life of George Barker*, (London: Jonathan Cape, 2002)

98 I had been having treatment: Farson, *Soho in the Fifties*, p. 144

98 He sounded weak: *Salvage of a Soho Photographer*, Analogue for Channel 4

98 I had to go down and identify the body: Bacon interview, Colony Room audio recording

98 I said, 'Was it horrible: *Salvage of a Soho Photographer*, Analogue for Channel 4

99 He was marvellously witty: Bacon interview, Colony Room audio recording

99 I know just what that means: Farson, *Soho in the Fifties*, p. 145

99 Of course, I did give him: ibid.

99 The natural romantic: Bruce Bernard, 'Face to face with John Deakin': *Sunday Times Magazine*, 7 October 1984

100 I was very pleased: *John Deakin: The Salvage of a Photographer* (London: Victoria & Albert Museum, 1984), p. 8

CHAPTER 4: GAMBLERS EPONYMOUS

101 If you feel like gambling: Norman and Jeffrey Bernard, *Soho Night and Day*, p. 90

101 I like the atmosphere: *The South Bank Show: The Life and Career of Francis Bacon*, Francis Bacon interviewed by Melvyn Bragg, London Weekend Television, 9 June 1985

102 nothing is more wonderful: Sinclair, *Francis Bacon: His Life and Violent Times*, p. 104

106 Soon after I met Francis: https://www.francis-bacon.com/content/francis-bacon-and-reece-mews

107 We'd talk about everything: Mick Brown, 'Eggs, Bacon and Jellied Eels', *Daily Telegraph*, 19 February 2002

108 If people wanted to talk: conversation at Colony Room bar

108 one night he won £15,000: Brown, 'Eggs, Bacon and Jellied Eels'

110 The only reason: Lord, *Just the One*, p. 326

110 The most depressing remark: ibid., p. 145

113 [Lucian Freud] was a gambler: Nicholas Wroe, 'Frank Auerbach: "Painting is the most marvellous activity humans have invented"', *Guardian*, 16 May 2015

113 Have you ever driven: Nancy Schoenberger, *Dangerous Muse: A Life of Caroline Blackwood* (London: Weidenfeld & Nicolson, 2001), p. 98

117 Because in a sense it cordons you: Bacon and Farson interview, Colony Room audio recording

120 The only way you can give up: Jeffrey Bernard radio interview, Classic FM

121 I'm not a shit. I'm a cunt: conversation at Colony Room bar

125 Carmel, if she liked you: Isabel Rawsthorne, *Memoirs*, private collection, London.

130 frail and frightened: Jon Lys-Turner, *Visitors' Book: In Francis Bacon's Shadow* (London: Constable, 2016), p. 307

131 Would you commit suicide: Bacon and Farson interview, Colony Room audio recording

132 Jeff [Bernard] and I gave the addresses: Farson, *Soho in the Fifties*, p. 184

132 It was George Melly: Fawkes, *The French*, p. 33

133 we all went back to the club: Smart, 'The High Priestess of Camp'

133 1980 without Muriel: Smart, 'The High Priestess of Camp'

135 I think of Muriel as a woman: conversation at Colony Room bar

CHAPTER 5: IDA BOARD: THE REIGN OF TERROR

143 Ian had a great way with words: Whittington, *Colony Room Club 50th Anniversary Exhibition*

145 Fuck me, here come the scrubbers: conversation at Colony Room bar

149 Michael Clark was an art student: Porter, 'Muriel's Academy', p. 222

152 One afternoon: Whittington, *Colony Room Club 50th Anniversary Exhibition*

166 heard ideas and opinions expressed: Will Self, *Evening Standard*, 9 September 2008

166 Bacon and I are at opposite ends: Ted Morgan, *Literary Outlaw: The Life and Times of William S. Burroughs* (London: Pimlico 1991)

167 Francis began a long dialogue: Hilary Spurling, *The Girl from the Fiction Department* (London: Hamish Hamilton, 2002), p. 138

167 Sonia had a habit: Moynihan, *Restless Lives*, p. 53

168 When Francis Bacon's lover: Spurling, *The Girl from the Fiction Department*, pp. 155–6

172 By 1980, I had a collection: Jay Landesman, *Jaywalking* (London: Weidenfeld & Nicolson, 1992), pp. 160–161

175 I was so fond of Paul Potts: ibid., p. 142

176 It is a great honour: Francis Bacon, Moscow exhibition catalogue, 1987

177 Everything had been closed up after 1917: Farson, *The Gilded Gutter Life*, p. 232

177 [The Russians] respond particularly well: Bruce Bernard, *Independent Magazine*, 8 October 1988

CHAPTER 6: CRIMES AND MISDEMEANOURS

181 Not being, like the pub: MacInnes, 'At Mabel's'

182 As a matter of fact the London gangster: Norman, *Norman's London*, p. 203

183 We all have our Soho memories: Whittington, *Colony Room Club 50th Anniversary Exhibition*

186 Ian was as brave: ibid.

190 We met at nine: Melvyn Bragg, 'Who's that with Melvyn? From Olivier to Tracey Emin – 30 years of South Bank encounters by Melvyn Bragg', *Daily Mail*, 6 September 2008

199 I knew Ian better than most people: Whittington, *Colony Room Club 50th Anniversary Exhibition*

203 Muriel and Carmel had the largest: Porter, 'Muriel's Academy', p. 222

205 When I first began to go there: Norman and Jeffrey Bernard, *Soho Night and Day*, p. 10

205 You have to look at it: Sinclair, *Francis Bacon*, p. 206

208 Francis was an excellent cook: conversation at Colony Room bar

210 Ian might infrequently decide: Whittington, *Colony Room Club 50th Anniversary Exhibition*

CHAPTER 7: LAST ORDERS

211 The industriousness of the old school: Fawkes, *The French*, p. 52

216 Well, Lucian is extremely gifted: Sinclair, *Francis Bacon*, p. 275

217 Dressed like a piece of rough: Joshua Compston's diary, private collection, London

222 When she [Eddi]: Fawkes, *The French*, p. 46

223 Being a Lord is crucial: Daniel Farson, 'Lord and Disorder', *Tatler*, January 1992, p. 158

228 Deakin was . . . not: Farson, *The Guilded Gutter Life*, p. 261

230 I don't go about shouting: Andrew Sinclair, 'Last Days of the Rage', *Sunday Times*, 5 September 1993

234 [Jeffrey] was a short: Waterhouse, *Last Orders for Jeffrey Bernard*

234 Jeffrey and I go back: *The South Bank Show: Arts Review '89*, Peter O'Toole interviewed by Melvyn Bragg, London Weekend Television, 29 December 1989

237 I was somewhat childishly pleased: Jeffrey Bernard, *Reach For The Ground: The Downhill Struggle of Jeffrey Bernard* (London: Duckworth, 1996), p. 20

CHAPTER 8: DEATH IN BOHEMIA

251 What do you think: Bacon and Farson interview, Colony Room audio recording

257 Friendship isn't easy: Michael Wood, 'How We Met: Ian Board and Daniel Farson', *Independent on Sunday*, 3 January 1993

257 We have always had a warm: ibid.

257 It's just like trench warfare: ibid.

258 I've dedicated my book: ibid.

261 What is one to say: Alan Hall address at the funeral of Ian Board, 1994

269 I don't like doctors: Jeffrey Bernard radio interview, Classic FM

271 Yes, I am still vain: ibid.

272 Jeff's funeral was packed: postcard from Marsh Dunbar to John Baker

274 I met Damien: Farson, *Never a Normal Man*, p. 374

276 Never heard of him: Sinclair, *Francis Bacon*, p. 301

276 marvellous good humour: Bernard, *12 Photographs of Francis Bacon*

277 I have loved Soho passionately: Farson's opening speech, Soho Village Fete 1997

CHAPTER 9: FINGS AIN'T WOT THEY USED T'BE

299 Daddy I like music: Andrew Motion, *The Lamberts: George, Constant and Kit* (London: Chatto & Windus, 1986), p. 271

299 Just to succeed in life: Simon Napier-Bell, 'Kit Lambert', *Sunday Times Magazine*, 1997: www.simonnapierbell.com/kit_lambert.html

CHAPTER 10: NO POST-MORTEMS

317 We went mad in a fantastic, anarchic: Darren Coffield, *Factual Nonsense: The Art and Death of Joshua Compston* (Leicester: Troubador, 2013), p. 89

Bibliography

In addition to the sources cited in the notes, the following texts have
been useful in the making of this book.

BOOKS

Amis, Kingsley, *Memoirs* (London: Hutchinson, 1991)

Balon, Norman, *You're Barred, You Bastards!* (London: Sidgwick &
Jackson, 1991)

Buckle, Richard (ed.), *Self Portrait with Friends: The Selected Diaries of
Cecil Beaton, 1926–1974* (London: Weidenfeld & Nicolson, 1979)

Carter, Miranda, *Anthony Blunt: His Lives* (London: Macmillan, 2001)

Edwards, John and Perry Ogden, *7 Reece Mews: Francis
Bacon's Studio* (London: Thames & Hudson, 2001)

Farson, Daniel, *Sacred Monsters* (London: Bloomsbury, 1988)

Frewin, Leslie (ed.), *Parnassus Near Piccadilly: The Café Royal
Centenary Book* (London: Leslie Frewin, 1965)

Grove, Valerie, *A Voyage Around John Mortimer* (New York: Viking
Press, 2008)

Heath, Michael, *The Complete Heath* (London: John Murray, 1990)

Lloyd, Stephen, *Constant Lambert: Beyond the Rio Grande* (Woodbridge: Boydell Press, 2014)

Melly, George, *Revolt Into Style: The Pop Arts in Britain* (London: Allen Lane, The Penguin Press, 1970)

Norman, Frank, *Stand on Me: A True Story of Soho* (London: Secker & Warburg, 1959)

Parkin, Molly, *Moll: The Making of Molly Parkin* (London: Gollancz, 1993)

Richardson, Nigel, *Dog Days in Soho* (London: Gollancz, 2000)

Steward, Samuel, *Parisian Lives: A Novel* (London: St Martins Press, 1984)

ARTICLES

Alvarez, Maria, 'The New Colonials', *Telegraph Magazine*, 9 October 1999

Barrett, Sara, 'Loudmouth Langan and the Saga of Caine and Table', *Daily Mail*, 14 April 1988

Bennett, Oliver, 'Liquor-ish Allsorts', *Guardian Weekend*, 16 January 1999

Bragg, Melvyn, interview, *Guardian*, 6 May 2009

Davies, Russell, 'Tales from the Colony', *Telegraph Magazine*, 5 November 1994

Dovkants, Keith, 'Battle for the Colony Club', *Evening Standard*, 26 September 2008

Gebler Davies, Clancy, 'Celebrating with the Booze Brothers', *Evening Standard*, 25 October 1988

Hall, Allan, 'Look', *Sunday Times Magazine*, 23 August 1970

Jacobi, Carol, 'Cat's Cradle – Francis Bacon and the Art of "Isabel Rawsthorne"', *Visual Culture in Britain*, 10:3, 2009

Pattenden, Sian, 'Life in a Rogues' Gallery', *Independent*, 11 May 2005

Richardson, Maurice, 'Nightlife Under the Credit Squeeze', *Observer*, 5 March 1967

Richardson, Nigel, 'A Furnace Fuelled by Drink and Despair', *Telegraph*, 19 September 2000

Sinclair, Andrew, 'The Lover Who Blew Bacon's Millions', *Sunday Times*, 5 September 2004

Wojas, Michael, 'A Members' Club for Outsiders', in Philip Beadle, *Making Links: Fifteen Visions of Community* (London: Community Links, 2007)

OBITUARIES

'Ian Board', *Independent*, 28 June 1994

'Henrietta Moraes', *Guardian*, 8 January 1999

'Bruce Bernard', *Guardian*, 31 March 2000

'Graham Mason', *Telegraph*, 9 April 2002

'John Edwards', *The Times*, 6 March 2003

'Michael Wojas', *The Times*, 8 June 2010

CATALOGUES

Artists of the Colony Room Club: A Tribute to Muriel Belcher at Michael Parkin Fine Art, 1982

2001: A Space Oddity, Colony Room Club Exhibition (London: 2001)

Colony Chronology

1948   Muriel Belcher's mother Ida dies in September. Muriel uses her bequest to purchase the lease on 41a Dean Street, Soho, which she names the Colony Room Club. Brian Howard brings Francis Bacon to the club on 14 December, the day before it officially opens. The next day the opening night is so quiet, Bacon and co. entertain themselves by playing a game of dice on the bar. Yorke de Souza is the pianist. Bacon becomes Muriel's 'hostess' and introduces people to the club.

1949   Francis Bacon introduces Denis Wirth-Miller, Isabel Lambert (Rawsthorne) and Lucian Freud. Wirth-Miller brings in Nina Hamnett and a group of artists, labelled the Neo-Romantics: John Minton, Jankel Adler, John Craxton, Keith Vaughan, Robert Colquhoun and Robert MacBryde (The Two Roberts). Ian Board becomes barman. Jeffrey, Bruce and Oliver Bernard become part of Minton's 'Soho circus', which also includes Rodrigo Moynihan and his wife Elinor Bellingham-Smith. Minton brings his students to the club: Bobby Hunt, Sandy Fawkes, Peter Dunbar and Owen

'Oska' Wood; Carmel Stuart introduces Indian Amy (Cynthia Blythe) and Hermione Baddeley (wife of David Tennant, founder of the Gargoyle Club) brings Tennessee Williams, who describes London as 'full of middle-aged fags'.

1950 Bacon brings the art critic David Sylvester to the club, and throws a wedding reception for Michael Wishart and Anne Dunn in his studio; Muriel supplies the alcohol; David Tennant hails it as 'the first real party since the war'. Henrietta Moraes (Audrey Wendy Abbott) becomes a life model at various London art schools; she meets her first husband, filmmaker Michael Law, and moves with him into an attic in Dean Street. Leonard Blackett replaces Bacon as club 'hostess'. Laurie Lee, Dylan Thomas and Donald Maclean, become regulars. Henrietta marries Michael Law and frequents the Colony. Mike McKenzie is the club pianist.

1951 Bacon's nanny, Jessie Lightfoot, dies. Mike McKenzie composes 'Strange Love'; Bacon claims it is his favourite song. The ballet, *Tiresias*, composed by Constant Lambert, opens at the Festival of Britain; Constant dies soon afterwards. Donald Maclean and Guy Burgess defect to the Soviet Union and are denounced as traitors in the British press. Bacon paints Lucian Freud and exhibits his *Screaming Popes* at the Hanover Gallery.

1952 Eduardo Paolozzi helps form the Independent Group, a forerunner of the Pop Art movement. Freud has an affair with Henrietta Law (Moraes). Henrietta and her husband are involved in a street brawl; Rodrigo Moynihan intervenes, leading to the *Daily Express* headline 'QUEEN'S PAINTER ARRESTED'. Freud paints portraits of Henrietta, Lady Caroline Blackwood, John Minton and Francis Bacon. Isabel

Lambert (Rawsthorne) paints Muriel's portrait. Henri Cartier-Bresson photographs Bacon who takes him to the club. Mike McKenzie marries the actress Elizabeth Emslie-Thompson. Colin MacInnes and Francis Bacon are both best man; Muriel and Carmel attend the wedding; Bacon gives the couple £25 as a wedding present and pays for the reception at the Colony. Leonard Blackett introduces Bacon to Peter Lacy at the club; Bacon falls in love for the first time and Lacy becomes club pianist whilst Mike McKenzie is on honeymoon. John Deakin photographs Bacon for *Vogue*.

1953 Coronation of Queen Elizabeth; Mike McKenzie composes 'Jazz Jubilee'. Daniel Farson, Lady Rose McLaren and Patrick Swift, 'The Poet's Painter', frequent the Colony. Dylan Thomas dies. Lucian Freud and Lady Caroline Blackwood marry. Ian Board leaves the Colony to become a valet for the actress Florence Desmond at Dunsborough Park, where he meets Hollywood stars Elizabeth Taylor and Tyrone Power. Ian is replaced at the Colony by Frank the Barman.

1954 Colony members Lord Montagu, Peter Wildeblood and Michael Pitt-Rivers are jailed for committing homosexual acts; extensive press coverage. In response, Lord Wolfenden chairs the Departmental Committee on Homosexual Offences and Prostitution. Molly Parkin frequents the club. Bacon and Freud represent Britain at the Venice Biennale.

1955 Nina Hamnett is banned from the Colony for urinating on the furniture. Society photographer Baron brings Princess Margaret to the club. Peter Wildeblood publishes *Against the Law*, campaigning for reforming the law on homosexuality. Isabel Lambert marries composer Alan Rawsthorne. Farson sacked from *Picture Post* magazine over his homosexuality. Frank the Barman leaves and Ian Board returns as barman. Muriel's former business partner, Dolly Myers, dies.

1956   John Deakin brings in his new boyfriend, David Archer. Archer's Panton Press bookshop, designed by Germano Facetti, opens at 34 Greek Street; Henrietta, Bruce Bernard and the poet Martin Green all work there. Archer introduces his circle of poets and writers to the club: W. S. Graham, George Barker, David Gascoyne. Lady Caroline Blackwood's marriage with Lucian Freud breaks down. Farson becomes a TV personality: his scandalous interview with Dylan Thomas' widow, Caitlin, is front-page news. After meeting Colin Wilson (*The Outsider*) in Archer's bookshop, Farson announces in the press that a 'post-war generation' of 'angry young men' has emerged; Farson and Bacon visit Kingsley Amis in Cardiff. Deakin's first exhibition, *Paris*, opens at Archer's bookshop. Joan Littlewood's production of Brendan Behan's *The Quare Fellow* transfers to the West End; Littlewood and Behan frequent the club. *This is Tomorrow* exhibition opens at the Whitechapel Gallery featuring Germano Facetti and Eduardo Paolozzi. Henrietta marries Minton's lover, actor Norman Bowler. The photographer Baron and Nina Hamnett die.

1957   John Minton commits suicide. *Encounter* magazine publishes Colin MacInnes' homage to Muriel, 'See You at Mabel's'. David Archer takes Henrietta to the Colony to discuss (future husband) Dom Moraes' poetry and publishes Moraes' A Beginning; Deakin designs the cover. Michael Andrews becomes a tutor at the Slade School of Art and redecorates the club from cream to Buckingham Green. He also installs a mural, a copy of Bonnard's *Terrasse à Vernon* originally commissioned for the visitors' tea room *at* Ebberston Hall, North Yorkshire. Farson is widely reported in the press as arrested for being 'drunk and disorderly'. The Wolfenden Report recommends partial decriminalisation of homosexuality between consenting adults. David Archer's bookshop closes.

1958 Jeffrey Bernard brings in Frank Norman and Michael Heath. Dom Moraes wins the Hawthornden Prize. Sonia Orwell marries Michael Pitt-Rivers. Farson interviews Bacon for television show, *The Art Game*, in Wheeler's restaurant. Bacon signs with Marlborough Fine Art to stem severe gambling debts and introduces William Burroughs to the Colony. The club throws a party to mark its 10th anniversary on 15 December.

1959 Ian moves into the same apartment block as Muriel: Russell Court, Woburn Place. Daniel Farson is impersonated on TV by Benny Hill in a parody of his Barbara Cartland interview. Publication of Colin MacInnes' novel, *Absolute Beginners*. Michael Andrews makes sketches for his painting, *The Colony Room I*. Joan Littlewood produces Frank Norman's *Fings Ain't Wot They Used T'be* at Stratford Theatre Royal, with music and lyrics by Lionel Bart; all three frequent the Colony. Prostitutes are removed from the streets of Soho following the introduction of the Street Offences Act. Mike McKenzie performs with Cleo Laine at the West Indian Gazette Carnival, a precursor to the Notting Hill Carnival. Bacon rents a studio in St Ives; Muriel and Carmel visit; he befriends the painter Roger Hilton, a notoriously heavy drinker and difficult character, who becomes a Colony member. William Burroughs moves to London.

1960   The poet Martin Green and Henrietta get engaged; Bacon pays for a 'pre-nuptial honeymoon' in Dublin, where Green realises his mistake. Henrietta and Diana Moynihan (Melly) arrested outside South African Embassy protesting against the Sharpeville massacre. Frank Norman pays the fine for Henrietta's release. Muriel, Carmel and Ian holiday in Mombasa, Kenya, their regular summer holiday destination for the next decade.

1961   George Melly meets his future wife, Diana Moynihan (wife of John Moynihan), at the Colony. Todd Matshikiza, composer of the all-black jazz musical *King Kong*, becomes the pianist. Gambling is legalised and betting shops appear in Soho. Henrietta marries Dom Moraes and succumbs to drug addiction. Sonia Orwell moves to 153 Gloucester Road, Kensington, which becomes her literary salon.

1962   Farson buys the Waterman's Arms; the opening is attended by numerous Colony members; he introduces Joan Littlewood to the Kray twins. Michael Andrews completes his painting, *The Colony Room I*. Bacon's retrospective opens at the Tate Gallery as news arrives of Peter Lacy's death; his wake is held next day at the Colony. Robert Colquhoun dies of a heart attack. Robert Fraser Gallery opens. Ian Board moves to 124 Clare Court, Judd Street, with Leonard Blackett.

1963   Patrick Caulfield frequents the Colony as an art student. Bacon meets George Dyer at a gay club; they concoct a story that they met whilst Dyer was burgling Bacon's home. Bacon commissions Deakin to photograph his Soho circle of friends as reference for his paintings and paints Henrietta Moraes in

Lying Figure with Hypodermic Syringe. Gerald McCann opens his boutique on Upper Grosvenor Square, Mayfair; photographed alongside Mary Quant and Jean Muir for *Life* magazine's 'brash new breed of British designers'. Christine Keeler and the Profumo affair leads to the trial of Stephen Ward, who later commits suicide.

1964   Muriel and Carmel move to 4 Wellington Court, Shelton Street; the interior is designed by 'Lady May'. Tom Driberg MP introduces Jay Landesman and Ronnie Kray to the Colony. Graham Mason and David 'Maid' Marrion become members. Deakin banned for spreading malicious stories about Muriel. Freud paints Deakin's portrait. Farson resigns from television over his homosexuality; he is bankrupted over the failure of the Waterman's Arms and moves to Devon. Elizabeth Smart gets Jeffrey Bernard his first job in journalism at *Queen* magazine. Joan Littlewood and Frank Norman attend Brendan Behan's funeral in Dublin. Julian Maclaren-Ross dies.

1965   1964 Licensing Act comes into force, leading to the withdrawal of the special licensing hours for afternoon drinking clubs. They must now operate under pub hours closing between 3 p.m. and 5.30 p.m. Muriel pretends to serve food to continue to sell alcohol. John Latham introduces fellow artist Barry Flanagan to the club. Colony habitué and designer Jean Varon (John Bates) designs the outfits for Diana Rigg's Emma Peel in *The Avengers*. Frank Norman and Jeffrey Bernard get 'drunk for a year' for research purposes. Giacometti retrospective at Tate Gallery; Giacometti attends the club with Bacon, Isabel Rawsthorne and David Sylvester. Publication of Francis Bacon catalogue raisonné with Muriel's portrait on the cover. Thea Porter opens her interior design shop in Berwick Street, Soho. Leonard Blackett dies.

1966 Publication of *Soho Night and Day* by Frank Norman and Jeffrey Bernard, featuring the Colony and Muriel. To circumvent the new licensing laws, Lord Goodman advises Muriel to change the Colony from a proprietorial club to a committee-led members' club, relinquishing her proprietorial powers but retaining ownership of the building's lease; this legal change will cause havoc in later years when trying to save the club. The 'world's richest woman', Olga Deterding, frequents the club. Jean Muir launches fashion label Jean Muir Ltd; her muse and model is Joanna Lumley. Thea Porter's shop moves to Greek Street. Robert MacBryde killed in a car accident.

1967 The Hon. Michael Summerskill brings Mumsie (Moyna Pearmaine) to the club. Bacon paints *Portrait of Isabel Rawsthorne Standing in a Street in Soho*. Artist Barry Evans brings in Catherine Shakespeare Lane. Len Deighton mentions Muriel and the club in the guidebook, *London Dossier*. The Sexual Offences Act decriminalises homosexuality in England and Wales. Robert Fraser arrested with Mick Jagger for drug possession. Henrietta Moraes jailed at Holloway Prison for attempted burglary. Muriel, Bacon, Lady Caroline Blackwood, Sonia Orwell, David Sylvester and Diana Melly raise £1,000 to help Henrietta upon her release.

1968 Big Eddi (Eddi McPherson) and the author Irma Kurtz frequent the Colony. Muriel and the club are mentioned in the *Millionaire's Diary 1968*. The publisher Peter Owen commissions Allan Hall to write a biography of Muriel. Isabel Rawsthorne exhibition at Marlborough Fine Art.

Bacon gives George Dyer an apartment in Kensington and £20,000 to stay out of his life. Ian Board bakes Muriel a hashish cake as a 60th birthday present; Barry Evans unwittingly consumes some and goes on a drug-fuelled rampage at a reception at Thea Porter's boutique, attacking the buffet. Muriel suffers a stroke, is hospitalised in the London Clinic and Bacon pays her medical bills.

1969   Publication of *Norman's London* by Frank Norman, featuring Muriel and the club. David Hall, a director of the *International Times*, is arrested for conspiring to outrage public decency for publishing a lonely hearts column for homosexuals, regularly used by Ian Board to pick up 'trade'; Ian finds his boyfriend 'Suzy Wong' through its advertisements. Robert Fraser Gallery closes. George Dyer breaks into Bacon's studio and destroys his paintings.

1970   Muriel and Ian Board model clothes by Gerald McCann and Thea Porter for Allan Hall's feature, 'Look', in the *Style* section of the *Sunday Times*. Bacon's home is raided and he is arrested on drugs charges.

1971   Frank Norman writes the play *Rough Trade*, based on the Colony, and marries Geraldine. *Oz* magazine accused of conspiracy to 'debauch and corrupt the morals of children and young persons'; the trial features club members George Melly as expert witness and John Mortimer QC for the defence. Judge Argyle asks Melly, 'Well, pardon me, for those of us who did not have a classical education, what do you mean by this word "cunni-linctus"?' (pronounced as if it were a cough medicine), to which Melly replies 'as we said in my naval days, "Yodelling in the canyon", your honour'; the trial becomes the most entertaining show in town and the courtroom antics are published by Colony member Anthony Blond. Jeffrey Bernard prepares his speech for presenting the *Sporting Life* Cup in the Colony, arrives inebriated at the ceremony and passes out before presenting the prize; this confirms him as a Soho legend and *Sporting Life* sacks him. David Archer visits the Colony on 15 October before committing suicide. George Dyer commits suicide on 24 October. Bacon's exhibition opens at the Grand Palais, Paris, on 26 October; guests include Muriel, Ian Board, John Deakin, Thea Porter, Rodrigo Moynihan, David Sylvester, Sonia Orwell, Michel Leiris, Isabel Rawsthorne, Denis Wirth-Miller and Dickie Chopping.

1972   Bobby Hunt brings Miss Whiplash (Sara Waterson) to the club. Adam Stevenson becomes the pianist. George Melly's album *Nuts* is released. Kenneth Anger finishes *Lucifer Rising*, with Sir Francis Rose playing himself ('Lord Chaos'). John Deakin dies. First Gay Pride rally held in London. The Soho Society is formed, supported by Muriel, Frank Norman and Norman Balon; over 200 people attend a meeting to halt developers and have the Soho area declared a conservation zone.

1973   Bacon hires Robert Carrier's country hotel, Hintlesham Hall, for a weekend party to celebrate Muriel's 65th birthday; Colony members can be found randomly passed out at odd angles on the lawns. For the club's 25th anniversary, a group photo is taken for a *Sunday Telegraph* feature, sculptor Hubert 'Nibs' Dalwood creates an edition of commemorative bronze ashtrays and Daniel Farson writes '"Open Your Bead

Bag, Lottie!'" for Paul Raymond's *Club International* magazine.

1974 Jeffrey Bernard assaults Big Eddi and gives up drinking out of remorse. Maid Marion introduces John Edwards to the club. Lucian Freud retrospective, Hayward Gallery; Freud falls out with Bacon and stops visiting the Colony. The BBC casts Tom Baker as 'Doctor Who' and Baker frequents the club. BBC Radio 3 broadcasts Daniel Farson's tribute to David Archer, *A Gentleman of Soho*. Julian Ormsby-Gore commits suicide. Muriel suffers another stroke and breaks her femur while at The London Clinic; Bacon pays for her hospital bills; Wirth-Miller and Chopping visit Muriel in hospital, she looks 'frail and frightened'. William Burroughs returns to the United States.

1975 Muriel considered too ill to continue working; Ian Board takes over and Maid Marion becomes the barman. Bacon takes Jeffrey Bernard to Wheeler's for lunch and asks: 'Now that you have lost your looks, Jeffrey, what will you do?' Muriel experiences financial difficulties during her illness and instructs the club's accountant, Aunty Fred, to chase members for unpaid bills; he sends a letter demanding £34 to Frank Norman, who disputes it and is barred from the club.

1976 Hamish McAlpine joins the Colony. Freud paints Frank Auerbach's portrait. Jeffrey Bernard begins as a columnist at the *Spectator* and eventually falls off the wagon, drinking a bottle of Scotch in two hours with Eva Johansen and Frank Norman. Allan Hall organises Muriel's 68th birthday party in the Café Royal cellars and is sued for non-payment of the £17,500 bar bill. Nibs Dalwood dies. Colin MacInnes dies;

Frank Norman and Fiona and Martin Green attend his burial at sea on a Folkestone fishing boat.

1977 Jay Landesman introduces Pam Hardyment to the club. Muriel, Ian, Aunty Fred and Thea Porter travel to Paris for Bacon's exhibition at the Galerie Claude Bernard. Keith Vaughan commits suicide. Michael Clark frequents the Colony and draws Muriel's portrait.

1978 Merilyn Thorold helps nurse a bedridden Muriel for the last two years of her life. Frank Auerbach retrospective at the Hayward Gallery. Jeffrey Bernard begins writing his 'Low Life' column. Michael Wishart brings James Birch and John Maybury to the Colony.

1979 Mumsie brings in Jim Moore and Jay Landesman introduces Tom Deas to the Colony; John Edwards moves into Muriel's apartment. Jeremy Thorpe trial shocks the nation; his accuser Norman Scott frequents the Colony; Landesman publishes Farson's parody of the Thorpe scandal, *The Dog Who Knew Too Much*, under the pen name, 'Miss Matilda Excellent'. Muriel dies on Halloween, is cremated on Bonfire Night and her memorial service is held at St Paul's, Covent Garden on 29 November. Sir Francis Rose dies.

1980 Muriel leaves £28,644 and bequeaths the lease on the Colony to Carmel; Ian Board and the club are now Carmel's subtenants; she forces them to pay her £3,500 in instalments for her 'loss of office', although she never held one. The landlord doubles the club's rent to £3,250 a year. Barney Bates is the new pianist and Ben Trainin is the new barman. Bacon buys Muriel's flat from Carmel for John

Edwards. Sonia Orwell dies bankrupt, trying to protect George Orwell's legacy from an unscrupulous accountant; Bacon pays off all her debts. Frank Norman dies.

1981   Michael Clark's portrait, *Muriel Belcher Ill in Bed*, is exhibited at the Royal Academy. The Indecent Displays Act stops sexual material from being displayed in shop windows in an attempt to regulate Soho sex shops. Kit Lambert dies. Michael Wojas takes over as barman. Thea Porter Ltd goes into liquidation and her store closes. She meets Peter Langan in the Colony and they decide to do a fashion show together in Langan's Brasserie. December sees the first recorded case of AIDS in the UK.

1982   Infamous brothel owner 'Madam Cyn' Cynthia Payne frequents the club. Ben Trainin moves to a squat in Brixton with Will Self. Jeffrey Bernard's 50th birthday after-party is held in the club. Michael Parkin Fine Art exhibits *Artists of the Colony Room Club: A Tribute to Muriel Belcher* and Thea Porter writes a feature about it, 'Muriel's Academy', for *Harpers & Queen*.

1983   Neal Slavin takes the members' group photo with the world's largest polaroid camera for his photographic series, *Britons*. Jeffrey Bernard writes about meeting Anthony Burgess, author of *A Clockwork Orange*, in the Colony. Thea Porter's second fashion show at Langan's Brasserie is a financial disaster; potential clients are too intimidated by Langan's louche drunken behaviour. Robert Fraser's second gallery opens. Eva Johansen dies smoking in bed.

1984   *John Deakin: The Salvage of a Photographer* exhibition at Victoria & Albert Museum.

1985   Daniel Chadwick, Marc Quinn and James Moores frequent the Colony. The club is filmed for the *South Bank Show* documentary on Bacon. The Groucho Club opens next door. Bacon's second retrospective at the Tate Gallery; the after-party is at Langan's Brasserie; JAK draws a cartoon of the private view, which Ian Board buys for the club. Ben Trainin and Carmel Stuart die.

1986   Jay Landesman publishes Jeffrey Bernard's book *Low Life*. Robert Fraser dies of AIDS; wake held at the Colony. Bookshop Billy organises a coach trip to Derby Day at Epsom Racecourse. Transgender prostitute, Vicky de Lambray, found dead in mysterious circumstances. Frank Auerbach represents Britain at the Venice Biennale.

1987   Birch & Conran Fine Art opens at 40 Dean Street. Publication of Daniel Farson's book, *Soho in the Fifties*, dedicated to Ian Board. *School of London: Six Figurative Painters* exhibition tours the UK. Twiggy (Michael Peel) commissions Gavin Jones to paint a double portrait of Ian Board and Michael Wojas, which hangs in the club for the next twenty years.

1988   Lucian Freud's retrospective at the Hayward Gallery. Licensing laws change to allow afternoon drinking in all public houses leading to the closure of many afternoon drinking clubs. Margaret Thatcher introduces Section 28 of the Local Government Act, prohibiting the 'promotion' of homosexuality by schools and local authorities. Bacon exhibition opens in Moscow. Elinor Bellingham-Smith dies. Michael Clark exhibition opens at Birch and Conran featuring portraits of Colony members. Club's 40th Ruby Anniversary Party is held with decorations by Michael and Elaine Woods and a

commemorative book published by Florian Denk. Joshua
Compston and Darren Coffield frequent the club.

1989   Bacon has a cancerous kidney removed. Gaston Berlemont
retires from the French House; Lesley Lewis and Noel
Botham become the proprietors. Jeffrey Bernard and Keith
Waterhouse spend an evening in the Colony promoting their
play, *Jeffrey Bernard is Unwell*. Peter O'Toole becomes the
barman for the evening. *Francis Bacon: Loan Exhibition in
Celebration of his 80th Birthday* at Marlborough Fine Art.

1990   The landlord of 41a Dean Street applies to the council for
change of use to convert the building into offices. Paul Potts
and Rodrigo Moynihan die.

1991   'Save the Colony Campaign' overturns the landlord's
application for change of use at Westminster City Hall.
Bacon is admitted to hospital for another operation, not
expecting to survive. Michael Dillon leaves the Colony
committee to become the proprietor of Gerry's club, Soho.
Michael Andrews exhibits his *Ayers Rock* series at Whitechapel
Gallery. Dan Farson brings Gilbert & George to the Colony;
book launch of Farson's *Gilbert & George in Moscow* at the
Groucho Club. Damien Hirst visits the Colony; Marc Quinn
exhibits his 'blood head' sculpture at the Grob Gallery; Joshua
Compston launches the Courtauld Loan Collection at the
Courtauld Institute. Lucian Freud paints Mick Tobin to clear
a gambling debt. Kate Braine sculpts Ian Board's bust. Ian
Board spends Christmas in Goa, India.

1992   Death of Isabel Rawsthorne. Same-sex desire no longer
classed as a mental illness by the World Health Organisation.

Damien Hirst exhibits 'shark' sculpture at the Saatchi Gallery. Francis Bacon dies; the wake is held in the club. Joshua Compston opens Factual Nonsense gallery in Shoreditch. Channel 4 broadcasts Ian Board interviewing Damien Hirst in his Turner Prize nomination film. Freud paints Bruce Bernard. Actor Denholm Eliott dies of AIDS.

1993   Ian Board taken to court for criminal damage to 'Baby Face' Scarlatti's mobile phone. Joshua Compston organises *The Fete Worse than Death* and introduces Langlands & Bell, Gavin Turk and Tracey Emin to the club. Publication of Farson's biography, *The Gilded Gutter Life of Francis Bacon*. Orlando Campbell opens his private drinking club, Green Street, in Mayfair. The décor is based on the Colony and it becomes the hub of the Britpop and YBA art scene.

1994   Westminster City Council demands a fire lobby to be built on the club's staircase, which would cut the Colony in two. Ian Board dies; memorial at St Paul's, Covent Garden. Ian bequeaths the club's lease to Michael Wojas and his insurance money to Michael Clark. London Weekend Television documentary on Joshua Compston filmed in the club. Publication of Henrietta Moraes' autobiography. Michael Clark stops frequenting the club. Frances Slowey becomes the Colony's first female bartender.

1995   Vivian Stanshall's wake is held at the Colony. BBC buys rights to *The Gilded Gutter Life of Francis Bacon*. Michael Andrews dies and his portrait by Deakin is hung in the club. Damien Hirst wins the Turner Prize. Jean Muir dies.

1996   Lady Caroline Blackwood, Mumsie (Moyna Pearmaine), Michael Wishart and Joshua Compston die. Sebastian Horsley joins the Colony. *John Deakin* exhibition at the National Portrait Gallery.

1997   Daniel Farson opens the Soho Village Fete and publishes his autobiography, *Never a Normal Man*. Michael Wojas asks John Payne to repaint the club from its trademark Buckingham Green to lurid leaf green. *Sensation* exhibition opens at Royal Academy featuring the YBAs. Mick Tobin, Bill Mitchell, Daniel Farson and Jeffrey Bernard die.

1998   John Edwards starts court proceedings against Marlborough Fine Art over Bacon's estate. *The Colony Room Club: 50th Anniversary Art Exhibition* at A22 Projects, London; Michael Wojas commissions a TV documentary on the Club. Sarah Lucas offers to work behind the bar every Tuesday. Release of biopic of Francis Bacon, starring Daniel Craig, Derek Jacobi and Tilda Swinton.

1999   Orlando Campbell's private drinking club, Green Street, closes; the Britpop and YBA art scene relocates to the Colony. Sarah Lucas' stint behind the bar morphs into a weekly performance bar night featuring: Alex James, Phil Dirtbox, Langlands & Bell, Rachel Howard, Darren Coffield, Tracey Emin, Mat Collishaw, Damien Hirst, Maia Norman, Daniel Craig, John Maybury, Suggs, James Moores, Orlando Campbell, Pam Hogg, Justin Mortimer, Kathy Dalwood, Adrian Searle, Jay Jopling, Sam Taylor-Wood, The Wilson Twins, Tim Noble and Sue Webster. Merilyn Thorold, Henrietta Moraes, Lionel Bart and Mike McKenzie die. Matt Cogger becomes the barman.

2000   *Showtime* nights are held the first Sunday of every month compèred by Phil Dirtbox; performers over the years include Tracey Emin, Salena Godden, Sebastian Horsley, Jupiter John, Clifford Slapper, La Celine, Jock Scot, the Rubbish Men, Abigail Lane, the Magic Numbers, Badly Drawn Boy, Chas Smash and The Alabama 3. Bruce Bernard, Thea Porter and the Duke of Sutherland die. Jake McLellan becomes barman.

2001   John Edwards is diagnosed with cancer and settles his dispute with Marlborough Fine Art out of court. David Sylvester and Marsh Dunbar die. Michael Wojas finds a working till, identical to the original in the Colony, in a Lithuanian social club near Bow; suburban hairdresser, Dave the Hair, refurbishes it in the manner of a Damien Hirst artwork and it becomes the club's new till. Colony Room exhibition, *2001: A Space Oddity*, A22 Gallery. Publication of *A Pickled Nose*, by Zinovy Zinik, featuring the Colony and Ian Board's nose. Simon Crabb becomes the club barman.

2002   Graham Mason, Joan Littlewood, Michael Elphick and Joe Strummer die. Lucian Freud retrospective at Tate Britain.

2003   Death of John Edwards; wake held at the Colony. The club's 55th anniversary exhibition and auction, *What's It Worth!*, held at Elms Lesters Painting Rooms.

2004   Percy Gabriel Lynch is born. His father, Laurence, introduces him to the Colony; less than one day old he becomes the club's youngest member. The Civil Partnership Act grants same-sex couples the same legal rights as married 'straight' couples. Dick Bradsell becomes the club barman.

2005   Dickie Chopping and Denis Wirth-Miller become one of the first same-sex couples to have a civil partnership. Le Gun art collective frequent the club, which becomes part of their subject matter. The Colony slides into financial difficulties. Sandy Fawkes, Sir Eduardo Paolozzi and Lady Rose McLaren die. Michael Wojas breaks into the vacant premises above the Colony and begins squatting there.

2006   The film set of the Colony Room Club from *Love is the Devil* is reconstructed in the basement of Selfridges department store in Oxford Street for a punk festival featuring the Buzzcocks and the Slits; Michael Wojas mans the bar. Lord (Jago) Eliot dies.

2007   *Showtime* is taken on the road and plays at various festivals in the UK. A national smoking ban comes into effect. Publication of Sebastian Horsley's *Dandy in the Underworld*. Bobby Hunt, Michael Meakin and George Melly die.

2008   Alix Coleman, Dickie Chopping and Alan Haynes die; Angus Fairhurst commits suicide. Publication of Will Self's *Liver*, containing the satire 'Foie Humain' about the Colony. Suggs films the TV series *Suggs in the City* in the club. The lease expires on the club's premises and the landlord applies for it to be terminated. The club committee send out a letter stating that Michael Wojas is retiring and the club will have to relocate. An auction of Colony artworks is held at Lyon & Turnbull; the club's mural by Michael Andrews is sold to his widow, June Andrews. An Annual General Meeting is called and fails to halt the club's closure. Colony Room Club's 60th anniversary party, Monday 15 December; the final closing party for members is Friday 19 December.

Colony Room Exhibitions

1982

Artists of the Colony Room Club: A Tribute to Muriel Belcher, Michael
  Parkin Fine Art

Exhibitors: Jankel Adler, Craigie Aitchison, Michael Andrews, Frank
  Auerbach, Francis Bacon, Tim Behrens, Elinor Bellingham-Smith,
  Peter Blake, Peter Bradshaw, Robert Buhler, Edward Burra, Michael
  Clark, Robert Colquhoun, John Craxton, Hubert Dalwood, John
  Deakin, Barry Driscoll, Anne Dunn, Sally Ducksbury, Martin Fuller,
  Lucian Freud, Nina Hamnett, Robert Hunt, JAK, Augustus John,
  Robert MacBryde, John Minton, Rodrigo Moynihan, Eduardo
  Paolozzi, William Redgrave, Edward Seago, Clare Shenstone, Stan
  Smith, Keith Vaughan, Karl Weschke, Denis Wirth-Miller, Edward
  Wolfe and Owen 'Oska' Wood.

1998

The Colony Room Club: 50th Anniversary Art Exhibition, A22 Projects, curated by Michael Wojas and James Birch.

Exhibitors: Chris Battye, Kate Braine, Paul Broadbent, Jo Busuttil, Patrick Caulfield, Daniel Chadwick, Brian 'Dawn' Chalkley, Darren Coffield, Keith Coventry, Clem Crosby, Kathy Dalwood, Peter Davies, Arif Djan, Barry Driscol, Tracey Emin, Barry Flanagan, Paul Freud, Francis Fry, Neil Hedger, Damien Hirst, Gavin Jones, James Krone, Stephen Lees, John Maybury, George Melly, James Moores, Justin Mortimer, Ray Natkiel, Jake Paltenghi, Marc Quinn, David Remfry, Catherine Shakespeare Lane, Lisa Stansfield and Ed Winters.

2001

2001: A Space Oddity, A22 Projects, curated by Michael Wojas and James Birch.

Exhibitors: Hugh Allen, Tom Baker, John Beasley, Peter Blake, Andrew Campbell, Rob & Nick Carter, Mat Collishaw, Peter Denmark, Sally Dunbar, The Lord Eliot, Angus Fairhurst, Paul Fryer, Clancy Gebler Davies, Anthony Genn, Sarah Herriot, Sebastian Horsley, Rachel Howard, Gary Hume, Alyson Hunter, Mark Inglefield, Fred Ingrams, Langlands & Bell, Pascal Latra, Sarah Lucas, Shane McGowan, Dan Macmillan, Tim Noble & Sue Webster, Amanda Ooms, Mark Reeves, Liz Rideal, Karen Selby, Jo Self, Paul Simonon, Nic Tucker, Gavin Turk, Kathryn Weatherell, Charlie Westerman and Jane & Louise Wilson.

2003

What's It Worth!, Elms Lester Painting Rooms, organised by Michael Wojas and Suzanne Bisset.

Exhibitors: Tom Baker, Sir Peter Blake, Dan Chadwick, Darren Coffield, Keith Coventry, Clem Crosby, Peter Denmark, Tracey Emin, Angus Fairhurst, Abigail Lane, Sarah Lucas, Dan Macmillan, Justin Mortimer, Tim Noble & Sue Webster, Jake Paltenghi, Sam Reveles, Karen Selby, Bob & Roberta Smith, Sam Taylor-Wood, Gavin Turk, Jessica Voorsanger and Zoltar the Magnificent.

Index

Unbound is the world's first crowdfunding publisher, established in 2011.

We believe that wonderful things can happen when you clear a path for people who share a passion. That's why we've built a platform that brings together readers and authors to crowdfund books they believe in – and give fresh ideas that don't fit the traditional mould the chance they deserve.

This book is in your hands because readers made it possible. Everyone who pledged their support is listed below. Join them by visiting unbound.com and supporting a book today.

Greg Abbott

Megan Ashcroft

Roddy Ashworth

Didier Avignon

John Baker

Michael Baker

Adam Bancroft

Martin Barrett

Adam Baylis-West

John Beasley

Chris Beckett

Giles Bennett

Terry Bergin

Stefanie Bergot

Bruno-Roland Bernard

James Birch

Suzanne Bisset

Charlotte Black

Geraldine Blake

Elaine Board

Dirk Bollen

Guy Botham

Ailsa Boyd

Alex Braid

Caroline Bray

Cecily Brown

Paul Brunton
Delicia Burnell
Katrine Cakuls
Andrew Campbell
Orlando Campbell
Fiona Cartledge
Daniel Chadwick
Brian Clivaz
Madeline Clow
Mat Clum
Chris Coffield
Ewa Coffield
Stevyn Colgan
Glen Colson
Emily Compston
Athena Constantine
    Constantinou
Mark Cooper
William Corbett
Simon Crabb
John Crawford
Aidan Cross
Derek Cross
Emma Cuthbert
Richard Dacre
Mark Daniels in memory of
    Barry Daniels
Zoe Darling
Barbara Davenport
Stuart Davidson
Clancy Davies
David Davies

Alasdair Deas
Tom Deas
Robert Dee
Adrian Deevoy
Ian Devaney
Stephen Dilworth
Stephen Douglas
Kealan Doyle
Sally Dunbar
William Dunbar
Martin Edmonds
David Edmunds
Marc Edmunds
J Eliot
Tomas Eriksson
Kate Fawkes
David Fielder
Hester Finch
Paul Fisher
Hercules Fisherman
Keith Ford
Bertie Forster
Michele Foulger
Richard Fowler
Nick Franco
Ian Freeman
Liz Friend
Vanessa Fristedt
Paul Fryer
Tom Galloway
Rita Gayford
David Gentle

Marc Glendening

Fiona Green

Anne Gruen

Di Hall

Alexis Harding

Pamela Hardyment

Eileen Haring Woods

Amanda Harris

Pete Harris

David Hayles

Jonathan Haynes

Anthony Heath

Michael Heath

Zebedee Helm

Alice Herrick

Danielle Hesketh

Gary Hill

Cheska Hill-Wood

Dannielle Hodson

Jacqueline Houtved

Gary Hughes

Patrick Hughes

Alyson Hunter

Jason Hutton

James Hyman

Ian Irvine

Clare Jenkins

Clive Jennings

Simon Jerrome

David Johnson

Alun Jones

Jackie Joseph

Pauline Kane

Martin Kelly

Dan Kieran

Des Kilfeather

Benedict King

Mark Kirby

Kate Kotcheff

Joanne Koukis

Art Lavelle

Stafford Lawrence

Sophie Le Filleul

John Leahy

David Lee

John V Lennon

Maria Lennon

Fiona Lensvelt

Bronwen Lenton

Paul Levy

Lesley Lewis

Julian Lloyd

Sarah Lucas

Clare Lynch

Seonaid Mackenzie-Murray

Charles Maclean

Dan Macmillan

Philippa Manasseh

David Marrion

Darcia Martin

Rees Martin

David Matkins

Derek Matravers

Lisa-Marie Matta

Hamish McAlpine

Fiona McAuliffe Artist
Forte

Jessica McBride

Clare McCaldin

Liza Mccarron

Niall McCormack

Polly Fiona McDonald

Seamus McGarvey

Dominic McGuinness

Jonathan C. M. McLeod

Eddie McPherson

Rod Melvin

Mervyn Metcalf

Dutch Michaels

Sean Michaels

John Mitchinson

James Moore

James Moores

Stewart Morgan

Tiernan Morgan

Robert Morris

Tim Motion

Ray Natkiel

Carlo Navato

Roo Newton

Per Norström

Craig Oldham

Colin Overall

Michael Paley

Francesca Peel

Michael Peel

Hilary Penn

Martin Perry

Mike Pitt

Justin Pollard

Philippa Potts

Dameon Priestly

Richard Proctor

Julie Pryce

David Prys-Owen

Nigel Pugh

Peter Quinn Davis

Brendan Reaney

Alistair Renwick

Glen Reynolds

Rob Reynolds

Ian Richards

John Richardson

Yvonne Ridley

Guy Ripley

Jill Ritblat

Hedley Roberts

David Roger

Martine Rose

Robert Rubbish

Darren Russell

@samschulzstudio

Mark Samuelson

Mark Sanderson

Sukhdev Sandhu

Sicily Scarlet

Arthur Schiller

Dick Selwood

Dale Shaw

Fiona Sheridan

Mandy Sim

Clifford Slapper

Frances Slowey

Daryl Smith

Joe Soave

Colin Stanley

Lisa Stansfield

Jessica Stevens

Paul Stolper

Alastair Stratton

Georgie Sutcliffe

Rich Sutton

Mary Swan

Dave Taylor

Samantha Taylor

Ken Thomson

Roger Thorp

Pete Thurlow

Phil Tidy

Gawain Towler

Mimi Trainin

Kelvin Trott

Gavin Turk

Yulia Vennard

Nick Vivian

Harriet Vyner

Sara Waterson

Gary Waterston

Christopher Webb

Andy Whale

Oliver Whitford-Knight

Rae Williams

Zoë-Elise Williamson

Ludger Wilmott

Dominic Winchester

Bob Winsor

Edward Winters

Dylan Woodward

Zinovy Zinik